MEDIA MANAGEMENT:
A Casebook Approach

COMMUNICATION TEXTBOOK SERIES
Jennings Bryant — Editor

Journalism
Maxwell McCombs — Advisor

BERNER • Writing Literary Features

FENSCH • The Sports Writing Handbook

TITCHENER • Reviewing the Arts

FENSCH • Writing Solutions:
Beginnings, Middles,
and Endings

SHOEMAKER • Communication
Campaigns About Drugs:
Government, Media,
and the Public

STEPP • Editing for Today's
Newsroom

BOGART • Press and Public: Who
Reads What, When, Where,
and Why in American
Newspapers, Second Edition

FENSCH • Associated Press Coverage
of a Major Disaster: The
Crash of Delta Flight 1141

GARRISON • Professional
Feature Writing

FENSCH • Best Magazine Articles: 1988

DAVIDSON • A Guide
for Newspaper Stringers

GARRISON • Professional
News Writing

SLOAN • Makers of the
Media Mind: Journalism Educators
and Their Ideas

FENSCH • Nonfiction for the 1990s

LESTER • Photojournalism: An
Ethical Approach

PROTESS/McCOMBS • Agenda Setting:
Readings on Media,
Public Opinion, and Policymaking

McCOMBS/EINSIEDEL/WEAVER • Contemporary
Public Opinion: Issues
and the News

PARSIGIAN • Mass Media Writing

GARRISON • Professional
News Reporting

GARRISON • Advanced Reporting:
Skills for the Professional

MAURO • Statistical Deception
at Work

LACY/SOHN/WICKS • Media Management:
A Casebook Approach

MEDIA MANAGEMENT:
A Casebook Approach

Stephen Lacy
Michigan State University
Ardyth B. Sohn
University of Colorado
Jan LeBlanc Wicks
Indiana University

Contributing Authors:

George Sylvie
University of Texas at Austin
Angela Powers
Northern Illinois University
Nora J. Rifon
Michigan State University

 LAWRENCE ERLBAUM ASSOCIATES, PUBLISHERS
1993   Hillsdale, New Jersey   Hove and London

Lawrence Erlbaum Associates, Inc., Publishers
365 Broadway
Hillsdale, New Jersey 07642

Library of Congress Cataloging in Publication Data

  Media management : a casebook approach / [edited] by Stephen Lacy . . .
  [et al.].
      p. cm.
    Includes bibliogaphical references and index.
    ISBN 0-8058-0659-8 (cloth). — ISBN 0-8058-1308-X (pbk.)
    1. Mass media—Management—Case studies. I. Lacy, Stephen, 1948—

  .
  P96.M34M4 1993
  302.23'068—dc20   92-34734
                                                                CIP

Books published by Lawrence Erlbaum Associates are printed on acid-free
paper, and their bindings are chosen for strength and durability.

Printed in the United States of America
10 9 8 7 6 5 4 3 2 1

Contents

8   MARKETING AND RESEARCH   **251**

9   BUDGETING AND DECISION MAKING   **282**

10   TECHNOLOGY AND THE FUTURE   **308**

EXTENDED CASE STUDIES   **336**

Introduction

Ardyth B. Sohn
University of Colorado

This book grew out of the collective needs of media management educators to explore through case analysis the theory and practice of the field. Although research studies exist in several different scholarly journals, and applicable cases are available through various sources, this work represents one of the first efforts to combine the broad concerns of the field with relevant cases. This book provides a framework and materials for analysis, discussion, and problem solving within various media (including advertising agencies, cable companies, magazines, newspapers, public relations firms, radio, and television stations). However, all cases are designed to illuminate not only the differences present in management environments, but also the similarities between media companies.

The goals of the book are: (a) to provide access to a seldom-used approach for discussing media management, and (b) to supplement current available materials concerning issues relevant to managing a media organization. Practice in evaluative and descriptive analyses is provided in the book, which seeks to suggest questions for individual research and provide more formal classroom debate and discussion.

The book is arranged to cover both internal and external media organization environments. Chapters on market analysis and research, strategic planning, law and regulation, and technology address the external concerns. Chapters on budgeting, organizational structure, leadership, and worker motivation focus on internal matters. Cases involve large and small media organizations with corporate-level issues included. Chapters begin with an overview of the topic and concerns in the field. Mini-cases follow the overview and serve to illustrate problems in each chapter. In addition, three comprehensive cases at the end of the book involve issues from several chapters. These more complex cases require the consideration and balance of several appropriate theories and applied practices.

The book includes original cases researched and written by the authors who have been managers and/or employees in media organizations.

THE CASE STUDY APPROACH

For quite some time the business, legal, and medical professions have used case study in one form or another to discuss important issues in their fields; however, the use of case analysis in the study of media management is fairly new. The Harvard Business School is well known for its role in the development of management case studies. From 1909 to 1919 the presentation was largely verbal and personal with business executives asked to come to classes and present problems for students to analyze (Leenders & Erkskine, 1973). In 1921 the first book of written cases by the Graduate School of Business Administration at Harvard Business School was published (Towl, 1969). Since that time, cases have assumed a larger role within the business setting to illustrate the environment of decision making. Although several definitions of case analysis exist, perhaps the following most aptly fits this particular book's goals: "A case typically is a record of a business issue which actually has been faced by business executives, together with surrounding facts, opinions, and prejudices upon which executive decisions had to depend" (Gragg, 1954, p. 6).

This definition is what guided the authors in selecting the kind(s) of cases to be included in the book. Cases should provide a vehicle by which reality can be assessed. Cases are meant to be pulled apart and examined from as many perspectives as possible so that the general as well as specific situation can be understood. In addition, cases offer the opportunity to explore different attitudes or ways of thinking about situations. Case study is not a passive learning experience but rather is built upon the assumption that learning will occur through active participation. Extensive discussion is expected because ideas are shared via conversation that also is subjected to open debate and criticism. The challenge is to discover the core issues and to determine the most practical and effective procedures for dealing with the problems and opportunities presented in the case.

Kinds of Cases

The methodology of cases can be organized in several ways, however all cases have three dimensions: (a) analytical aspects, (b) presentation aspects, and (c) conceptual underpinnings (Leenders & Erskine, 1973). A case's degree of sophistication turns on how these three dimensions are combined. It is typical that cases are rarely pure in their analytical sophistication, and so readers must be astute in figuring out the core concerns and in focusing on the issues to be resolved. The cases appearing in this book vary in their complexity, but all of them demand knowledge of theory as well as practice. It is assumed that students and teachers will go beyond the case facts presented. That is, there is no perfect answer to any of the case problems. The resolutions may draw on as many creative resources as the readers are capable of introducing. The central structure and most reasonable avenues of discovery are suggested by the authors of the cases, but readers need not feel constrained to limit their thinking to only those avenues suggested by case authors.

Analytical Aspects

Typically, the most simple kind of case begins by introducing a problem and suggesting solutions. The reader is expected to decide if the suggested solutions are suitable and to consider alternatives. Case 3.2 is an example of this kind of analysis. Readers are asked to assess the leadership responsibilities of management after an episode of ethical concern has occurred at a television station.

A second kind of case provides only a problem and asks the reader to suggest an original solution. An example of this is Case 1.1, which requires readers to evaluate past behaviors in light of decision theory, which is reviewed in the chapters.

The most difficult kind of case provides a situation and asks the reader to identify the problem and formulate a reasonable solution. The longer cases are examples of this. In "Facing the Competition in Mount Pleasant," for instance, readers are provided background and asked to analyze the organization and market conditions and to make decisions about the problems confronting a media organization.

Presentation Format

The least sophisticated case provides data in a straightforward way with little extraneous material, whereas the most challenging presentation contains large amounts of extraneous yet important information that is not organized in a way that allows ready and easy consideration. Although this format is difficult to work with, it is perhaps the closest to "real" work situations, which rarely present themselves in precise and direct terms. All several presentation formats are included in this book.

Conceptual Underpinnings

The underlying principles of a case can be so obvious that they require little explanation. However, other cases contain several values and ideas that collide or are worthy contenders in the final analysis. One way to categorize conceptual difficulty is to consider how much clarification is needed to understand the basic problem. That is, if little explanation is needed to understand the concepts under study, the case is a fairly simple one with primary goals evident. However, if extensive clarification and involvement are required to grasp the issues, then the concepts under study are apt to be difficult to summarize and balance without a great deal of supporting evidence and explanation. Ground-breaking or exploratory cases fall into this category because they often require the extension of existing tangentially related theory or practices. Cases in this book lend themselves to consideration of allied business and communication theories, and readers are challenged to go beyond the materials presented to confront the basic issues inherent in the cases.

No matter what mental mechanics and abilities are necessary to resolve a case, all are written to satisfy particular needs for understanding. Cases are valuable in that they require a focused approach to thinking about media companies and allow an in-depth, realistic consideration of decision-making processes. Even the most simple case format provides practice in defining and synthesizing information.

CASE CONTENT

Case data can include materials that have been collected informally as well as systematically. For instance, cases in this book include informal conversations as well as generalizable empirical data. Readers must determine which data are most valuable and relevant to the decisions being considered in the case. Among the questions that might be reasonably considered by readers are:

1. What global-encompassing values are shared among those who are participants in the case? That is, do nearly all members of the community under study have the same level of awareness about common concerns? Misunderstandings between various groups can occur because basic information is not accessible to all participants in the decision process, or all members may not share the same set of priorities concerning values. Case writing and analysis demand careful attention to basic underlying agendas that are built upon world-view realities held by members of the group being studied. For example, even if all members of a company can agree that the goal is to earn a particular profit margin, there will be conflict and/or tension if some managers make decisions that violate basic professional or personal value systems of other workers.

2. What are the confining boundaries of participants in a particular case setting? Data should be examined from the point of view of what is potentially possible given the circumstances and values shared by the community under study. A solution to a case may be theoretically brilliant but inappropriate because of practical limitations that can be grounded in economics, human behavior, or organizational constraints. That is, a company that is in an entrepreneurial or building phase may be able to

adopt a new set of practices more quickly than a company that is grounded in long-held traditions and has stockholders who do not like changes.

3. What situational-specific meanings are shared and utilized by participants in the case under study? Are there boundaries or opportunities that are truly unique to a particular situation that cause peculiar data? When attempting to make generalizations from one case situation to another, it is important to know if organizational, economic, or other constraints exist.

4. What phases or steps of meaning occur among participants? Are there predictable patterns of behavior due to shared meanings about not only content, but actions within the setting? (Lofland, 1971). If the managers in the case always interpret a particular situation or set of behaviors in one way, then resolutions for the case must take this into account.

Case data generally represent days, weeks, months, or years in which behaviors and conduct have been under observation. Case subjects usually have been observed over a long period of time in which routine as well as extraordinary activities have been recorded in a regular, systematic way that includes confidential and intimate conversations as well as very public and open encounters (Lofland, 1971).

PARTS OF THE CASE

Case content includes what Lofland (1971, p. 19) called phase analysis "leading up to a single class of performed act." This effort includes identification of the stages through which action occurs. The data leading up to a single act are analyzed and/or the stages or phases of (or within) a single performed act are analyzed. The action, the people, and the events or activities themselves are all part of the data. The challenge then is for the observer to "find out what is fundamental or central to the people or world under observation" (Lofland, 1971, p. 4). The data collection includes close observation and notation of several variables, which can have static as well as dynamic qualities that may interact or remain separate from others. Among these are the following:

1. *Acts.* These, according to Lofland, are events or activities of short duration (a few seconds or minutes or, at most, hours) that hold either single or collective connections to the participants.
2. *Activities.* Data classified as activities include action that is of a more major duration (weeks, days, months) and provides sustaining interest or importance to the participants and the setting under study.
3. *Meanings.* Verbal pieces of information that define and direct action are considered meanings for participants who may share collective or individual understandings of these meanings.

4. *Participation.* Holistic involvement in or adaptation to situations and settings under study provide context for collective and individual behaviors that are noted.
5. *Relationships.* The interactions and interrelationships among several persons as they simultaneously respond to and work with one another are valueable pieces of data about the case under study.
6. *Settings.* The data analysis should include information about the entire set of variables mentioned previously so that the collective information gathered about Items 1 through 6 include a generalized description of the "whole" (Lofland, 1971).

Although any of the variables just listed can be utilized as a single descriptive vantage point, all of them are necessary components if a complete understanding of the case is to effectively occur. Data collection includes written, internal, formal documents as well as unwritten, but understood, and shared information gained through systematic interviewing or informal, free-flowing observation and conversation. The presentation format can include relatively short reports from 2 to 10 pages or book-size analyses that include several documents or sets of raw data.

CASE ANALYSIS

Several types of case analysis can be utilized, including the systems approach, the behavioral approach, or the decision approach.

In the systems approach, the organization is viewed as engaged in a process of converting inputs to outputs. Processes within the system can be viewed in circular patterns with feedback mechanisms analyzed. In general, this kind of case would describe a media organization's goals, which would be written clearly. A timetable would be set for meeting the goals and the case would state what kind of data would be collected to measure the success in reaching the goals.

The behavioral approach focuses on how inputs become outputs through and with people involved. The values, the norms, and the social structure of protagonists are examined. The decision approach looks at different business alternatives and what events must occur before an alternative can be realized (Ronstadt, 1980).

The cases that follow demand varying degrees of sophistication in data analysis and synthesis. They attempt to remind the readers of both the similarities and differences between media organizations as well as the current and future problems and opportunities for those who choose to contribute to the field through media management practice or theory building. The authors have attempted to unite the scholarly and pragmatic concerns they see facing the field.

1
Managerial Decision Making

Managers usually make decisions the way people breathe, without thinking about the process. Yet decision making is at the heart of the managerial process, just as breathing is central to life. It is difficult to think of any important aspect of running a media organization that is not connected to decisions. Herbert Simon (1960), probably the most noted scholar in the area of decision making, equated the process of decision making to the process of managing.

Making decisions without considering the process works reasonably well on a day-to-day basis. However, decision making is a skill. Just as breathing can be improved with practice, so can decision making. If managers want to improve their abilities to make effective and efficient decisions, they must think about the process they use to decide.

The purpose of this chapter is to introduce material about decision making as a guide to using the cases in this book. The cases provide decision-making practice in a number of managerial areas. This practice will be more effective if a person understands the decision-making process.

DEFINING DECISION MAKING

Definitions of decision making abound. For example, Simon (1960) wrote, "Decision making comprises three principle phases: finding occasions for making decisions; finding possible courses of action; and choosing among the courses of action" (p. 1). Harrison (1987) defined a decision as, " . . . a moment, in an ongoing process of evaluating alternatives for meeting an objective, at which expectations about a particular course of action impel the decision maker to select the course of action most likely to result in obtaining the objective" (p. 2).

Scholars have taken different approaches to decision making. Huber

(1980) distinguished between decision making, choice making, and problem solving. He used problem solving as the broadest term and said it involved anything from dealing with identifying problems to monitoring, maintaining, and reviewing solutions to the problems. He said decision making involved identifying problems, generating alternative solutions, and evaluating and choosing among the solutions. Choice making included just the evaluation and choosing process of decision making.

Many of the traditional approaches to decision making concentrate on the process as a rational one that involves a person or group with common goals. However, Taylor (1984) emphasized the role of social and political context of organizations and their environments. This approach suggests that decisions are not as deliberate as often assumed, but occur more from interaction among people and groups with sometimes conflicting goals.

The range of definitions for decision making suggests that defining this process is somewhat arbitrary. However, some concepts are common to most definitions. For example, decisions almost always involve some forms of resources; they usually address goals or objectives; they always involve people, either as individuals or in groups; and the environment in which these people work almost always affects decisions.

With these common concepts in mind, we define decision making as the allocation of scare resources by individuals or groups to achieve goals under conditions of uncertainty and risk.

This definition has six terms that need discussion. First, *allocation* simply means that things have been distributed among alternatives. Just as a family allocated its income for food, clothing, housing, transportation, and entertainment, media managers must decide how to distribute their resources.

Scare resources means a manager never has all of the resources she would like. Available resources are time and money. To a degree, these two resources are interchangeable. If you have money, but need time, you can hire others. If you have time, but need money, you can sell that time. Certainly, other forms of resources are available, but all are related to time and money. For example, technology is a way of increasing the effectiveness and efficiency of time and is acquired with money. In effect, other forms of resources are derivative of time and money, or they are ways of improving the allocation of time and money.

The word *scarce* is just as important in this term as resources. If resources were not scarce, decision making would not be central to management. Scarcity limits trial and error. With a limitless supply of money and time, people simply could try every alternative until they found the one that worked best. Scarce resources limit the time and money spent on a decision.

The third term is *individuals and groups*. Decisions can be made by one person or by two or more people functioning as a unit. All other things equal, it takes less time for one person to decide than it does a group. However, ease of decision is not the same as effectiveness of decision. Groups make some decisions better than do individuals.

Goal is the fourth term. Goal means a decision has a purpose. The nature of business goals is complex and has been the subject of much debate and research. The cases in this book may or may not state specific goals, but no decision can be made adequately without considering the goals of that decision and the overall goals of the organization.

Because decision making is woven into the fabric of management, it is not surprising that goals of specific decisions and the overall goals of organizations fit into the same general categories. At the highest level of abstraction, goals fall into *rational* and *nonrational* goals. Organizations are considered rational when their goal is to maximize some aspect of business. Simon (1957) defined a rational decision as occurring when a decision maker confronted with alternatives selects the one that has the highest return. This definition of rationality is the basis of classical economic theory and has resulted in the idea that business should maximize some goals, whether it be profits, revenues, or sales.

The assumption of rationality began to crumble after World War II, as scholars began to recognize the limits of the "rational man" approach. Cyert and March (1963) said the profit maximization assumption for businesses was not realistic because people within organizations do not have single-minded purposes. People pursue a variety of goals. Cyert and March also added that firms do not have the perfect knowledge necessary to maximize profits.

In place of this rational assumption for decision making, Simon (1957) suggested the principle of *bounded rationality*. This principle recognizes that humans cannot be rational in the traditional sense because of physical and mental limits. However, Simon was not willing to say people act randomly. Rather, he proposed that humans pursue goals in a purposeful manner but this pursuit is limited by the nature of people and by the social environment in which they live. As a result, people will seek goals and make decisions that work to satisfy instead of maximize their benefits from the decisions. This *satisficing* approach means people adopt goals and decision outcomes that are acceptable within the constraints faced by the organizations.

Uncertainty is the fifth term of the definition that needs discussion. Uncertainty means all decisions are probabilistic. No decision outcome is 100% certain. At best, people can estimate the likelihood that a certain decision will cause a certain outcome. Uncertainty is generated by many factors and is the central problem facing decision makers.

The use of the term uncertainty here is different from that of traditional literature on decision making. Historically, uncertainty has been classified into three conditions: certainty, risk, and uncertainty (Kreitner, 1986).

Certainty meant the outcome of a decision could be predicted accurately. *Risk* meant that probabilities of outcomes could be calculated. *Uncertainty* meant that no reliable information was available to predict outcomes.

The distinction among these three conditions has been criticized for being inconsistent with empirical research and for having little practical use (Bass, 1983; Taylor, 1984). In reality, the calculation of objective probabilities, a term associated with the traditional definition of risk, is impossible. All probabilities associated with decision making deal with future events; yet they are based on past events. All objective probabilities have subjective elements because of assumptions necessitated by the nature of time and measurement. Measurement of any phenomenon is limited, and the future is a change from the past, even though patterns of behavior may show similarity.

In lieu of the traditional approach, uncertainty is used here to mean a level of subjective probability based on information and analysis. These estimates of probability may be as crude as a statement that an outcome is more likely than not, or they may be as sophisticated as a mathematically derived statement of probability. However, all estimates share two characteristics: (a) They are based on analysis of information; and (b) they also are based on assumptions about measurement and time that limit their objective nature.

Uncertainty then rests on a continuum from 0% to 100% uncertainty about a decision outcome. This is shown in Fig. 1.1. As discussed earlier,

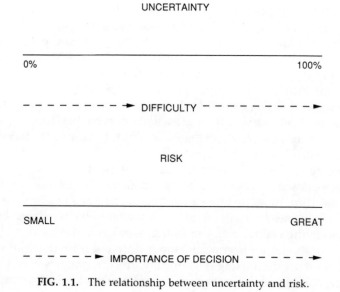

FIG. 1.1. The relationship between uncertainty and risk.

0% uncertain decisions do not exist, and a 100% uncertain decision would be a random solution. As Bass (1983) pointed out, in the absence of other information, people fill in with their experience or that of their acquaintances. As uncertainty increases, the difficulty of making an effective decision increases.

The word *risk* is used differently here than in traditional decision literature. Risk refers to the amount of resources committed to accomplishing a goal and, therefore, the amount of resources that might be lost. Risk also exists on a continuum, shown in Fig. 1.1. The risk runs from small to great. Small means few resources are allocated, whereas great means a large amount of resources are involved. As with uncertainty, rarely will organizations operate at the ends of this continuum. Few organizations will allocate a large percentage of their resources to a given project, much less a single decision. One should remember that risk is a relative term. Allocating $1 million would be a huge proportion of resources at most weekly newspapers, but a relatively small proportion of resources at a large group, such as Gannett. The greater the risk, the more important the decision.

Figure 1.1 can be used to illustrate the importance and difficulty of decisions to a media organization. A decision that concerns a relatively great risk and a high level of uncertainty is important and difficult. In fact, such a venture might not be undertaken. A decision that has little risk and uncertainty would be relatively unimportant and not very difficult to make.

TYPES OF DECISIONS

Decisions fall into two types: *programmed* and *nonprogrammed* (Simon, 1960). A programmed decision sets up a rule that states an action will take place once a certain condition has been reached. A nonprogrammed decision is one that cannot be made by referring to a rule. Programmed decisions tend to be highly structured, with established goals and channels of information. Nonprogrammed decisions have poor structure, vague goals, and ambiguous information. Determining an employee's pay every month is an example of a programmed decision. Publishers at a newspaper do not have to decide how much money to pay their employees at the end of each month. The amount and form have been set up in advance, usually on an annual basis. The exact hour for issuing checks may be the only monthly decision. In many cases, larger organizations have computers that will issue the checks. Selecting a new network news anchor is an example of a nonprogrammed decision. A classic illustration is the process by which Dan Rather was chosen to replace Walter Cronkite in 1981. No rule could have told the managers at CBS who should take Cronkite's place. This type of decision happens too infrequently to develop an effective policy.

The distinction between programmed and nonprogrammed decisions is an important one. If a decision can be programmed effectively, it is wise to do so. The greater the number of programmed decisions, the more time a manager will have to spend on more difficult nonprogrammed decisions. Whether or not a decision can be programmed depends on the uncertainty and the risk involved. The lower the uncertainty and risk, the more likely a programmed decision will work.

The clear-cut distinction between programmed and nonprogrammed decisions might lead managers to the erroneous conclusions that all programmed decisions are alike. This is far from true. All decisions vary as to uncertainty and risk. Some, however, are certain enough and have levels of risk that they can be programmed. This is the equivalent of drawing a line across the two continua in Fig. 1.1 and saying all decisions to the left are programmed and decisions to the right are nonprogrammed. The programmed decisions closest to the line may be those that soon become nonprogrammed because the rule ceases to be effective in a changing environment.

THE DECISION PROCESS

Despite variation in the names given to the steps in the decision process, most models of decision making are similar. For example, Drucker (1983) gave six steps: classify the problem, define the problem, specify what the decision must do, seek the right decision, build in the action to carry out the decision, and use feedback to test the effectiveness of the decision. Huber (1980) listed five steps in problem solving: explore the nature of the problem, generate alternative solutions, choose among alternative solutions, implement the chosen alternative, and control the solution program.

Griffin and Moorhead (1986) offered a model that has advantages over these others. First, they developed a practical version of the traditional rational decision-making model. Second, they incorporated in their model the difference between programmed and nonprogrammed decisions. Third, in their model they acknowledged the role of information at each step.

The model shown in Fig. 1.2 is called a *decision wheel* because it represents the cyclical nature of the decision process. The decision wheel is similar to other models, but it differs from the Griffin and Moorhead (1986) model in two ways. First, it does not include the idea of programmed versus nonprogrammed decisions. Programmed decisions, although important, are not the basis of the case study approach. Although creating a policy may be the solution to a case, this solution results from a nonprogrammed decision process.

A second difference between the decision wheel and other models is the

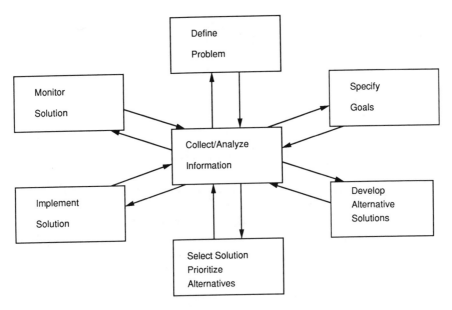

FIG. 1.2. The decision wheel.

central placement of the collection and analysis of information. Just as decision making is the heart of management, the collection and appropriate analysis of information is the hub of decision making. All steps of the decision-making process must involve the collection of information and its appropriate evaluation. The Griffin and Moorhead (1986) model acknowledges the use of information in each step, but the collection of information alone does not result in effective decisions. Analysis, which breaks down the information and then examines and classifies it so it can be used, is a key to effective decisions. Correct analysis with little information often is more useful than poor analysis with abundant information. The importance of the collection and analysis of information is shown in Fig. 1.2 by its central location.

Defining the Problem

The first step is defining the problem to be solved. It involves the collection of information about some form of behavior, either inside or outside the organization, that is a problem for the media firm. This information must be analyzed in a way that allows the managers to frame the problem appropriately. For example, a television news department that is losing audience has a problem. To define the problem behind this decline in ratings, management must develop a list of possible causes and collect information about them. Then the information about the potential causes must be analyzed to decide what the cause may be. Perhaps the audience does not like the hard-news focus of the news shows, or they may not like the anchors. Each problem holds several possible causes. In many cases, problems may have more than one cause. The ability to reverse the sliding ratings, however, will depend on management's ability to define the problem in a way that the causes can be identified correctly.

Specifying Goals

After the problem is defined, the next step is specifying the goals of the decision. The goals need to be concrete. Vague statements about reversing a trend will not allow for effective decision making. The goals should be as specific as the problem and available data will allow. Usually the decision process will address multiple goals. All goals should have some time frame for accomplishing them.

In the television news example, the station president and news director may decide that the station should increase its early evening news ratings by 3 points and its late evening news ratings by 2 points within the next 6 months. These very specific goals allow for better monitoring and force a manager to use detailed analysis of data. It may be that several goals are set up across time. So, the station management may want a 1-point increase in ratings within 3 months and an additional 2-point increase during the following 3 months. The crucial aspect of goal setting is the degree of specificity. To do this, one must collect as much information as possible and analyze it effectively.

Developing Solutions

The third step in the decision wheel is developing alternative solutions. The first effort in this step should develop as many alternatives as possible. Inadequate solutions always can be rejected, but a solution that has not been considered never can be selected. A weeding out process follows the listing of the solutions. Here, the obviously unsuitable solution can be dropped, leaving those that have some possibilities for accomplishing the goals. Just as with all steps, the narrowing process requires the acquisition of information and its analysis. Two questions for developing this short list are: (a) Will the solutions actually accomplish the goals? and (b) will the costs of the solution outweigh the gains to the organization? If the answer to the first question is no, then the solution should be dropped. If the answer to the second question is yes, then the solution should be dropped.

Using the problem of declining ratings, we can list possible solutions to this situation:

1. Hire new anchors.
2. Increase the time devoted to weather.
3. Increase the time devoted to sports.
4. Introduce new segments to the newscast, such as a health information segment.
5. Buy a satellite news-gathering vehicle that would allow more live coverage from distant locations.
6. Change the nature of the news by presenting more feature material and fewer hard-news stories.
7. Hire a new sports announcer.
8. Hire a new weather announcer.

These are just some of the possible solutions. We give only a few of these serious consideration, but it is useful to consider all of the alternatives when decisions must be made.

We can apply the two-question test to eliminate some of the alternatives listed. First, based on a recent viewer survey, the news director rejects Solutions 1, 7, and 8 because all of the on-camera talent received good evaluations from the viewers. Solution 5 can be dropped because the station does not have the money needed to purchase and maintain a satellite news-gathering truck.

Selecting a Solution

With a short list of solutions, a manager moves to Step 4, which involves the selection of one solution to the problem. The solution may be a combination of more than one alternative solution, but the next step requires a decision to pursue a specific solution.

The collection and analysis of information is crucial at this point. Tools and techniques of information collection and analysis are discussed later, but whatever methods are used, one plan emerges. The alternate solutions should not be forgotten, however. Often the original solution does not work as well as management would like. As a result, managers have to return to the problem and either generate new solutions or choose one of the solutions dropped in Step 4. It is a good idea to list the solutions not used in some form of priority for solving the problem, based on the information and analysis in Step 4. This may save time if the chosen solution fails.

Selecting solutions is always a matter of costs and benefits. Often, more than one solution will work, so the correct option is the one with the best return. This means balancing costs with the benefits. One solution may generate more viewers than another, but the costs would be so high as to consume the entire increase in profits from getting more viewers. At the same time, a solution may be inexpensive, but the results will not reach the specified goals.

Returning to the television news department, we find the managers considering the four solutions that remain after Step 3. They reject changing the nature of the news because a recent survey of viewers indicated they generally were pleased with the mix of news being carried. The three remaining solutions all involve the allotment of time. The comparison then becomes one of costs versus expected audience increase. Adding time to weather and sports would not require additional reporters because these two segments already have more material than they use now. The potential for increasing audience exists, based on the recent viewer survey, but the survey also revealed a significant segment of the viewers who did not care much for sports.

Based on the potential negative impact of more sports, the managers narrow the solution to either more time for weather or a new daily segment about health. Either solution will require the expense of promotion and advertisements. The costs of the health spot include loss of time for other news and the expense of training a reporter to cover health issues. The potential for an audience increase appears greater for the health spot for three reasons. First, no other station in the market has such a spot, which means it could be promoted and advertised effectively. Second, this type of spot has attracted viewers in other markets. Third, research has indicated a growing awareness of health and environmental issues by the general population in the United States. On the other hand, the increase in weather coverage cannot be promoted as well because another station in the market already broadcasts more weather information and cable has a 24-hr weather service.

The managers decide that a daily segment devoted to health issues would be the best way to increase their ratings. As a back-up approach, they decide an increase of about a minute each for sports and weather would be best. However, they delay the decision about the exact content to be included in the new health spot. They want more information about what types of health news other stations have included in their spots.

Implementing the Solution

Once the solution has been selected it must be implemented. This is the fifth step in the decision wheel. The solution means nothing unless it is applied correctly. This requires a detailed plan of action with a timetable for specific actions, a budget, and a breakdown of who has responsibility for carrying out the changes. The details should be as specific as possible.

Again, the collection and analysis of information is important at this stage. Much of the information at this point deals with internal organization issues. The budget, timetable, and delegation of responsibility reflect the resources within the media company. It is important to note that the people with the responsibility for carrying out aspects of the solution must be given the power and budget to do so. Responsibility and power always should be connected.

Our television managers, for example, have selected one of their reporters to be in charge of the daily health spot. This reporter was a science major in college and has an interest in this area. The reporter will work directly with a particular producer. The spot will be introduced in 3 months, following an extensive promotional effort, and will occupy about 2 1/2 min every weekday on the early and late evening newscasts. The spots on the two newscasts may or may not cover the same topic, but they always should have different angles. The time will be taken mostly from the news hole, but a half minute will come from the sports segment. About $5,000 has been set aside to fund workshop attendance by the reporter, and about $10,000 has been allocated for researching viewers' responses.

Monitoring the Solution

The final step is monitoring the implementation in light of the goals. This monitoring should provide feedback on a regular basis to judge progress toward the goals and be part of the implementation plan. For example, the television news managers have decided to evaluate the effectiveness of the spot on a monthly basis, as well as through informal weekly discussions with the producer and reporter. Every month, the managers will have a meeting with those involved to discuss the content and any problems. After 3 months, the managers will have meetings with several small groups of viewers to get their comments on the new segment. Also, after each ratings period, the data will be analyzed to determine if the new spot is having an impact on the ratings.

Crucial to the monitoring system is a timetable. A solution that is not working should be given an adequate test period, but a media organization should not remain committed to a solution once it becomes obvious that it will not work. Times should be established during the implementation process at which the managers must decide to continue or end the plan.

This monitoring process makes the entire decision process cyclical. If the solution is not working, this becomes a problem that starts a new cycle of decision making. The same steps are taken in a new cycle but some may take less time and effort because the previous decision process already provides relevant information. However, managers always must be careful not to assume that they have all the information they need. An effective manager continues to acquire information until the cost of additional information outweighs the probable benefit from having that information.

CONSTRAINTS ON THE DECISION PROCESS

The decision wheel is an ideal. It is a blueprint that seldom is followed exactly. The process is affected primarily by two types of constraints: size of decision group and time.

Decision Makers

Decisions can be made by individuals or groups. Whether a group or individual makes the decision influences the efficiency and effectiveness of the decision. In some cases, individuals may decide best. In other cases, group decisions work better. Huber (1980) listed three advantages and four disadvantages of group decisions, whereas Harrison (1987) gave nine strengths and four weaknesses. Griffin and Moorhead (1986) presented six advantages of group decision making and three advantages of individual decision making. Table 1.1 presents a summary of several lists of advantages and disadvantages of group decision making and categorizes them under the headings of timing, uncertainty, and goals.

Interestingly, weaknesses of group decision making also can be strengths. For example, one of the advantages and disadvantages of group

TABLE 1.1
Advantages and Disadvantages of Group Decision Making

Advantages	Disadvantages
TIMING	
Slower decision process task	Slower decision process
Division of labor for complex task	Disagreement over goals may result in no decisions
UNCERTAINTY	
Larger amounts of information and knowledge generated	Political behavior of group members reduces acceptance of information from others
Fewer errors in analyzing information	Groupthink – The tendency of group members to think the group is infallible
More alternatives generated	
GOALS	
Groups can clarify goal understanding	Groups sometimes act in ways inconsistent with
Participation increases acceptance of group goals	Groupthink

decision making is the slow process it involves. Group decision making usually increases the time needed for a decision because of problems in organizing meetings and in the long process of forming consensus among people with conflicting positions. An individual decision maker does not have these timing problems. Whether the time element is an advantage or a disadvantage depends on the decision. If timing is crucial, individuals are better. If timing is not crucial and risk and uncertainty are high, a slower process has advantages.

Deadlines exemplify the timing importance in news departments. Stories do not get used if they are not ready by the printing or broadcast deadlines. So, individuals make most decisions about what stories will run. However, exceptions to this rule often involve important stories. An example of a group decision involving a news story is the case of the Pentagon Papers. The Pentagon Papers were a secret report about the history of the Vietnam War. They were prepared in the late 1960s for Secretary of Defense Robert S. McNamara, who served for President Lyndon Johnson. *The New York Times* got the report from Daniel Ellsberg, who helped prepare it. After four installments of the Papers ran in *The New York Times* in June 1971, a federal court issued a restraining order. Meanwhile, *The Washington Post* had obtained a copy of the report. A group of 10 managers of the *Post* met for 12 hr to discuss whether they should publish parts of the report. They published (Witcover, 1971).

The inherent lack of speed in group decisions is not the only advantage or disadvantage of groups. When complex tasks are involved, groups have the advantage of division of labor. Dividing tasks among group members actually can speed up the process because no one person must learn the wide range of complex information required for complex decisions. Buying a new computer system for a newspaper is an example. Because such systems often serve several departments, it would make sense to include in the decision-making process someone from each of these departments who is familiar with the departments' computer needs rather than expect one or two people to learn about the computer needs of all the departments.

Another problem with the timing of groups is that they may not reach a decision at all. Disagreement over the goals of an organization or over the particular goals of a group can lead to no decision. This tends to be rare because management generally will not accept indecision from groups. But under extreme conditions this can occur, with the resulting need to start the decision process all over again.

Advantages and disadvantages of group decisions also fall under the heading of uncertainty. Group decision making can reduce uncertainty in three ways. First, having more than one person will increase the amount of information and knowledge brought to the process. Second, it will decrease the number of errors. The cliche' "two heads are better than one" applies here. Having more people also can reduce information errors because people can evaluate each other's information and analysis. Third, groups generate more alternative solutions. The ability to compare alternatives against each other can result in better solutions.

Although uncertainty can decline with groups, it can increase. The probabilities that develop from the satisficing approach are subjective. This subjectivity is influenced by the attitudes and perceptions of other group members. Political behavior among group members can create doubt as to appropriate goals and desirability of solutions. For example, when both a city editor and a sports editor each tries to persuade other group members that her department is key to improving quality, the very process of persuasion can cast doubt on either department being effective at attracting readers. The result is uncertainty of actions.

Just as dangerous as political behavior, which can divide, is the phenomenon of *groupthink*. Groupthink occurs when group members are so set on sustaining unanimity among themselves that they fail to properly appraise the alternative solutions (Janis, 1982). Although the group feels they have reduced uncertainty because they agree on the best alternative, they actually have decreased the probability that any one solution will work. The solution does not get an adequate evaluation.

The final heading in Table 1.1 is Goals. Because of the numbers of people involved, groups often will develop a better understanding of the organization's and decision group's goals. Reading a statement of goals adopted by an organization does not mean automatically that the employees understand those goals. Hearing others discuss the goals can help clarify them.

Another advantage is that participation in group decision making will increase acceptance of the goals and solutions that are adopted. Increased acceptance can translate into increased effort in accomplishing the goals. People tend to accept more readily those decisions in which they participated.

A disadvantage of group decisions with respect to goals is the tendency of some groups to develop their own goals that may be inconsistent with the organization's goals. For example, a group set up within a media organization to develop ways to cut costs may decide that cost cutting is not a proper goal. The result will be a conflict of goals between management and the decision group. Resulting decisions are less likely to accomplish the aims of management.

The many advantages and disadvantages of group decisions create problems for deciding when groups or individuals should make decisions. Vroom and Yetton (1973) said that individual managers are likely to make decisions themselves when the problem is well structured, information is plentiful, a previously successful solution to a similar problem is available, and time constrains require a quick decision.

Time and Decision Making

In addition to classifying by the size of the group involved, decisions can be broken down on the basis of time available. Three general timing patterns seem appropriate. Nonprogrammed decisions can be classified as *immediate*, *short-term*, or *long-term*. Immediate decisions must be made quickly. The time that is available between Step 1 and Step 5 in the decision wheel is measured in hours or even minutes. Story decisions on deadline are the prime examples in media.

As a result of deadlines, it is common to find individuals making content decisions at newspapers, magazines, and television news departments. However, the deadline pressure hides the danger that individuals will begin making all decisions quickly and alone out of habit. No decision should be made before time requires it. If a decision need not be made immediately, participation of others, either in the actual solution selection or in other steps of the process, should be sought.

Short-term decisions are ones that need not be made immediately, but they must be made within a reasonable period of time. At a newspaper, the plans for a breakdown of news and advertising space for the coming week would be short-term.

Small groups usually make these decisions, even if one person has responsibility. For example, the publisher, who has final authority for space in a newspaper, may meet with the advertising manager and editor to determine news holes for a week. Often the publisher has determined a breakdown for the year between news and advertising space. The meetings are monitoring sessions by which the three managers discuss news-editorial needs in light of the year's goal, previous use of space, and the newsroom's space needs for the week.

Long-term decisions are those that affect the organization over a period of years and, therefore, warrant a longer decision-making process. This type of decision ranges from the television news ratings problem discussed earlier to format changes at a magazine or newspaper. Because of their complexity, these decisions require participation by a large number of people in groups and as individuals. In effect, a long-term decision, such as what next year's budget should be, requires hundreds or thousands of smaller decisions.

Overall, time acts as a constraint on the process shown in the decision wheel by limiting the time available for each of the six steps. These limits determine how much information can be collected, how much analysis can be conducted, and how many people can participate in the decision. For example, immediate decisions allow very little time for each step and for information collection and analysis. Long-term decisions should include adequate time for each step.

The timing of various types of decisions places a premium on different types of managers. When an immediate decision is needed, a satisfactory solution is more important than an optimal solution. So the person who has command of a great deal of information in an area and who can analyze quickly will perform best. This person need not be as good at working with people as a manager who deals with short- and long-term problems.

A manager faced with short-term decisions needs both people skills and the ability to reach decisions within a reasonable time. On the other hand, managers who must make long-term decisions are better served by skills that allow them to work with people and that allow them to examine a problem from several angles. This person should be good at analysis, but it is analysis with a different time frame. This manager must be good at developing many alternatives and evaluating them against each other. The variation of needed skills explains why some people make better upper level managers, such as editor, than lower level managers, such as assistant city editor.

The key to effective decision making is to put people in positions where their abilities will serve them best and then to train them in the areas where they are weakest. The ability to understand and handle time constraints is essential if a person is to be promoted within the media organization.

TOOLS OF MANAGEMENT

Just as decision makers and time constrain decision making, so does the quality of information and analysis, which relate directly to the skills of the decision maker. As with all skills, collecting and analyzing information can be improved through learning. This section will address briefly the sources of information and some of the tools of analysis.

Sources of information

Because information plays so important a role in all six steps, it is useful to examine where one gets information. Basically, information comes either from one's own efforts or from the efforts of others. The efforts can take various forms, however, and those forms can affect the quality of information. The two main types of efforts are *experience* and *research*. Experience means participating in events or processes, and research is the application of generally accepted systematic methods of examining events or processes. If you work at a news magazine, you have experience in magazine journalism. If you conduct a survey of news magazine reporters, you are conducting research about magazine journalism. Experience differs from research in that it does not have accepted standards for analyzing data. Experience is inseparable from the person having the experience. But a researcher, if conducting research properly, should have a minimal impact on the events or processes being studied.

In effect, research should be more objective and systematic than experience. Should be are important words because quality of research depends on the researcher's skills, just as quality of experience depends on the wisdom of the person experiencing the event. Experience can be analyzed systematically and somewhat objectively by a manager, just as a researcher inadvertently can alter the result of his research through poor use of methods.

Managers have roughly four sources of information: their own experiences, the experiences of others, their research, and the research of others. By reading, watching, and discussing, managers learn about other people's experience and research. Because the quality of the information relates to the skills of the person producing it, managers should be able to evaluate information and people providing the information. This is important because people who have something to win or lose from a decision will try to influence decisions with biased information.

For example, good research always should include a detailed description of the method of collection and analysis. Included in this are the weaknesses of the research as perceived by the researcher. Information that does not give its limits should be considered suspect.

One of the most important tests of any information or source of information is the ability to predict. High-quality information will allow one to predict the outcome of decisions with some degree of accuracy. If a manager gets information from a source that results in a decision that accomplishes her goal, she will be likely to use information from that source in the future.

The tendency among media managers is to depend on their experiences and the experiences of trusted colleagues. Experience has the characteristics of being detailed and specific to a particular situation. This can be an advantage when a decision must be made about a situation similar to previous events. However, using one's experience becomes a liability when that experience is applied to a problem that differs from the original experience. The result in such cases is often a poor decision.

Managers should know the value of all forms of information and seek many diverse sources of information, especially in the monitoring step. A successful manager analyzes past decisions so the next decision can be made more effective. The results of every decision should become information for future decisions, but the usefulness of this information depends on the ability to use tools of analysis.

Analysis Tools

A manager with few analytical skills or with little knowledge and experience will end up depending on others to judge the reliability and validity of information. This can be a problem. Managers who understand analysis are in a better position to select information appropriate for decisions. Analysis involves ways of processing information. Several different types of analysis, which vary in complexity, are available. Three of the approaches are mentioned here as examples of how these formal analysis systems work.

Perhaps the most recognized analytical tool is *cost-benefit analysis,* which is an attempt to estimate the costs and the benefits that would result from alternative actions. McKean (1975) listed five steps: (a) identifying benefits to be achieved, (b) identifying the alternatives that will reach the goal, (c) identifying the costs for the alternative methods, (d) developing a model or set of relationships that explain the impact of alternatives on the costs and benefits, and (e) a criterion, involving both costs and benefits, for selecting the preferred alternative. These steps sound familiar because they correspond to steps of the decision wheel.

The traditional approach to cost-benefit analysis is to place a monetary value on all costs and benefits and compare the resulting differences (Huber, 1980). Because this is difficult to do with many types of costs, cost-benefit analysis may include the "dollar-equivalency technique" (Huber, 1980, p. 80), which is the development of money equivalents for costs that are difficult to measure in dollars. Obviously, this becomes problematical when costs and benefits involve human behavior.

Two concepts are useful in dealing with the nonmonetary aspects of cost-benefit analysis: *opportunity costs* and *intangibles.* Opportunity costs are the expenses that accrue from giving up alternative actions. It is an example of the old saying, "There's no free lunch." For every alternative selected, a person loses what she would have gained from another alternative. For example, a manager is hiring a reporter and must pick from two candidates. The first is stronger at writing and the second at reporting. If the first is hired, an opportunity cost is the reporting ability that will be lost from not hiring the second. If the second is hired, an opportunity cost is the writing skill that will be lost from not hiring the first.

Intangibles are the things that cannot be measured well. This may be leadership in a manager or the ability of some people to raise morale in an organization. Whatever the attribute, a dollar amount cannot be assigned adequately. These intangibles often are ignored in formal tools of analysis because they cannot be measured well.

Opportunity costs and intangibles are the Achilles heel of cost-benefit analysis and most other types of formal analysis. These two concepts relate to all decisions, although sometimes they are more important than at other times. Despite these two problems, cost-benefit analysis can be useful even if it simply allows a manager to think more clearly. The following example demonstrates the potential use of cost-benefit analysis in a situation where quantification is difficult.

The *Times-Leader* recently conducted a readership survey in which 48% of the readers said they would like to have more in-depth local coverage. Managing Editor Jane Smith has been assigned to come up with a plan for doing this. Her first observation is that it can be done either by hiring a new reporter or by using existing staff. She comes up with the benefits and advantages presented in Table 1.2.

The monetary benefits for either alternative are equal in Table 1.2 and amount to $54,000 per year. These benefits are based on retaining 250

TABLE 1.2
Cost-Benefit Analysis of Increasing In-Depth Reporting at the *Times-Leader*

	Alternatives	
Costs	*Hiring a Reporter*	*Using Existing Staff*
Monetary	$30,000 a year salary $5,000 a year expenses for travel & research $13,000 for 26 additional pages at cost of $500 per page	$10,000 a year additional overtime $5,000 a year expenses for travel & research $13,000 for 26 additional pages at cost of $500 per page
Opportunity	Dissatisfaction among existing staff because they will not be allowed to do in-depth work Editing time lost on day-to-day coverage due to increased editing needs of in-depth coverage	Use of staff for in-depth reporting will reduce time for day-to-day reporting Editing time lost on day-to-day coverage due to increased editing needs of in-depth coverage
Intangible	Possible negative impact of new reporter in newsroom	Added effort needed to balance in-depth coverage among existing staff
	Benefits[a]	
Monetary	Save $4,000 needed to gain 250 lost readers Save $50,000 in advertising revenue that could be lost with decline of 500 readers	Save $4,000 needed to gain 250 lost readers Save $50,000 in advertising revenue that could be lost with decline of 500 readers
Intangible	Increased morale among staff from increased quality of newspaper Promotional value of expected recognition from in-depth coverage	Increased morale among staff from increased quality of newspaper Promotional value of expected recognition from in-depth coverage Increased staff morale for those who do in-depth reporting

Note. The goal is to increase the amount of in-depth coverage by an average of one page every 2 weeks.

[a]Benefits are based on an estimated retention of 250 readers and attracting 250 new readers as a result of increased in-depth coverage.

readers a year and attracting 250 more readers annually as a result of increased in-depth coverage. Two main areas of monetary benefits are saving $4,000 from not having to replace the 250 readers and making $50,000 in advertising revenue that would be lost if the 500 readers were not taking the newspaper.

Both approaches also have intangible benefits in the form of staff morale and the promotional advantage of having in-depth coverage that will generate recognition of the newspaper's journalistic efforts. The use of existing staff has an added advantage in that it will increase morale of the staff because they will be allowed to spend time on more lengthy projects.

Monetary costs of hiring an additional reporter are about $20,000 more a year because the new reporter would earn $30,000 a year, whereas overtime needed to use existing staff would only amount to $10,000. Both alternatives have opportunity costs. Each alternative would require about the same amount of additional editing, which would have to come from the time spent on editing of day-to-day stories.

Two opportunity costs and two intangible costs stand out as important factors. First, hiring a new reporter could create dissatisfaction among the existing staff members who would like to pursue in-depth reporting. In-depth work usually is looked on by reporters as a kind of reward because it is more satisfying and interesting than most day-to-day coverage. On the other hand, taking time from day-to-day coverage has the opportunity cost of reducing the amount of space and effort spent on everyday reporting. This could negatively affect circulation.

The intangible costs also involve the staff's reaction to a new plan. If a new reporter is hired, he or she may alter the chemistry among people in the newsroom. This impact, combined with the possible resentment, may have negative consequences. On the other hand, a new reporter might add to the newsroom chemistry. Whether this becomes a cost or not would depend on who is hired as the new reporter. The use of existing staff means an added cost for the editors because they must ensure that the in-depth assignments are distributed fairly. Otherwise, staff resentment could develop.

By examining Table 1.2, a manager could see that the question of which approach to take comes down to whether the additional $20,000 cost of a new reporter and the potential newsroom disruption exceeds the impact of reducing the day-to-day coverage in the newspaper. This, in turn, is related to the adequacy of the current staff. If the newsroom already is understaffed, expanding the work required could be disastrous. More readers might drop the paper because of poor day-to-day coverage than would take the paper because of increased in-depth reporting. In order to make an appropriate selection, a manager needs to have an understanding of the nature of the reporters currently working and an awareness of the informal organizational setting in the newsroom.

An important point of this illustration is that many of the costs and benefits are not quantifiable. But this should not lead to these costs and benefits being ignored. A second point is that the analysis is only as good as the information that goes into it. The monetary costs and benefits should be accurate, but the knowledge of the people in the newsroom needs to be just as reliable and valid.

A second analytical tool is the *decision tree*. Huber (1980) defined a decision tree as "a graphic model that displays the sequence of decisions and the events that comprise a sequential situation" (p. 118). Just as cost-benefit analysis can be formal with involved mathematics, so can decision trees (Harrison, 1987; McCreary, 1978). The mathematical use of decision trees involves assigning probabilities and monetary values to various outcomes so they can be compared as to payoff.

Decision trees need not be mathematical to be useful, however. Non-mathematical trees can be beneficial because they graphically represent the decision process at hand and because they allow a manager to list possible outcomes and see how they are related.

Figure 1.3 shows an example of a nonmathematical decision tree. It contains information from Table 1.2. In this case, Jane Smith is using a decision tree to analyze the potential impact of opportunity and intangible costs. In the example, the squares represent a decision fork and the circles an outcome fork. Each fork has branches. The branches of the decision fork represents possible actions, whereas the branches of the outcome fork represent different results. At the end of the outcome, branches are either payoffs of the solution or additional decision forks (Huber, 1980, pp. 118–130). When numbers are used in a decision tree, these payoffs are profit or loss outcomes, which are compared to select the best solution. Because Fig. 1.3 is not a mathematical decision tree, the payoffs are nonmonetary.

Figure 1.3 shows the impact on day-to-day reporting of hiring or not hiring a new reporter. The two decision branches are hire a new reporter or use existing staff. The three outcome branches of these two decisions are increased day-to-day reporting, no effect on day-to-day reporting, and decreased day-to-day reporting. The only outcome branches of interest are decreased day-to-day reporting, because the other two outcomes require no action. Because hiring a new reporter will not reduce day-to-day reporting, the top outcome branches need not be pursued. However, the reduction of day-to-day coverage from using existing staff requires a second decision fork, which is what to do about the reduced day-to-day coverage. The options are to increase overtime to make up for coverage decline, do nothing, or hire a new reporter to make up the lost coverage.

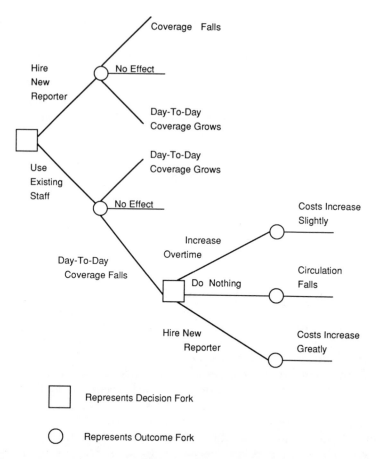

FIG. 1.3.   A decision tree for using existing staff or hiring a new reporter to increase news coverage.

The payoff for the first is a slight increase in costs, whereas the second results in a circulation decline. The third outcome payoff is a great increase in cost because the result would be the same as if she had taken the other original decision branch.

The decision tree is a way of examining the decision points and possible solutions for decisions. A nonmathematical tree will not provide numbers to compare, but it will allow a clearer picture of possibilities. In this case, the manager either must spend more money to make up for lost day-to-day coverage, either through overtime or hiring a new reporter, or must accept the drop in circulation from reduced coverage.

By using a series of decision trees that explore the possible outcomes in several areas, Jane can better analyze the two options and be prepared to take action to correct any negative repercussions of her decision. A manager who has a good knowledge of her staff and newsroom can then make a better estimation of the outcome of a decision and take action to head off the problems that will result.

Another approach to making decisions is *utility theory,* which states that managers attempt to maximize utility from a decision by applying subjective estimates of benefits from outcomes and subjective probability estimates that the outcomes will happen. Utility can be measured in three ways:

1. *Nominal utility* assigns descriptions to outcomes. The descriptions can be numbers or simply adjectives. For example, one outcome may be described as good and another as bad.
2. *Ordinal utility* involves involves ranking outcomes as either more or less desirable.
3. *Cardinal utility* means assigning a numerical value to outcomes. An example of this would be estimates of profits from increasing advertising rates (Harrison, 1987).

Utility theory is the basis for the rational decision-maker approach discussed earlier in the chapter. It has all of the limitations associated with that approach. However, it can prove useful when it is combined with the concept of *expected value* and used in situations where decisions can be quantified accurately (Taylor, 1984). Expected value means a person combines the quantifiable outcomes of a decision with the probability of the outcomes to get an estimate of what one might expect from making the decisions (Harrison, 1987).

An example of expected value is shown in Table 1.3. The decision to increase in-depth coverage by using existing staff has two possible outcomes: (a) an increase in circulation that would lead to increased profit of $26,000 a year; and (b) a loss of $15,000 because of dropped circulation due to loss of day-to-day coverage. The decision to increase in-depth coverage by hiring a new reporter has two possible outcomes: (a) an increase in circulation that would lead to increased profit per year of $6,000; and (b) no effect on circulation.

Based on the reader survey conducted earlier, Jane Smith estimates the probability of the outcomes at 50% each for the two that involve using existing staff. The probabilities for the outcomes of hiring a new reporter are 60% for the increase in profit and 40% for no effect. The probability of the outcomes for a given decision always equals 100%.

Table 1.3 shows how the monetary outcomes are multiplied by the probability to get an expected value of the solutions. In this case, the expected value of using existing staff is $5,500, compared to the expected

TABLE 1.3
Expected Value of Increasing In-Depth Coverage

Decision	Expected Profit	Probability of Profit	Expected Value
Use Existing Staff			
Outcome A	+$26,000	.5	+$13,000
(Increase in circulation)			
Outcome B	−$15,000	.5	−$ 7,500
(Drop in circulation)			
			+$ 5,500
Hire New Reporter			
Outcome A	+$ 6,000	.6	+$ 3,600
(Increase in Circulation)			
Outcome B	− −	.4	000
(No effect)			
			+$ 3,600

value of $3,600 from hiring a new reporter. All else being equal, Jane Smith would increase in-depth coverage by using existing staff.

The points upon which the decision turns are the money estimates and the probability estimates. For example, if hiring a new reporter only cost $25,000 a year, instead of $30,000, the expected value of this option would equal $5,500. The $5,000 difference in salary would be added to the profit and multiplied by the probability of .6. As a result, the two options would have equal expected value.

If the probabilities associated with using existing staff were less (say .4 and .6), the expected value of that option would be only $1,400. This results because the $26,000 would be multiplied by .4, which equals $10,400, and the loss of $15,000 now would be multiplied by .6, which equals $9,000. This takes place because the probabilities have to equal 1.00 (100%). After subtracting the possible loss of $9,000 from the possible profit of $10,400, one is left with an expected value of $1,400 from using existing staff. With the change in probabilities, the option of hiring a new reporter becomes the best option because $3,600 expected value is greater than $1,400 expected value.

Because this approach depends so heavily on the accurate estimate of monetary payoff and probabilities, it is of limited use for decisions that involve a great deal of intangibles and opportunity costs. Yet it can be useful even in these decisions for exploring the monetary results of a decision, as long as it is used cautiously.

Successful use of these formal analytical tools depends greatly on the quality of the information being fed into them. Poor information will result in poor decisions. However, another analytical tool is available that can improve the quality of information, whether it be from experience or research. This tool is called *theory*.

Social science theory is a system of abstract statements that describes a set of behaviors. Theories can provide one or more of the following: (a) a method of classifying behavior, called a typology, (b) predictions of future events and behavior, (c) explanations of past events or behaviors, (d) a sense of understanding about what causes events, and (e) the potential to control events or behavior (Reynolds, 1971). The usefulness of a theory depends on how many of and how well these functions are fulfilled by the theory. All of the five possible functions of theory would be useful to a manager in making decisions because they help reduce uncertainty.

Useful theories can be found in sociology, psychology and economics, and many of these are discussed in this book. One example of applying theory would be the use of equity theory. Equity theory states that people evaluate how fairly they are being treated by an organization in four steps. First, a person evaluates how he is being treated. Second, the person evaluates how a "comparison-other" is being treated. This other is someone the individual considers to be equivalent to himself in some way from the organization's perspective. Third, the individual compares the treatment of himself and the other. Fourth, the individual feels he is being treated either equitably or inequitably (Griffin & Moorhead, 1986).

As a result of the comparison, a person who feels equity is motivated to continue the current situation, whereas the person who feels inequity may take several different steps to reduce the inequity feeling. An important implication of this theory is that the absolute amount of a pay raise given a person is not as important in many cases as the evaluation of the raise with respect to others in the organization.

Equity theory is one of many behavioral theories. The point here is that it can be used to analyze behavior. For example, if an employee displays lack of motivation or poor performance following a pay raise, it may be a result of inequity feelings. A manager who explores this possibility may be able to work with the employee by examining her approach to equity. It may be that the person's comparison-other is inappropriate, that the comparison-other got a large raise because of something unusual, or that the inequity feeling was justified. Whatever the case, theory can be useful in classifying and understanding the behavior of people in an organization.

The use of theory for decision making takes five steps. First, a person must be familiar enough with theories to identify which are useful in a given situation. Usually, behavior may fit more than one theory. Second, a manager applies several theories and selects the one that might be useful in understanding the given behavior. Third, more information is collected to better fit the behavior to the theories and narrow down further. Fourth, the behavior is examined in light of the appropriate theories. Finally, the resulting information is fed back into the decision wheel process.

Across time, managers will find some theories more useful than others in explaining behavior. However, they should be careful not to apply a theory just because it worked in other cases, and they should make an effort to keep up with theories that develop.

SUMMARY

Decision making is the heart of managing. Decisions fall into either programmed, which means the solutions take effect under prescribed conditions, or nonprogrammed, which requires attention to the individual problems that must be solved. Nonprogrammed decisions are more difficult to make. All programmed decisions originally were set up by nonprogrammed decisions.

Reaching decisions has an abstract form presented here as a decision wheel. The steps in this wheel occur to some degree in all effective decisions, although the time and effort devoted to the individual steps varies with the conditions surrounding the individual problem.

Just as decision making is at the heart of management, so analysis and information collection are the hub of decisions. Lack of information or poor analysis of information account for a high percentage of decisions that fail to achieve their goals. Several tools are available to improve analysis and information collecting, including theories and formal techniques for evaluating decision outcomes.

As with the majority of human endeavors, management can be made better with thought and practice. The remainder of this book is designed to facilitate thought and provide practice through cases. Each chapter also presents background to help explore the cases. The theories and research presented in the early part of the chapter should be used to analyze the information that either is provided with the case or needs to be collected from outside sources. In all cases, the decision process applies.

CHAPTER 1 CASES

Case 1.1

Assignment: Looking at Past Decisions

People very often make important decisions without properly preparing or fully examining the decision process. The purpose of this assignment is to have you think about your decision-making process by concentrating on a specific decision. Select some important decision (choosing a college or college major, moving in with someone, etc.) that you made during the past few years that has disappointed you. Think for a few minutes about how you made that decision and why you were disappointed. Now, using the decision wheel from chapter 1 try to remember the actions you took that would have fit into the various steps in the wheel.

Your assignment is to write a brief summary of the decision, and then answer the following questions:

1. Did you take all of the steps in the decision wheel? If not, which ones were not taken and why?
2. Did you complete each step as thoroughly as you should have? If not, which ones were not completed thoroughly and why?
3. If you could make that decision over again, what would you do differently to improve your decision?

Case 1.2

Assignment: Future Decision Making

Although not all decisions require the use of an elaborate decision-making process like the one outlined in the decision wheel, some important and risky decisions are made better using such a model. This assignment is designed to have you think about applying this model to an important decision.

Pick an important decision that you will be making within the next few years. For example, you may want to think about a career decision or one concerning where you will live. With this decision in mind answer the following questions:

1. What are the goals of this decision?
2. Where can you collect information about your options?
3. What alternatives do you think you will have?
4. What types of considerations will help you prioritize these alternatives?
5. What criteria will you use to determine if it is a good or bad decision?
6. How might you change your decision-making strategy, if at all, as a result of this chapter?

Case 1.3

Assignment: Programming Decisions

Decisions can be divided into those that are programmed and those that are nonprogrammed. Programmed decisions save time and effort because they involve sets of rules that more or less automatically make decisions. The purpose of this assignment is to help you understand the difference between the two.

Think about the decisions you have made during the past couple of days. List the ones that best fit under the heading of programmed. List the decisions that best fit under the heading of nonprogrammed. Now go over the list of nonprogrammed decisions and see if any of these types can be turned into programmed decisions. Explain why or why not for each of the decisions on the list.

2
The Structure of Media Organizations

Many people believe that a good employee should be able to perform well regardless of the structure of the organization. Others believe that in the right organizational structure, anyone should be able to perform well. The truth is probably somewhere in between.

The structure of media organizations defines the tasks, communication, and authority relationships within the organization. An organizational chart illustrates how the parts of an organization fit together. Structure can also be viewed as the informal influences within an organization, such as the persons and things that motivate members to achieve goals. Taken together, organizational structure exists to order and coordinate the actions of employees to achieve organizational goals.

This chapter analyzes various aspects of structure and the effects of such structure on media organizations. First, organizations are viewed as formal, classical systems. Next, organizations are analyzed as informal, humanistic systems. Then, a combination of the informal and formal approaches are presented. Finally, studies of media organizations are presented to demonstrate the effect structure has on situational variables of media organizations.

CLASSICAL APPROACH

Classical approaches to studying organizational structure are based on a carefully developed chain of command and efficient division of labor. In a formalized structure, positions are specified, roles are defined, and role relationships are prescribed independently of the personal characteristics of members. Organizations are designed to attain specific preset goals and are less concerned with the selection of those goals than with their attainment. Formalization serves to make the goals and relationships of an organization appear to be objective. The organizational structure is viewed as a means to an end that can be modified only to improve performance.

Taylor's (1947) scientific management theory and Weber's (1921/1947) theory of bureaucracy are two classical theories of organizational structure that stand out. They developed the importance of formal structure and concerned themselves with specifying the nature or content of that structure.

Scientific Management

Taylor (1947) believed it was possible to scientifically analyze tasks performed by workers and thereby discover procedures that would produce the maximum output with the minimum input of resources. He transformed the role of the manager from arbitrary decision maker to one who makes decisions based on analytical, scientific procedures. For example, workers would be selected scientifically to perform tasks for which they were best suited. Scientifically determined procedures would allow them to work at optimal efficiency for which they would receive top pay. Table 2.1 summarizes four prescribed techniques on ordering the workplace.

Managers would devise appropriate work arrangements and salaries based on the prescribed techniques, and workers would cooperate. Communication was to be formal and hierarchical. Its purpose was to increase productivity and efficiency. Overall, Taylor viewed communication as one-sided (from managers to subordinates) and task oriented (Taylor, 1947).

This scientific approach proved less than successful. Employers questioned it because it undermined workers' good judgment. They saw the system as an unnecessary interference and an attempt to standardize every aspect of their performance. Workers also rejected incentive systems requiring them to perform continuously at optimal levels (Bendix, 1956).

TABLE 2.1

Taylor's Techniques for Ordering the Workplace

---

1. Each task is examined with a time and motion study to find the best way to permit the largest average production during a day.
2. Workers are given a financial incentive to work in the best way.
3. Specialized experts are used as functional foremen to instruct and supervise the workers on aspects of their work: methods, speeds, tools, task priorities, discipline, quality, machine maintenance.
4. Managers should not arbitrarily change the standard production rate.

Note. Adapted from Tausky (1980).

Bureaucracy

Prior to Taylor's scientific management school was the work of Max Weber (1921/1947). Weber developed the bureaucratic model of organization design. He viewed a bureaucracy as a logical, rational, and efficient form of organization. He developed the model as a normative framework where organizations strive for one best way of administration. A simple list of these administrative characteristics present in bureaucratic forms are listed in Table 2.2.

The bureaucratic model of organization has several strengths. Elements such as division of labor, reliance on rules, and hierarchy of authority may improve efficiency and are still used today in organizations. The model was also the starting point for later research about organization design. The bureaucratic model also has several disadvantages. It tends to be rigid and inflexible. The human-relations aspects of the organization are neglected. Some of Weber's (1921/1947) assumptions about loyalty and impersonal relations are also unrealistic. However, the bureaucratic model of organization design was an important development of management theory and continues to shape definitions of the central elements of administrative systems.

Formal organizational theories were concerned with basic questions of structure. They proposed principles applicable to all types of organizations that managers ideally should follow. Although these are no longer viewed as universal principles, they highlight the important structural variables to

TABLE 2.2
Bureaucratic Components

1. Fixed division of labor among participants—Each office's duties are clearly specified.
2. Hierarchy of offices—Each office is subject to discipline from a superordinate office only in regard to the duties of the office. An official's private live is free from organizational authority.
3. Set of general rules that govern performance—Impersonality, not personal relationships, regulates activity. Specific and general rules regarding subordinates, peers, rank and file members, and clients are binding.
4. Separation of personal from official property and rights—Officeholders are employees. The "means of administration" are attached to the office, not the officeholder. The officeholder cannot gain personal rights to the office.
5. Selection of personnel on the basis of technical qualifications—Hiring and promotion are based on competence, as measured by certificated training or performance in office.
6. Employment viewed as a career by participants—Bureaucracy membership is a career with distinct ladders of progression.

Note. Adapted from Weber (1921).

be considered in designing organizations including (a) unity of command, (b) span of control, (c) division of labor, and (d) departmentation.

Unity of Command

The unity of command principle argues that a subordinate should have only one superior to whom she is directly responsible. To have more than one superior would create the possibility that subordinates would face conflicting priorities. However, in broadcast newsroom situations, reporters are responsible to several supervisors. News directors judge their overall job performance. Assignment editors evaluate their coverage of a news story. Producers are concerned with how stories are visualized and organized.

Research suggests that when unity of command has to be violated, there should be a clear separation of activities and a supervisor responsible for each. In today's media organizations, strict adherence to the principle of unity of command would create inflexibility and hinder performance.

Span of Control

Span of control addresses the number of subordinates a manager can direct efficiently and effectively. Early researchers agreed that the number of people who report directly to a manager should become smaller at succeedingly higher levels of the organization (Davis, 1957). For example, the span for top executives should range somewhere between three and nine. The span for middle managers should be between 10 and 30.

The span of control is a major determinant of how many levels an organization has and the number of managers that are needed. Ideally, the wider or larger the span, the more efficient the organizations. For example, as Fig. 2.1 indicates, differing spans result in varying numbers of managers. If one media organization had a span of three and the other a span of nine, the wider span would have three fewer levels and 272 fewer managers. If the average manager earned $40,000 a year, the wider span would save more than $108 million a year in management salaries. However, questions remain as to whether wider spans are as effective.

Managers can give subordinates more attention when they have narrower spans of control, which indicates that managers should consider carefully adding subordinates. However, this represents only one variable, and there are a number of contingency factors that could affect this relationship. The complexity of the work to be done affects the amount of time managers spend with subordinates. Also, the degree of similarity of tasks being performed, the degree of standardization of work activities, the training and general capability of subordinates, and the amount of initiative these subordinates demonstrate all affect how the optimum span of

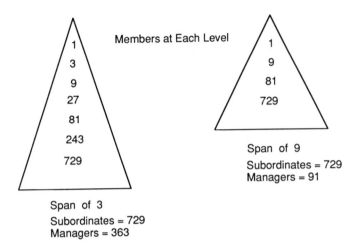

Members at Each Level

Span of 3
Subordinates = 729
Managers = 363

Span of 9
Subordinates = 729
Managers = 91

FIG. 2.1. Contrasting spans of control.

control is determined (Mintzberg, 1979). Because the early writers did not recognize these contingencies, research on span of control continues.

Division of Labor

Division of labor is the extent to which jobs are broken down into a number of steps with the responsibility for each step being assigned to specific individuals. Instead of being responsible for an entire activity, employees specialize in doing part of an activity. In unionized television stations, videotape editors are solely responsible for editing videotape. They perform this same standardized task over and over again.

Division of labor is an efficient way of utilizing employees' specific skills. In media organizations, some tasks require highly developed skills. Others can be performed by untrained individuals. However, if all employees were engaged in each step of producing a newscast, all would have to hold skills necessary for performing both the most demanding and the least demanding jobs. This would be an inefficient method of utilizing workers' skills.

Other efficiencies also are achieved through division of labor. People's skills at performing a task increase through repetition. Efficiency also is exhibited in reducing time spent in completing tasks as employees become more expert. Training workers to perform specific and repetitive tasks is also less costly. Finally, division of labor increases efficiency and productivity by encouraging specialized creativity.

The belief that organizations should be designed with a high degree of division of labor has been a widely accepted principle. However, this principle can be carried too far. The disadvantages are that too much division of labor causes boredom, fatigue, and stress—and may lead to inefficiency. Although it can be a valuable goal in planning performance in organizations, division of labor is no longer a universal principle.

Departmentation

Division of labor creates a need for coordination of specialists. Departmentation (or departmentalization) describes how specialists are placed together in departments under the direction of a manager. The creation of departments usually is based on (a) the work functions being performed, (b) the product or service being offered, (c) the target customer or client, and (d) the geographic territory being covered.

Function. Functional departmentation occurs when organization units are defined by the nature of the work. Newspapers have about five departments based on function: the news-editorial, advertising, circulation, production, and business departments. These departments, as well as departments of other media organizations, are engaged in functions such as (a) preparing information, (b) reproducing information, (c) distributing information, (d) promoting the product (newspaper, newscast) to readers and advertisers, (e) financing operations of the firm, and (f) coordinating the other five processes (Lacy & Simon, 1992).

As Fig. 2.2 indicates, large media companies, including the broadcast corporation illustrated, can be organized according to function, as well as geography. The chart and the following job descriptions describe the function of typical managers in broadcast media organizations:

1. The Chief Executive Officer (CEO): The CEO is responsible for overall performance of the corporation. Primary responsibilities are for the media's relations with their perspective communities and audiences. The CEO also must coordinate the efforts of all departments and oversee the allocation of resources to each. This would be a coordinating position.

2. The Chief Financial Officer (CFO): The CFO is responsible for relations with outside bankers and financial institutions. Most media organizations must borrow money for expansion or capital improvements. The CFO is responsible for financial planning, cost control, and overall efficient financial management for each department. This would be a position concerned with the financing operations of the firm.

3. General Manager: The general manager is responsible for the overall management and operation of the individual station. General managers are concerned with matters such as income, expense, budgeting, forecasting, and long- and short-term planning. General managers hire the managers of other departments within the station and oversee the activities

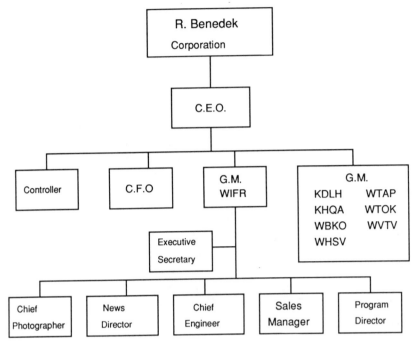

FIG. 2.2. Organization chart for Benedek Broadcasting.

of each department. This would be a position concerned with coordination, as well as finance.

4. News Director: The news director is responsible for the entire news operation and everything that airs during the newscasts except commercials. The news director supervises everyone in the newsroom including anchors, reporters, sports and weather announcers, producers, and assignment editors. News directors also have administrative duties such as budgeting and conducting staff meetings. This is a position concerned with preparation of information and reproducing information.

5. Chief Engineer: The chief engineer is responsible for keeping the station signal on the air. This includes performing special tests required by FCC regulation. This person is responsible for maintenance of technical equipment and for ordering new equipment. This is a position concerned with distributing information.

6. Sales Manager: The sales manager is responsible for all sales activities of the station. This person assigns account executives to particular areas or accounts and supervises their activities. Sales managers also set the rate for the sale of advertising time. They must be knowledgeable of market data, retail statistics, audience research, and all other marketing and advertising concerns. This would be a position concerned with financing operations.

7. Program Director: The program director is responsible for all local, network, and syndicated programming that is broadcast by the station. The program director selects and schedules all programming. Program directors also must be knowledgeable of Federal Communication Commission (FCC) regulations to ensure programming complies. This would be a position concerned with coordination and preparing information.

The primary advantage of functional departmentation is that it allows for specialization. It also provides for efficient use of equipment and resources. The disadvantages may be that members of a functional group may develop more loyalty for the group's goals than the organization's goals. If the two are not mutually supportive, problems may result. Conflicts also arise when different departments strive for different goals.

Product. Departmentation by product allows employees to identify with a particular product or service and develop cohesion or allegiance to the product or service. For example, the lead anchorperson at WBBM-TV in Chicago, Bill Curtis, directs his own production staff for special assignments. All activities necessary to produce and market a product or service are under one manager. Departmentation by product enables each product or service to act as a distinct profit entity. Problems can arise if departments become excessively competitive. Another potential disadvantage is if facilities and equipment have to be duplicated. Usually large multiproduct organizations, such as those that produce different magazines, are the ones to adapt product departmentation.

Customer. Customer departmentation is based on division by customers served. One example would be a newspaper organization that has one department to handle home deliveries and another to handle industrial customers. These departments would be structured according to division by customers served. This type of departmentation has the same advantages and disadvantages as product departmentation. For example, if the home deliveries group becomes too competitive with the industrial customers group, cooperation between the two departments will diminish and the organization's overall performance could decrease.

Geographic. Geographic departmentation occurs in organizations that maintain physically scattered and independent operations or offices. Departmentation by territories permits the use of local workers and/or salespeople. Some major newspapers would be an example of media companies organized by geographic departmentation. The *Chicago Tribune* has branch offices to serve suburban editions of its newspaper. Such departmentation creates customer goodwill and an awareness of local issues. It also provides a high level of service. The disadvantage is that too many geographic locations can be costly.

An examination of most contemporary media organizations reveals numerous formal management principles still in operation. These organizations not only have hierarchies and chains of command, but also the transfer of power is governed by rules and regulations similar to those Weber (1921/1947) proposed. However, more contemporary schools of thought have attempted to shift the emphasis from the structure of organizations, work design, and measurement to the interactions of individuals, their motivations, and influence on organizational events. This informal approach to organizational structure views organizational design and function as reflections of basic assumptions about human behavior.

HUMANISTIC APPROACH

The humanistic approach to organizational structure is based on the assumption that work is accomplished through people. It emphasizes cooperation, participation, satisfaction, and interpersonal skills. To describe the characteristics of this informal approach to organizations, the work of five researchers is presented—Elton Mayo, Chester Barnard, Douglas McGregor, William Ouchi, and Rensis Likert.

The Hawthorne Effect

Mayo (1945) was interested in expanding the understanding of the work environment as had been described by Taylor's (1947) scientific management approach. Mayo studied ways to improve the physical working environment for increased productivity. For example, like Taylor, Mayo studied individual characteristics such as fatigue to determine the optimum length and spacing of rest periods for maximum levels of productivity. The Chicago Hawthorne plant of the Western Electric Company was the site of the research.

Management at the Hawthorne plant was aware that severe dissatisfaction existed among workers. Mayo and his colleagues began to experiment with changing physical conditions to determine which condition would increase productivity. They worked with variables such as lighting, noise, incentive pay, and heating. They found little support for the expected relationship between improved working conditions and improved productivity. Mayo (1945) summarized these surprising results:

> The conditions of scientific experiment had apparently been fulfilled—
> experimental room, control room; changes introduced one at a time; all other

conditions held steady. And the results were perplexing . . . Lighting improved in the experimental room, production went up; but it rose also in the control room. The opposite of this: lighting diminished from 10 to 3 foot-candles in the experimental room and the production again went up; simultaneously in the control room, with illumination constant, production also rose (p. 69).

Mayo (1945) observed that work output increased no matter how the physical variables were changed. Mayo came to realize it was the attention the researchers were paying to the workers that resulted in increased productivity. The workers were so pleased to be singled out for special attention that they tried to do the best they could for the researchers and the company. This effect became known as the "Hawthorne effect," and was the first documented realization of the importance of human interaction and morale for productivity.

Additional studies revealed that individual workers did not behave as rational actors but as complex beings with varying motives. Informal status hierarchies and leadership patterns emerged that challenged formal systems designed by managers. The research indicated a complex model of worker motivation based a great deal on social psychological patterns rather than economic concepts. As a result of the Hawthorne studies, productivity no longer could be viewed as solely dependent on formal organizational structure.

Cooperative System

Barnard's (1938) ideas also contributed to human relations approaches. Barnard was not a researcher but an executive of a telephone company. He stressed that organizations are basically cooperative systems that integrate the contributions of their individual participants. Barnard defined an organization as "that kind of cooperation among men that is conscious, deliberate, purposeful" (p. 4).

Barnard (1938) believed that goals were imposed from the top down, whereas their attainment depended on the willingness to comply from the bottom up. However, Barnard did not believe that authority always came down from above, noting situations where leaders claim authority but fail to win compliance. Rather, he believed that authority depended on subordinates' approval.

Barnard (1938) was one of the first theorists to signify the importance of human motivation as crucial to production. Material rewards or economic motives sometimes were viewed as weak incentives that must be supported by other types of social and psychological motivations. The most critical ingredient to successful organizations was the formation of a collective purpose.

Overall, Barnard (1938) believed that when formal organizations came into operation, they created and required informal organizations. Informal structures facilitated communication and maintained cohesiveness.

Theory X and Theory Y

McGregor (1960) was interested in the basic assumptions about human nature inherent in both formal and informal theories of management and structure. He developed two attitude profiles about the basic nature of people. These attitudes were termed Theory X and Theory Y. McGregor believed that managers subscribe to either Theory X or Theory Y. A Theory X manager believes the average person dislikes work and will avoid responsible labor whenever possible. These managers must respond to this attitude with controls such as punishments if employees fail to produce. Theory X managers also assume that employees prefer to be directed in order to avoid responsibility. Theory X managers were based on scientific management theory.

McGregor (1960) proposed a Theory Y manager as an alternative to Theory X and as a way to understand motivations and interactions of individuals in the organization. Theory Y managers believe that employees find work as enjoyable as play. They are self-motivated and self-directed. Because employees are committed to organizational goals, they do not need the threat of punishment to be productive. Theory Y workers seek responsibility and are creative in solving organizational problems. Although the beliefs of Theory X and Theory Y managers are quite opposite, McGregor assumed these to be a range of behaviors. Managers can draw on both sets of ideas depending on the situation.

Theory Z

Among the more popular of recent approaches to informal organization structure is Ouchi's (1981) Theory Z. Theory Z makes assumptions about the culture of organizations as McGregor's (1960) Theory X and Y made assumptions about individuals.

First, Ouchi (1981) contrasted American organizations (Type A) with Japanese organizations (Type J). He stated Type A organizations are characterized by short-term employment, specialized career paths, rapid promotion, formal control, and individual responsibility. They value individuality over group membership. Social needs are provided by institutions such as churches, neighborhoods, and schools rather than the formal work group. Type J organizations, in contrast, are characterized by lifetime employment, slow advancement, informal control, consensus decision making, and generalized career paths. Loyalty to groups is of primary concern and more important than individual achievement. Japanese companies reduce incentives to leave the organization and do not rapidly advance employees.

The Theory Z organization that Ouchi (1981) proposed attempts to blend the best of both worlds by retaining individual achievement and advancement but also by providing a continuing sense of organizational community. Theory Z is important because it draws attention to the human relations approach to management.

One drawback of the theory is that it does not take into account additional situational variables that come into play. For example, the impact of the environment on the internal organization is overlooked. Management theories must be comprehensive to reflect the real world successes and failures that media industries face.

Participative Management

Likert (1961) conducted research to determine the differences between successful and less successful organizations. His theory of participative management was based on effectively functioning groups linked together structurally throughout the organization. His research, consisting of interviews conducted with 24 supervisors and 419 subordinates at the Prudential Insurance Company in Newark, New Jersey, indicated that supervisors of high-producing work groups were likely to:

1. Receive general rather than close supervision from their superiors.
2. Like the amount of authority and responsibility they have in their job.
3. Spend more time in supervision.
4. Give general rather than close supervision to their employees.
5. Be employee oriented rather than production oriented.

Supervisors of low-producing groups had the opposite characteristics and techniques. They were production oriented and closely supervised their employees.

The research indicated management processes should depend on participative groups formed to have overlapping individual membership among groups. Likert (1961) believed that increasing participation by organizational members at all levels would help build productive organizations.

The formal and informal approaches to structuring media organizations are somewhat at variance because each focuses on a different end of a single continuum representing the range of organizational forms. At one end of the spectrum, some organizations are highly formalized and centralized. They pursue clearly specified goals. At the other end, some organizations are less formalized and rely greatly on the personal qualities of participants. The two extremes should be viewed as different forms of organizations that are determined by the type of environment to which the organizations must relate. Etzioni (1960) argued that the more homogeneous and stable the environment, the more appropriate will be the formalized and hierarchical form. The more diverse and changing the task environment, the more appropriate will be the less formalized structure.

Initially, researchers analyzed both formal and informal approaches to structuring media organizations to increase efficiency and productivity. Their studies indicate that both play an important part. Furthermore, no one organizational structure is suitable for all situations. Appropriate organization structure depends on many situational variables. What may work in a small-town newspaper may not work in a large-city advertising agency. The knowledge that there is no best way to structure has led to a contingency or situational approach to organizing.

A CONTINGENCY APPROACH

Tannenbaum and Schmidt (1973) contended that different combinations of situational elements require different management behaviors. They suggested that there are three important factors that organizations must consider: forces involving the manager, the subordinates, and the situations. All of the forces are interdependent. Forces acting on the manager include his or her value system and personal leadership inclinations— whether they are authoritarian or participative. Forces acting on the subordinates include their need for independence, their readiness to assume responsibility, and their degree of understanding and agreement with organizational goals. Forces that act on the situation include type of organization, time pressure, demands from upper levels of management, and demands from government, unions, or society. Successful managers understand not only themselves but also the other persons in the organizational and social environment.

The path-goal theory of leadership attempts to define the relationships between a managers's behaviors, the subordinates' performance, and work activities. House and Dessler (1974) argued that managers can enhance the psychological state of subordinates, which results in greater motivation to perform or in increased satisfaction with the job. The theory distinguishes between varying degrees of relationship-oriented and task-oriented management behavior. Relationship-oriented behavior is the extent to which the behavior of the manager is indicative of friendship, mutual trust and respect, and good human relations between the manager and group. Task-oriented behavior is the extent to which the behavior of the manager tends toward organizing and defining the relationships between himself and the group, in defining interactions among group members, establishing ways of getting the job done, scheduling, criticizing, and so forth (Fleishman, 1956).

The theory also identifies situational variables that moderate the effect of managers' behavior on subordinates' satisfaction and productivity. Such categories include the personal characteristics of subordinates and the environmental characteristics subordinates must cope with to accomplish work goals and satisfy personal needs.

Personal characteristics include the subordinate's perception of his or her own ability. People who perceive that they are lacking in ability may prefer directive managers to help them understand path-goal relationships. However, they may resent directive managers if their perception of their own ability is high. Personal characteristics also include education, experience, and age. Hersey and Blanchard (1972) argued that effective management behavior varies in conjunction with the personal characteristics of subordinates. As employees' maturity level, age, and experience increase, management behavior should be characterized by a decreasing emphasis on task behaviors and an increasing emphasis on relationship behaviors.

Environmental characteristics include factors outside the subordinate's control including the subordinates' task, the formal authority system of the organization, and the primary work group. If tasks are straightforward, attempts to direct by the leader will be redundant and seen by subordinates as unnecessary. The higher the degree of formality, the less directive management behavior will be accepted by subordinates.

The nature of the work group also affects appropriate management behavior. When the work group provides the individual with social support and satisfaction, relationship-oriented management behavior is less critical. However, research indicates that relationship-oriented management behavior has the strongest positive impact on satisfaction and productivity for those subordinates who work on stressful or frustrating tasks (Schriesheim & Schriesheim, 1980).

The popularity of contingency approaches and Japanese management theories has lead to what advocates say is a "feminine" model of sharing information and encouraging participation in organizations. Rosener (1990) found that men were more likely than women to describe themselves as task oriented. They view job performance as exchanging rewards for services rendered or punishment for inadequate performance. The men were also more likely to use the formal authority and power that comes from their organizations.

Women, on the other hand, described themselves as being relationship oriented. They were able to get subordinates to transform their own self-interest into the interest of the group through concern for a broader goal. They credited their power to personal characteristics such as charisma, interpersonal skills, hard work, or personal contacts rather than to organizational stature. Women were found to make their interactions with subordinates positive for everyone involved. Women also encouraged participation, shared power and information, enhanced other people's self-worth, and excited people about their work.

Not all men or all women lead in a particular manner, and leadership styles are not mutually exclusive. Women are capable of managing organizations by adhering to the traditional, task-oriented model; some men are relationship oriented. The larger issue concerns the need for organizations to be willing to question whether traditional command-and-control management is the only way to get results. As the work force continues to demand participation and the economic environment increasingly requires rapid change, relationship-oriented behavior may emerge as the management style of choice for many organizations.

THE EFFECT OF STRUCTURE ON MEDIA ORGANIZATIONS

Organizational influences on media organizations come from many sources. This discussion focuses on formal and informal influences on media organizations. Also, a contingency approach to structuring media organizations that considers formal and informal variables is presented.

Formal Influences

Little research has focused on formal organizational influences on media organizations. Much of what has been written has dealt with the function of media managers.

As early as 1958, the National Association of Broadcasters became interested in outlining the functions of managers. Three basic elements of the management job were determining policy, executing policy, and checking results for control and planning purposes (Tower, 1958).

Rhea (1970) expanded the list of functions with information gathered from a survey of media managers. His findings of the primary objectives of broadcast media organizations are listed in Table 2.3

Newspaper managers spend their time in similar ways. Lavine and Wackman (1988) listed how managers spent their time in a group of newspapers published by one of the authors. Most of their time was spent supervising (20%-30%), planning (13%-25%) percent), and coordinating (15%-18%). The rest of their time was spent, in descending order, in evaluating, investigating, negotiating, staffing, and public relations.

Other media-related research on the formal structure of media organizations has focused on the relationship between size of the organization and communication within the organizations. Johnstone (1976) found that in newspaper organizations, face-to-face communication declines as orga-

TABLE 2.3
Objectives of Broadcast Media Managers

---

1. To make an optimal profit.
2. To increase the station's share of the audience.
3. To maintain the station's position in the market.
4. To increase the gross revenue of the station.
5. To serve the general needs of the community.
6. To produce new and innovative programming.
7. To keep the station growing and expanding.
8. To maintain high quality transmission and production standards.
9. To protect the stations's license to operate.
10. To promote social change in the community.
11. To provide superior informational programming to the community.
12. To promote good employee relations and have satisfied workers.
13. To develop employees in order to promote from within.
14. To attain a position of leadership in the business community, as well as the broadcast
    industry.

Note. Adapted from Rhea (1970).

nizations increase in size. He also found that communication in large news organizations flows primarily down the organizational ladder.

Howard (1973) found that large corporations encouraged the flow of communication and that extensive communication existed; however, much of it was written in the form of reports, memos, and newsletters. Annual evaluation of management performance was required, as were weekly and monthly reviews of station departments.

Phillips (1976) also concluded that organizational structure within television corporations may be prescriptive of communication channels and leadership at lower level management positions. The influence on the corporate leader in establishing responsibilities and a climate for work and communication was felt throughout the organization. The corporate leader had an impact on the behavior of middle and lower level management. He also found that profits and ratings affected leadership activity.

The research indicates that the larger the media organization, the more formal the communication between managers and subordinates becomes. Also, the management behavior of higher level executives sets the tone for communication at lower levels of the organization. For example, a news director at WGN-TV in Chicago, Paul Davis, said he preferred a "hands-off" management style. However, the general manager of the station advocated a participative approach. Therefore, the news director and other middle-level managers felt pressured by upper management to become much more involved with the day-by-day procedures (Powers, 1990).

Other determinants of formal structure of media organizations also exist. Bantz, McCorkle, and Baade (1980) listed the following factors as ones that affect the news process:

1. The nature of news staffs: Reporting procedures are standardized to quicken the news-gathering process.
2. Technology: The complexity of the technology, especially satellite technology, requires preplanning and scheduling in order to meet deadlines.
3. Consultants: News must conform to the guidelines presented by consultants.
4. Profit center: News organizations must consider ratings, circulations, and sales.
5. Product: The factors just listed combine to create a product that is judged by members of the audience and members of the media.

Lavine and Wackman (1988) concurred that technology, as well as the mission of a media firm partially will determine organization structure. For example, if a radio station defines its mission as one of providing local news coverage to a community, then it must invest in news-gathering equipment and qualified journalists. Also, when stations have access to helicopters and satellite transmissions, then coverage area is likely to expand. Technology also affects chains of command. Formerly, television reporters consulted producers on ways to package news stories. With the high cost of satellite transmissions, news directors also must be consulted when using expensive technology.

Although some interesting findings on formal structure of media organizations have emerged, the field is open for additional research. Some questions to be addressed include:

1. What is the optimal span of control for large and small media organizations?
2. What are efficient ways to departmentalize news personnel and other media employees?
3. Is increased division of labor at larger media organizations productive?

The answers to such questions will surface as more students, researchers, and practitioners become involved in analyzing formal structures of media organizations.

Informal Influences

Informal organizational influences on the media include (a) the socialization process that takes place within organizations, (b) the degree of professionalism within organizations, and (c) management behaviors and the effects of such behaviors on employees.

Socialization Process. As early as 1955, Warren Breed asked how policy in newsrooms is established. Through interviews with 120 newsmen, Breed learned that journalists usually were not told formally of policy; rather, corporate indoctrination was a result of an informal "socialization" process. Journalists were left on their own to discover and internalize responsibilities. For example, one reporter spoke of his experience of writing a series about discrimination practices at hotel resorts. He was called in by his superior and told the story was unfavorable. Although the manager did not command the story be dropped, it never appeared in press. The unspoken message from upper management was to avoid coverage of certain controversial stories at that time.

Breed (1955) listed six environmental factors that informally influenced policy at newspaper organizations. These included the following:

1. Institutional authority and sanctions: The publisher owned the paper and had the right to expect obedience of employees.
2. Feelings of obligation and esteem for superiors: Respect and gratitude was felt for managers who hired the employees.
3. Mobility aspirations: Reporters feared that challenging authority would make it more difficult for them to advance in their careers.
4. Absence of conflicting group allegiance: Reporters never collectively opposed policy.
5. The pleasant nature of the activity: The newsrooms were friendly places. Employees discussed stories with managers. Work was interesting. Reporters were proud of their profession.
6. News becomes a value: Energies were channeled into getting more news rather than into challenging policy.

Professionalism. Controlling journalists' behavior is difficult, because reporters work outside of the newsroom much of the time. However, through informal influences, journalists come to agree on acceptable behavior. Researchers have studied how journalistic professionalism affects the gathering and reporting of news. Professionalism has been defined as "the exercise of autonomy, the right of workers to control their own work, frequently with reference to norms developed by professional agencies external to the organizations in which they work" (Tuchman, 1978, p. 65). Beam's (1990) examination of ethics codes suggests that professional behavior for journalists would include the following expectations:

1. Journalists are educated liberally and they maintain a commitment to continuing education, either formal or informal.
2. Journalists adopt a disinterested or impartial approach in dealing with the phenomena about which they write and edit.

3. Journalists place a strong emphasis on producing factually accurate work.
4. Journalists participate in occupational organizations, associations, or activities dedicated to the advancement of the occupational group's collective interests.
5. Journalists work to assure their access to sources of information, particularly information in the possession of government agencies.
6. Journalistic work serves the public interest.

Soloski (1989) looked at how journalistic professionalism affects the gathering and reporting of the news. He found that organizations control the behavior of reporters and editors through professionalism. Although management could control them with elaborate rules and regulations, this bureaucratic form of administration would not be efficient because:

1. The rules would have to cover all possible situations that journalists might encounter, including rules to deal with situations not covered by the rules.
2. Elaborate rules are prescriptive and would limit a journalist's ability to deal with the unexpected, which is the essence of news.
3. The news organization's management would have to establish an expensive and time-consuming system for teaching its journalists the rules and regulations.

Reliance on professionalism rather than bureaucracy relieves organizations of the responsibility for controlling employees. On the other hand, professionalism also provides journalists with a power base that can be used against management policies. In Table 2.4, Breed (1955) identified five factors significant in a reporter's power to bypass policy.

For example, loyalty to journalistic integrity may conflict with management's profit motives. Management may resist printing a controversial story that involves an advertiser. However, the journalist may be compelled to print the story and resist managements' warnings against doing so, because the journalist believes the public has a right to know. As such, organizational structure and professionalism are both likely to affect news content. Tuchman (1978) stated that newsworkers create a news product that mirrors society through their perceptions of social norms. News organization structure influences news content through its impact on the perceptions of social norms.

Management Behavior. Another informal influence is management's relationship with employees. One management problem that continues to surface in media organizations is that of too little opportunity for subordinates to be involved in the decision-making process. Dracos (1989), a

TABLE 2.4
How Reporters Bypass Policy

1. Many norms of policy are vague and unstructured. Because policy is covert, it has large scope and permits a range of deviation.
2. Executives may be ignorant of particular facts, and reporters who gather information can use their superior knowledge to subvert policy. Reporters pick sources, and both personal belief and professional codes can affect these choices. Reporters also decide what questions to ask, which quotations to note and which to bury, and what tone the story will take.
3. In addition to exploiting executives' ignorance of facts, stories can be planted. Although a paper's policy may prevent coverage of an issue a reporter can pass the story to another newspaper or wire service through a friendly journalist. Then the reporter can submit it to his editor and plead the story is now too big to ignore.
4. News can be classified into four types on the basis of source of origination: the policy or campaign story, the assigned story, the beat story, and the story initiated by the reporter. In the latter two types, the reporter has the power to initiate stories.
5. Journalists who are "stars" can transgress policy more easily than those who are not.

Note.   Adapted from Breed (1955).

former television news reporter, said news directors must learn to manage newsrooms effectively and involve journalists in the decision process. Ray (1988) reported dissatisfaction among employees, communication problems between management and subordinates, and motivational deterrents exist within broadcast news operations because most news managers have had no formal training in management procedures.

In field observations of broadcast news departments, Ray (1988) found three distinct manager philosophies: (a) an "X culture" where the manager controlled the environment with his own value system, (b) a "Y culture" where the manager allowed departmentalization to shape the direction of the station, and (c) a "Z culture" where the manager directed all departments with a single set of station-wide goals.

To identify preferences of such philosophies, Adams and Fish (1987) surveyed television news directors, general managers, and sales managers and found that participative, or democratic, leadership behavior related to higher levels of job satisfaction. Additional research also has indicated that work dissatisfaction exists when management makes most decisions. An increase in centralization and bureaucratization fosters job dissatisfaction because of diminished autonomy (Joseph, 1983; Polansky & Hughes, 1986).

Fowler and Shipman (1982) noted similar findings within the newspaper industry. They found that newspaper managers evaluated employees on a regular basis and interpersonal communication was the preferred and most often used means of communication. They also found that the perceived atmosphere of the newsroom was related to the amount of participation in which reporters were involved on matters of importance to reporters. The atmosphere was better when reporters participated in decision making.

Perceptions of environments also influence how satisfied employees are with their jobs. Researchers have found that journalists who felt they had little autonomy would be more likely to leave news organization. Furthermore, among those under 40 years of age, esteem for the job the news organization was doing and frequent feedback from supervisors were the most important predictors of satisfaction (Weaver & Wilhoit, 1986). Likewise, Bergen and Weaver (1988) found that an important predictor of job satisfaction among 308 newspaper journalists was feedback from managers. Taking a quote from Argyris' (1974) study of the organizational structure of a major newspaper, one reporter commented, "Reporters are an irrational bunch. And the ego is high. You need to hear you're doing well" (p. 49).

Another important contributor to job satisfaction may be how likely employees feel they are able to advance in their positions. Barrett (1984) suggested this is of particular importance to news managers who want to maintain high job satisfaction among women journalists.

These studies indicate that the informal structure of media organizations is formed through socialization, professionalism, and employee relationships. Media personnel are likely to be satisfied when they have more autonomy and are involved in the decision-making process. Job satisfaction also increases with additional feedback from supervisors and with opportunities for advancement.

A Situational Approach

The previous studies identified differences between formal and informal influences on media organizations. However little research identifies the effects of both influences on media organizations. In Fig. 2.3, Powers and Lacy (1992) presented a model of television newsroom management that modifies the situational path-goal framework.

The model divides factors affecting job satisfaction into four groups: individual factors, market factors, organizational factors, and leadership. According to the model, these four types of factors influence journalists and their perceptions of how successful their organizations are at attaining goals such as profit, good human relations, and quality news. If journalists believe their organizations are successful at attaining these goals, their level of job satisfaction increases.

Indeed, results of the study indicated that numerous factors related to employees' perceptions of how successful their news departments were in attaining certain goals. A negative relationship between market size and perceptions of successful relations suggested that local television journal-

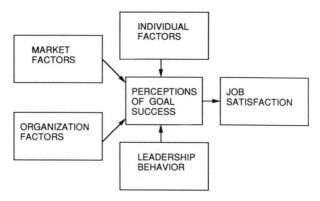

FIG. 2.3. Model of job satisfaction for local television news departments.

ists in large newsrooms perceived less human relations success than did those in newsrooms located in smaller markets. Because the size of the organization often is associated with bureaucratic behavior, this was not surprising and was consistent with results found by Johnstone (1976), Howard (1973), and Polansky and Hughes (1986).

Of equal interest was the negative relationship between the organizational factor of group ownership and profit success. Local television journalists at group-owned stations did not perceive more success at making a profit than did those at independently owned stations.

The most important result of the study for predicting job satisfaction among local television journalists was the relationship behavior of the news directors. Employees were more satisfied with democratic-oriented managers than with management that was autocratic in nature. This does not imply necessarily that news directors cannot make their own decisions, but rather that many, if not most, decisions also should include participation by the journalists.

Lawrence and Lorsch (1967) broadened the same path-goal framework used by Powers and Lacy (1992) by including additional situational variables. In their studies of organizational structure and environment, they concluded that different organizations in different environments require different kinds of organizational structures at various stages in their growth. Variables that can effect the most appropriate organizational structure include the stability of the environment, the objectives of the organization, the tasks involved, the size of the organization, the management approach, the culture, and the characteristics of the work force.

SUMMARY

The structure of media organizations is influenced by a wide variety of variables. Formal approaches to structuring media organizations are concerned with how the parts of an organization fit together in terms of unity of command, span of control, division of labor, and departmentation. Informal approaches to structuring media organizations are concerned with the human-relations aspect and the assumption that work is accomplished through people.

Owners and managers of today's mass media base the structure of their organizations on many internal and external factors. Internal factors of consequence include the functions of the managers, the size of the organizations, the available resources and technology, and the mission of the organizations. Organizations also are concerned with the effects of socialization, professionalism, and the behaviors of managers and subordinates.

External factors of consequence include advertisers, the government, the competition, the business community, and the public. The media marketplace may be described as increasingly competitive. With the proliferation of cable, independent television stations, magazines, and suburban daily newspapers, competition for audience attention and advertiser dollars has increased. This downturn in advertising revenue has resulted in a need for budgetary austerity.

Media organizations are coping with the tightened economies in various ways. Operational budgets are being watched more closely. Expenses such as telephone charges, travel expenses, satellite time, helicopter usage, and overtime have been trimmed in many newsrooms. In essence, media managers are being asked to do the same job they always have done, with less money. Inefficiency has no place in today's media organization.

With a contingency approach, managers analyze the relevant variables and then choose the appropriate structure. Because these variables are constantly changing, managers periodically must reanalyze and evaluate the efficiency and effectiveness of their structure.

CHAPTER 2 CASES

Case 2.1

The Case of Learning about the Bottom from the Top

Easternhouse Broadcasting Corporation owns 12 television stations, 12 AM radio stations, and 12 FM radio stations in the eastern United States. The corporation is divided into two geographic divisions; the Midwest Division has five television stations, six FM stations, and seven AM stations and is headquartered in Chicago. The remaining stations are in the Atlantic Division, with headquarters in Philadelphia. Each division has a president and two division vice presidents, one for television and one for radio.

Answering to the regional vice presidents in charge of radio and television are the individual station general managers. Easternhouse also has a corporate headquarters in Washington, DC, with corporate heads for both radio and television. The Midwest Division president is Harvey Milton.

When Milton arrived at work on Monday, he had a message to call Wilson Gaddy, chief executive officer of Easternhouse Broadcasting Corp. The message was marked urgent, so Harvey called right away.

"Willie, this is Harvey. What's going on," Milton said when Gaddy picked up the telephone.

"What in God's name is happening at WGHT in Cleveland?" Gaddy asked in an accusing tone.

Milton was taken aback by the tone and the question. "What do you mean?" he asked defensively.

"I was at an Eastern Foundation Trustees meeting in Columbus last Friday and all I heard about was the problem with Melinda Raven. What's this all about?"

Milton considered bluffing his way through the conversation, but he knew Gaddy would realize the truth. He replied meekly, "Willie, I don't really know what is going on, but if you give me a couple of hours, I'll get back to you and fill you in."

"I'll go with that Harve. But make it this afternoon. I've got meetings the rest of the morning," Gaddy said as he hung up.

Background.   WGHT has been in a tight race with WETA for the lead in the early evening local newscast ratings race for 2 years. WGHT was able to take the top spot by 1 ratings point during the last two rating periods. Much of this success has been a result of the anchor duo of Jim Haversham and Melinda Raven. After 2 years as a team, they have had an excellent rapport. The market surveys show a steady growth in viewer loyalty to the team.

Sandra Godby has been general manger of WGHT for 4 years and has done well in moving it toward being the top station in the Cleveland market. She worked her way up through the advertising department at the station, but she has a good sense for what viewers want. As has been Milton's custom, he has not dealt directly with Godby; rather, he has followed the chain of command and had Larry Jamison, regional division vice president for television, deal with her. On a couple of occasions, Jamison had mentioned a tendency on Godby's part to be slow in filing reports and providing information about the station.

After Gaddy hung up the phone, Milton called Jamison and asked him if he had heard anything about Melinda Raven. Jamison said he had not, but then he had not talked with Godby or visited Cleveland in about 3 weeks. Milton mentioned his call from Gaddy to Jamison and then hung up.

He immediately called Godby to find out what was going on.

"Sandra, Harve here. I'm a little distressed about some rumors concerning Melinda Raven. What can you tell me about them?"

Following a 30-sec pause, Godby began: "Well, you used the right word; they are only rumors. I think it may be a negotiation ploy."

"Why don't you tell me about it," Milton prompted.

"The newspaper ran a story about 10 days ago saying sources inside the station had reported that Melinda was unhappy with her role at the station," Godby explained. "The story said she felt she was playing second fiddle to Jim, and she didn't like it. I asked Melinda about the story, and she said she wasn't sure where the story came from. Then she added that she did feel that Jim was condescending to her sometimes.

"Two days later, *Cleveland Metro Magazine* ran a short blurb in its 'What's Hot in Cleveland' column saying Melinda wants to move to WETA. Again, I asked what gives, and she said I paid too much attention to gossip.

"I'm not sure what is going on," Godby said, "but her contract is up in 6 months, and I have a meeting scheduled with her in 4 weeks. It seems the two might be related."

"Why haven't Larry or I heard anything about this before now?" Milton asked.

"Well, like you said, they're rumors," Godby said. "I didn't want to bother Larry or you with something that may have no substance. If a problem had developed, I would have faxed Larry a memo, as I have in the past."

Assignment

Answer the following questions:

1. What should Milton do at this point concerning Godby?
2. What should Milton do at this point concerning Gaddy?
3. Is there a communication problem in the Midwest Region of Easternhouse Broadcasting? If there is, what causes are behind the problem?
4. What can Milton and others in the Midwest Division do in the future to avoid such surprises?

Case 2.2

The Case of the New Editor

The Bloomington Mercury-News rapidly was becoming one of the best suburban dailies in the Midwest when its editor, Jim Westley, took a job as a business writer for *The Detroit News*. The news staff of eight reporters and two assistant editors at the *Mercury-News* had been together for about 18 months. During that time, the staff had developed a spirit of teamwork that had made them friends and improved the newspaper. The *Mercury-News* had been named the best daily newspaper under 25,000 circulation a month earlier by the Michigan Press Association (MPA).

The circulation of the paper had gone from 14,000 to 17,000 during Westley's 2-year tenure as editor. The advertising linage also had increased 35%. Publisher Janet Gaylord attributed much of the financial improvement to the work of the editorial staff. At the MPA awards banquet, she mentioned that Westley not only brought skills as an editor, but his ability to work with people had resulted in the longest period of staff stability in the paper's 25-year history.

The *Mercury-News* staff was saddened by Westley's leaving, but they knew it was a big break for him. They felt they would continue to remain a close-knit staff. The natural curiosity of the staff about their new editor was answered when Gaylord announced Steve Smith, a former assistant city editor for the *Dallas Morning News*, would be the new editor.

Smith seemed to be a nice guy. He had worked in newspapers for about 6 years – the last 3 in Dallas. He had a degree in history from the University of Michigan. He explained to one staff member that he took the new job to get back to his native state.

Relations between Smith and the existing staff went well for a week. On the Thursday afternoon of the second week, reporter Leslie Bridges came into the newsroom and pounded her desk. When asked what was bothering her, she said, "Our new leader butchered my story to the point that it is unintelligible. I'll be surprised if we don't get sued by someone."

The story involved a lawsuit filed against the local school board by a parents' group over teaching handicapped children. The group contended the board was violating federal law by not providing adequate facilities for their children. The board argued in turn that it did not have the facilities to teach some of the more severely handicapped students. Bridges had written a 30-column-inch review of the case to run the day the court hearing was scheduled start. Almost half of the story had not made the newspaper.

When Bridges asked Smith about it, he mentioned almost casually that he had miscounted the inches in laying out the story. He said the *Mercury-News* five-column format had thrown him off. Smith told her to rework the story and he would run it on Sunday.

Relations did not improve the next week. During the staff's informal weekly lunch gathering, Dave Simmons, who works general assignment, told the other staff members about what had happened the day before. He had been following a controversy involving 60 homeowners in Bloomington and the builder of their homes. The homeowners said they had been sold houses that were not complete and that had many serious structural problems. The builder said the houses were fine when the deals were closed. Simmons had wanted to attend the homeowners' demonstration, which would be in front of the builder's offices. Smith, however, said no one was really interested in that sort of thing and assigned Simmons to cover the Chamber of Commerce luncheon, where the Chamber was about to reveal its new promotion campaign for a better Bloomington. Simmons had suggested another reporter be assigned, but Smith said rather sharply that he wanted Simmons to do it.

The next 4 weeks saw similar conflicts arise between the new editor and other members of the staff. The weekly luncheons, which had been attended by the old editor but were not attended by Smith, had become gripe sessions. Each staff member tried to outdo the others with a horror story about Smith.

Susan Moore, one of the assistant editors, told the group about the day Smith was writing one of his weekly columns. "He turned to me and asked, 'How do you spell Negaunee?' I said I didn't know and told him to look on the map. He just shrugged, said 'Never mind,' and kept typing. He ended up misspelling Negaunee in the paper."

Five days after the luncheon, the publisher called Moore and the other assistant editor into her office and showed them an unsigned letter complaining about Smith. It said he had undermined staff morale, had shown sloppy work habits, and had shown poor news judgment. The letter went on to say several of the staff had decided to find other jobs.

Assignment

1. What are the basic issues in this problem?
2. What should Janet Gaylord, the publisher, do now? Explain.
3. What could Gaylord have done to avoid this situation?
4. What would you do if you were a staff member? Explain.
5. If confronted with the feelings of the staff, what could Smith do to solve the problem? Why would your suggestions work?

Case 2.3

The Case of Helping Reporters at the Brighton Light

The *Brighton Light* publishes 6 days a week, Monday through Friday and on Sunday. It serves a four-county area in the Southeast that has an economy based on industry and agriculture. Its circulation, which has declined about 10% during the past 5 years, is 15,506 in a market with 40,000 households. The four counties also are served by two weekly newspapers, both of which are free distribution papers. The *Light* has varied in quality over its 70-year history, going through periods when it was not very good and periods when it won state press association competitions for best small daily newspaper. The 10 years that Sam Davidson has edited the paper have produced good, but not outstanding journalism. Some individual reporters and photographers have won awards during that period.

The newsroom organizational chart for the *Light* is given in Fig. 2.4. Under Davidson are three desk editors, who supervise a total of 16 full-time reporters. Two photographers work directly with Davidson.

One morning, Publisher Darlene Hampton asks Davidson to come into her office.

"Sam, I'm concerned about the quality of writing and editing coming from some of our staff," Hampton said to Davidson. "Sandra Hipsome, the English teacher at the high school said she counted 20 grammar, punctuation, and spelling errors on the front page last Sunday. She said she didn't want her students to read the paper because they would learn bad habits. I'm embarrassed. What's going on here?"

"I agree with her, to a degree, although last Sunday was a big exception," Davidson replied. "Two editors were out, one was on vacation and the other caught chicken pox from her kid. But we do have a problem, and it comes from several sources. As you know, we've got a really young staff of writers; five of them have been out of school for less than a year, and another three have been with us for less than 2 years. It also seems like the youngsters we've been hiring aren't as good at the mechanics as they use to be, but I don't know why.

"The other editors and I would like to work with them, but we don't really have the time to edit well, much less sit down for a session on

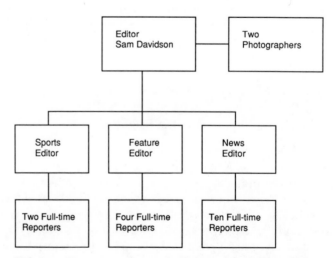

FIG. 2.4. Newsroom organizational chart of the *Brighton Light*.

writing. We've been averaging about 17 pages of news per day the last few months and that's way above what we use to have. We're just having a devil of a time keeping up," Davidson concluded.

"I understand," Hampton said, "but we have to do something about this. I want you to take some time during the next week and write some recommendations for improving the writing and editing at the newspaper. We can spend some money, but your request for funds needs to be reasonable or I can't get it past the owners. Tell me in detail what you think we can do to improve. We'll get back together this time next week."

Assignment

Your assignment is to write a report for Hampton detailing ways that the writing and editing can be improved at a reasonable cost. Give details of at least three options for improvement and explain how and why these would improve the writing and editing.

Case 2.4

The Case of How Much Work in the News Bureau

Megan Kenyon had just started her 4th week in the News Bureau at Megastate University (MU). This was her first job after finishing her journalism degree at MU. She had done well in school, with a B + average and a newspaper internship at a metropolitan daily. So far, she felt the job had gone well. John Silverstein, the head of the News Bureau, had dropped her a note saying he liked the story she wrote about the new telescope acquired by the Astronomy Department. The note had complimented her on her ability to make the technical aspects of a large telescope easy to understand.

Megan had been trying to produce about four stories a day, with one of them being a longer personality feature. Her "beat" covered some of the less prestigious departments at MU, but as one of her journalism instructors had told her, "Everything and everyone has a story, it is up to the journalists to find it and make it interesting."

As lunch time approached, Megan started thinking about her three colleagues who had asked her out to eat. They seemed so much older, all in their forties, that she was a little nervous. But her concern passed quickly as they got to the restaurant and settled into eat. Bob Hammer was the oldest of the group at age 49. He had been at the News Bureau for 5 years, after working 12 years at the local daily newspaper as a staff writer. Joan Collars had been at the News Bureau longest of all the staff, having started right out of college 23 years ago. The final member of the lunch group was Beverly Thomas, who had been a staff writer for the News Bureau for 8 years.

Conversation was cordial as the four ate their lunch. As they sat drinking coffee after finishing lunch, Joan started talking about Megan's work.

"We have been amazed at your work, Megan. Your copy is clean and your story ideas are fresh," Joan said. "We're delighted to have you on staff, but we're curious about how you like being part of our little group."

"The job is just great," Megan said. "The work is interesting, and I've got all sorts of ideas I want to work on."

"We're glad to see your youthful enthusiasm, dear," Beverly said, joining the conversation, "but we are a bit concerned about your work pace. Four stories a day is an awful lot of work. I would hate to see you burn out from too much work. Maybe you should try to pace yourself."

"Oh, I enjoy writing," Megan said, as a feeling of uneasiness crept over her. "I don't think I'll burn out."

"That's how everyone feels at first," Joan said. "But you've been here less than a month. After several years, it's a little different. You get a better understanding of what management wants."

"I think what Joan's trying to say is that you don't quite know the lay of the land yet, Megan," Bob added. "The seven of us who have been here a while know the setup pretty well, and we have to be careful with the way we work. MU is one giant bureaucracy you know. Once you set up work patterns, they will continue to expect you to work at that level."

"Bob's right, dear," Beverly said. "We're concerned that you not put yourself in a bad situation in the future. We hope that you hang around for a while, so we're just trying to help out."

"Generally, we aim at 10 to 12 stories a week, including one nice personality piece," Bob said. "Take it from an old newspaper man, the news media won't use even that many stories. We'd be wasting paper by writing too many press releases."

Megan was taken back by all of this. She managed to say she understood and thanked the three for their concern and interest. She left the lunch with a sense of uneasiness, of being on trial. That evening all she could do was think about the conversation at lunch. She wasn't really sure what was going on, or what it all meant to her future. About 9 o'clock, she decided it would help to talk with someone, so she called her old school roommate, who was working on a newspaper in another city. As her friend said hello, Megan blurred out, "I think I've got some problems here and I need your advice."

Assignment

Your assignment is to provide Megan with the advice she seeks. You can do this by answering the following questions:

1. Given what has happened, what do you think is going on?

2. What can Megan do to find out what all of this means?
3. If you were Megan, would you change your work habits? If so, in what way?
4. What could be the repercussions of changing work habits?
5. How will the relationship with her co-workers affect her relationship with her boss?

Case 2.5

The Case of Paper Glut at the Herald-Telegraph

Henry Peterson, publisher of the *Herald-Telegraph*, had figured the monthly department heads' meeting would be a quick one. No major problems had come across his desk during the past few weeks. The meeting started at 3:30 pm and he had a 5 pm tee time for golf. He never reached the golf course.

These meetings had been held the first Monday of the month for the past 3 years at the 200,000 circulation newspaper. As usual, the first 45 min had been somewhat dull. Marie Laraby, the editor, discussed the need for replacing two assistant editors who recently quit. Lynn Madison, the circulation manager, told the other heads about the district manager who had left town with a week's worth of receipts. Robert Atkins, production manager, told the others about the recent problems in color registration.

Larry Lynch, the advertising department manager, was last as usual. Peterson asked what he had to report.

"There is one thing," Lynch said haltingly. "I was concerned about the story that ran in yesterday's paper about how to bargain with auto dealers. It created quite a stir among the local dealers. I'm afraid we might be facing an ad boycott."

Peterson leaned forward in his chair and asked, "What do you mean?"

"Well, right now, the three largest car advertisers have said they don't plan to run their ads next Sunday. Together that amounts to about five full pages. That's a serious loss of money," Lynch said.

"What's their beef?" Peterson asked. "Was there something wrong with the story? I glanced through it Sunday and thought it was straightforward."

"The problem is that they felt it undermined their bargaining positions and that some of the points would be applicable to dealerships back East but not out here," Lynch explained. "They were especially angry that it ran on the same day that the annual auto tab ran."

"Marie, what do you think about this?" Peterson asked.

"A tempest in a teapot," the editor replied. "It was an accurate and useful story. In fact, we got about a dozen calls today from readers thanking us."

"I'm afraid I don't quite consider losing $10,000 a tempest in a teapot," Lynch shot back. "It could get worse."

"Who wrote the story?" Peterson asked. "I don't recall."

"It was a wire story," Laraby said. "We ran it inside in the business section. It was well written and had pertinent information. If the car dealers can't handle the truth, I say too bad."

"Running the story is one thing, but running it on the day they spent a combined $20,000 on an advertising section is another," Lynch said. "Why couldn't you have held the story? It wasn't all that timely."

"I can understand your being upset," Laraby said, "but I don't dummy the business section. Besides, why didn't you tell me about the tab?"

"I did tell you, or at least I sent you a memo. Besides I send out a list of advertising sections and the dates they will run at the beginning of every year. Then I sent a reminder in my weekly memo," Lynch said. "Don't you read your memos?"

"To be honest, I don't read all of the memos that come across my desk," Laraby said. "Listen, we're working short-handed now. Losing two assistant editors this month leaves us understaffed by three assistant editors and one desk editor. I even worked slot last week. I don't have time to read the mountain of memos you and David send. If you want me to know something, tell me to my face, or give me a call."

"You're not the only person short-handed," Lynch replied. "We're missing a sales rep, and I don't have time to call you and repeat messages I have already sent to you. We send memos so you will have some tangible message you can refer to."

"But those memos get lost in all the paper that comes from the various department and the corporate headquarters, not to mention all the press releases I get," Laraby said. "Besides, I can't ask a memo any questions. If you'd talk to me, I think we'd have a better understanding of what was going on around here."

"You know, I have to side with Marie," Atkins broke in. "It does seem like some people in our organization hold stock in paper mills. What happen to the paperless society our computer systems were suppose to create?"

Peterson, who had been listening to the argument between Lynch and Laraby, interrupted. "We've got a problem here, and it's not just with the auto dealers. We've got to do something about it."

Assignment

1. What problem is Peterson talking about?
2. What might be creating the problem?
3. How can the problem be solved?
4. Who will play the main role in solving the problem?

3
Leadership and the Work Force

This chapter reviews the literature concerning media leadership as well as the overall theories and context for organizational leadership. Issues like professionalism, demographic trends, and the implications for media companies are covered. Major work force changes are discussed including figures projected by the Bureau of Labor Statistics. For instance, the numbers of women working will continue to rise to 63% by the year 2005, compared to 58% in 1990. Overall women will make up 47% of the work force by 2005. Hispanic men, who are most likely of all men to work now, are expected to maintain their standing, and by the year 2005 some 82% of them are expected to work compared with 76% for White men, 75% for Asian men and 70% for Black men (Crispell, 1991). The implications of such demographic projections are explored in the pages that follow. The challenges for the future are clear, and it is the purpose of this chapter to outline not only the history but the future needs of media company leaders.

The chapter is divided into the following sections: the media business setting; theoretical background; and current issues in the media management field.

GENERAL PROFILE OF MEDIA COMPANIES

The media, like other businesses, face profound workplace challenges in the next 10 years. Companies will be focused on: (a) profit margin, (b) competition, and (c) employee needs. Media companies that survive and prosper during this coming era will have leaders who are astute in accommodating the tensions that exist among these factors and making use of resources, the most valuable of which are employees.

It has been some 30 years since Milton Friedman (1962) wrote that business has only one social responsibility—to increase its profits. Indeed, profit has been a prominent variable in the management of media companies, which have enjoyed profit margins of up to 30% and more, whereas other businesses have had to be content with a standard that generally does not rise above 12%. Although managers have struggled to achieve a reasonable balance between bottom-line considerations and the media's responsibility to the public, the high-yield media properties too often have been seen by stockholders as opportunities only for expansion and takeover rather than opportunities for development of exemplary products and internal management practices within the organization.

Competition for media audiences, which has meant broadcast network managers facing cable and video erosion of their audiences and newspaper executives dealing with decreasing advertising lineage and segregated customers, will continue to be a priority. However, these new developments do not overshadow the traditional goals of media companies, which have been to provide products that appeal to mass audiences. Indeed, the competition to control large national markets has driven the movement in the past decade for a few megacompanies to own most of the media.

The media differ from other businesses in terms of their economic markets. Media are joint commodities that tend to be natural monopolies. As pointed out by Lacy and Simon (1992), media companies are joint commodities because they serve two economic markets with one physical product. The two markets are (a) advertisers who are seeking to reach (b) readers and viewers of the media. Because subscription fees or other revenue for media companies usually result in less revenue than the production costs, advertising revenue must cover costs as well as produce profits for the business. Natural monopolies exist when one firm is so efficient that all other firms within the geographic market go out of business (Lacy & Simon, 1992). Such monopolies are attributed to economies of scale, which happens when per-unit costs decrease as more of the product are produced. For instance, because much of the printing costs for newspapers are accrued for the first copy, the cost per copy decreases as additional copies are printed.

Although economies of scale contribute to media monopolies, the joint commodity issue is more responsible for the phenomenon. Customers attend to media to scan advertising as well as news or entertainment items, and so as advertising increases so do circulation and audience numbers. Most media firms must operate in two connected markets: information and advertising. As a result, they are joint products because they sell in two markets.

Newspapers struggle with the economic realities and attempt to hold revenue losses to a minimum and broadcast networks do battle for audiences not only with each other but with cable television and home video records. Care and attention to the bottom line will continue to be central in importance for media managers in the next decade. Media companies will expect managers to understand the tensions and provide effective leadership that meets economic as well as societal needs.

Media companies have become so centralized that now some 23 corporations own 25,000 media outlets in the United States (Bagdikian, 1990). Although economics have dictated coordination of group-owned media properties, there is evidence that the centralization of the media has not always brought internal organizational gains. For instance one study shows that, "An increase in centralization and bureaucratization, often a result of media concentration, tends to breed job dissatisfaction because of diminished autonomy" (Gaziano & Coulson, 1988, p. 880). Another effect involves employee commitment and loyalty to the media corporation. Gene Del Vecchio (1991), a senior vice president and director of planning and research for an advertising agency in Los Angeles, wrote about such impacts on his 10th anniversary at the same advertising agency: "It [loyalty] spoke to a sense of family and an unspoken commitment to see one another through hard times. The notion of loyalty conjured up an image of brotherhood, flowing both ways between worker and boss" (p. 8). He went on to speculate that such a mirage of loyalty served corporations well—until times changed and profits dwindled. As large companies swallowed smaller ones, the idea of loyalty to a particular company was stripped of its former meaning:

> The loyalty we thought existed has been replaced with a sober understanding. On the company's part, that understanding means hiring individuals to do a specific job at a marketplace wage, training them if needed, keeping their wages up to performance standards, then keeping them employed and advancing as long as their performance is maintained and the company can afford it. On the employee's side, that understanding means staying on the job as long as the working conditions are suitable, the pay commensurate with the marketplace, the training available and the opportunities for advancement open. (p. 8)

Other media managers agree they see and hear less about "team" effort or work force continuity and more about machinelike individuals who can preserve the company's advertising revenues, market share, or audience ratings as economic pressures increase. This lack of emphasis on relationships within the workplace is not only common within the media business but prevalent throughout U.S. corporations.

According to Blonston (1991), "In a poll of non-managerial white-collar people, the proportion who told Roper Organization pollsters they found their workplace very 'humane and fair,' 'open and frank,' 'enjoyable,' and 'progressive,' fell from the mid 40 percent range in 1980 down into the mid-30's today" (p. B1). These feelings translate into less devotion and corporate "loyalty" by employees to their immediate supervisors and to their corporation. Many describe themselves as "betrayed" by their company. The same people who say they willingly have worked overtime to fix or update equipment or to find a creative solution to a corporate problem say they now feel reluctant to expend that same energy. They say they feel little personal commitment to their company or bosses. In fact, 90% of 1,000 company officials polled by Opton's Exec-U-Net organizations said they feel "far less" loyalty to their firm than they once did.

The reality is that employees in the next decade will be individuals who may hold loyalties to a profession or belief in a product, but probably not to a company. For managers this means supervising employees who are committed for limited time periods—not entire careers. The notion of company loyalty is not tenable when economics seem to dictate regular company as well as employee turnover. Media managers who believe commitment and loyalty to group, if not company goals, are important to the development of successful products will need to introduce and foster them through specific strategies.

A publisher who started a small magazine that grew into a successful enterprise said he knew many of his young staffers would leave after his magazine was viable:

> I knew they were committed to the idea and ideology of the magazine, and they pumped all the professionalism they had into it. However, I also knew that while they cared about the product, because it represented their individual work, they wouldn't stay here out of loyalty to this particular magazine. We weren't a family wedded for life but rather a group of individuals that came together for a particular time and purpose (personal communication, September, 1989).[1]

This certainly does not mean that media managers will not have employees who want to work for them forever or who develop loyalties to their company. It simply means that media managers cannot count on such loyalty motivating the next decade of workers. Media managers may want to discuss more thoroughly the motivations of workers and job conditions during the hiring phase. For instance, it is not unreasonable to contemplate managers asking prospective employees what would cause them to resign and what their overall professional goals are. Such blunt and direct conversations about expectations rarely have occurred outside of mandated or written union understandings. However, it makes sense for managers—and employees to initiate such conversations before employment commitments are made. One media manager said such a discussion

---

[1]Several of the interviews with media managers referred to in this chapter took place with an agreement that their names would not be used. These interviews are referred to as personal communications and only a general date is given.

is now a part of all his interview conversations with prospective employees. He described it this way:

> My company can't afford employees who are expecting long-term job security. I can't compete with larger groups that can offer increased salaries and benefits for seniority. I need employees who are planning to use the experience here to move on to other media with greater resources. What I can offer is entry-level experience and opportunity to learn on the ground floor. After a couple of years, I expect the employees to move on with my blessing. It's simply a mistake for someone to come here expecting long-term employment. I explain this to everyone I interview, and that way there are no misunderstandings or false assumptions. I expect those I interview to be equally candid with me (personal communication, September, 1989).

In addition to the centralization movement of U.S. media companies, managers need to consider the implications of international ownership thrusts into the U.S. market. The 1990 MCA purchase of not only film but other U.S. media properties provides an example of the magnitude of international interests in U.S. media companies. Although Canadian companies like Thompson have sold U.S. properties in order to invest in European media, Australian-based Murdock and MCA have expanded significantly into the U.S. market. This competition for and with international interests will add dimensions to the media economic climate that have yet to be analyzed or dealt with by media managers. Fears that foreign ownership dramatically will change news products have not been substantiated, and so far U.S. management teams have not been replaced systematically by international executives. However, the phenomenon is too new for anything but preliminary speculation concerning management trends related to the ownership shifts.

Technological media advancements also are regarded as competitive tools that affect not only the options open to audiences but provide managerial opportunities for entrepreneurial development within media companies. Investments in information services go beyond providing traditional news or entertainment to mass audiences. Knight-Ridder, through such services as INFOCALL, has offered information delivery and retrieval systems for specialized customers who want to know about some 100 different categories covering the latest development on their favorite soap opera to stock prices. United Press International, a traditional news delivery system, has experimented with newspaper formats for airline commuters between New York and Washington, DC. The search for audiences and markets is intense as electronic media explore print options and traditional print organizations invest in cable and other nonprint delivery systems. The stakes have been raised as media companies walk the line between remaining a mass medium and becoming a class medium.

Although the past strategies have included the baseline need to provide information to the largest numbers for the longest time period, the next decade will see efforts by current and new media managers to determine products that appeal to important segments of audiences that have the economic strength and vitality to justify the efforts to reach a specialized and elite audience.

It is clear that the recruitment, training, and motivation of employees, who can help with the product opportunities mentioned earlier present the greatest current and future challenges for media managers.

LEADERSHIP THEORY

No distinction in this chapter is made between a manager and leader with the assumption being that managers are leaders in the work place. Although it is true that not all managers have assumed the responsibilities and opportunities of leadership, it also is assumed that it should be the goal. A manager may be defined as one who oversees tasks, is accountable for meeting goals, and pays attention to profit objectives, whereas a leader is someone who does all the former but also has a "vision" of where the company is going and why.

Interesting early research in the field includes the Michigan Leadership Studies (Likert, 1961), which involved interviews with managers and subordinates to determine effective management behaviors. The studies isolated and identified at least two major supervisor orientations. They were: (a) job-centered or task-oriented behavior, and (b) employee-centered or relations-based managerial behavior. Researchers assumed the two types of managerial orientations were exclusive and represented two ends of a continuum with managers being either one or the other but not both.

About the same time, researchers at Ohio State University were conducting similar leadership studies. The research, which included data from military and industrial institutions, focused on relations-based decision making. The studies identified at least two typologies which were called *consideration behavior* and *initiating-structure behavior*. In the former, the manager considers the needs and ideas of subordinates before making decisions. In the latter, the manager clearly defines the duties of the subordinates and communicates their functions to them. Unlike the Michigan scholars, the Ohio State researchers suggested that managers were not necessarily one kind of leader. Rather, they concluded that a manager could possess more than one orientation and successful managers could and did alternate styles as circumstances changed.

Although the research described previously was helpful in identifying leadership behaviors, it was not complex enough to account for different organizational settings or individual deviations. Fiedler's (1967) contingency theory suggested that leadership effectiveness is related to a leader's personality and the situation. His research proposed that leaders have basic personality preferences that make them task versus relationship motivated, and that these preferences are constant and measurable for leaders. However, all media managers must fit their personalities to an existing culture when they join a company. The cultural context, therefore, bears important consideration in all discussions of leadership behavior.

As media companies expand into national and international arenas, it makes sense to understand the various dimensions for cultural analysis. That is, consensually understood symbols, language, task definitions, and acceptable behaviors vary between and among various countries as well as between different media. Culture is a construct that underlies behavior and beliefs within a company and the society in which it operates. It guides, explains and predicts processes and products of a media company.

Organizational culture can be "observed" through categorizing and noting patterns of behavior, styles of dress, backgrounds of those hired and promoted and so forth. Culture also can be defined in terms of shared values or assumptions workers hold about the world and human nature. Such common belief systems result in predictable behaviors and confirming rituals. Hofstede (1980) noted that North American and West European countries stress individualism rather than collectivism. This impacts how workers and managers regard their own relationships as well as those between the company and the individual. If organizational culture is seen as opposed to individualization or as something that impedes or diverts the individual then supervisor–subordinate conflict is sure to occur in companies where Western values are prevalent. Such conflict affects morale and in turn employee production.

Early research by Lewin, Lippitt, and White (1939), who studied boys' clubs, found that autocratic leadership produced the largest number of airplane models, at least while the leader watched, but morale was best under democratic leadership. Interestingly enough, mixed and different results were found when the study was replicated outside the United States within different cultural contexts. For instance, Misumi (1985) found that, in Japan, the democratic style was effective if the task was easy, but the autocratic style was preferred if the task was difficult. Meade (1967) found in India that the autocratic style was best on all criteria.

Other studies have found similar differences between cultures – and between types of businesses. For instance, Heller and Wilpert (1981) found that Sweden and France were consistently more participative in their management decision making than were Britain, the United States, West Germany, and Israel, and that participative styles are more characteristic of the oil and electronics industries than of banking and public transportation. Such studies serve to remind us that leadership styles must be considered within the context of worker values and expectations that may be tied to national, professional, and personal cultural orientations. Quite simply, "effective" leaders are not necessarily interchangeable across industries or international borders.

Regarding media news cultures, a shared U.S. value is high regard for competition. The cultural context for this competition includes the notion that being first with the news is being best, and being best translates into more market share and higher profits. Competition can entice managers into considering as appropriate behavior almost anything short of lying. Media companies informally monitor one another, and through professional groups sometimes even design codes and agreements for themselves that temper the cultural support for such values as competition. There are also unwritten "rules" that occasionally have resulted in excommunication of members who violate them. Within large media companies it is likely there is a dominant culture that aligns itself with national norms as well as self-styled ones. In addition, several subcultures define the advertising/marketing, news, entertainment, distribution, production, personnel, and accounting departments, to name but some. There even may be countercultures within the organizational setting.

Historically, rich local cultural systems can change as quickly as it takes for corporate mergers to occur. For instance, a top manager at one large media company that recently moved from private to public ownership summed up the culture of today's newspapers in the following way: " . . . the phenomenon of newspapers going public has changed the nature of the industry. Newspapers are no longer newspapers. They are now in the same rat race as any other Fortune 500 company, and they are trying to adjust a culture that is not quantifiable to quantifiable precepts . . . " (personal communication, October, 1990). But the question remains, who sets the culture? Who defines and leads the culture? Is it a top-down process? Is culture something that is inserted upon a company by senior managers?

It is the perspective of this chapter and author that the culture can be changed and defined at any level of the organization—senior management, line workers, middle managers and so forth. All that is necessary to "set" the culture is agreement and communication on the symbolic meanings by a collective group within a media company. Although unexpected events or social changes sometimes can create a culture, more likely the culture is recognized and managed by company executives who determine the appropriate beliefs and behaviors and reinforce them. Leaders, according to Schein (1985), have the ability to communicate organizational culture in at least five different ways: (a) by focusing on and measuring and controlling variables; (b) by how they react to crises or other important events; (c) by coaching and teaching; (d) by reward and status conferring; and (e) by promotion, recruitment, and excommunication. If leaders are consistent in actions supporting these five criteria and if they embellish these actions with stories, myths, and formal statements, the culture can be "managed" and maintained quite effectively.

Cultures can be upset by contrary evidence that the criteria in place are wrong or inappropriate, by the emergence of a charismatic leader that readjusts the value system or by the current culture's failure to meet expectations in some important way. That is, if a media company has as one of its major values community service, and employees have an abiding understanding of that value, the products the employees help develop will reflect that value. However, if for some reason the products become unimportant to the community, or the employees decide because of leadership or self-initiative that the internal value should not be community service but social responsibility, which they see as the antithesis of community service, the company culture could change dramatically.

Another confounding variable in this discussion is the fact that the success of managers in determining and defining culture is not understood universally. The typical model is of managers "acting on" less powerful subordinates who gain their understanding of culture from supervisors. In media companies where the work force is generally well educated and possesses professional mores and allegiances, corporate culture can be influenced by emergent leaders who are not traditionally recognized power holders through title or position. Culture can be defined by individuals who do not hold official power positions but who are well liked and respected and thus influential in setting cultural norms regardless of management mandates. Such a situation easily can occur and be enhanced when official leaders distance themselves from subordinates or if morale is poor and cultural indicators ambiguous. In such situations workers tend to turn to consensual leaders who emerge because of their expert or well-respected status.

Although research on culture and its significance to the work place continues, it is important for media companies to recognize that workers and organizations must share some basic premises. The cultural context provides the foundation for day-to-day operations as well as overall goals of the company. Basically, corporate culture tells workers and managers "who we are" and "what we do." Confusion, and even anarchy, can occur when management is unclear in communicating values. Managers must not be isolated from employees, and corporate values must be understood and supported by employees for consistent products to emerge.

Group Dynamics

Historically, discussion of leadership generally included the notion that leaders hold "influence over others." This influence was said to occur because of either social and organizational context or because of inherent personal abilities or charisma. These notions have been challenged recently by social science research advancing the concept of team or group dynamics rather than individual dominance. Tannenbaum and Schmidt (1973) pointed out that research cast doubt on the efficiency of highly directive leadership and that more attention was paid to motivation and human relations.

Research suggests that today's effective leaders choose from a menu of styles that range from authoritarian, in which managers determine and then announce expected behaviors, to participative, which calls for active decision making by subordinates. Indeed, House (1977) suggested that effective leaders use authoritative tactics when resistance is encountered and invite employee participation in decision making when compliance is assured. This model assumes that the leader and followers are not linear and directive but rather interactive. That is, the leader still is asserting power actively on subordinates, but the leader is adaptive to the subordinates, the situation, and the criteria for success. In this model leaders exercise influence over subordinates, but subordinates dictate appropriate influence tools.

Managers who are flexible can adopt an approach that considers their personality, the situation, organizational constraints and employees' needs. Research by Tannenbaum and Schmidt (1973) supports these views, adding that managers are influenced and choose an approach based upon their value systems, their confidence in subordinates, and/or their own leadership inclinations. Situational concerns include the values and traditions of the organization and how the organization regards various styles of leadership. Other factors include the nature of the problem, and the amount of time available to resolve it as well as the type of training and expertise held by employees. If leaders feel subordinates are qualified and expect to participate they are more likely to share decision making and to be less authoritarian.

Researchers suggest that the most effective leaders are those who are aware of the forces that affect their decision making and act in accordance with those forces. They say successful leaders are those who are flexible and cognizant of their choices, directing when necessary and allowing freedom when possible (Tannenbaum and Schmidt, 1973).

Another related leadership approach mentioned earlier is the path-goal theory (House & Dessler, 1974). This theory focuses on developing the motivation and job satisfaction of subordinates through relationship or task-based behavior. Relationship-oriented behavior refers to the tendency of leaders to utilize mutual respect and good human relations to manage others. Task-oriented behavior refers to leaders who manage by defining the jobs and scheduling and establishing procedures for the work to be completed (Fleishman, 1956).

Research by Powers and Lacy (1992) modified the path-goal model to illustrate how (a) factors within journalists (that is, individual variables), (b) leadership characteristics, (c) organizational settings, and (d) market factors affect a local television newsroom. All four factors should affect the perception of goal accomplishment or effectiveness, which in turn affects job satisfaction. Powers and Lacy found that employees are more satisfied with democratic-oriented leadership than with leadership that is autocratic in nature. They suggested that "this does not mean news directors cannot make their own decisions, but rather that many, if not most, decisions should also include participation by the journalists" (p. 18).

If leadership is seen as a dynamic activity, then managers will need to explore intellectually and pragmatically what is effective for the moment as well as for the long-term corporate climate.

Sources of Power

Power is defined in several ways, however within the context of this discussion, it means the ability to accomplish an act or event or to influence an outcome. Media managers are expected to have the authority, ability, and influence to provide expected or desirable outcomes.

The bases of leadership influence were identified by Weber (1921/1947) as: (a) rational or resting upon legal or normative rules; (b) traditional, resting on the legitimate status of those exercising authority; or (c) charismatic, which could involve leadership arising out of devotion or heroism. In addition, Griffin and Moorhead (1986) suggested a fourth base called (d) expert power, which allows leaders to control via expertise or information they hold that others need

This chapter includes discussion of all four kinds of leadership because they all exist in the modern work force. That is, although the first two (legal authority and traditional authority) leadership types are recognized most easily because they possess titles, fulfill functions on an organizational chart, and have hierarchical recognition, the third type may operate informally and without institutional identification. This type of leader can develop out of positive needs for entrepreneurial development within an organization or out of negative or oppressive situations where workers feel disconnected, unappreciated, and devalued. The fourth leadership power arising out of expertise is dependent on a leader being able to convey, in a subtle, nonthreatening way, her possession of information. In addition, sometimes unauthorized leaders emerge out of situational factors that provide platforms for recognition. These types of leaders might be considered "renegades," especially if they threaten traditional, hierarchical corporate authority.

Much of the early leadership work focused on studying "current" leaders, and then identifying the steps on their rise to power. These studies found that people accept or are chosen for legal and traditional leadership positions because they possess certain cultural backgrounds that are acceptable to the current organization. It is still not clear how important personality is in the leadership formula, but it is clearly a variable related to the organizational situation as well as the level of expert competency required for the position. It also is clear that "leaders" who are named through static bureaucratic or institutional edict and are successful within that context may be very different from leaders who "emerge" because of dynamic situational factors growing out of crises or special need.

Likewise, it is quite possible for a leader to score high on meeting the needs of subordinates but not high on meeting the needs of supervisors and vice versa. Within the media context, this might mean that a publisher who favors internationalizing the news pages would be supported by supervisors at corporate headquarters, where international news is considered a high priority. However, this same publisher might receive low ratings and meet resistance from subordinates if they perceived that international news was displacing local news, which always had been a priority for them. Another example is the market "sweep" months, which regularly occur in television. During these times programming is developed to increase numbers of viewers and thus provide proof of audience to advertisers. Although a manager who develops programming that provides high viewership might be considered effective by supervisors, quite an opposite evaluation might be given by subordinates if they feel the programming is not of high quality. Obviously, leaders are ranked highest by both groups when there is a strong relationship between the goals of subordinates and supervisors.

Rosemary Stewart's (1976, 1982) work differentiates between the "demands" of management versus the "choices" of management. That is, although different levels of management might require different patterns of behavior and communication, managers have considerable flexibility. Effective managers combine their own personal intuitive styles with the role demands of their title, corporation, and particular responsibilities. Stewart advocated managerial creativity in situations such as those described earlier. She suggested combining bottom-line concerns with increased communication and participation with subordinates. Or, if a situation can be anticipated, then it makes sense to think through all the possible options. That is, sweeps weeks do not have to mean shoddy or sensational programming. Managers can discuss with subordinates ways to meet corporate obligations without sacrificing critical employee values.

ISSUES IN MEDIA MANAGEMENT

Media Professionals

Many media employees tend to be college-educated individuals who are loyal to a professional or creative standard that may be even more important to them than the organization that pays their wages. This sense of autonomy can result in episodes of individualized decision making that are not understandable from a traditional managerial perspective but are reasonable if examined within the framework of professional codes. That is, a newsroom manager "knows" that it is not unusual for a journalist to continue working on a story until either a deadline or dead end are encountered. What drives the journalist to continue working overtime without extra pay is not a tough or inhumane boss but rather a commitment to a professional code of responsibility.

For instance, in the 1991 Persian Gulf War, CNN journalist Peter Arnett chose to stay in Baghdad after other Western journalists had departed, and a CBS crew risked death to cover the war from inside hostile borders. Certainly the news organizations paying these journalists did not require them to endanger their lives. Although some might have called these journalists overly competitive fools, attention seekers, or even threats to national security, there was understanding and even grudging respect within journalistic ranks. It was agreed that at least part of what was causing the behavior of these journalists was their sense of professional commitment.

It is hard to imagine other workers being so committed to professionalism as to remain in a war zone to get out the last shipment of goods if threatened by bombs. Indeed, although Arnett remained in Iraq by personal choice, Arab Amoco was dismayed by U.S. employees who refused to remain in combat conditions as requested by the oil company.

Such independence and commitment to a professional code also can manifest itself in noncrisis daily situations. Media managers have found themselves dealing with employees who might walk off a television set or out of a newsroom over "infringement" of their rights or professional responsibilities. As mentioned previously, media managers must deal with the fact that some employees may feel less loyalty to their employer because of economic uncertainties. This phenomenon also may occur because of professional alliances. Hacker (1980) suggested that professionalism means a journalist is not completely loyal to her organization. That is, workers who feel professionally aligned with others in their field present particular management challenges. In mass media, these professional alliances may develop because of similar educational background/training, motivations for or feelings about the importance of the profession to society, or even shared experiences within work climates.

Whatever the reasons behind the connection to professionalism, it is clear that some managers believe such a phenomenon exists, and media managers often point to news workers as the most difficult to control. The personnel manager of one large metropolitan newspaper claims that newsrooms are like no other department within the organization. Although accounting, advertising, circulation, marketing, production, and other departments will pull together over common corporate goals, he says news departments are fiefdoms unto themselves. He described it this way in a conversation in 1991:

> . . . But one of the worst managed departments in any newspaper is the editorial department. It really truly is. There is not a lot of management there; they are loyal only to journalism; they practice journalism, and (they think of management as the opposition). They really do. Editorial reporters really are very skeptical about everything and are always digging for what's really behind things, and that sort of thing. It creates an environment where you don't become real trusting (personal communication, October 1991).

Communication theorists and historians agree there are significant professional differences between media workers and suggest such differences can be traced to the early origins of each medium. For instance, advertising theory and practice grew out of understanding and adherence to principles tied to profit margins, and the radio and television industry developed from entertainment interests. Newspapers, however, are the products of historical institutional clashes. Typically newspapers have crusaded against political/government entities, business organizations, religious groups, military structures, and others. Indeed, in the United States the First Amendment is written specifically to protect what America's founding fathers felt was a crucial voice of future dissent. Therefore, the conflict between the news department and all other departments of a medium is to be expected and supported, some scholars say.

Journalism professor and media critic Ben H. Bagdikian suggested such tension between the news department and all other departments is a necessary ingredient in media companies: "Everything the newspaper does, except news, can be done better by another medium" (personal communication, April 1991). And, according to Bagdikian, the health of the industry depends on corporate support of the uniqueness of the news department in both broadcast and newspaper companies:

> The traditional, centralized hierarchical alignment of different departments in some corporations should stop at the newsroom door with the acknowledgement that both for social reasons for the country at large and long-term viability of news organizations . . . the newsroom is different with a separate professional ethic from all other divisions of the corporation . . . . It's inevitable in a highly organized hierarchy that there is a militaristic supposition that it is imperative that all orders will be obeyed once the decision is made. If that should extend to journalists individually in organizations and news executives that decide what is news and the priority of news, then the professional news as we know it sooner or later will become discredited not only with its own audience but within the place of news and the First

amendment within the values of the country (personal communication, April 1991).

The tendency for news editorial employees to be skeptical, untrusting, and suspicious even of colleagues within their own news organization, as charged by the personnel director referred to earlier in this chapter, then may be seen as an historical "condition" sanctioned by professional expectations of those within the field.

Indeed, the former editor of the same newspaper described earlier, readily and proudly agreed that the editorial office of a newspaper is a "subculture" within the larger newspaper culture. He said he hates the "Harvard MBA approach to newspapering." He believes a newspaper ultimately must be a reflection of some personality who is "willing to become identified with and take a stand for what his product is and what his product is not" (personal communication, September, 1990). This notion of personalizing the newsroom and making it a reflection of the vision held by a charismatic leader rather than the result of a carefully molded set of corporate goals is an intriguing one, but not a new one for management scholars. The role of charismatic leadership is dealt with next.

The Personalized Management Style

Weber (1921/1947) distinguished his concept of charismatic leadership by defining it in terms of a psychological need of followers to become committed to a leader who might guide them out of a difficult situation. It is beyond hero worship, Weber said, and has a base in the idea that the charismatic leader should recognize this quality and act on it. He went on to say that this devotion by followers can arise out of enthusiasm, despair, or hope.

It appears then, that charismatic leadership would not occur in a traditional corporate setting unless employees are ripe for deliverance via personality-based leadership. Also, the bond between charismatic leader and follower requires a unidirectional model in that followers are seen to be acted on by a leader. That is, followers tend to see themselves as subordinate to the professional abilities and strategic thinking capabilities of the leader. Charismatic leadership is recognized as a legitimate category that is distinct from more routine definitions of managers or administrators. Charisma is often discussed in terms of transactional and transforming leadership. The former is defined as an exchange between leaders and followers that could be built upon economic, political, or psychological bonds that continues only as long as leaders and followers find it mutually beneficial. Transforming leadership involves the initiation of a relationship with followers that has each encouraging the other through motivation and morality. Interactive relationships suggest that leaders do not act on followers but that followers somehow agree to the relationship because it is a satisfying one. Yet, it is still clearly the leader who is the definer of what is important. That is, goals are set by the charismatic leader—not by the leader and followers working together.

Efforts to quantitatively measure the effectiveness of charismatic leadership have been mixed and generally disappointing (Bass, 1985). However, charisma retains powerful anecdotal meaning within the context of media and other businesses, so it is included here as one of several legitimate recognizable leadership styles. Several media executives have been known as charismatic leaders, including Henry R. Luce, who died in 1967 after forging an enormous publishing empire, Al Neuharth, who gave life and direction to the Gannett organization, and Ted Turner, head of CNN and Time magazine's 1991 Man of the Year. In summary, the research on leadership has been built upon several theoretical assumptions presented by Smith and Peterson (1988):

a) Criteria for measuring "successful" leadership vary. They can include but are not limited to: task completion or production quotas; they can be be derived solely from goals set by supervisors and organizations; or they can be subordinate morale centered.

b) Certain leadership characteristics are thought to be identifiable and measurable and thus capable of being studied and taught.

c) Leadership criteria cannot be assumed to be culturally adaptive, and differences in findings between and among different cultures are present.

d) Personality factors are thought to contribute to leadership.

e) Situational as well as legal, traditional, task and charismatic leadership are recognized.

CURRENT ISSUES

Among the tensions facing all businesses are the anticipated declines in available employees. According to recent projections, the work force in the year 2000 will be older and include more cultural diversity with people of color and women increasing in numbers. Competition for the "best and the brightest" in the employee ranks will be intense. Specifically, by the year 2000 retirements from baby boom generation workers will mean that fewer workers are available. That is, the market for employees is projected to be a competitive one in which companies will need to provide not only fair pay, benefits, and working conditions but also other incentives to attract qualified employees. It is reasonable to assume that this competition will foster the development of stimulating environments in which creative, enlightened, and effective leadership is synonymous with management. Job satisfaction will be key to hiring and maintaining the most able and attractive work force. This will occur not because media institutions have become suddenly proemployee as well as proprofit, but because company survival will depend on it.

Johnston (1987) said, "We are about to experience the oldest work force in recorded history. Career ladders are becoming crowded and opportunities for the 'baby boom' generation of 25 to 44-year-olds are reduced. The 'baby bust' generation of potential employees aged 16-24 is fewer in number and in great demand. The result is that, through 1995, significantly fewer workers will be available to fill entry-level jobs" (p. 1). Johnston predicts a seller's market for entry-level workers because not only will there be fewer people entering the work force, but present trends indicate there will be more jobs to fill.

The Bureau of Labor Statistics stated that the 35- to 54-year-old age group will make up almost 50% of the labor force in the year 2000. This is up from 38% in 1986. According to Redwood (1990), this has several implications for U.S. companies. Traditionally, businesses have considered middle-age employees less adaptable, flexible, dynamic, and responsive to new ideas and technological changes than younger workers. However, because there will be fewer available workers and competition for them will be intense, media companies will need to readjust their appraisals and adapt their work climate to the needs of the middle-age worker. For instance, older workers tend to react best to organizational structures that are less authoritarian and hierarchical, and companies that traditionally have not operated on a participatory model will need to reconsider their management practices. In addition, salary schedules that are based on seniority will be most effective with older workers. Likewise, compensation packages that include retirement packages and long-term health care benefits will be popular with older workers.

Meanwhile, younger workers will be interested in vacation benefits and leisure opportunities as well as long-term salary opportunities that are not affected by compression.

It is clear that media companies will need to develop training and adult education programs for both the middle-age workers and younger employees. Middle-age employees will need retraining in technological developments and general skill upgrading. However, younger workers may need basic educational tools because school reform has not kept pace with the needs of business, and the "gap between the education schools provide and the education workers need is widening" (Redwood, 1990, p. 75). According to one researcher, American businesses lose $20 billion each year due to illiteracy in the work force (Pilenzo, 1990). Media companies will need to invest in the development of employees who may need training before they can even begin to work.

Other demographic work force changes relate to gender and color. The current work force is made up of 41% women, whereas only 24% of the officials and managers are women. Likewise, minorities represent 21% of the work force, yet only 9.5% of all officials and managers are minorities. A 1990 study of Fortune 500 industrial corporations showed that minorities and women hold less than 5% of the senior management positions, and there has been only a 2% increase in minorities and women in top executive positions in America's 1,000 largest companies in the last 10 years (Dominguez, 1990). Media companies that expect to survive will provide access to management jobs for women and people of color who previously have faced sex and color barriers.

The Bureau of Labor Statistics projected an increase in the female labor force participation rate from 55% in 1986 to 61.5% by 2000 (Redwood, 1990). Women's growth in the work force is expected to increase support for such innovations as flex-time, flexi-place, flexi-scheduling, shared jobs, alternative career paths, telecommuting, extended leave and employer supported day care.

The Bureau of Labor Statistics projected the Hispanic labor force to increase 74% whereas African-American labor force participation will increase by 29%, compared to an increase of 15% in the White labor force between 1986 and 2000 (Redwood, 1990).

Joseph Radigan, senior vice president at The Equitable Financial Company, said all companies that plan to survive and thrive in the next decade will need "courageous leadership committed to the belief that compassionate treatment of all employees is as important to the integrity and success of a corporation as quality performance and customer service" (Fishman and Chernis, 1990, p. 205). This means that discrimination will not be tolerated, and that managers will understand the importance of vacation and other benefits to employees. If the 1980s were a time of fast-track work ethics, the 1990s will be quite different. As Shames (1980) put it:

> . . . in the eighties, people were supposed to approach their jobs—their Careers [sic]—with the utmost seriousness and involvement, the highest and sometimes most exclusive commitment. . . . In the eighties, people were supposed to bring their real selves to the office, and the office, in turn, would provide the backdrop against which those real selves could strut their stuff (p. 129).

The promise for the work force in the next decade is somewhat different with families and work being combined by more women and men. National research shows that leisure time—not money—will become the status symbol of the 1990s (Robinson, 1990). For instance, a recent study indicated that 50% of those polled would sacrifice a day's pay for an extra day off each week and 77% said spending time with family and friends is a major goal for them (Robinson, 1990).

The media employees of the next decade not only will be interested in flexible work schedules and day-care facilities, but managers will have to pay careful attention to such issues as discrimination and fair working practices. The competition for qualified workers will demand job inducements revolving around such concerns. Diversity as a reality and not just rhetoric will dominate mangerial discussions in the 1990s. The next section covers some of the more obvious managerial concerns.

Affirmative Action

Media leadership in the next 10 years will be focused on hiring, evaluation and retention policies. Companies will need written procedures that tie managerial evaluation to humane practices within the workplace. (For a discussion of the legal requirements for these procedures see chapter 5.) No media companies will survive the challenges ahead without clearly written job descriptions for hiring as well as equitable and measurable performance objectives for evaluation. Although companies needed written procedures in the 1980s, in the next 10 years accountability for reaching goals will be required.

The quality of the work climate is also an important consideration for most employees, and media managers must be aware to guard against hostile or discriminatory settings—particularly as diversity becomes a measurable goal of media companies. During the fall of 1991, historic hearings for Supreme Court nominee Clarence Thomas, the U.S. Senate and American public listened as stories of sexual harassment were described in vivid detail by Professor Anita Hill. Although the accuracy of the charges against Thomas never was determined, it became clear that all companies need clear written policies that articulate acceptable behavior. According to the Equal Employment Opportunity Commission (EEOC), sexual harassment is" 'unwelcome' sexual attention, whether verbal or physical, that affects an employee's job conditions or creates a 'hostile' working environment" (Adler, 1991, p. B1). The EEOC guidelines were issued in 1980 and unanimously affirmed by the Supreme Court in 1986.

Many companies not only have a written statement about harassment but also require training sessions to be certain supervisors understand the meaning and spirit of the policy. Although most companies would establish programs and policies to deal with harassment out of humane reasons, it also is clear there are legal/financial inducements to do so. According to a *Newsweek* account, sexual harassment costs a typical Fortune 500 company nearly $7 million a year in terms of legal settlements.

MGM-Pathe Communications Co. is one media company that has written guidelines and distributes its sexual-harassment policy to all employees and includes it in orientation materials for new employees.

According to Sally Suchil, senior vice president of corporate legal affairs, the policy has improved men's behavior (Lublin, 1991).

Managerial Implications

As mentioned previously, future managers will include more women and people of color. The managerial diversity trend is two decades old. Between 1965 and 1985, the number of female managers quadrupled, whereas the number of male managers increased by only one-fourth (Powell, 1988). What will this mean in terms of management style? Of course, no one knows for sure, however a survey of American Management Association members found that female managers were more committed to their careers, as opposed to their family or home lives, than were White male managers with equivalent ages, salaries, educations, and managerial levels. Several studies of women in newspaper management have found that women tend to be single and without families. Some women managers say this is so because the demands of the job require full commitment, and they simply find it difficult to combine personal relationships and outside work.

It is not clear how those demographic differences will affect the workplace, or if such "sacrifices" for the job will continue to be so evident as the managerial ranks include older individuals. What is clear, however, is that the experiences that women bring to the management arena are somewhat different from those of white male counterparts. Women who have broken through barriers to look up through a glass ceiling and women who have juggled family, work, and personal agendas have different professional experiences and perspectives to bring to the managerial ranks, and it is reasonable to anticipate not all of them will follow the white male models now in place.

Sheppard (1989) concluded that research indicates that women and men experience organizational life differently. As Morgan (1986) explained:

> The links between the male stereotype and the values that dominate many ideas about the nature of organizations are striking. Organizations are often encouraged to be rational, analytic, strategic, decision-oriented, tough and aggressive, and so are men. This has important implications for women who wish to operate in this kind of world. For insofar as they attempt to foster these values, they are often seen as breaking the traditional female stereotype in a way that opens them to criticism, e.g., for being "overly assertive" and "trying to play a male role" (p. 79).

It is difficult to analyze management data on a gender basis because so little of the research thus far has included women managers. Most of the management models were developed by studying White male managers. Some theorists claim women have a more circular consensual style of leading than men who tend to use linear models. They predict that women will create a new working climate by their tendency to spend more time with subordinates, listen more carefully, and develop more participative management environments than men. They even contend that women's presence in the workplace will transform organizations into androgynous workplaces.

The term androgyny comes from the Greek words *andr* (man) and *gyne* (woman). Androgyny could be seen as offering media managers the option of operating in a way that uses the strengths and abilities of both sexes. Sandra Bem and others developed the psychological concept and tools for androgyny through a series of studies (Bem, 1974; Berzins, Welling, & Wetter, 1978; Spence & Helmreich, 1978). Controversy surrounding the methodology, theory and findings of androgyny continues, however Bem (1974) suggested that gender should not be a classifying category but rather that everyone should be free to be themselves regardless of stereotypes about how men and women "should" behave.

The research concerning nonWhite managers is also largely underdeveloped and anecdotal. However, the few media executives who have crossed the color barrier are instructive in their observations. One Hispanic media manager said his supervisors had difficulty when he adopted a style of management that was comfortable for him and his Chicano staff members. He said it was "natural" and effective to develop a working climate built upon affiliation rather than authority. He used a model that was closer to a "family" than a hierarchy. Although the leadership style he used worked well for his staff and took into consideration the ethnic culture from which they emerged, his traditional White male supervisors were uncomfortable and questioned his sense of closeness with the staff because he did not distance himself from the staff. He added that even at a corporate training session on leadership there seemed no understanding of the wisdom of adapting corporate climates to employee needs. He said the management training session was set up to indoctrinate executives into a preconceived management model. There was little room or time for discussion or acceptance of styles that were diverse or deviated from the White male traditions.

Leadership is a dynamic activity, and the next decade will hold even more examples of challenge to the traditional corporate model as diversity within the ranks increases. As more women and people of color merge with White males in work situations, the lines of differences may become clearer, and the opportunities greater for developing more complex and encompassing leadership models. The experiences, needs, and cultures of women and people of color will become dominant rather than silent features of media management practices.

SUMMARY

The human resources needs of the next decade for media companies are consistent with those of all businesses. The changing demographics of workers, including the emergence of women and people of color into management, will influence not only the "look" of the office but the concerns of the business. Although competition and profit margin will continue to drive decision-making models, the choices considered by managers are bound to be influenced by their work histories and experiences.

Styles of leadership are bound to be shaped by the types of people who assume responsibility. Authoritarian, controlling models with top-down management styles probably will not disappear. However, it is possible for many other models to develop as well. If media companies continue the trend toward developing merged informational products, the historical roots for an individual medium will be blurred as well. Clear-eyed visionaries who can deal with crises and yet maintain the consensual workplace favored by well-educated, committed professionals will be needed. Leaders who can draw the most able and brightest to the field when fewer entry-level workers are available will be valued as will leaders who can develop these new workers into outstanding contributors.

And finally, the cultural context for leadership will become more and more important. The symbols, language, and behavior of the workplace will reflect the technological, competitive, and demographic changes anticipated. Leaders of the future will need to understand the new meanings and how to redefine and articulate them within the work place. Subcultures, countercultures, professional, and international cultures will become unified, and successful leaders will find ways to merge the tensions inherent in the work force.

CHAPTER 3 CASES

Case 3.1

The Case of Management in Transition*

Introduction. The *Timely News*, in the heat of a pitched battle with *The Daily Mirror* for control of the Metropolis newspaper market, made a strategic decision in the late 1980s to change its management style. That

---

*This case is from a larger study by Jim Redmond. Names have been changed although quotes and facts are derived from research conducted at an actual large metropolitan newspaper.

change was dictated by the conviction among the paper's senior management that ultimately only one major daily can survive in the Metropolis market. There are two reasons cited by *Timely News* management. First, Metropolis has always had a boom or bust, cyclic economy and is currently in a serious downturn. This economic situation has intensified competition between the two major dailies for advertising dollars which have not increased enough to keep pace with inflation. Secondly, the daily newspapers are competing with a myriad of other media which have steadily chipped away at their advertising revenues by convincing advertisers to divide their expenditures among the over 40 radio stations, four major commercial television stations, cable television, several weekly newspapers, billboards, and various other advertising outlets such as display cards on the sides of buses.

Against the backdrop of what *Timely News* management describes as a flat economy with market advertising dollar revenue also flat, with parallel intensification of multimedia competition, the *Timely News* looked inward for the impetus to expand its circulation lead on *The Daily Mirror*. Management became convinced that eventually Metropolis must surrender its status as one of the few major markets with two significant competing dailies, and become another one-newspaper city. Senior management, certain the traditional, autocratic style of management had to be replaced by one more suited to pulling the work force together as a team, hired Express, a management-consulting group, to facilitate the change.

This case looks at the effort by the *Timely News* to increase competitiveness through adjustment in the way the newspaper is managed. To consider issues of management style and leadership technique it is helpful to review the development of modern management theory.

The Managers and the Problem. John Day, who is, chairman of the board of directors, began at the *Timely News* in 1952 in the dispatch department, working his way up through advertising and labor relations. He was president and general manager for 20 years and has considerable pride in the growth of the newspaper during that period. He pointed out that, "when I became manager of the paper in 1970 we were operating with 14 units of press, and today we have 56." He said his newly created position of chairman of the board was created to allow a smooth transition to a new publisher as he phases into retirement.

Director of Personnel Harold Lippman has been at the *Timely News* for 25 years. He said his father, who spent 31 years working at a newspaper, influenced his decision to enter the newspaper business.

Frank Hale is the least optimistic of the three about the speed of change in management style. A former sports writer and editor, he believes that management style change is extremely slow because it deals with people's ingrained habits.

Robert Jarvis is a former editor of the *Timely News* and grandson of one of the newspaper founders. He supports an editor-dominated philosophy of management rather than the more participative style currently being developed at the *Timely News*.

On the surface, the battle between the *Timely News* and *The Daily Mirror* appears to be an economic effort to sustain publication. However, the *Timely News* management is focused on more than bottom lines and hopes to marshal the powerful forces of human motivation as a tactic to prevail against its competition. Developing human-relations themes within the *Timely News* culture is seen by senior managers as a critical part of achieving a competitive edge. Convinced they are in a fight not only for market dominance, but their very survival, they believe more participative management and employee involvement will provide the newspaper with increasing momentum to achieve the economic goals. It is their perception that their competitor has the same newspaper technology so, they are focusing on managerial superiority as the key to success.

All three current senior managers agree the *Timely News* is in the midst of changing its management style from a version of the traditional Theory X model, to a more contemporary, humanistic approach. The newspaper appears to be aiming toward a combination of Theory Y and Theory Z approaches with teams and quality circles favored. However top management also wants to retain a clear line of authority.

It is obvious that top management has been influenced to implement change through workshops and seminars conducted with its consultant, Express.

Top managers tend to use the same language to describe the work force and their goals. For instance, Day said, "Probably 10% of the people really make the place go . . . You'll get 85% of the people who are good, solid employees . . . And then you get what I call the 5 percenters. And if I could get rid of the 5 percenters we'd be a lot better off." Personnel director Lippman agreed using similar language. He said, "About 10% really run the place and 5% are absolutely trying to destroy the place. And the rest of them are pretty much indifferent."

Managers at the *Timely News* are interested in developing a consistent management style. Lippman said:

> We really have as many management styles as there are managers. That's the real truth of the matter. What you have to do is have everybody work within certain parameters and understand those things and the key is really in the selection process. You can tell really whether someone is people oriented or not. You can also test to determine certain things that will create problems for managers. A lot of people who are in management have very dominant personalities. A lot of people in newspapers and broadcast media have very inflated egos. That very combination makes for some deadly personalities. . . . And you have to watch people because everybody has a backup

style and if you're a very dominant personality, and that's why most people in management have dominant personalities. They're the people who want to be the scratchers, the people who want to get there and be the best and that sort of thing so they are the ones who excel; end up in management. You have to school those people well because when push comes to shove, what are those going to do? They are going to be like steamrollers and go right over people if you are not careful.

Frequent meetings, at approximately monthly intervals, are held with mid-level managers to indoctrinate them into the new management approach. Those sessions, with about 50 managers normally in attendance, usually are held in the company auditorium. Robert Jarvis does not like the trend he sees developing. He believes newspapers require dominant editor personalities, not the more participative effort embraced by current management at the *Timely News*. As he put it, "I understand that there are more meetings at the *Timely News* now, every day, than we would have in a month. We used to have a daily staff meeting around 4 in the afternoon and anybody could come to it. It was no big deal."

But to current management the increased use of meetings, to convey not only day-to-day information but a philosophy of running the newspaper, is crucial. Lippman said, "We are getting a lot more committees than we had before. But we have people in charge of those committees . . . . And the ground rules are you are not here to run the place necessarily. You're here to make suggestions. And once you make a suggestion you are entitled to an answer. Yes, we will do this or no, we won't, and this is why we won't. And if you treat people like that you continue to have that effort . . ."

The literature on management and leadership reflects the difficulty of effectively motivating employees. And doing that within creative environments is particularly tricky, according to Managing Editor of Administration Frank Hale:

> I believe that no one, virtually no one, ever performs to their full potential. And I believe that the greater the talent in a person, the farther from their potential they perform. And so, I believe that if you take people of average ability, or limited ability, and motivate the hell out of them, and, and work with them and encourage them, their desire is so great, to do as well as they can, that you have a much higher chance of getting the most out of them than you do getting the most out of a great talent. If a great talent excels, that great talent excels, I think, for two reasons. One, because they are motivated, not because you motivate them. And because you have found a way to tolerate them, to interact with them in a way that allows them to take their own motivation in a direction that they want to go.

Hale sees the organization as complex, that it is not a single thing but an intricate collection of extremely diverse individual human beings that requires careful communication across organizational boundaries:

There is one fundamental that applies to all talent levels and all personality levels and all of that. And that is to communicate to the individual that they are important and that you respect what they value. I have a philosophy that I try to live by in managing people. And that is: If it's a problem for you, even if I think it's the stupidest thing in the world, it's a problem for you, and I can't communicate to you that I think it's dumb. I have to respect that it matters to you, and I have to help you deal with it. I have to show an interest in you, in your well-being, in you as a person.

With change in the operational environment requiring different approaches and skills has come an effort by management to measure success and failure. Hale said:

As far as performance appraisals we really use a system that's called personnel dynamics profile [PDP]. It's done as something we buy. The reason we use that is it's easy and consistent throughout the plant. The only place it's not used is in the editorial department or in some in the production areas where they have refused to allow us to do it. Because the reality is when you're dealing with labor law that's a mandatory subject of negotiation, so you can't just unilaterally implement performance appraisals in union-covered areas without negotiating it with the union, and in production areas, that is something they fear a great deal.

One way to reduce that fear is to make clear what is going on. Employee involvement is seen by senior managers as a solution to the problem of fear and uncertainty. It requires top to bottom integration within the organization, Day said: "We are trying to get as many people involved in the quality of what we are doing as we can and trying to push down the level of decision making as far as we can push it to the degree that the individual has the knowledge to make the decision."

That has meant considerable emphasis on training both managers and production employees to work in a more participative environment. Day added:

We've had some management-training sessions, and in those meetings where we brought in a trainer to help in management techniques and, we had a series of teams there, and I insisted the teams be mixed, that there be representatives of different departments on each team so that we didn't have all advertising people and all production people, and that gave a lot of these people the awareness of what goes on in other departments, and what their problems happen to be, and the things that frustrate them the most.

Such forced integration of manager and worker increases the need for a kind of socialization, de-emphasizing command and control while expanding person-to-person relationships. Lippman said, "I think the key we need for the future of management is, if you are not a people person, you should not be in management. That's an over-used term, but there's a lot of people in management that really do not care about people. They say they do, but they really don't. They have trouble putting themselves in somebody else's position."

The managers emphasize that changing the management style of the *Timely News* is a process that, in its third year, has only begun and will take a considerable time to complete. According to Lippman, "I think it may have made a few changes in a few little ways. But I can't say that there has been any dramatic transformation yet. It just doesn't happen that quickly, in my view. I don't think that all of our, all of the what we call directors, those people who are the heads of all the various divisions of this company, I'm not sure that they all are yet managing in a new style."

Day identified one effort that began in the business office and expanded to other departments within 4 months:

> They started a program called "Quest," and their objective was to improve the quality of service to our customers. In this case our customers being the advertisers not the subscribers. But as they developed theirs, they then thought they had it to a point where they made a presentation to all department heads and invited participation from all the other departments. So that has pretty much permeated the whole building—who are your customers and how can you perform for them? And if you look at it in this way, the subscriber is the customer in the circulation department, but the circulation is really the customer of the press room. Because if the press room doesn't get those papers in time, they're not doing their job. And the platemakers, the pressroom is their customer, and it's that concept that has worked all over the building. So a lot of this is bubbling up from the bottom.

Senior management's push is driven by pragmatic concerns triggered by a corporate ownership that has changed from a privately held company, to a public corporation. As Day said, "It increases the pressure on the local property from the standpoint of more reports, more financial reports, all sorts of things that financial analysts are questioning all the time, so that is the thing that drives corporate the most."

As newspapers have changed from closely held family operations to huge media conglomerates, there are those who fear the emphasis on financial numbers is transforming the newspaper industry into just another retailing business without the journalistic fire of a passing era. One of those is Jarvis, who charged flatly that, "there are heads of media companies who themselves are so numbers oriented, they are kind of Bob Cratchit types; number crunchers; that's what they are, Bob Cratchits."

With the change of newspaper culture from family business to public conglomerate, Jarvis believes, has come the dilution of decision-making power that has led to the need for a wider base of decision makers. He sees participative management as serving to make accountability more difficult when things go wrong. And, he also believes erosion of editor power softens the personality of a newspaper and is contrary to the key operating guide of his family's newspaper used in its private company days.

Current management, however, sees such a view as an anachronistic, out of touch with a changing employee environment. An element of the shift in decision-making from authoritarian editors to employee participation is seen as symptomatic of the changing social environment. As Day said:

> There are a lot of people who are just working to have a job. They don't have any great career. It's true; they don't have any great career goals . . . . There are a lot of people who are in two income families, where they got the job to help with the family income. In fact, in one session we had, our editor was talking about career women, and we had a focus of the paper on that, and I simply made the comment let's not make the mistake of thinking that all working women are career women. They're not. There are a lot of them, but a lot of them are just women trying to supplement the family income. They come in every morning, they do a good job, and they're first ones out of here at 5 o'clock. That's fine.

Such a perspective of varying motivations among employees requires a recognition that workers have different personal viewpoints and approaches to the work environment that need attention. Lippman said, "One of the things I discover constantly around here in management, one of the things we don't do very effectively, and I am not doing it now at all probably, is listen. When I test people in management as to their ability to listen and comprehend what's said, we don't do very well. And I don't think much of management does really because we have not learned to listen. We have learned to tell or sell and not really get the input from our employees." Interestingly, in the effort to change management style at the *Timely News*, the last department still to be integrated is the news editorial department, which continues to avoid substantial influence from the personnel department. Lippman said:

> We screen in all the other areas except editorial. Screen means when we send somebody to them, we are satisfied based on our interviewing and testing of them, different tests in different areas, to see if this person hopefully could perform in the top 25% of the employees in a department. The editorial department is all by itself. Quite honestly, if you suggested to most reporters that they go to a personnel department they'd figure I don't want to work there; those people are nuts. Those people don't even know what's going on. That's the attitude, and that's not going to change overnight.

The change in approach has been easier to achieve in higher ranking managers. That may be because it involves a smaller number of people.

Also, middle and upper level executives may be more likely to see profitability and performance as mutually compatible. Lippman said:

> Now we have some vice presidents. But there are only two of them, and that's a new concept for us because the only vice president that ever existed in the past was corporate. The *Timely News* is working towards vice presidents . . . . We have started meetings recently with mid-management people where we get 50 in the auditorium once a month and put together a program with them to communicate better with them and feel part of the team and everything else. They are part of the team but they haven't necessarily been handled as part of the team in the past because the form of communication was we'll tell the directors and let them tell their people. The good ones, that communicate well, did; the bad ones didn't so we decided well, we can't take this chance anymore, we'd better communicate directly at that level.

The time frame for completion of the shift in management style is not clear. Senior managers indicate the process is still in the infant stage and predict no calendar target, for reaching the goals. And it is clear a large metropolitan daily newspaper is a very complex organization within which to attempt to affect such change. As Jarvis said, "A newspaper is a culture and within a newspaper are many subcultures . . . . There is the subculture of the editorial office which ought to be ultimately the subculture of the editor himself, but there is an interrelationship on some newspapers between the editor's office and the publisher's office, and there's another subculture downstairs. And then you have a subculture of the marketing department." The list could continue through all the other departments from advertising to circulation to stringers, each with a different perspective, a different vested interest in management's decisions, with different managers who have varying skills and personal agendas. Lippman said:

> We have around here right now the same kind of problems that all management has. We have finger pointers; we have managers who cannot admit that they have ever made a mistake in their lives and probably don't make many because they probably talk to somebody else and have them make the decision or they talk to lawyers and get the lawyer's advice; they're ultimately responsible for their decisions but they'll never admit that. They'll blame their failures on somebody else, and they'll finger point, and we certainly have that here. We have managers who are incapable of making decisions; we have managers who are Jekylls and Hydes. In front of their superior they are very friendly and seem to be part of the team, but they don't believe in it; they haven't bought into it. You find out about that when you do exit interviews for some of their employees in their departments and start working with them, and realistically, you have to go through the same process with managers as you do with employees. You don't hire people to fire them, but on the other hand, if they can't change their attitudes, then you

have to go through progressive discipline and give them warnings and give them so much time to correct or else and, if need be, eliminate them. It's not pretty, and you don't do it all overnight, and it's not the way you want to manage change, but sometimes it's the way you eliminate someone who can't change.

Assignment

1. How would you describe the management style being developed at the *Timely News*? Use the descriptions provided in the case and in chapter 3 to label and support your answer.

2. Utilizing information in chapter 3 and in the case, discuss and analyze what probable outcomes will occur as a result of the efforts being made by top managers. Consider the competition the newspaper is addressing, its institutional history, and the personal styles and beliefs of the managers.

3. Given what you know about the managers and their feelings about the newspaper and its employees describe the "perfect" management style for this newspaper. That is, what would work best in this environment and why? Be specific, using examples and quotes as necessary.

Case 3.2

The Pit Bull Case

Award-winning TV reporter Wendy Bronson worked for network-owned KCCC in Denver, which was in an intense competition for first place with another station. Bronson was well known in local circles for her reporting projects, which included one in which she went undercover as a homeless person to report how life is on the street. She had earned four local Emmies.

Bronson was researching a dogfighting story for possible airing during fall sweeps, when important audience-ratings are collected. Sweeps, especially in a competitive market like Denver, can create a frenzy to win, win, win. Some stories are run that might not make the airwaves during other times, because advertising rates and the ability to sell advertisements are affected by the ratings taken during sweeps.

While working on the project, Bronson knew she needed pictures and strong visuals to tell her story. A source offered to help Bronson attend a dogfighting match. Bronson gave him $50, which the source said he needed to settle a bad debt. Bronson and two photographers attended a backyard fight, which they videotaped.

The story was scheduled to air in November 1990. However, when it was learned that dogfights and attendance at them are a felony in Colorado, the station decided not to show the dogfight. The tape's bloodiness also bothered station managers who believed it might offend viewers and overstep the boundaries of good taste. Bronson, however, still believed the story was a good one.

"I will get the story back in the running for May sweeps. Who knows, maybe an anonymous 1/2-inch tape with scenes from a dogfight will arrive in the mail one day. And you can bet it will get some big numbers in the ratings," she wrote to her news director who later said he had mislaid the memo and not read it until months later.

In mid-April of 1991, a tape appeared at the station with an anonymous letter. The tape was edited by the station to eliminate some of the brutality in it. The station decided because the tape has arrived anonymously, it could legally air it. The tape was shown during 1991 spring Sweeps.

Animal-rights activists immediately complained to the station about the content of the tape. Rumors begin circulating among other local media that the tape had been "staged." Local and county law enforcement agencies began investigating the circumstances to determine if laws had been broken by the network that owned the station.

Bronson assured her supervisors and later a grand jury that the dogfight came to the station through anonymous sources, and that she and station photographers did not stage the dogfights. However, the grand jury saw it differently, and in September of 1992 the grand jury indicted Bronson and two photographers on several dogfighting and conspiracy charges. In addition, Bronson was indicted on two counts of first-degree perjury charges. She admitted later that she dubbed and redubbed the original tape and added the anonymous letter. In addition, she and the photographers added footage.

The grand jury did not indict the station managers, although the network reprimanded the station manager for poor supervision.

Assignment

1. Bronson, who was considered an experienced and award-winning journalist, primarily worked alone on the development of the pit bull story with little supervision from management. What were management's leadership roles and responsibilities in terms of this story?

2. When the anonymous tape arrived, what should management have done?

3. Assume you are a manager at Bronson's station. Develop a set of decision-making standards for your station.

ACKNOWLEDGMENTS

The authors thank Professor Sue O'Brien for the use of materials in the preparation of this case.

CASE 3.3

The Case of Managing a Corporate Task Force: Repositioning "Live at Five"

Case Background

"Live At Five" is a human interest news program that has been in existence for the past 15 years. It airs 1 hr before the main newscast. The program is a product of WSIC-TV, a midwestern large-market television station. The program had been initiated during the height of the television news years in the 1970s when money for such programming was plentiful. Audience research indicated that viewers could not get enough news. In addition, the leading station (WSIC's major competitor) broadcast an early news program, featuring human interest stories, prior to their main newscast. The trailing station, the third station in the market, was soon to follow and implemented an additional half hour of news, although it was a more traditional format of hard news.

To differentiate itself from the other stations in the market, "Live At Five" included on-set interviews, in addition to packaged reports, with the newsmakers. Although audience feedback had been enthusiastic from the start, the program was never able to beat out the leading station in market shares.

Julie Roberts is an intelligent, sharp producer at WSIC-TV. She has all the skills and formal training that the company requires of her. For the past 3 years, she has worked hard and successfully for the television station. She has received three promotions and held management responsibilities for the past year. Her personnel file contains shining reports about her accomplishments.

Early this year, the general manager of the station put her in charge of a special task force that was to reposition the lagging "Live at Five" early news program. It had dropped to number three in the ratings for the past 2 years, and top management was eager for it to improve so that advertising sales would increase. This was the sort of management opportunity that Julie had been waiting for. She knew that one avenue to top management positions came by increasing ratings through effectively managing a special task force.

The general manager gave Julie the authority to assemble whatever human resources were necessary to complete the task. Julie thoughtfully planned the task force and called the first meeting.

She selected the news director Duane who had been (and still was) her supervisor since she came to work at the station. She was certain he would support her, and that his 10 years of management experience would be a valuable asset.

Julie invited two salespeople, Bill and Bob, who had been involved in selling advertising time for that particular program for the past 10 years. She believed they would be able to provide a client point of view, as well as provide information about the news program when it had been more successful in past years.

She also invited two sharpshooting marketing executives, Keith and Kent, who were fresh from graduate school. They were chosen for their ability to promote products, including news, as well as their ability to do statistical analysis on the effectiveness of the news program.

Finally, she included a reporter, Christine, who had previously anchored the "Live at Five" program. Christine had been taken off the anchor position because of poor ratings. However, she was an excellent journalist, and Julie was sure she would be able to provide sound suggestions as to how the program could be improved. Julie was also pleased to include another woman on the task force.

Case Log

Julie personally contacted her six task force members by phone. All were enthusiastic about participating. However, Duane, the news director seemed slightly hesitant. Julie arranged a meeting place, set a time, and consulted everyone's schedule. She then distributed a printed agenda and the list of all the task force members. She felt positive that all premeeting details had been covered, and she was looking forward to the first weekly meeting.

Meeting 1. Julie was ecstatic with the results of the first meeting. However, it had started with considerable nervous conversation, and she had initially imagined failure. The two marketing experts, Keith and Kent, had sat on one side of the table huddled in private conversation. The two salespeople, Bill and Bob, sat together on the other side of the table. Christine, the reporter, sat by herself and nervously smoked cigarettes. Just when things looked hopeless, Duane came to the rescue. He started telling one humorous story after another about what had been happening in the newsroom that week. Soon everyone was laughing and talking about humorous situations within their own departments. Julie took this ice breaker as an opportunity to open discussion on the planned agenda.

The group then worked for about 1 hr and agreed upon the broad goals outlined by Julie. They also agreed that their task should be able to be completed within the next 6 months. The group congratulated each other on their initial accomplishment and expressed satisfaction that the group had been formed. Even Duane, who had first seemed hesitant, congratulated Julie on what a fine job she had done in organizing the task force.

Meeting 2. The next meeting did not run as smoothly as the first. Julie was not surprised, however, because she purposely had included people from different departments with differing viewpoints. For example, she knew that the marketing and the salespeople would most likely have different viewpoints concerning news program format. However, she never imagined that the two pairs would split so quickly. Each group suggested they knew more about putting a successful news program together than the other. There were undertones of resentment and lack of respect. Even more frustrating was the fact that Christine, who should have provided a journalistic perspective, seemed more withdrawn than ever. Luckily, Duane continued to try to smooth out the situation by telling humorous stories. Julie became worried about her role in terms of resolving conflicts between the salespeople and the marketing people.

Meeting 3. This meeting was more disastrous than the last. The salespeople really got into it with the marketing people about why the news program was doing so poorly. Julie tried to resolve the conflict, but to her surprise, all four of the fighting parties disregarded her. Julie defended herself by presenting projects that she had produced that had received acclaim. But the marketing people were not convinced because she had no statistical support. And the salespeople were not convinced because she had not been around long enough to know what had worked in years past. Once again, Christine just sat there and took no position whatsoever. However, Duane was able, once again, to resolve the conflict for the moment. Although Julie was pleased, she resented his challenge to her position of authority. Despite all of the conflict, Julie's planned agenda for the meeting was left untouched.

Meetings 4–6. Conflict continued between the marketing people and the salespeople. Christine continued to remain quiet and somewhat resentful. Julie felt more and more ineffective. Duane continued to settle disputes. Julie began to wonder if Duane was not trying to overly influence the group because the news program was ultimately his responsibility. He always had supported her in the past, but now she felt betrayed. More and more she began to feel like an outsider.

Meeting 7. Prior to the meeting, Julie distributed a written agenda suggesting that the following items be addressed.

MEMO

To: Duane, Bill, Bob, Kent, Keith, and Christine

From: Julie

Subject: Task Force Meeting Agenda

The following items must be addressed at our next meeting. Please refrain from excessive criticism of one another so that some progress will be made. Thank you for your support.

1. A comparison of ratings and shares from competing newscasts must be made for the month of May (see attached sheet).
2. Continue discussion of changing the format from onset interviews (as scheduled by the assignment editor and the producer), to a summary of the top news of the hour and human interest stories and investigative reports, as suggested by reporters.
3. Discussion of audience research of receptiveness of anchors.

To her surprise, Duane approached her right before the meeting and asked that he be removed from the task force. The last thing that Julie wanted, however, was for people to start quitting. So she begged Duane to stay and assured him that the group would work out its problems. The meeting got underway and the conflict continued. The marketing people insisted that the numbers showed the new anchors were right for the job. The salespeople argued that the "hot shot" researchers had done the program a disservice by providing faulty data that suggested the old standby anchors be replaced. Duane continued to challenge Julie's authority. Julie's suggestion that reporters be given more say in the types of stories they cover was met with disapproval because the news director believed the reporters had enough to do with just covering the stories they were assigned to each day. Besides, he thought that the in-studio interviews set their news program apart from others in the market. Julie was angry with herself for letting Duane remain on the committee. She thought that if Duane were gone and she could get Christine to side with her, then progress could be made. So after the meeting, Julie privately asked Christine for her support and Christine agreed. Julie then asked Duane to lunch where they agreed that Duane should step down from the committee.

Meeting 8. Christine confided in Julie that, for various reasons, she had felt awkward being on the committee with Duane. After all, Duane had been the one to pull her from the anchor slot on the "Live At Five" news program. She was now happy to be able to voice her opinions and support Julie. The meeting, however, was even less productive than when Duane was attending. The men were clearly in opposition to the women. Furthermore, Christine's sudden support of Julie was rather obvious.

Week 9. Rather than meet face-to-face, and to avoid conflict, Julie produced agendas this week and asked group members to work on the items individually and provide written suggestions. Unfortunately, the work that came back was of poor quality and was produced with little thought. Most of the work load fell into Julie's and Christine's hands.

Meeting 10. In an attempt to resume actual meetings, Julie was unable to find a time when all members could gather. Unwillingly, Julie went to the general manager who had appointed her to the committee and explained the difficulty she had been having over the past couple of months. He knew of the problems and informed Julie of the company's decision to bring in an outside consultant. He asked Julie to submit a report of the proceedings of the task force, at which time her responsibilities for the group would be concluded.

Assignment

1. How was this task force formally structured?
2. How was this task force informally structured?
3. What forms of communication were used? Which were more effective?
4. Were the conflicts between the salespeople and marketing people to be expected?
5. Why was Duane a source of conflict for Julie? Should he have been included on the committee?
6. Should Julie have asked for Christine's support?
7. Should Julie have asked Duane to leave the task force?
8. What were some of the underlying problems with the management of the "Live At Five" news program?
9. Based on these problems, what suggestions would you make for improving the news program?
10. What could Julie have done to avoid the failure of the group?
11. How could the task force been better structured so that it would have been more successful at accomplishing its goals?

Case 3.4

The Case of Sagging Morale

Up until 3 years ago, WUPY had the finest news operation in the two-county area. It dominated the four-station market of about 250,000 viewers. The news staff had won more than its share of broadcast journalism awards during the 10-year period preceding its sale 3 years ago. The station was sold to David Hansen by the family that started it in 1955.

During the next 3 years, Hansen slashed costs in every way possible. His apparent purpose was to squeeze as much profit out of the station as possible for a few years and then to sell it. This is exactly what happened. The station now ranks third in overall ratings in the market behind the other two network affiliates. It was only slightly ahead of the independent. The early evening newscast was fourth in ratings during the last sweeps week, just behind reruns of "Gilligan's Islands." The 10 pm newscast ranked third.

Last week Hansen sold the station to Munson Communication Corporation (MCC), a privately held corporation with four dailies, five weeklies, and two cable systems in the state. MCC is headed by Linda Munson, the granddaughter of Alvin Munson, who started the corporation 50 years earlier with two daily newspapers.

The first step Munson took was to hire Todd Wainwright as general manager of the station. Wainwright had been the general manager at a station in a neighboring state. He had a reputation for being a people-oriented manager and for taking low-rated stations and turning them into quality stations that make money.

Munson told Wainwright before hiring him that she wanted a quality station with the top-rated newscast in the market. "This company was founded on good journalism, and it will continued to be known for its quality," she said.

Munson said Wainwright had 5 years to regain WUPY's dominance of the market. She added that he would get double last year's operating budget to start with and that he should prepare a prioritized list of technological needs and a timetable for acquiring them. Munson said she did not expect a profit during the next 3 or 4 years.

Wainwright was satisfied with Munson's commitment to quality and with the financial commitment she had made. He felt that the 5-year time frame was sufficient because the network WUPY was affiliated with was the leader in prime-time ratings. His first job was to assess and develop his personnel and the way the station was organized. Morale was about zero, and he wants that to change.

Organization structure and communication

The station's existing structure is shown in Fig. 3.1. The general manager's position was held by Hansen, who left the day-to-day operations to the assistant general manager, Susan Hampton. Hampton came to WUPY with Hansen.

The communication system that went with the structure was linear, with most communication coming from Hampton in writing and moving along the structure through the department managers. Hampton's messages were looked upon as coming directly from Hansen.

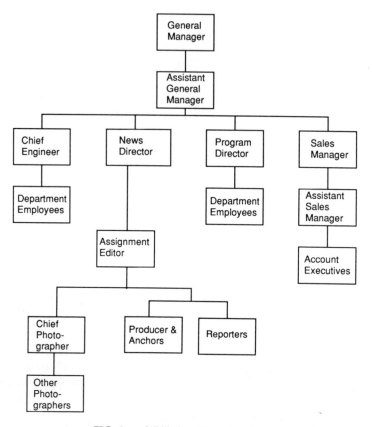

FIG. 3.1. WUPY's existing structure.

Personnel

The following are descriptions of station personnel based on Munson's review of their personnel files and his interviews with them. Personnel included here are limited to department heads and the news department.

Program Director. Sam Waterman has been at WUPY for 30 years, the last 5 as program director. He is 60 years old and about 4 years from retirement. He is friendly and enjoys camping, hunting, and fishing. He is well liked by almost everyone at the station. He is married, and his three children all have graduated from college.

His work as a program director has been adequate, but not spectacular. The syndicated programs he has bought during the past 5 years have catered more toward an older than younger audience. The programs he bought also represented the slim programming budget he had under

Hansen. The budget is now 20% below what it was 3 years before, without adjusting for inflation.

Sales Manager. James Edson is the sales manager. He is 32 years old and has held the position for about 2 years. His promotion came after the last sales manager resigned because of the drop in program quality and ratings. He was selected because the advertising billings he sold during the previous 2 years were three times that of the remaining sales staff. He continues to sell even though he is manager because he enjoys it. In fact, some of his sales staff complains that he takes all the best accounts for himself. Edson is a native to the area. He is not likely to leave the market because his wife is also a area native who works as an assistant principal at a local elementary school.

Overall advertising revenue has declined during his 2 years, but this reflects the declining ratings that have come from the reductions in budget. He has an assistant sales manager, Delaine Duncan, who helps with managerial duties and also sales advertising. She is very much involved with the day-to-day operation of the sales staff, which has three other salespeople.

Two of the three salespeople have been there for only about a year, and the third for about 2 years. All are women under 30 years old. The rapid turnover in the sales department is related to low commission rates, compared to other media in the market, and the difficulty of selling ads for a station with declining ratings in almost all areas. In addition, Edson, although a good salesperson, is not very good at teaching sales techniques. He thinks salespeople are born not made.

Chief Engineer. David Jackson, 26 years old, has been chief engineer for about a year. He worked at a small station in the state for 3 years before joining the WUPY staff. He has a staff of four, all of whom have been with the station for 5 years or more. The staff is at a bare minimum, which means Jackson does a lot of hands-on work himself.

Jackson is doing an adequate job as chief engineer. He is knowledgeable enough, but he is an inexperienced manager. Because of the small staff, members often work overtime, but they have been discouraged from reporting too much overtime because of the expense. WUPY is not a union shop. His problems with managing reflect a lack of training in dealing with people and the fact that he is 10 years younger than the next youngest staff member and 35 years younger than the oldest staff member.

There is a high probability that Jackson will move to larger markets as he becomes a better manager. He is single and not from the market area.

News Director. Sally Vaneer, 33 years old, has been news director for about 3 years. She was promoted from a reporter's position when the last news director quit following Hansen's acquisition of the station. She had been a reporter for 5 years and had never held a management position until this one.

Vaneer is well liked as a person, but she also lacks training as a manager. The news department is understaffed, and she feels stress from the problems that result. She has good news judgment and potential to become a good news director. She is not likely to move anytime soon because her husband recently started a local computer business. She has a daughter who is about 9 months old.

News Staff. Vaneer's staff includes an assignment editor, two producers, a chief photographer, five other photographers, two anchors, a sports reporter, a weather reporter, and three other general-assignment reporters.

Jason Williams is the assignment editor and is second in command of the news department. He was promoted from reporter at the same time as Vaneer. He is about 5 years older and had been working at the station for about a year when he was promoted. His salary is equal to Vaneer's because, as he said, he has more experience. His work is adequate, and he has ambitions to move to a larger market, as a news director, but it may be a difficult because of his age and abilities.

The male coanchor is Stephen Ludsford. He is about 40 years old and has been the anchor for 2 years. He was promoted from a reporter position when the previous male anchor was fired because of slipping ratings. He had worked as a reporter at a competing station before moving to WUPY 10 years ago. He won several statewide awards for his reporting over the years. He prides himself on being a good journalist. He is reasonably well liked by the viewers who report watching WUPY and has no plans for moving to a larger market. His salary as anchor is considerably below his counterparts at the other stations in the market and below the salary of the previous male anchor.

The female anchor, Samantha Wilson, is a 24-year-old African-American. She is unmarried and took the job as coanchor 3 months ago after working for 2 years as a reporter in a smaller market within the state. She has a bright future because of her good news judgment and on-air personality. She is the only African-American coanchor in a market with a population of 18% African-American, 10% Hispanic and 5% other ethnic groups. A shift of ethnic viewers toward WUPY was seen in the latest ratings report. Wilson has plans to move on to bigger markets, but the plans are not definite.

The weather person is Amy Alltree, 35 years old. She has been at the station for 13 years and is a well-known person in the community. She is active in several charity organizations and is genuinely interested in helping those less fortunate than herself. She is a meteorologist and happy with her job. She is unmarried.

All three general-assignment reporters have been with the station for less than a year. William Lacey, 24 years old, came to the station from a smaller market. Sondra Levitt, 23 years old, took the job right out of college, as did Janice Deven, also age 23. All three are fairly good reporters for beginners, and all have aspirations of moving on to larger markets or maybe the networks. Lacey and Levitt want to continue as reporters, whereas Deven aspires to be an anchor. She doubles as anchor on the weekend newscasts.

James Davis, 55 years old, is chief photographer and has been for 12 years. He reports to Williams, even though not all the camera work involves the news department. The six photographers that work for Davis do the photography for all interview and children's shows as well. Before Hansen bought the station, photography was a separate department with 10 photographers, a secretary, and Davis as the department head. Hansen fired the secretary and four photographers and placed the photography department under the news department.

Davis is likely to stay in the market because of family commitments, but he possibly could move to other stations. He is good at his job, but he does not always get along with other people, especially Vaneer.

Assignment

Wainwright is starting with the assumption that everyone can do her or his job well if they are motivated. He will not fire anyone or reassign anyone during the next 6 month, unless he or she asks for reassignment. His job is to improve communications and morale by restructuring, if necessary, and developing ways of motivating the staff. Your assignment is to explain how he could do this by answering the following questions.

1. Would you restructure the organization at WUPY? If so, how and why?
2. What type of leadership behavior should you pursue? Why?
3. What could you do to improve performance preconditions at WUPY? How and why would these changes help individuals to perform better?
4. Taking the information about individuals given earlier, how do you think these people could be motivated? What types of rewards would motivate the various people? Why would these rewards work as motivators? (Develop at least one type of reward for each person mentioned previously.)
5. Which of these people might be motivated by participatory management? Why would they be? How could you promote increased participation?

4
Motivation

Motivation often is thought of as an effort to manipulate employees into doing what the company wants. Unfortunately, this impression is all too often an accurate one. However, at an abstract level, *motivation* is the collection of cognitive processes that make people behave in specific ways (Griffin & Moorhead, 1986; Kreitner, 1986).

On a more practical level, motivation involves efforts by managers to channel these cognitive processes in a way that will benefit the organization and the individual employee. The negative connotations that have become attached to motivation result from efforts by some managers to benefit the company at the expense of the employee. This is not necessary. The proper use of motivation by a manager results in improved work satisfaction for the employee and better performance for the organization.

Motivation, as with all human processes, is complex. A similar behavior by two individuals may have entirely different motivating factors; just as the same motivating factors may result in totally different behaviors by two individuals. Add to this complexity the relatively primitive understanding about motivation we have, and it is understandable why managers often make mistakes in working with employees.

The best way to reduce managerial mistakes is to develop understanding. This section of the chapter aims at increasing this understanding by examining theories about motivation.

MOTIVATION PROCESS

Several models exist concerning the motivation process that occurs within individuals. These vary in complexity from the four steps presented by Van Fleet (1991) to the 11-step model developed by David A. Nadler and Edward E. Lawler III (1977) and presented in French (1986).

A compromise between these extremes is the Griffin and Moorhead (1986) motivational framework. This framework is a five-step, circular process. Within the framework, *needs* are defined as internal factors that "push" behavior. They drive people to act a certain way. For example, a need for food might push someone to make a sandwich. Griffin and Moorhead defined *motives* as factors that "pull" people to act in certain ways. For example, a person may want to become a foreign correspondent for the prestige that goes with the job. This prestige is a need. This person will have a better chance of fulfilling this need if she earns a college degree. The motive for enrolling in college is the need to achieve prestige by becoming a correspondent.

In other words, needs become motives, which are either primary or secondary. *Primary motives* involve nonlearned needs, such as hunger, thirst, sex, and sleep. *Secondary motives* are those that are learned, such as power and achievement.

Needs and motives work as stimuli in the first step of the Griffin and Moorhead (1986) motivation framework. The second step is to identify goals that will satisfy needs. The third step is goal-directed behavior, which is followed by the actual level of need satisfaction coming from goal attainment, the fourth step. This need satisfaction reinforces initial needs and motives, which is the final step that completes the cycle. In the framework, motivation is not the only factor that affects performance. The ability of individuals and the environment also affect the possibility of satisfying needs and motives.

Individual ability and environment are crucial factors in the level of performance. A person can be highly motivated and not succeed because he does not have the skills required to complete a task, or because the conditions are not conducive to high performance. For example, a reporter hears a rumor about the city mayor playing high-stakes poker with land developers once a month. If true, this story would certainly raise conflict-of-interest issues. This reporter may be motivated to get the story and may have the ability, but getting hard facts will not be easy. It is in the interest of all participants to remain silent. In this case, motivation becomes secondary to the environment in attaining a goal.

Ability and environmental factors can be grouped under the term *performance preconditions*, which means factors that are necessary for motivated individuals to attain a desired goal. The role of managers in motivating people is not just to help identify the motives and needs of individuals, but to help create favorable performance preconditions. This means developing skills and providing the equipment, time, and money necessary to perform well.

Figure 4.1 combines the Griffin and Moorhead (1986) framework and the Nadler and Lawler model (French, 1986) with the idea of performance preconditions to illustrate how motivation works. First, needs and motives

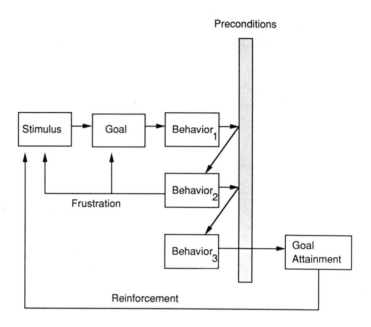

FIG. 4.1. The motivatin process.

provide a stimulus, which leads to the identification of a goal. The identified goal leads to behavior, which may or may not be successful at attaining the goals. This success is determined by the performance preconditions, which include but are not limited to ability and environment. In effect, the preconditions can form a barrier to goal attainment.

If the initial behavior, shown as behavior1, is unsuccessful, the person often will pursue different behavior, represented here as behavior2 and behavior3. If the behavior does not result in goal attainment after a given number of behaviors are tried, the individual can revise the goals and try again, or the person can reexamine the importance of the need or motive. If a successful behavior is found and the goal is attained, the initial needs and motives are reinforced.

This model illustrates some important aspects of motivation. First, motivation to act is only the first step in the process of reaching a goal. Second, attaining a goal requires decision making to find the right behavior. The decision-making process also may involve trial and error. Just how many behaviors are tried depends on the nature of the needs and motives, the difficulty of attaining the goal, and the favorability of the performance preconditions. Third, frustration can affect the goals and the needs and motives. The extent of the impact depends on the nature of the goals, needs, and motives and on the nature of the individual performing the task. Fourth, the level of reinforcement will depend on the difficulty of attaining the goal and the nature of the needs and motives.

In understanding this model, two particular performance preconditions are worth examining, although they are not the only ones. The first deals with the fit between employees and jobs, and the second concerns journalists and their motive of autonomy.

Argyris (1957) developed a theory concerning the relationship between the formal structure of an organization and the personality of the individual worker. He postulated that individuals develop along continua for several personality characteristics from a state of immaturity to a state of maturity. The immature person tends to be passive, whereas the mature person tends to be active in dealing with her environment. These personality characteristics include dependency on others, number of behavior responses, attention span, time perspective, position of subordination, and self-awareness.

Various types of organization structures require various personality types to successfully reach organizational goals. If the structure and people do not match, the organization can become dysfunctional. For example, the top manager in an organization should have a long-term time perspective; otherwise strategic planning will not be effective. Investigative journalists will perform better if they are independent and have a variety of behavior responses they can use in various situations. On the other hands, performance on tedious and repetitive jobs, such as taking classified ads, will be higher for people who are not motivated by independence and who do not have a long-term time perspective.

The match between individual personality and the demands of a particular job structure is a performance precondition and thus can affect motivation. If the personality and job requirement do not match, it will be difficult to attain any goals. The performance preconditions will create frustration. This frustration can lead employees to defensive reactions, absenteeism, creating informal groups that work against organizational goals, lower productivity, and leaving the organization. Such frustration most certainly will change the ways in which employees can be motivated.

When the match is inconsistent, a manger has several options. He can allow the individual to grow into the job with training and proper supervision, or he can move the individual to a more suitable job. It is important to note that Argyris (1957) was dealing with personality and not ability. Both are areas that can be developed, but the types of training differs.

Argyris' (1957) work can be extended specifically to journalists in the area of autonomy. In a national study of journalists in the early 1980s, Weaver and Wilhoit (1986) found that perceived autonomy was an important predictor of job satisfaction. They also found the perceived autonomy of journalists was lower than that found in a similar study 12 years before.

Autonomy is a performance precondition for the more mature journalists. These are the ones who have the potential for the highest performance. A manager who wants high journalistic performance would be advised to promote autonomy for her journalists.

MOTIVATION GOALS

As Fig. 4.1 illustrates, goals are an important part of the motivation process. The goals flow from the motives and needs and become the target of the behavior. The level of success in attaining the goals will affect future behavior. Motivational goals include both organizational goals and individual goals. The two can be consistent or inconsistent, but either way they affect organizational performance.

Organizational goals should be stated formally and include financial and product goals. The financial goals involve profit, revenue and costs goals, and are discussed in chapter 7. The product goals usually aim at a level of quality for the company's service or product. In media, these product goals generally relate to the content.

Individual motivational goals vary from person to person, but job satisfaction is generally a catchall for how often these goals are reached. *Job satisfaction* is how a person feels about her job and represents how well the job is fulfilling the needs and the motives of the employee. The concept of *quality of work life* is related to job satisfaction, but it deals more with the interaction of individuals and the organization than looking at the feelings of individual employees.

Walton (French, 1986) listed eight dimensions for analyzing the quality of work life. These are: adequate and fair compensation, safe and healthy working conditions, opportunity to use and develop human capacities, opportunity for continued growth and security, social integration in the work organization, rights to privacy and due process, balanced role of work in worker's life, and socially beneficial and responsible work. These criteria are useful for managers as an inventory of work life at their organizations. The criteria do not reveal how a particular individual feels about her job or the organization, but an organization with a low quality of work life is likely to have a number of dissatisfied employees.

Job satisfaction is one of the most researched concepts in motivation. This extends to the field of journalism, where several studies have tried to identify what makes journalists satisfied with their jobs. The Weaver and Wilhoit (1986) study mentioned earlier found that journalists older than 40 years of age were motivated by different factors than those under 40. The important factors for those under 40, in order of importance, were rating of performance by employing news organization, frequency of comments about work from supervisors, extent of freedom to select news stories to work on, and salary. Important factors for those over the age of 40 were editorial staff unionized, editorial policies, marital status, majoring in journalism, importance of autonomy, and salary level.

Autonomy also was found to be important in job satisfaction for television journalists (Joseph, 1983). Additional factors in determining job satisfaction for journalists are degree of participatory leadership (Adams & Fish, 1987; Powers & Lacy, 1991), how well the public is being informed (Bergen & Weaver, 1988), and the nature of structure and communication in the organization (Howard, 1973; Johnstone, 1976; and Polansky & Hughes, 1986).

These studies illustrate the variety of factors that affect job satisfaction for employees, and the role that performance preconditions, such as communication and leadership, play in the motivation process. Some employees face the problem that managers are not always convinced the goals of the organization and employees are compatible. Many managers believe that employees should be motivated only by the pay they receive and any other expense to develop employees is wasted. This scientific management approach is discussed in chapter 2 and is far too simplistic to explain employee behavior, especially in jobs that involve some creativity. Making money is not the only, or even the primary, goal that motivates most workers in media organizations.

The relationship between performance and job satisfaction is a complex one. The human-relations approach to management was based on the assumption that satisfied workers are more productive. French (1986) reported that the relationship appears to be that motivated employees perform better and that higher performance leads to satisfaction, which in turn can reinforce the motivation. The problem of defining the relationship between job satisfaction and performance may be one of definition and measurement because the concept of job satisfaction is rather vague.

Although the exact relationship between job satisfaction and performance remains unclear, research indicates that dissatisfaction has a negative impact on performance. Dissatisfaction can lead to defensive behavior, sabotage, absenteeism, and high turnover—all of which interfere with reaching the financial goals of an organization.

Before examining approaches to motivation, the role of perception should be discussed. Whether a manager is dealing with ways of motivating or the degree of job satisfaction, she should remember that these involve processes that go on inside a person's brain. These cognitive processes act on information that is filtered by a person's selective exposure, selective perception, and selective retention. A manager who assumes that an issue or problem will be perceived the same by himself and the employee is in trouble. Not only do people perceive differently, but the roles that managers and employees must act out guarantee differences in perceptions. Even different managers will perceive issues differently.

The way a manager deals with varying perceptions will play an important role in determining her success. The best approach is to develop empathy for other people, so that a manager can better understand the impact of perception on communication and consequently on motivation. Often disagreements among people will disappear if they make the effort to understand differences in perceptions.

MOTIVATION APPROACHES

Early theories about motivation can be categorized as either need theories or conditioning theories. The former assumes that people have basic needs that motivate them. The key for managers is to understand which basic needs are important and channel those needs toward goals that a person can attain. The second approach assumes that behavior primarily is learned through conditioning a person with rewards and punishment. Motivating people depends on developing the proper reward system for attaining specific goals.

Several theories have been developed within each of these approaches, and process theories have emerged more recently. These two approaches are examined and then more recent theories are explored.

The Need Approach

The study of need theories of motivations starts with Maslow's (1954) hierarchy of needs. He said people have five types of innate needs that are arranged in a hierarchical order. In effect, these needs form a ladder, shown in Fig. 4.2. The bottom three needs—physiological, security, and belongingness—are called deficiency needs. These needs must be satisfied before a person can fulfill the growth needs, which are esteem and self-actualization.

Physiological needs include the need for food, water, and sex. Security needs include the need for physical and psychological security. Belongingness needs include the need for acceptance, affection, and love. Esteem is the fourth level and includes the need for a sense of self-worth and recognition from others. The final need is self-actualization, which involves creativity and fulfilling one's potential.

Maslow (1954) argued that a particular need was a motivator until it was satisfied, then a higher level need was necessary for motivation. For example, a person would not be as interested in fulfilling security needs until the physiological needs were fulfilled. In the workplace, an employee

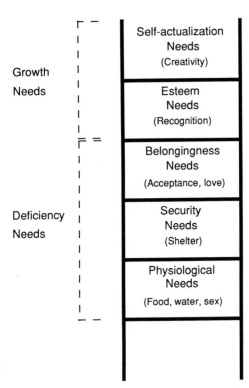

FIG. 4.2.   Maslow's hierarchy of needs.

might not be motivated by a promotion, which would represent esteem needs, until the need for belongingness, friends within the company, was met.

Maslow's (1954) hierarchy is worthwhile because it recognizes the various types of needs that can motivate and it establishes some order among the needs. However, it also is limited in its application to everyday work life. First, Maslow does not discuss what happens if lower level needs cease being fulfilled. For example, what happens to an employee whose company goes bankrupt? Does he return to lower levels of need motivation? Second, the idea of a rigid hierarchy is inconsistent with some behavior. People will sacrifice fulfillment of lower level needs in order to achieve self-esteem or self-actualization. For example, an entering freshman might pursue journalism as a major instead of prelaw despite the lower pay of journalism. Certainly, law would provide the person with more security and fulfill a higher level of physiological needs.

The limitations of Maslow's (1954) theory are addressed by Alderfer's (1972) ERG theory. He postulated three basic needs: existence, relatedness, and growth (ERG). Existence needs are similar to the physiological and security needs of Maslow. Relatedness needs are analogous to Maslow's belongingness needs. Growth needs correspond to the esteem and self-actualization needs of Maslow's hierarchy.

Alderfer's (1972) theory was an advancement over Maslow's (1954) for two main reasons. First, it stated that a person could be motivated by more than one need at a time. For example, a producer in a local television newsroom could be motivated by the existence needs, such as the need for good retirement benefits, and by growth needs, which might be training in management techniques.

A second advantage of the ERG theory is the inclusion of a frustration component that explains what happens if needs are not met. Alderfer, just as Maslow, said that if lower level needs are met, a person will be motivated by higher level needs. However, the ERG theory also explains that if higher level needs are not met, the person may regress to lower level needs as motivators. For example, if a television news producer works for a promotion to news director to fulfill a growth need but the promotion goes to someone else, she no longer will be motivated by that level of need. She is more likely to become motivated by an existence or relatedness need.

This frustration component is important for managers to recognize because it means that the types of needs that motivate an employee change as a result of managerial action or inaction. For example, the decision to hire inside or outside an organization when a managerial position opens carries a message to employees about the future of their professional growth within the organization.

A final theory of motivation relates to the assumptions about job satisfaction. The two-factor theory developed by Herzberg and associates (Herzberg, 1968; Herzberg, Mausner & Snyderman, 1959) rejects the assumption of other need theories that satisfaction and dissatisfaction are ends of the same continuum. This assumption implies that satisfaction and dissatisfaction are affected by the same needs and motives. Herzberg said that satisfaction and dissatisfaction were separate continua that are affected by different needs and motive.

Dissatisfaction is affected by hygiene factors, such as salary, security, and interpersonal relations. Satisfaction is affected by needs motivators, such as recognition, achievement, and responsibility. The hygiene factors can reduce dissatisfaction, but they will not motivate people to superior performance. However, motivation is not likely to occur if hygiene factors are lacking.

Figure 4.3 shows the relationship between the two dimensions and the factors that affect them. Research concerning this theory is inconsistent. Some research, mostly that using the same method as Herzberg (1968; Herzberg, Mausner & Snyderman, 1959) used in his studies, has supported the theory, but other research has not (Griffin & Moorhead, 1986).

As with the ERG theory, the two-factor theory is analogous to Maslow's

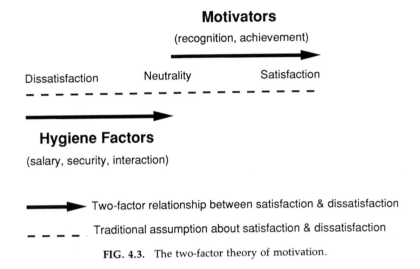

FIG. 4.3. The two-factor theory of motivation.

(1954) hierarchy. Herzberg's (1968) hygiene factors are similar to Maslow' three lower level needs–physiological, security, and belongingness–and to the ERG existence and relatedness needs. The motivation factors are similar to the self-esteem and self-actualization needs found in Maslow and the growth needs found in the ERG theory (Giles, 1988; Griffin & Moorhead, 1986).

Two other theories are notable for their contribution to the need approach. McClelland (1961) identified three basic needs that motivate people: the need for achievement, the need for affiliation, and the need for power. The need for achievement means people seek to reach goals. The need for affiliation involves the need for friendship and affection. The need for power involves the need for control, which can be control over others or over one's own environment. McGregor's (1960) Theory X and Theory Y discussed in chapter 2 also deal with motivation. Theory X assumes that people are motivated by the need for financial resources, whereas Theory Y assumes that motivation comes from needs other than those that can be fulfilled with money.

Conditioning Approach

No doubt exists that motivation is far more complex than just paying money for work. However, the idea that we have needs that are our primary motivators is not the only approach toward understanding why people act as they do. The conditioning approach assumes we learn patterns of behavior through a series of rewards and punishments. This approach does not deal with internal cognitive processes, but rather emphasizes that behavior is determined by making the wanted behavior patterns successful at attaining goals.

Various types of reinforcements and punishments work to varying degrees with various individuals. The particular reward and/or punishment schemes may reflect either primary or secondary motives. An important assumption of using conditioning for motivation is that managers need not understand the needs of the individual employees as long as they provide the types of rewards that will get employees to act in certain ways.

Conditioning processes fall into two types: *classical conditioning* and *operant conditioning* (Hamner & Organ, 1978). Classical conditioning involves associating a conditioned stimulus with an unconditioned stimulus that causes a reflexive response. The reflexive response originally associated with the unconditioned stimulus then will be associated with the conditioned stimulus.

Classical conditioning was developed by Pavlov (1902) while he was studying digestive reflexes. He rang a bell before serving a dog with food. A natural reflex to food is salivation. After repeated bell ringing followed by food, the dog began to salivate at the sound of the bell. He had been conditioned to respond to the bell in the same way he had been responding to food.

Operant conditioning, which was explored primarily by Skinner (1953, 1972), assumes that the individual is active within her environment. A person will act to achieve goals that have pleasant results and avoid actions that have unpleasant results. Just which actions result in pleasant or unpleasant responses often is discovered through trial and error.

Figure 4.4 shows the process of operant conditioning, which is also called reinforcement theory. A stimulus results in a response. The response leads to a consequence. The consequence of the response will reinforce the behavior, if the consequence is positive for the individual, but the consequence will not reinforce the response, if the consequence is

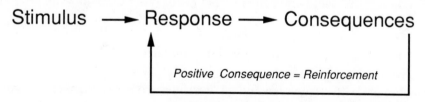

FIG. 4.4.   Operant conditioning.

negative. Reinforcement increases the probability that the same stimulus will elicit the same response, whereas nonreinforcement will decrease the probability that the same stimulus will result in the same response. Repeated exposure to the same stimulus will create a pattern of behavior.

The difference between classical and operant conditioning is that classical conditioning involves an involuntary response, such as salivating, whereas operant conditioning involves voluntary responses in reaction to the environment. A person is more active with operant conditioning.

An example of operant conditioning is helping a writer improve his writing. When an editor or news director works with a journalist on his writing, the comments and instructions become the stimulus. The response concerns the quality of future writing. If improvement in writing results in praise, promotion, raises, or other positive rewards, the journalist has been conditioned to respond to suggestions about writing in a positive way. If the improvement in writing is not rewarded, the tendency of the writer will be to ignore future suggestions about writing.

Operant conditioning involves four types of reinforcements: *positive reinforcement, negative reinforcement, extinction* and *punishment*. Positive reinforcement involves rewarding the desired response with something pleasant. For example, high performance of a job is rewarded with a raise, a promotion, or an award. Negative reinforcement, also called avoidance, occurs when a desired response results in the removal of something unpleasant. For example, a reporter whose editor screams at her for missing deadline, will avoid being screamed at if she turns stories in on time. Extinction is the process of eliminating unwanted responses by not rewarding them. This is often what happens with behavior that once was desired and rewarded but no longer is wanted. For example, if working overtime to get stories has become too expensive, journalists can be told that they will not be paid for overtime. Some may continue to work on their own, but many will cease working overtime. Punishment means presenting unwanted responses with negative consequences. For example, misspelling a person's name on a public relations release can result in a verbal reprimand for the writer.

Generally, the most effective way of getting people to behave in a desired way is through positive reinforcement. Second best is negative reinforcement, and extinction is third. Punishment is the most ineffective way of changing behavior. It builds resentment and often only has a temporary impact on behavior.

Positive reinforcement can take place on a variety of schedules. Two main types of schedules are continuous and partial (Hamner & Organ, 1978). Continuous means the response is rewarded after every occurrence. This reinforcement schedule results in quick learning, but the response disappears quickly after reinforcement is removed. Partial reinforcement does not occur after every response. It results in slower learning than continuous reinforcement, but the response is retained longer than with continuous reinforcement.

Partial reinforcement has different schedules (Fester & Skinner, 1957) that are useful for establishing different types of behavior. The particular type of reinforcement schedule will vary with the individual and with the type of behavior sought. The intervals fall into fixed, which means they occur regularly, and variable, which means they are not predictable. Generally, variable reinforcement produces higher levels of performance, but the intervals between reinforcement should not be long.

Not everyone accepts the use of operant conditioning as appropriate for management. Hamner and Organ (1978) pointed out that some scholars argue its use ignores the individuality of humans, that its use restricts freedom of choice, and that its use ignores the fact that the job itself can motivate people. The ethical issues and limitations of operant conditioning should be understood before managers attempt to motivate employees. If employees believe they are being manipulated, or even that an attempt to manipulate them is underway, management will find it extremely difficult to regain the trust of those employees. The company may lose some of the most creative people as a result.

Hamner and Organ (1978) presented six rules for using operant conditioning:

1. Do not reward all people the same. Managers should differentiate rewards on the basis of performance.

2. Failure to respond has reinforcing consequences. Not rewarding a behavior can affect future behavior as much as rewarding the behavior.

3. Be sure to tell a person what he or she can do to get reinforced. Operant conditioning will work better if the person knows the desired behavior.

4. Be sure to tell a person what he or she is doing wrong. A person should know how not to act as well as how to act.

5. Do not punish in front of others. Punishment should be used sparingly, and when it is used, it should address specific behavior. Punishment in front of others means ridicule before peers and does not address the undesired behavior.

6. Make consequences equal to behavior. If a manager underrewards employees, the desired behavior may not take place. Overrewarding employees may create guilt in the employees receiving the reward or resentment among other employees.

Operant conditioning occurs whether managers want it to or not. Because managers have the power to reward, the method used to administer these rewards will affect employee behavior. The best approach to rewards is an open and conscious effort to promote behavior that benefits the organization and its individual members. The importance of participatory management discussed in chapters 2 and 3 applies to rewards as well. People who are affected by rewards should be involved in setting up the systems of rewards.

PROCESS THEORIES OF MOTIVATION

A drawback of the need approach to motivation is that it deals more with factors that cause behavior than with the process by which behavior occurs. The limitation of the operant conditioning approach is that it is somewhat mechanical and overlooks the role of a person's needs and motives in behavior. Griffin and Moorhead (1986) discussed a collection of theories they called process theories, which deal with the process by which people are motivated. Three of these—*equity theory, expectancy theory,* and *goal setting theory*—are discussed here.

Equity theory (Adams, 1963) assumes that people compare themselves with their peers to determine how fairly they are being treated. Individuals compare their return from their inputs into an organization with the return on inputs of the peers they have selected for comparison. The comparison is shown by the equation:

$$\frac{\text{Outcome for self}}{\text{Input by self}} = \frac{\text{Outcome for other}}{\text{Input by other}}$$

Inputs include contributions to achieving the organization's goals, such as time, loyalty, and experience. Outcomes are the rewards that are given for the inputs, such as money, recognition, and interpersonal relationships. The ratio of input to output is expected to be equal for an individual and the selected others of comparison. If they are not equal, the employee is left with a feeling of inequitable treatment and reacts to the situation.

A person can react seven ways after evaluating his equity. If the person is satisfied that he is being treated equitably, he will be motivated to continue his present situation. If the person has a feeling of inequity, he faces six options:

1. He may change his inputs. For example, a reporter might cut back on his efforts if he feels unfairly treated.
2. He may change the outcomes. The reporter might ask for a raise.
3. He may alter his perception of himself. The reporter might decide that his inputs are not as great as he originally thought.

4. He may alter his perception of others. The reporter may decide that the other people actually did work harder than he did.
5. He may change comparisons. The reporter may decide that he has been comparing himself to the wrong peer.
6. He may leave the organization. The reporter may decide that he is not appreciated and find another job.

Research has tended to support equity theory in situations of underpayment (Griffin & Moorhead, 1986), and most people have experienced a feeling of inequity at some point in their careers. It is important to note, however, that feelings of equity and inequity are based on perceptions, and these perceptions may reflect inaccurate information. For example, rewards that another is receiving may be underestimated because the information is gained through rumor. The relative amount of effort by a peer may be underestimated. But the perceptions must be dealt with, even if they are incorrect. A manager cannot assume all employees have complete and accurate knowledge of the performances and rewards of other employees.

Many organizations attempt to keep salaries and reward schemes secret because they know people make comparisons. This practice is questionable because it is based on two assumptions that are not true. These assumptions are that people will not make equity evaluations if they have incomplete information and that all people are motivated by money. Honesty about the level of reward, explicit explanation of how the rewards were determined, and participation of employees in determining rewards is a better solution in the long run than secrecy for media organizations. Trying to keep secrets from journalists only will present a challenge to them.

Vroom's expectancy theory (1964) states that motivation is a result of how likely a behavior will lead to a reward and how important that reward is to the person. This theory has three important variables (Giles, 1988): Instrumentality is the probability that an effort will result in the desired performance, expectation involves the probability that the performance will result in the reward, and valence is the desirability of the reward. This relationship is shown in Fig. 4.5.

This theory is almost an extension of the decision-making process discussed in chapter 1. The motivation of an individual to perform is based on the probabilities that performance will result in a goal of value to the individual. This theory shows the importance of making sure individuals have the ability to perform at the desired level, of creating favorable preconditions to achieving goals, and of designing reward systems that meet the needs of individuals. If any of these steps break down, the employee is less likely to be motivated to achieve the goals.

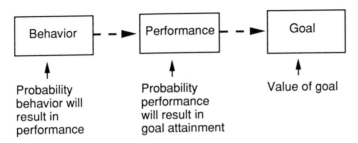

FIG. 4.5. Expectancy theory.

Locke (1968) developed goal-setting theory on the assumption that behavior is a conscious effort to attain goals. He suggested that the level of performance was based on two aspects of goals: goal difficulty and goal specificity. Goals should be high to motivate performance, but not so high as to frustrate employees. Goals also should be specific, which means they should be stated in quantitative terms. Specific goals provide better feedback on performance.

Locke later expanded his model (Latham & Locke, 1979) to include goal acceptance and goal commitment. Acceptance is the degree to which an individual adopts the organization's goal as her own. Commitment is the degree to which she wants to attain the goal. Commitment and acceptance are influenced by participation in setting goals, the degree to which goals are challenging but realistic, and the perceived chance that the goals will lead to valuable results.

PARTICIPATION

An important element of the process approaches to motivation and operant conditioning is participation by employees. Participation plays a role in organizational structure (chapter 2) and leadership (chapter 3). Participation lies at the center of modern management, yet managers find it difficult to allow employees to participate in a meaningful way.

As contingency leadership models point out, the role of participation varies with the individual and the situation. At media organizations, participatory management will not work well when decisions must be made on deadline. However, most creative and educated employees, such as journalists, want a role in decisions that affect them.

The challenge to media managers is to develop ways that allow employees to participate, while retaining some power for necessarily quick decisions that judging news often requires. Although day-to-day participation should be a part of media organizations, two other types of participation suggest themselves as possibilities for media organizations: *quality circles* and *task forces*. Quality circles are groups of volunteer employees who meet regularly to identify problems, analyze the causes, and make recommendations to eliminate the problems. A task force is a group of employees assigned to deal with long-term problems and issues that affect the organization.

Both of these employee groups allow participation and deal with important problems, but they vary somewhat in the makeup and use. Table 4.1 compares these two approaches to participation. Quality circles are voluntary, whereas task forces can be voluntary and appointed. Quality circles continue for as long as they are effective, but task forces usually have a time period after which they are disbanded. Quality circles work on production and quality problems, usually at the department level, whereas task forces can address a wide range of issues and problems at any level of the organization. Quality circles usually meet weekly, whereas task forces vary in the regularity of their meetings. Both types of groups engage in identifying and analyzing problems and recommending changes to solve them. Quality circles usually have about 6 to 10 members, whereas task forces vary in size. However, with all groups, an increase in size past 6 to 10 members makes successful completion of the assigned task more difficult.

Generally, quality circles monitor an on-going process for problems, whereas a task force is formed to deal with long-term problems, such as strategic planning and dealing with industrial changes. It is important that participation in both be genuine. Disguising efforts to manipulate employees as participatory management can create long-term problems between management and employees. When it comes to motivating people in mass-media organizations, true participatory management is better than

TABLE 4.1
Comparison of Quality Circle and Task Force

	Quality Circle	Task Force
Formation	Volunteers	Volunteer or appointment
Duration	As long as effective	Set time span
Level of Use	Departmental	All levels
Functions	Identify, analyze and solve problems	Identify, analyze, and solve problems
Types of Problems	Production and quality problems	A wide range of problems
Meeting Schedule	Usually weekly	Variable
Size	Usually 6–10	Variable, but small size works best

autocratic management or classical management disguised as participatory management.

COMMUNICATION AND MOTIVATION

Communication and motivation belong together because a manager cannot motivate without communicating, and a manager's communication will have little impact if employees are not motivated. As discussed earlier, structure affects communication, but structure alone cannot ensure communication. Communication ultimately involves how well one person conveys a meaning to others.

Communication can be defined in many ways. Cooley (1909) said it is "the mechanism through which human relations exist and develop—all the symbols of the mind, together with the means of conveying them through space and preserving them in time" (p. 61). Although this is an eloquent definition of a complicated concept, it includes a much larger range of topics than can be addressed here. So for this chapter, *communication* will be defined as the exchange of information and ideas by two or more people.

The process of communication starts with a sender, who transmits a message through a channel to a receiver. This message transmission is subject to noise. The sender constructs the message in her brain and encodes that message into symbols. The symbols are then sent either face-to-face or using some mechanical form of transmission to a receiver. The receiver then decodes the symbols in the message and gives them meaning. The symbols can take any number of forms, from words to photographs to body configurations called "body language."

An important aspect of the communication process is *noise*. Noise acts to interfere with communication and can take two forms: *channel noise* and *semantic noise*. Channel noise is some interference due to the transmission mechanism. For example, static on a telephone line is a form of channel noise. If channel noise makes the message difficult to understanding, it reduces the probability that the decoding process will give a similar meaning to the one intended in the encoding process. Semantic noise involves difficulties in understanding due to variations in the meanings of symbols. Semantic noise is addressed in more detail later.

The selectivity of cognitive processes plays an important role in communication. Both encoding and decoding reflect the experiences, memory, ways of understanding, and other cognitive processes and properties of the individuals communicating. The cognitive processes are affected by four forms of selectivity (Severin & Tankard, 1992). *Selective exposure* means that people help to determine the messages they consider. They tend to expose themselves to messages that are consistent with their beliefs and experiences. *Selective attention* means that people will pay attention to particular parts of a message, usually those parts that are consistent with their beliefs and experiences. *Selective perception* means that people's understanding of a message is influenced by their beliefs, needs, attitudes, and experiences. In other words, not everyone interprets the same message in the same way. *Selective retention* means that people recall portions of messages based on their, needs, beliefs, experience, and attitudes.

Severin and Tankard (1992) said these four processes can act as defense rings that filter psychologically threatening information. In effect, selectivity works as a way of reducing feelings of psychological inconsistency brought on by communication. Selectivity as a defense is not necessarily a conscious activity, although the process of selecting often is seen as such by an individual. Because of this, selectivity can be a problem for managers. Managers need to select information based on its usefulness in making decisions. As mentioned in chapter 1, adequate amounts of information and accurate analysis of that information are necessary for effective decision making. Managers must make an effort, therefore, to resist the impact of selectivity on encoding.

Communication Problems

Communication problems are those that come from channel noise and semantic noise. Correcting for channel noise is relatively straightforward. It involves identifying the sources of the channel noise and correcting the cause. Semantic noise is far more difficult to deal with because it involves cognitive process that are not observable.

Haney (1973) examined 10 types of communication problems, some of which could be called semantic noise. These problems are not unique to organizations, but they certainly create problems for organization communication. Three of these problems that are common and, therefore, are of particular interest to journalists are discussed here.

The first problem is *bypassing*, which occurs when a word means something different for the sender and the receiver, or when the sender and receiver use different words to mean the same thing. For example, at newspapers the term beat has more than one meaning. Recent usage of beat means an area of coverage, such as police or state government. However, a more traditional meaning for beat was getting a story before the competition. An editor telling a reporter he has an idea for a beat could mean two different things depending on the reporter's background. This type of misunderstanding often can occur between reporters and sources.

The impact of bypassing varies from situation to situation. The results are the appearance of agreement when there is really disagreement, or vice versa. In either case, the impact is usually slight and even can be humorous, which very often occurs with headlines. For example, a 1975 headline in *The New York Times* read: "Antibusing Rider Killed by Senate." This is bypassing with little consequences. However, some bypassing can be potentially more damaging, even leading to libel suits.

The second problem is *allness*. Allness occurs when a sender does not realize he is abstracting and assumes what he is saying is absolute and all there is to know about the subject. *Abstracting* is the process in communication of concentrating on certain details while ignoring others. Abstracting is an essential part of language because communicating all details of an object or idea would be too time consuming. The problem is that some people do not realize the characteristics they choose to abstract are not the only important characteristics.

Allness can have a negative impact on decision making. For example, if ratings of an early evening newscast are falling, a station manager might assume that it is a result of dissatisfaction with the anchors. Such a conclusion could come from chatting with some acquaintances at a party. Allness occurred when the general manager assumed that this is the reason and does not explore other possibilities. In effect, the general manager is ignoring the importance of information searching in decision making. People can remind themselves of the allness problem by saying to themselves "maybe not" after making generalizations.

A third problem is *polarization*, which is the tendency to deal with problems and situations as dichotomous. It leads to statements such as people are either good or bad. Polarization creates problems because it fails to distinguish degrees of variations in a situation. In reality, few problems are either/or in nature. Reporters often assume government officials are either crooked or not. They, therefore, conclude that poor performance is because of malfeasance. Most poor performance in government is due more to incompetence than to any evil intent.

The English language contributes to the polarization problem because it has few intermediate terms. Most adjectives tend to be bipolar in nature, such as success-failure and honest-dishonest. Polarization is a serious problem in journalism because journalists tend to look for "both" sides of an issue when in reality issues have many sides.

The impact of polarization on decision making is similar to allness because it tends to reduce the quest for information that would provide alternative points of view. A manager might decide one alternative is the correct one and then consider all others as incorrect. This prevents analysis of various options to find the one that *probably* will work best. The term *probably* is italicized because polarization denies the variation found in the concept of probability.

SUMMARY

Motivation of individuals is an essential function of managers. An organization cannot accomplish its goals effectively and efficiently without motivated employees, and they cannot be motivated unless the organization has an adequate communication system.

Communication can take many forms. Two important steps in promoting effective communication are solving the semantic and perception problems that can interfere and selecting patterns of communication that work toward the organizational goals.

The two traditional approaches, needs theory and operant conditioning, have given way to more complex process theories. These theories emphasize the role of employee participation and the provision of working conditions that will allow employees to attain their goals. It is important to remember that people vary in the factors and rewards that motivate them.

These theories have practical uses to managers as tools that can be used in two ways. First, the theories can help managers to understand employee behavior and motivation. Second, theory can help managers to design reward systems and organization structures that will help motivate employees.

An important decision for management is the degree to which employees will participate in management decision making. If participation is high, which it should be for many departments in media organizations, the system of communication must be open enough to share information adequately. Otherwise, participatory management will not work.

CHAPTER 4 CASES

Case 4.1

The Case of the Sluggish Quality Circle

Randy Miller, the publisher of the 30,000-circulation *Morristown Citizen Tribune*, organized the quality circle in the circulation department after attending an ANPA convention and hearing a speaker from the *Detroit Free Press*. Miller was impressed with the results reported by Jim Smith of the *Free Press* and felt a quality circle might help solve some of the circulation problems facing his evening daily.

After returning from the convention, Miller called Janet Lafore, the circulation manager, into his office and told her to set up such a circle at the *Citizen Tribune*. He explained that he wanted the circle set up with Lafore as head. It would meet every week to brainstorm about ways to solve problems that Miller felt were important. The circle would be composed of six circulation employees selected from and by the 16 district and assistant district managers. The group members would be given $10 a week for their participation.

The first week, the six employees attended and were asked to come up with ways of solving the increasing number of stops. The *Citizen Tribune* had been losing almost 1% of their readers per month during the past 6 months and Miller wanted it stopped.

The quality circle also was told to figure out ways of reducing the turnover among the news carriers. Of the 160 carriers, less than half had been with the newspaper for a year or more. Miller felt this was related to the stops and thought that the group might be able to take care of two problems with one solution.

Six months passed before the quality circle submitted their report on these two problems to Miller. During that time, they had suggested a few changes in the circulation department that had made things slightly more efficient, but Miller had decided his support for the continuation of the quality circle was going to depend on what the group suggested about these two big problems. The day after he got the report from the circle, he called Lafore into his office.

"Janet, I can't tell you how disappointed I am in what this quality circle has done," Marshall said. "I had expected a more creative approach than they were willing to give. You've seen what they gave me. What do you think?"

"Well, Randy, I'm not so sure they haven't hit on something. They worked real hard on this report," Lafore replied. "I think . . . "

"They said the circulation problem was due to poor quality of reporting," Miller said as he interrupted his circulation manager. "If I had wanted to know about the news staff I would have set up a circle there. I wanted them to address the problems in circulation that have continued during the 6 months they were supposed to be solving the problems."

"But Randy, they had some excellent ideas about retaining carriers. The idea of limiting route size is a good one, as is the idea of setting up college scholarships for the carriers that work for 7 years or more. I think these two changes will help keep these boys and girls."

"Yeah, but at what cost? What they have planned may cost more than it does to train all of the new carriers we get. I'm just not pleased with this at all. Go back to them and tell them I want something better."

The following week, Lafore visited Miller and told him that the quality circle had voted to disband. She also said the other people in the circulation department had declined to participate in a new quality circle.

"I guess what works in Detroit doesn't work in Morristown," Miller said with a shrug.

Assignment

1. Is Miller's final assessment correct? Explain.
2. What went wrong with the quality circle in Morristown?

3. What would you have done differently in setting up the quality circle?

4. What are some of the factors and conditions that could affect the success of quality circles and other such participatory programs? What type of impact could these factors and conditions have?

Case 4.2

The Case of Big Egos in Broadcasting

XYZ-TV in San Antonio has a big lead over its closest competitor in ratings for both the 6 pm and 10 pm news. The group-owned station had a 51 share for the evening newscast and a 48 share for the 10 pm newscast. Its closest competitor had 25 and 22 shares during the latest Nielsen ratings period. The anchors of the XYZ-TV newscasts are Bill Hammond and Marie Osborne. Hammond is 42 years old and Osborne is 29 years old. Both anchors score well in viewer surveys, but Hammond is unquestionably the star.

Hammond has been in the San Antonio market for 20 years and an anchor at XYZ-TV for 5. He is compared with Ted Koppel and has a solid background as a reporter. He is more than just a talking head. Osborne is still new at the job. She has been a coanchor for 6 months after coming to the station for that purpose from Austin, Texas. She has been well received by the audience, but it is Hammond who draws viewers.

The two newscasts have been big moneymakers for the station. All the time slots are sold a year in advance. The possibility of extending the news to an hour from its current half-hour format also is being discussed.

Although Hammond is often given credit for the large profit the station is making from the news, Jan Michaels, the top ad executive on the advertising staff, is considered by her co-workers to be the real reason behind the sold-out slots on the newscasts. The rates are high even for the good ratings. Members of the ad department say it is Michael's way with people that has accounted for the sold-out spots.

Michaels is 35 years old and has been with the station for 10 years. She has been offered the position of ad manager at the station twice and turned it down both times because she likes to sell. She is liked and respected at ad agencies and by the ad managers in companies throughout San Antonio. She has won numerous awards for her contributions to the community.

Jim Lackey, president of XYZ-TV, has seen his station become one of the biggest and best in the Southwest. Jim has hopes of moving into group management sometime soon, as a reward for his station's success. He had not anticipated problems over money.

The Problem

Hammond's contract has just ended and during the first negotiation meeting he told Lackey that he wanted to be the highest paid person at the station. Hammond was already making $200,000 a year, and Lackey had anticipated giving him a $25,000 pay increase. When Hammond was told about the 25% raise, he was not impressed.

"Bill, you are already the highest paid talent in the market. I don't understand the problem," Lackey said.

"Jim, I don't make as much as Michaels," Hammond said. "I know her cronies in the ad department say she is the reason my newscasts are making so much money, but you and I know it's because of the work I do. So, why aren't I making more money than she is?" "But Jim, her base salary is considerably less than yours. She makes the rest in commissions and incentives. I can't control her commissions, and she won't like the $1-more-a-year type of contract you're asking for."

"I don't care about that. Coming up with a way to do it is your job. I'm sure you've heard about the job offers I've gotten from the network and from other markets. All I want is what I'm worth, and I'm worth more to this station than she is."

Assignment

1. As station president, how do you respond to what Hammond has said? Explain your response.
2. What is at issue in this case?
3. Is Hammond's demand justified? Why or why not?
4. As station manager, is there a way to meet Hammond's demands as stated without affecting the relationship you have with Michaels?
5. What are possible repercussions on the other members of the staff if you give in to Hammond's demands? How could you handle these repercussions?

Case 4.3

The Case of the Meandering Task Force

Diana Stocking leaned back in her chair and sighed. This was not what she had expected. She had been excited by the prospect of heading up the newspaper's task force for increasing circulation. But the first meeting, which was supposed to identify problems, was not what she had expected.

Stocking, who was managing editor of the *Lanesberg Lantern*, decided to read the transcript of yesterday's meeting. Her impression following the meeting was that the publisher's hand-picked group was having a problem communicating. She thought perhaps looking at the transcript might help her figure out what to do next at the next meeting. As she read, she underlined certain passages that seemed to illustrate some of the problems.

Sam Bolster, assistant circulation manager: "The problem is with the news. I've been having my district manager ask customers why they drop the paper, and the vast majority said it's the quality of the news. They just . . ."

Jan Peterson, a reporter: "Wait a minute, Sam. It's not news quality. Just last year we were named the best newspaper in the McLesh Group. We've already won several awards this year. A couple of people in my apartment complex said they dropped the paper because they didn't get it about every third day. I'd call that a circulation problem."

Sam Bolster: "That couldn't have been recently. For the past 3 months we've had the policy of delivering a paper within an hour to any subscriber who didn't get one. Sure we've had some problems in the past, but not anymore."

Dan Adams, an advertising account executive: "I don't think the people who live in apartment are a good example of our readers anyway. They all tend to move around so much and have such a limited community commitment that they're not a good market for newspapers anyway."

Jan Peterson: "I don't think that's necessarily true. After all, I live in an apartment."

Dan Adams: "Yes, but you're looking for a house right now, aren't you?"

Leslie Sampson, press foreman: "A lot of what people have said so far is true. Circulation is affected by the newspaper content and by delivery, and by price, and by print rubbing off, and by all the other problems we've talked about, but we need to start narrowing down the problems to a manageable number. I've read that people can be divided into two groups: reader and nonreader. The readers are those that have the newspaper habit, and the nonreaders don't for any number of reasons. We need to be able to identify the readers and go after them."

Dan Adams: "Leslie has a good point. It's useless to go after that group of people who just don't want to read newspapers."

Jason Smith, accountant: "I don't know if that's right, Dan. I'm not sure that the nonreaders aren't turned off by the type of news and writing we have in the newspaper. The paper's just not the quality it used to be."

Jan Peterson: "Here we go with the quality thing again. The paper's as good as it's ever been. I suspect we've got people who are so used to television that they've forgotten how to read."

Diana Stocking: "I recently read a research report sent out by the main office that said many people say they don't have time to read the newspaper. They tend to just stack the issues up in the corner, and then they feel guilty that they haven't been a good citizen. Subscribing to a newspaper and reading it are not the same thing."

Jason Smith: "I can identify with those folks. I often find myself just looking at the ads to see how they turned out and not reading the news because I don't have the time. That's what I meant about quality. Good quality should be compelling. It should make you want to read the paper."

Jan Peterson: "I suspect a lot of those people who say they don't have time are really saying they want short stories and lots of graphics. They don't really want news. All they want is color, so they can watch television on paper. Besides, our writing is compelling. We do a damn good job of making the news readable. I don't think that is our problem here. Maybe somewhere else, but not here."

Stocking put down the transcript. It was clear that the members of the task force were not communicating very well. All that first meeting had contained was argument over whose department was at fault. The next meeting must be more organized and some of the miscommunication needs to be eliminated.

Assignment

Your assignment is to suggest how the next meeting can be improved by analyzing the parts of the transcript you have been given. Answer the following questions:

1. What types of communication problems mentioned in the text can you find in the conversation? Give examples.
2. How could these problems have been overcome?
3. What steps can Stocking take to ensure that the next meeting is more productive?

Case 4.4

Assignment: Charting Participation

Divide the class into groups of two or three. Have each group select a different news organization to study. Group members should interview the top manager of the news organization (i.e., editor, managing editor, news director), a lower level manager (i.e., metro editor, sports editor, assignments editor), and at least three reporters in the organization. The topic of the interviews should be participation by reporters in making news judgments, in establishing organizational ethics, and in planning the future of the organization.

The purpose is to find out the organization's overall policy toward employee participation and to see if the people from the three levels are consistent in how they perceive employee participation. The interviewers of the managers should try to find out the reasons behind the organization's policy toward employee participation. The interviewers of the reporters should try to establish what the reporters think about their participation and whether they are satisfied.

Each group should prepare a report comparing the perceptions of the managers and reporters. If the managers and reporters see participation differently, the report should try to address why. The report also should address whether the level of participation is adequate from both the managers' and reporters' perspectives.

An additional assignment is to have the groups discuss their findings in class to see if news media vary in their level of employee participation.

Case 4.5

The Case of Mid-Career Motivation

David Everstone did not look forward to the meeting. He had never enjoyed the personnel management part of his job. He considered himself to be a journalist. He liked being managing editor because it allowed him to influence the entire content of *News*, a weekly news magazine. But he still did not like this part.

He picked up Kay Roberts' personnel file to refresh his memory, although he knew most of its contents. Robertson had joined *News* the year after he did, about 15 years ago. She had spent that entire time covering politics in Washington, D.C. He would not say he and Roberts were good friends, but they had worked several assignments together in the early years. He had not had much contact with her during the last 5 years as editor, but he always admired her work, at least until the past 6 months. This was the reason behind the meeting.

The yearly evaluation by Douglas Perkins, the political editor, had resulted in an unsatisfactory rating. Company policy called for a meeting between the managing editor and any employee who received such a rating. Two unsatisfactory ratings usually meant dismissal. Perkins said she had missed two deadlines, that her copy required too much editing, that she had been uncooperative with other reporters on team assignments on three occasions, and that she seemed not to be concerned about these problems.

Just then Everstone heard a knock at the door. It was Roberts.

"Kay, hello," Everstone said. "Come in and have a seat. It's good to see you, although I wish it were under better circumstances." "Hello Dave," Robertson responded. "How are you these days?"

"I'm fine. Would you like a cup of coffee?"

"No thanks. Perhaps we should get down to business and discuss Perkins' impression of me."

"OK. You've seen the evaluation. I noticed you didn't take the opportunity to write a reply. I've known you for 15 years, Kay. I know about the awards you've won, and all the shady politicians who wish you'd never come to Washington. Your past evaluations are glowing. Now, tell me what's behind this evaluation."

"Dave, I honestly don't know. It may be me; it may be the job; it may be a combination of several things. I do know that I don't look forward to coming to work like I once did. I find it harder every day to put up with the idiots and assholes that run Washington. Just last week, I was listening to Jim Batton ramble on about cutting the deficit when it occurred to me that my Irish setter probably knows more about economics than he does. It was hard to write that story."

"I understand how you feel," Everstone said. "Every reporter gets tired of dealing with their sources. But Perkins said you missed two deadlines and are having trouble working in teams. What's that about?"

"I'll admit to missing the deadlines," Roberts answered. "That won't happen again. One was a technical mix-up and the other was a miscommunication with Perkins. That stuff about not working with the team is bullshit. Basically, Perkins didn't like the way I angled a couple of stories, so he said change them. I told him he was wrong. I don't mind team writing and reporting, but the system has changed since we started here. It's not a team effort so much as it is an editor's story, the editor and the graphics editor. Their concern is selling the magazine, even if that means giving the reader less than she needs and deserves.

"I used to love to go after the crooks and incompetents, but it's hard to do kickass journalism anymore. Journalists should be making the decisions about stories, not editors. They're too far from the action, and a lot of them haven't seen enough action."

Everstone got up and went to the coffee pot. "Are you sure you don't want some coffee?" he asked.

"No, thanks," Roberts replied.

"Kay, it's not the time and place to get into news philosophy. Besides, I'm not sure I disagree with you entirely," Everstone said. "We need to address this evaluation. Do you have any other problems with Perkins?"

"The biggest problem is that twerp is threatened by anyone who has more experience than he has. That goes especially for women," Roberts said.

"Are you saying Perkins is sexist?" Everstone asked.

"That word's close enough," Roberts said. "Listen, Dave. Haven't you ever noticed how few women hold editing positions here? When I came here 15 years ago, about a half dozen women started with me. I'm the only one left. And the problem's not just here at *News*.

"Dave, I'm 42 years old. I've been a journalist, a good journalist, for 20 years, 15 of them here. But sometimes it seems things don't get better no matter what you do. You get a little tired of banging your head against the old glass ceiling."

"Kay, you are a good journalist—one of the best I've ever worked with. It's obvious that you have a lot going on in your mind. Are you due any vacation time?"

"I've got a couple of weeks that are overdue," Roberts said.

"I want you to take those 2 weeks as soon as you can finish up whatever you're working on," Everstone said. "I would like you to go somewhere and spend some time thinking about yourself, what you want, where you want to go with your career. I am going to think about what you've said and look into some of the things you mentioned today. We'll get back together after your vacation and talk some more."

Assignment

Using the previous discussion, answer the following questions.

1. What has happened to Kay Roberts? Why have all these issues become a problem now?
2. What are Roberts' career options at this point? What types of opportunities does she have?
3. Assume Everstone and Roberts decide that she should stay at *News*. What are some of the ways she can be motivated at this point in her career? Which of these ways might work best?
4. Discuss how these ways of motivating differ from Roberts' motivations when she first came to work at *News*.

5
Media Regulation and Self-Regulation

There are legal concerns that are similar to all media firms and others that are the domain of each type of media firm. Yet there are practices and principles that all kinds of media managers apply to help prevent legal problems. The goal of this chapter is to familiarize you with some of the major legal areas affecting the media. General principles for avoiding legal problems are presented first. Then, concerns important to all media organizations are discussed, followed by the types of problems that may occur in each type of firm. Finally, major media self-regulatory efforts are reviewed.

This chapter is not intended to be a comprehensive discussion of all areas of law that might affect media firms. It is intended to present briefly only a few major areas, focusing instead on the prevention and response to legal actions. Readers interested in more detail should review the appropriate legal publications referred to throughout the chapter.

PREVENTING LEGAL PROBLEMS

There are general principles and procedures managers at all kinds of media organizations can institute to minimize the occurrence of legal problems. (Procedures pertaining to specific legal problems are discussed in the appropriate sections to follow.) Managers should establish written procedures for dealing with all sorts of potential legal problems. Instruct employees to document their dealings with interviewees, news sources, business contacts, advertisers and free-lance writers, photographers, and artists. That way, a written record exists if any problems arise later.

Managers and their legal counsel should review important transactions to discern which potential pitfalls should be explained in clauses. Then, clauses spelling out details of possible concern can be included in all contracts. For example, agreements with free-lancers should be in writing and signed by both parties. Fees and expenses should be included in such agreements, as well as what the work's appropriate subject matter is and what its finished form should be. Prioritize any research suggestions in order of importance and make sure to note that payment depends on the ability to submit work that meets the appropriate standards on deadline. If the free-lancer balks at these conditions, the assignment should be changed or canceled (Rauch, 1991). Clauses appropriate to newspaper advertising contracts include terms and provisions on ad duration and timing to ensure both parties agree on when the ads will run. Self-renewing clauses, rate schedules in the event an advertiser fails to complete contract terms, and cancellation fees ought to be included. Advertisers also should be required to meet advertising acceptance standards (Sohn, Ogan, & Polich, 1986).

Media organizations should establish procedures for dealing with complaints because irate advertisers, public (or private persons who are the subject of stories), readers, listeners, and/or viewers contact such companies regularly. First, employees should be told to treat all complaints seriously. Employees should be as polite and conciliatory as possible, even if they believe the complaint is baseless, because courteous treatment often defuses a situation. Train employees to tell a telephone complainant that they are writing down the facts for internal investigation and then do so, without admitting anything, interrupting, or passing blame. Then, have the employee bring the complaint to the appropriate supervisor's attention, ensuring that a possibly defensive employee cannot complicate the situation by acting alone. The supervisor should determine whether the complaint has merit and then send a letter to the complainant, that day, that confirms the call, provides an explanation, proposes a solution, or provides a deadline by which she will contact the complainant. The same general procedure can be used for written complaints.

Different rules apply in the event of a serious complaint, when a lawsuit is threatened or discussed, and when the complainant is an attorney. Instruct employees not to admit anything and immediately refer the matter to top management, along with all available documentation. Top management then should contact an attorney before responding and allow the attorney to handle the problem, when necessary. In any event, employees must feel comfortable about reporting complaints to supervisors, especially complaints caused by employee error or misconduct. If a retraction or letter of apology is needed, an attorney must review it before dissemination. A retraction could repeat the offense and be viewed as an admission of wrongdoing (Fink, 1988; Rauch, 1991).

Finally, media organizations should publicize their policies internally and have training and/or discussion sessions regarding appropriate procedures and behavior. Never assume that all employees have the judgment and experience necessary for dealing with legal and ethical dilemmas; even long-term employees can lose their cool. The best way to prevent legal and ethical concerns is to anticipate common problems and prepare for them. The media provide information to the public; such organizations must never forget the legal and ethical responsibilities that accompany this role.

GENERAL AREAS OF LEGAL CONCERN

Managers at all kinds of media firms must be concerned with federal, state, and local regulations including labor, hiring and firing, discrimination, and other laws concerning antitrust and libel. Readers interested in more information might review Gillmor, Barron, Simon, and Terry (1990) and Lacy and Simon (1992).

Labor and Employment Issues

The major federal labor statutes are the Fair Labor Standards Act (FLSA) and the National Labor Relations Act (NLRA). The FLSA established the minimum wage and proscribed the maximum number of hours an employee may work. The FLSA regulates overtime pay, the employment of minors, and bans pay differentials based on gender. The NLRA governs collective bargaining, contract negotiations, and the assessment of behavior during contract terms. Its aim is to guarantee that employees are treated fairly when contracts are formed. NLRA media actions often include allegations of unfair labor practices such as firing an employee for trying to organize a union or for publishing comments criticizing the employer (Lacy & Simon, 1992).

Professional employees, defined as employees whose work is characterized by a variety of tasks that are primarily intellectual in nature, are not covered by the NLRA. Professional employees typically have specialized training and are granted some independence and discretionary authority. Nonprofessional employees work in jobs where an established procedure is habitually performed, such as routine mental or manual work. In newspapers, the exception for professionals has been limited mostly to managerial editorial employees or to employees who work independently without direct supervision (Lacy & Simon, 1992).

Managers should become familiar with these statutes and employment laws in their state and locality. It is also important to distribute a handbook explaining important company policies and practices to all employees. Make sure that all policies included in a handbook are meant to be binding and that this is clearly stated. The employee handbook should explain important terms and conditions of employment. Policies regarding benefits, vacations, hiring, firing, working conditions, and other company regulations should be included. However, firing procedures should not be stated in more detail than necessary, so the chances that a firing is not conducted as specified are minimized. All managers and supervisors should be trained in administering handbook policies and procedures, to ensure policies are enforced consistently. Fair and consistent treatment helps a company to avoid employee complaints and costly court actions. Examples of policies to include in a handbook are now explained.

In the past, an employer could fire workers at will who were not protected by collective bargaining agreements or civil service regulations. Exceptions to this "at-will" doctrine have arisen due to court decisions. Exceptions vary by locality, but fall into three general categories: contract, public policy, and the covenant of good faith and fair dealing theories. In a breach of contract case, the fired employee claims that something the former employer said or did created an implied contract permitting termination only for a good cause like poor job performance (Baxter, 1983a). So, if an employer wants to retain the right to fire at will, a written statement reinforcing that intent must be included in employee handbooks, application forms, and other company publications. Expert legal counsel should review such publications to avoid creating implied contracts limiting the right to terminate (Bushman, 1989).

Broadcast managers should pay special attention to personal services contracts. Contracts with star anchors and reporters typically limit the employee's ability to move to a competing station and give a station exclusive rights to the employee's services. Legal review is also needed to ensure that the employee is treated fairly and the station is protected (Lacy & Simon, 1992).

Public policy cases fall into four broad categories. In "whistle blower" cases, employees are fired for reporting an employer's unlawful conduct. In the second category, employees are fired for refusing to engage in illegal activities on the job. The third category involves employees who are fired for exercising a legal right or privilege like filing a workers' compensation claim. The fourth category involves employees who are fired for satisfying a legal obligation such as serving on a jury. Examples of covenant of good faith and fair dealing cases include firing an employee to avoid paying an accrued sales commission and terminating a long-service employee without legal cause (Baxter, 1983a).

Obviously, many problems can be avoided simply by treating employees fairly. Fair treatment includes giving periodic performance assessments that are handled with care and candor. Giles (1988) noted that a performance review is a formalized way of giving feedback of an employee's performance on the critical requirements of a job. What will be rated and how should be defined as clearly and in as much detail as possible, in advance. Managers should observe the work on which an employee is being rated. Evaluations should be objective and eliminate the opportunity for managers to include personal views. An example of a performance evaluation form for a reporter is included in Fig. 5.1.

Employees should be involved in the development of performance evaluations. Standards should also be based on critical job elements, defined in writing, and publicized to employees before an evaluation takes place. Written performance evaluations should be conducted at least once a year. Evaluation forms should allow a supervisor to recognize both unsatisfactory and excellent conduct realistically. Upper management should monitor the development and implementation of a performance appraisal system closely and be certain that all employees are familiar with the process. (See Giles, 1988, for more information on performance evaluation.)

Always use progressive discipline when unsatisfactory performance is reported in an assessment. With progressive discipline, the employee is notified that performance is unsatisfactory and given a chance to improve. A thorough and impartial investigation is conducted first. The employees involved and appropriate witnesses are interviewed. A written warning clearly outlining the unsatisfactory conduct and future consequences for failing to comply is given to the employee. Warnings are given before punishment for infractions like absenteeism, tardiness, and incompetency. Punish all violations of the same infraction in the same way to avoid discrimination. Special circumstances warranting a more severe reprimand than usual should be clearly explained and documented.

The employee is told privately by a supervisor and given a written copy of the warning. A copy also should be placed in the employee's personnel file and given to a union representative, if appropriate. Only other employees who actually need to know about the warning, like an immediate supervisor, are informed but directed to keep it private. That way, the employee's privacy is protected and the company does not risk defamation charges.

Using progressive discipline is desirable because it gives the employee a chance to improve performance. This is not only fair, but also may prevent a termination, which is unpleasant for everyone involved. On the other hand, if the employee disregards the warning, progressive discipline strengthens the case for firing the employee and documents the fact that the employee was treated fairly (Baxter, 1983b; Sohn et al., 1986).

However, sometimes employees must be fired without warning. Conduct such as intentionally creating a safety hazard, intoxication, or fighting on the job warrants an on-the-spot firing. Management must be sure that the employee is guilty before terminating employment. Employers also should develop an independent review process for all terminations. The reviewer must have the authority to revoke terminations if they do not meet company and/or legal standards and be familiar with the law and the firm's employment policies and procedures.

REPORTER PERFORMANCE EVALUATION

Name _____

Department _____

Job title _____

Grade level _____

Anniversary date _____

Time in present assignment _____

Review period _____

Next evaluation _____

☐Annual
☐Six-month (new hire)
☐Six-month (new assignment)
☐Other

ACCURACY	OUTSTANDING	COMMENDABLE	ACCEPTABLE	MARGINAL	UNACCEPTABLE	NOT APPLICABLE
Spelling, stylebook, typos	☐	☐	☐	☐	☐	☐
Attributing information to sources	☐	☐	☐	☐	☐	☐
Factually accurate information	☐	☐	☐	☐	☐	☐
Verifying identities, addresses	☐	☐	☐	☐	☐	☐
Using best possible sources	☐	☐	☐	☐	☐	☐
Calling errors to editor's attention	☐	☐	☐	☐	☐	☐
Grammar	☐	☐	☐	☐	☐	☐

RATING/ACCURACY: ☐   ☐   ☐   ☐   ☐   ☐

EVALUATING EDITOR'S COMMENTS:

FIG. 5.1

(continued)

REPORTING	OUTSTANDING	COMMENDABLE	ACCEPTABLE	MARGINAL	UNACCEPTABLE	NOT APPLICABLE
Gathering information	☐	☐	☐	☐	☐	☐
Approach to routine stories	☐	☐	☐	☐	☐	☐
Suggesting and developing story ideas	☐	☐	☐	☐	☐	☐
Producing enterprise stories	☐	☐	☐	☐	☐	☐
Developing sources	☐	☐	☐	☐	☐	☐
Depth, perspective, insight	☐	☐	☐	☐	☐	☐
Research	☐	☐	☐	☐	☐	☐
Awareness of the news	☐	☐	☐	☐	☐	☐
Community awareness	☐	☐	☐	☐	☐	☐
Legal awareness and sense of fairness	☐	☐	☐	☐	☐	☐
Judgment	☐	☐	☐	☐	☐	☐
Coverage of beat/assignment	☐	☐	☐	☐	☐	☐
News of minorities	☐	☐	☐	☐	☐	☐
Following stories	☐	☐	☐	☐	☐	☐
Suggesting picture and graphic ideas	☐	☐	☐	☐	☐	☐
Meeting daily deadlines	☐	☐	☐	☐	☐	☐
Meeting long-range deadlines	☐	☐	☐	☐	☐	☐
Managing time	☐	☐	☐	☐	☐	☐

RATING/REPORTING: ☐ ☐ ☐ ☐ ☐ ☐

EVALUATING EDITOR'S COMMENTS:

FIG. 5.1

(continued)

WRITING

	OUTSTANDING	COMMENDABLE	ACCEPTABLE	MARGINAL	UNACCEPTABLE	NOT APPLICABLE
Organizing story	☐	☐	☐	☐	☐	☐
Recognizing important story elements	☐	☐	☐	☐	☐	☐
Copy tightly written	☐	☐	☐	☐	☐	☐
Word selection	☐	☐	☐	☐	☐	☐
Writing under deadline pressure	☐	☐	☐	☐	☐	☐
Writing style	☐	☐	☐	☐	☐	☐
Opinion writing	☐	☐	☐	☐	☐	☐

RATING/WRITING: ☐ ☐ ☐ ☐ ☐ ☐

EVALUATING EDITOR'S COMMENTS:

COMMUNICATION

	OUTSTANDING	COMMENDABLE	ACCEPTABLE	MARGINAL	UNACCEPTABLE	NOT APPLICABLE
Working with editors to develop stories	☐	☐	☐	☐	☐	☐
Working with editors to improve stories	☐	☐	☐	☐	☐	☐
Using feedback for development	☐	☐	☐	☐	☐	☐
Working with other staff members	☐	☐	☐	☐	☐	☐
Contact with the public	☐	☐	☐	☐	☐	☐
Professional conduct	☐	☐	☐	☐	☐	☐

RATING/COMMUNICATION: ☐ ☐ ☐ ☐ ☐ ☐

EVALUATING EDITOR'S COMMENTS:

FIG. 5.1

(continued)

This rating represents the conclusion of your editors on your overall performance. A number of factors influence this rating. Some factors in your performance are more critical than others to your success as a journalist. Other factors may rank high only because, in the judgment of your editors, there is a need for immediate improvement.

In addition, your overall performance rating can be influenced by experience and by the relative degree of difficulty in the specific job you are performing. In no case is your overall performance rating determined by averaging the functions or categories.

	OUTSTANDING	COMMENDABLE	ACCEPTABLE	MARGINAL	UNACCEPTABLE
OVERALL PERFORMANCE RATING	☐	☐	☐	☐	☐

EVALUATING EDITOR'S SUMMARY:

The space below is available if you wish to respond in writing to this performance review. The spirit of performance reviews recognizes that differences of opinion about one's performance can exist. We believe that differences can be presented constructively, professionally and without risk.

YOUR COMMENTS:

FIG. 5.1

(continued)

139

PERFORMANCE DEVELOPMENT

Here are areas where, in the judgment of your editors, you can improve your performance.

☐ Improvements identitied as Priority A are considered essential to meeting minimum acceptable standards. Immediate and serious attention is required. Your editor will state on the form the period of time you will have to correct any such deficiencies. Failure to make such improvements carries the warning that your continuing employment may be in question.

☐ Improvements identified as Priority B are those that will contribute to raising your performance from an acceptable level to one which is outstanding or commendable.

☐ Improvements identified as Priority C are those that would fine-tune already excellent performance.

☐ Improvements identified as Priority D are those that can help you to be considered for larger responsibilities or new opportunities.

IMPROVEMENTS   PRIORITY

SIGNATURES

Your signature indicates that you have read this performance review and have discussed it with your evaluating editor.

EVALUATING EDITOR _____ DATE_____

MANAGING EDITOR_____

YOUR SIGNATURE_____

FIG. 5.1

(continued)

CAREER DEVELOPMENT

In addition to assessing your *current* performance, your editors are interested in encouraging you to think about career goals. To assist in this process, you are invited to indicate below your own ideas about jobs you may wish to hold in the future.

SHORT RANGE (One to three years)
☐ I prefer to continue in my current assignment.
☐ I am interested in other assignments. They are:

LONG RANGE
Here is what I would like to be doing in my job three or more years from now:

EVALUATING EDITOR'S ASSESSMENT:

Would you encourage the reporter to pursue the career goals outlined above?

☐ Yes
☐ No
Comments:

If the reporter is interested in a different position, is he/she:
☐ Ready to be considered now
☐ Expected to be ready in 1-2 years with additional preparation
☐ Unlikely to be considered
Comments:

Here are some skills and knowledge the reporter would need to meet his/her career goals, and some steps the reporter could take to acquire the skills and knowledge:

FIG. 5.1. Sample rating form for a reporter. From Giles (1988). Copyright 1987 by The Detroit News, Inc. Reprinted by permission.

Whether or not a firm implements a termination review process, all managers can ask themselves the following questions to ensure that a termination is fair. Baxter (1983b) stated that a termination reviewer should consider the following questions: What is the employee's overall record? Are there any mitigating factors that might explain or excuse the employee's misconduct or unsatisfactory performance? Are any statutory problems involved (e.g., regarding race, age, gender, etc.)? Were any job security representations made to the employee? If yes, is the termination consistent with those representations? Are there any public policy concerns? Has the employee received progressive discipline? Is the termination justified? Does it fit the offense?

Employers also need to be conscious of how they fire employees and consider ways to minimize the employee's frustration, anger, and embarrassment. Employees should be told privately why they are being fired, as candidly as possible. The supervisor should do so firmly, yet compassionately, without being apologetic. An apologetic demeanor may suggest the employer feels guilty and thus imply wrongdoing to the fired employee. Employers also should limit the amount of information provided to prospective employers calling for reference checks on fired employees. Only the fact and dates of employment and the positions held should be provided. Avoid providing negative information, as the former employee may sue if such information is publicized (Baxter, 1983b).

Managers also must remember that fellow supervisors, not just employees, may commit infractions. "White-collar" misconduct is more difficult to discover because managers often have the power and position to circumvent internal checks and controls. Other white-collar crimes like extortion or kickbacks paid by vendors are "off-the-books" and hard to detect. Although internal auditing controls are useful, upper level employees should be aware that colleagues could circumvent them (Bagby, 1990).

Discrimination

Discrimination at all levels of employment is prohibited. Title VII of the amended Civil Rights Act of 1964 proscribes employment discrimination (or treating an employee unfairly or unfavorably) on the basis of race, religion, gender, or national origin. Prohibited actions include refusing to hire employees based on race or gender, providing unequal conditions of employment, and providing unequal pay for the same job. Specific employer intent to discriminate is not necessary and even if the employer made a conscious effort to avoid discrimination a case can be prosecuted (Lacy & Simon, 1992; Sohn et al., 1986).

Media organizations must develop and act upon plans to increase minority employment at all levels for both moral and legal reasons. Morally speaking, men and women from all backgrounds deserve equal opportunities and all employees deserve to be judged fairly on job qualifications and performance, not race or gender. Although the number of minority employees in media has increased, many feel that there are few places to turn for support and encouragement, especially where career advancement is concerned. Changing demographics also makes a response necessary: Minorities will account for a larger proportion of workers in the future (Veronis, 1990). Finally, media institutions that report on the transgressions of others should not be guilty of such injustices themselves. How credible will the public perceive the media to be if they criticize others for discriminating, yet do so themselves?

Efforts can be made to hire and retain minority employees. Some media companies ask employees to visit local schools to encourage minorities and women to enter the field. Others have established multiracial committees to address minority staffers' concerns. Sensitivity training helps employees to appreciate and/or tolerate others with different perspectives and experiences. Mentoring programs also help to retain minority employees. Tying part of a manager's performance and salary review to progress in hiring and promoting women and minorities also encourages hiring and retention (Veronis, 1990).

Nowadays, employers must include a workplace policy in employee handbooks, company publications, or other written forms that clearly prohibits any sort of harassment. Employees should report incidents of harassment in writing, although employers should investigate all complaints. Appropriate action always must be taken when needed as harassment is a serious matter and should be treated accordingly (Rosenberg, 1991).

Employee Health and Safety

Employment health and safety are other important management concerns. Government and employee priorities in this area change, so managers should keep abreast with current developments in order to protect employee health and safety and comply with the law. Such concerns vary from dealing with repetitive motion injuries to developing drug-testing policies.

Repetitive motion injury (RMI) is caused by repetitive tasks, awkward posture, and inadequate rest and recovery time. RMI is of concern to media managers because the disorder has emerged among keyboard operators. Actions to minimize RMI include buying well-designed ergonomic furniture for people of different sizes, training employees about practices and exercises to avoid injury, and seeking out doctors who are experienced in dealing with the problem (Goltz, 1991; "OSHA begins," 1990)

Some media employers feel they should establish drug-testing policies to avoid attracting people from other industries that test potential employees for drug use. Berger (1990) pointed out that employers planning to implement a drug-testing system first should consider some important questions. For example, how will employee privacy and confidentiality be protected? Should only new applicants be tested or current employees as well? What is the relative cost-benefit advantage of implementing drug testing? Should counseling and treatment programs be recommended, and if so, which ones? Finally, what are the dangers of litigation if the drug test itself is incorrect?

Employers can take certain steps to minimize the likelihood of drug-testing suits. Be absolutely sure that a reputable lab is used for testing. If an applicant tests positive, conduct another, more sophisticated test as a check and give the applicant a chance to explain the result. Sometimes a medical statement can clear up a potential misunderstanding over a positive test. Applicants or employees who test positive should be referred only to licensed treatment centers. Employees also may need to sign releases so information may be shared with appropriate parties like insurance companies (Berger, 1990).

Require employees to sign a reentry agreement, covering a specific period such as 2 years, after completing treatment. Other suggested provisions include requiring the employee to: abstain from mood-altering drugs or alcohol, agree to random drug testing, agree to continue in follow-up treatment for a specified time, agree to submit a record of all such meetings attended for the employer to verify, and agree that the after-care treatment is the employee's and/or insurance company's expense (Berger, 1990).

The Americans with Disabilities Act of 1990 (ADA) also must be reviewed before implementing a drug-testing program. The act prohibits discrimination against disabled persons who otherwise are qualified to hold a job. Persons with AIDS, mental and physical impairments, and recovering alcoholics and drug addicts are covered by the act. Certain practices are prohibited, too. Employers may ask if job-related tasks can be performed but may not ask if an applicant is disabled. Job-related preemployment medical exams may be given only after the employee has been offered a job. The act also requires employers to make job sites more accessible to the disabled in the future, under certain conditions (Goltz, 1991; "OSHA begins," 1990).

However, employers are cautioned to conduct thorough background checks to avoid hiring a worker whose past record might indicate a likelihood of causing job injury, damage, or loss. Employers certainly want to avoid discrimination against persons with temporary or permanent mental and substance abuse problems on both moral and legal grounds. Yet employers also must protect other employees from likely potential injury (Rosenberg, 1991). This example underscores how employee health and safety concerns involve more than just machine maintenance and safe operating procedures.

Managers face a much larger variety of health and safety concerns on the job than discussed here. The importance of keeping up with regulations in the trade press and consulting with the appropriate legal expert for advice cannot be overemphasized. Finally, besides being good legal advice, the equitable and considerate treatment of employees is the "right" thing to do. Always remember that you are managing people. Consider how you would want to be treated in a given situation. Often, this is the best way to avoid problems, establish a good working relationship with, and retain good employees.

Antitrust

Antitrust is another major legal area of interest to media managers. The Supreme Court affirmed in *Associated Press v. United States* (1945) that antitrust laws apply to the media. The Sherman Act of 1890 prohibits contracts or conspiracies that restrain trade and governs the misuse of monopoly power, defined as "the power to control prices or exclude competition" (Gillmor, et al., 1990, p. 543). The Clayton Act of 1914 forbids certain practices when they might lessen competition substantially or create a monopoly. The act prohibits price discrimination or the sale of a product or service to similar types of buyers at different prices. Tying and exclusive dealing contracts, where the buyer must agree to no longer deal with a competitor as a term of sale, also are proscribed. The Robinson-Patman Act of 1936 limits large-company buying power by prohibiting price discrimination unless supported by cost savings or proven necessary to meet a competitor's price offer (Gellhorn, 1981).

The Newspaper Preservation Act (NPA) of 1970 gives certain daily newspapers a limited exemption from antitrust laws. Two newspapers within a market may form a joint operating agreement (JOA) when one is in probable danger of financial failure. Under a JOA, the newspapers' advertising, circulation, production, and administrative departments are merged, whereas their editorial departments are kept separate. Proposed JOAs must be approved by the U.S. Attorney General, although administrative hearings often are held before a decision is made. Readers interested in additional information on antitrust, the NPA, and JOAs might read Coulson (1988), Gillmor et al. (1990), Lacy (1988), and Lacy and Simon (1992).

Broadcasters have no such exemption from antitrust laws, however. The National Association of Broadcasters (NAB) Television and Radio Codes, which provided guidelines for advertising and programming practices, were abandoned as a result of an antitrust action. In 1979 the Justice Department filed a suit claiming that three TV Code provisions violated the Sherman Act: the commercial time restrictions, the limits on the number of ads airing consecutively in a break, and the prohibition of more than two products being advertised in a spot less than 60 sec long. Later, the two products per spot limit was ruled a per se violation of the Sherman Act (*U.S.*

v. NAB, 1982a). The NAB settled the matter by consent judgment rather than face trial on the other charges and risk further lawsuits (*U.S. v. NAB*, 1982b). The NAB abandoned both Codes in 1983 (Gillmor et al., 1990).

Media companies can avoid certain conduct to minimize the chances of antitrust actions. For example, it is inadvisable for a newspaper to force an advertiser to buy space in a shopper as a condition for buying space in the daily edition. Local newspapers or radio stations cannot agree to set advertising prices so low that other firms cannot enter the market or earn a profit. Pricing a product or service below cost in order to run a competitor out of business, while intending to make up losses afterward by raising prices, is illegal. Offering volume discounts or rebates to some advertisers but not others is unlawful. Finally, antitrust violations may occur when a daily newspaper buys weekly newspapers and shoppers within its market (Lacy & Simon, 1992; Sohn et al., 1986).

Media managers can take precautions to avoid antitrust suits. First, managers should familiarize employees with antitrust compliance rules and post them. If combination rates are offered for advertising placed in several editions, then the discount offered should reflect a true and reasonable cost savings. Companies should avoid forcing combination advertising rates on advertisers and should include news in zoned editions and shoppers. Circulation managers should make sure that the independent contractors who distribute the newspaper do not try to restrict or control routes. Newspapers considering a switch from independent distribution to company-controlled circulation should consult a lawyer. Finally, managers and employees should avoid putting anything on paper that implies an intent to monopolize because the question of intent is very important in antitrust cases (Gillmor et al., 1990; Lacy & Simon, 1992; Sohn, et al., 1986).

Libel

Defamatory statements are one of the limitations on First Amendment protections of freedom of speech. Defamatory statements subject a person to hatred, contempt, or ridicule and may injure a person's reputation. Written false and defamatory attacks on a person's reputation or character are libel and oral statements are considered slander. Defamation by broadcasters is libel when a written script exists (Gillmor et al., 1990). Zuckman, Gaynes, Carter, and Dee (1988) noted that "the essential elements common to both libel and slander actions are 1) the making by the defendant of a defamatory statement; 2) the publication to one other than the plaintiff of that statement; and 3) the identification in some way of the plaintiff as the person defamed"(p. 47). In other words, for libel to be actionable, a defamatory meaning about an identifiable person or persons must be published. A statement, broadcast, or written work is published when it is communicated and understood by a third party (DuBoff, 1987).

Individuals, groups of people, corporations, and partnerships can sue under libel statutes. Libel occurs in a variety of media, including printed material, photographs, cartoons, editorials, headlines, cutlines, paintings, motion pictures and film, audio and video tape, records, signs and signboards, bumper stickers, advertisements, effigies, skywriting, statuary, and gravestones (DuBoff, 1987; Gillmor et al., 1990; Sohn et al., 1986; Zuckman et al., 1988). Journalists should consult the most recent edition of *The Associated Press Stylebook and Libel Manual* (French, 1987) and/or the *AP Broadcast News Handbook* (Hood & Kalbfeld, 1982) for more information on libel.

A public official or figure bringing a libel case must prove actual malice. (There are a number of libel defenses that are not discussed in this chapter. See Gillmor et al., 1990, pp. 216-276). In *New York Times v. Sullivan* (1964), the Supreme Court ruled that a public official may not recover damages for a defamatory falsehood relating to official conduct unless it is proven that the statement was made with actual malice. Actual malice is defined as knowledge of, or a reckless disregard for, the truth or falsity of the published statement(s). Reckless disregard is when someone has serious doubts about the statement's truth (DuBoff, 1987). So, the public official must prove that the press knew that the information was untrue, or published it with complete disregard of its truth or falsity.

Actual malice also must be proven by public figures, of which there are two types. All-purpose public figures hold powerful and influential positions. Because they are considered public figures for all purposes, much of the media comment about them is protected. This category includes people who are frequently in the news but are not public officials, such as Madonna and Walter Cronkite. The second type of public figure voluntarily thrusts herself to the vanguard of public controversies to influence the resolution of the issues involved (*Gertz v. Robert Welch, Inc.*, 1974). For libel to be actionable for a limited public figure who is assumed to have access to the media, the defamation involved must be related to her role in the public controversy. However, an event is not a public controversy simply because it is newsworthy (*Time, Inc. v. Firestone*, 1976) or because there are different views on the propriety of an act (DuBoff, 1987).

There are steps media managers can take to avoid libel suits. At least one newsroom editor or manager must be knowledgeable about state and federal libel developments. Many situations can be avoided by using careful reporting techniques and thinking before acting. Reporters should be told to keep careful notes, have more than one source for potentially libelous accusations, obtain supporting documents for controversial statements, and obtain the appropriate court documents (such as complaints, cease-and-desist orders, and judgments) when allegations are made. Reporters also should repeat words like "alleged" and "allegation" in a story when a legal action is pending and be wary of publishing a story based on a district attorney's "intent" to charge or investigate. It may be more prudent to wait until charges are filed. Finally, potentially libelous stories should be reviewed by a legal expert before publication (DuBoff, 1987; French, 1987; Gillmor et al., 1990; Hood & Kalbfeld, 1982; Rauch, 1991; Sohn et al., 1986).

Managers also should be aware that any postpublication contact with a person claiming to be libeled should be handled carefully, as media response to such contact is an important factor in a decision to sue. Bezanson, Cranberg, and Soloski (1987) concluded that the "manner in which the press deals with plaintiffs following publication unnecessarily fosters litigation" (p. 229). Libel plaintiffs reported that "when responding to questions concerning media contact that the media were 'arrogant,' 'indifferent' to their situation, 'aloof,' and 'insensitive'" (p. 229). In addition, "the newspapers that were surveyed confirmed the press' shortcomings in the area of response to complaints" (p. 87). Obviously, employees should be told to treat a person claiming to be libeled with courtesy and respect.

However, media managers must avoid self-censorship if it does not serve the public. Lawyers may evaluate how much a lawsuit would cost rather than whether it could succeed. Small papers, and presumably other small media organizations, have become especially careful about what they publish for fear of surviving a costly libel battle (Garneau, 1991a, 1991b). Although prudence and care always make good sense, a manager must always consider whether the potential suit is meant to intimidate and whether the public interest would be served by publication or broadcast (America, 1991).

Privacy

The right of privacy encompasses "the right to be let alone" or to live one's private life free from publicity (Keeton, 1984). Privacy entitles an individual to prevent the use of, or interference with, personal and intimate aspects of life. Such invasions presumably have a negative effect on a person's psychological well-being (Gillmor et al., 1990).

Journalists may read more about privacy in the *AP Broadcast News Handbook* and *The Associated Press Stylebook and Libel Manual*, which state that once an individual is voluntarily or involuntarily involved in a news event, the right to privacy is forfeited. A journalist should be protected when writing about an individual involved in a matter of legitimate public interest, even if it is not a bona fide spot news event. But publication of a story or picture that "dredges up the sordid details of a person's past and has no current newsworthiness" may not be protected (French, 1987, p. 306; Hood & Kalbfeld, 1982, p. 44).

Privacy is composed of four different kinds of personal invasion:

intrusion, public disclosure of embarrassing private facts, false light in the public eye, and appropriation. Intrusion is an unauthorized interruption of physical solitude or seclusion, with an element of prying, by invading someone's home or illegally searching him. Eavesdropping with telephoto lenses, electronic listening devices, wiretapping, and other means in private areas like an individual's home or office are also intrusions. Such eavesdropping may result in criminal penalties, as the Electronic Communications Privacy Act of 1986 prohibits certain attempted or intentional interceptions of wire, oral, or electronic communications. However, an individual has no right to be let alone and may be reasonably photographed or recorded in a public place (Keeton, 1984; Prosser, 1960; Zuckman et al., 1988).

Publication is not essential to, and certain news-gathering techniques can be violations of, intrusion. For example, gaining access to a "healer's" home by deception, secretly taking pictures while the healer conducted a breast cancer examination, and then relaying tape recordings to law officers outside was found to be intrusion (*Dietemann v. Time, Inc.*, 1971).

Managers should discuss potentially actionable reporting techniques with employees to avoid intrusion suits. Using outright deception to gain access to public or private property should be avoided. Reporters and other employees should try to gain authorization before entering public or private property, if possible. Permission should be sought from relevant public officials to gather news in public buildings and/or from police and fire officials to accompany them onto private property when conducting official business, especially if the owner is absent. Managers and employees also should discuss whether there are situations when these guidelines might be suspended (Zuckman, et al., 1988).

The public disclosure of private facts involves giving objectionable publicity to truthful private information about a person. These cases are rarely successful because courts recognize a broad newsworthiness defense, tend to protect the publication of truthful matters of public interest, and often defer judgment to the media on what is newsworthy. Exceptions typically occur when the private facts involved outrage the community's sense of decency or when unreasonable media practices are used. Examples include publishing medical pictures of a person's intimate anatomy, revealing someone's debts, reporting embarrassing details of a person's characteristics or behavior, and publishing a photo of a woman emerging from a fun house with her dress blown above her waist by a jet of air (Gillmor et al., 1990; Keeton, 1984; Prosser, 1960). Obviously, " . . . journalists should approach the intimate and embarrassing facts of an individual's past or even present life with caution and exercise discretion in publishing such material. In this area good taste is the watchword" (Zuckman et al., 1988, p. 139).

Placing a person in a false light in the public eye involves creating a false image of an individual. The false light may not be defamatory, but must be something to which a reasonable person would object. Common examples include erroneously attributing authorship of an article or political views to someone, using a person's name on a petition without permission, accidentally juxtaposing photographs and headlines in news stories, using a person's picture out of context, and intentionally fictionalizing events involving identifiable persons. New or renewed releases should be obtained whenever a name or picture is used commercially for a different reason, in a different way, and/or at a different time (Gillmor et al, 1990; Keeton, 1984; Prosser, 1960; Zuckman et al., 1988).

Appropriation is the unconsented use of one individual's name or likeness for another's economic benefit or advantage (Keeton, 1984; Prosser, 1960). Appropriation thus "appears to protect something akin to a property right in one's own personality and image" (Zuckman et al., 1988, p. 120). The right of publicity developed from appropriation and protects the financial interests of those whose names, likenesses, and attributes are marketable, especially celebrities (Gillmor et al., 1990).

Appropriation can involve advertising, promotions, and merchandising uses. The best defense in an appropriation or right of publicity action is a signed consent or release from the person, parent or guardian of a minor, or heirs and assigns of deceased celebrity whose identity is used. A signed release should reflect accurately how a person's name or likeness will be used. Permission also should be obtained when news, feature stories, and photographs are republished for publicity or promotional purposes (Gillmor et al., Terry, 1990; Zuckman et al., 1988).

Media managers also should be concerned about "data privacy" or controlling the flow of computer and electronic data about individuals (Gillmor et al., 1990). Electronic and computer eavesdropping by individuals, government, and business may represent a major threat to privacy rights. Many consumers agree and have fought marketers' attempts to develop data bases including their names, addresses, telephone numbers, video rental habits, demographic profiles, and credit information (Radding, 1991).

Access to Government Information

Media organizations may obtain government information using The Freedom of Information Act, which established a process for requesting information from federal agencies. In many instances, government employees will comply with informal requests just because they know the Act exists (Zuckman et al., 1988). Often, making a few well-placed telephone calls results in quick, easy compliance. The act should not be used on a regular basis; responses to official requests often take time. The process is too slow for reporters working on breaking stories, but is useful to those working on long-term projects (Sohn et al., 1986). Managers also should familiarize themselves and their employees with state laws concerning access.

Copyright

Media managers can expect to deal with copyright issues. Copyright protection extends to almost anything authored, created, performed, or produced in a tangible or permanent way. Works fixed in the following media are protected: print, videotape, audiotape, sound recordings including those played on jukeboxes, musical compositions, television programs including but not limited to news programs and television taped at the time of transmission, film, motion pictures, photographs, advertisements, computer programs, data bases, art works, choreographies, maps, compilations, and newsletters (Gillmor et al., 1990; Zuckman et al., 1988).

Copyright protects the authors of published and unpublished original works at the instant of creation. The original author retains any rights that are not transferred specifically in writing. A work is the property of the author unless it is a work made for hire—then the employer is considered the author. There are two categories of works made for hire: (a) works prepared by an employee within the scope of employment; or (b) a specially ordered or commissioned work that is agreed to in writing and signed by all parties (Copyright Office, 1980; Gillmor et al., 1990).

Determining who retains copyright ownership in work for hire situations is complicated when free-lancers are used. Managers first should discern whether the free-lancer is considered an employee or an independent contractor. Factors to consider include where the work was done, who provided necessary supplies and equipment, the amount of discretion the employer had over the free-lancer's work hours and habits, how the matter is treated for tax purposes, and whether the free-lancer received employee benefits. If the free-lancer is an independent contractor, the employer who commissioned and paid for the work may not own the copyright. Thus, a company always should obtain a signed written agreement if it wants complete or partial assignment of rights (Soyster, 1991).

Copyright law protects the author of works published on or after January 1, 1978, for life plus fifty years. Works created before then may be protected, under certain conditions, for a total term of seventy-five years. The copyright owner has the right to do and/or authorize others to: (a) reproduce the copyrighted work by any means; (b) prepare derivative works based on the copyrighted work; (c) distribute copies to the public by sale, rental, lease, loan, or other transfer of ownership; (d) perform the work publicly; and (e) display the work publicly (Copyright Office, 1980).

Managers should be aware of their rights under copyright law. For example, a newspaper publisher is the author of all copyrightable material in each issue, unless an agreement to the contrary is worked out beforehand with a reporter or columnist. Publishers of magazines or collected works "acquire only the first serial and limited reprint rights to articles or photographs. All other rights are retained by the author" (Gillmor et al., 1990, p. 610). News and information are not subject to copyright and may be disseminated by anyone. Yet the manner in which news is organized, such as a reporter's choice of words and/or manner of presentation or expression, is copyrightable. Cablecasters also should be aware that they may retransmit programming without obtaining the copyright holder's permission, but must pay a compulsory license fee (Zuckman et al., 1988).

Although copyright law limits the use of works by the media, some relief is provided by the fair use defense. Fair use allows limited reproduction of a work for uses including news reporting, comment, criticism, and scholarship. Four factors are considered when determining whether a use is fair: (a) the purpose and character of the use, (b) the nature of the work copied, (c) the amount used in relation to the work's full size, and (d) the effect of the use on the work's market. The public interest in the work and the nature of the medium involved are also considerations (Gillmor et al., 1990; Zuckman et al., 1988).

Business regulations, libel, privacy, and copyright represent only a few of the many legal concerns which face media managers. There are many other areas of media law that are not discussed here. Interested readers might review Gillmor et al. (1990) and Zuckman et al. (1988) for more information.

SPECIFIC AREAS OF LEGAL CONCERN

Selected legal concerns of interest to managers at particular types of media companies are discussed in the following section.

Print

Postal Regulations. Historically, the press has received preferential treatment through lower postal rates. Second- and third-class rates traditionally were subsidized; the justification being that lower rates allow the public to buy publications to stay informed on current events. The subsidy continued after the Postal Reorganization Act of 1970, which required each mail class to bear its costs, because Congress appropriates enough money to cover revenue differences (Lacy & Simon, 1992).

Print managers and direct mail advertisers should keep abreast of changes in second- and third-class rates. To qualify for second-class status, a publication must (a) charge subscription costs above a nominal rate, (b) have a list of paid subscribers, (c) have more than 50% of mailed copies paid, (d) not be intended primarily as an advertising vehicle and devote no more than 75% of its total space to advertising copy on average, with not more than half of yearly issues to exceed the limit, and (e) must presort copies by zip code and pack them in bundles. In return, publishers receive "red tag" expedited delivery (Gillmor et al., 1990; Lacy & Simon, 1992).

Third-class mail, formerly for nonprofit organizations, has grown since it was opened to bulk mail advertisers. Direct mailers now perform more detailed sorting, bundling, and mail preparation than second-class permit holders do. Newspaper and magazine publishers argue that the postal service should not subsidize advertising and assert that third-class rates are too low, creating an unfair competitive advantage for direct mailers (Gillmor et al., 1990; Lacy & Simon, 1992).

However, newspapers can send free total market coverage (TMC) publications to just under half their paid subscription because the postal service only requires that more than 50% of a newspaper's copies mailed by second-class be paid subscriptions (Lacy & Simon, 1992). Publishers use TMC's to recover advertising dollars from third-class direct mail, providing advertisers access to subscribers and nonsubscribers (Sohn et al., 1986). And the battle between TMCs and direct mail reveals an important point about regulations that first appear to have a negative competitive effect. Some creative media manager came up with the idea to develop TMCs after third-class postal regulations were changed to accommodate direct mail advertisers. Often an appropriate and effective competitive counter strategy can be found simply by reviewing regulations with a creative eye.

Estate Taxes. Many family-owned newspapers are purchased by chains because inheritors cannot afford to pay the high estate taxes following the owners' deaths. Estate taxes are high because a newspaper's sale value typically exceeds its book value significantly (Lacy & Simon, 1992). It is important for family-held newspaper owners to decide whether to transfer ownership to their heirs before their deaths.

Such a decision is problematic for many reasons. It is hard to contemplate one's own death, much less give offspring control of a business built on hard work and personal sacrifice. Deciding which child inherits primary control is a highly emotional decision. And other children, especially those uninvolved in the business, may criticize their siblings' management and create problems at any time.

Owners must consider seriously the following questions when deciding whether to pass on a newspaper: Do the children really want to own and manage the company? Can they? Will excluded children become hostile shareholders? Will key employees stay with the company after the owner's death? And is the anticipated tax burden too much for the family to bear financially (Duscha, 1990)?

If family inheritance seems ill-advised, try to make the company financially attractive to potential buyers. Reduce debt and standardize auditing and financial reporting procedures in order to be prepared at any time to accept an attractive purchase offer. Establish employment agreements for key and/or loyal employees to protect their jobs if a sale occurs. Develop a list of potential buyers and rank them in order of preference. Finally, educate the family about buyer preferences and include these wishes in a will.

If family inheritance seems best, begin planning immediately, with the assistance of a tax lawyer. Consider developing a Grantor Retained Interest Trust, an irrevocable trust where the grantee receives all income for up to 10 years, then passes the property on to beneficiaries. Or the owner and spouse could give tax-free gifts each year to build their heirs' equity in the company and lower estate taxes. Also consider developing an employee stock ownership plan (ESOP) where employees buy stock for cash. Determine if proceeds from insurance policies can be excluded from the estate. Find out whether the company qualifies for deferred estate tax payment. And remember to educate family and key employees about all plans (Duscha, 1990).

Think for a moment how crucial it is for a family-held newspaper owner to be aware of estate tax laws. Then consider that there are numerous legal concerns that require exactly this sort of detailed knowledge. This is why it is so important to have good legal counsel who are competent experts in their areas of specialty.

Broadcast

Broadcasters also must retain expert counsel because stations are licensed by the Federal Communications Commission (FCC) to serve the public interest, convenience, and necessity. And the definitions of these public interest responsibilities change regularly. The FCC, created by the Communications Act of 1934, regulates commercial and noncommercial broadcasting. FCC activities include issuing licenses for and regulating stations by inspecting them to ensure operations meet FCC rules and technical provisions. Presently, radio station license terms are 7 years and television terms are 5 years. License applicants must be U.S. citizens, demonstrate that their proposed operation would be in the public interest, and meet certain legal, technical and financial qualifications ("ABC's," 1990).

The FCC monitors station performance by reviewing complaints from the public, competing stations, and parties competing for a station's license. Stations must retain certain records in a file open for public inspection including the license, ownership records, network affiliation contracts, letters from the public, employment records, equal opportunity employment records, and a quarterly list of programs that provided the most significant treatment of community issues ("ABC's," 1990). So, parties challenging a station's license renewal application look in the public file to see whether the licensee fulfilled its public interest promises and to prepare a case against renewal. Obviously, broadcast managers must ensure that the public file is completed faithfully and promises made therein are met.

Although most licenses are renewed, license challenges are possible and take time and money. The FCC chooses between mutually exclusive applicants, or parties competing for the same license, after conducting comparative hearings. In such hearings, the licensee's actual past program service is compared to the challenger's proposed service and ownership, and management and technical concerns also are considered ("ABC's," 1990; Gillmor et al., 1990).

Before deregulation, broadcasters used the *Report and Statement of Policy re: Commission en banc Programming Inquiry* (1960) for advice on meeting the public interest and discovering local tastes. The report noted that public interest programming included children's, religious, educational, public affairs, agricultural, news, sports, and entertainment programs. Political coverage and programs, editorializing, and service to minorities also were viewed as important public service components. These requirements grew in complexity when determining public interest was formalized as ascertainment, which included programming and advertising practices (Amendment, 1964). Two primers specified the appropriate methodology to use for ascertaining local programming needs (Ascertainment, 1976; Primer, 1971).

Many important changes in broadcast regulation occurred in the 1980s. Ascertainment and other policies were relaxed or eliminated when radio (Deregulation, 1981) and television (Revision, 1984) were deregulated. For example, the ban on program-length commercials and commercial time guidelines were rescinded, and maintaining program logs (which keep a record of all material aired on a station each day) is now up to station discretion. The FCC also relaxed deceptive advertising requirements (Elimination, 1985). The Fairness Doctrine, which required licensees to present alternate views on controversial issues in certain circumstances, is no longer in effect (Inquiry, 1987; *Syracuse Peace Council v. Television Station WTVH*, 1987).

Yet other regulatory responsibilities remain. With some exceptions, Section 315 of the Communications Act requires a station allowing one legally qualified candidate for public office to use its facilities to provide equal opportunities to all other legally qualified candidates for that office. It also regulates the rates candidates are charged for such uses. Section 312(1)(7) requires a broadcaster to provide reasonable access for or to permit purchase of airtime by a legally qualified candidate for Federal office. The FCC also has interpreted the public interest standard of Section

307 to mean that some access must be given to certain state and local candidates as well, although there are no clear-cut rules on how to do so. In addition, broadcasters cannot air lottery information or advertisements, unless regarding a lawful state-operated lottery ("ABC's," 1990; Gillmor et al., 1990; Zuckman et al., 1988).

Broadcasters must not air indecent, obscene, or profane material when children are expected to be in the audience ("ABC's," 1990). Indecency includes patently offensive descriptions of sexual acts, organs, or excretory activities. The use of "four-letter words" is also problematic (*FCC v. Pacifica Foundation*, 1978). Recent examples include a disc jockey inviting callers to provide alternate headlines for a tabloid story about a man on his honeymoon who lost a testicle down a hot tub drain ("FCC Puts," 1991) and telling homosexual jokes about the entertainer Liberace ("New Allegations," 1991). Yet a 24-hr ban against indecent material was struck down as unconstitutional, again demonstrating how broadcast regulation is ever-changing ("Court Throws," 1991; "Radio Broadcasters Seek," 1991).

Advertising and programming directed to children are also of historic regulatory concern. The FCC treats children as special audience members (Children's Television, 1974), although it did not adopt regulations (Children's Advertising, 1981) until 1991. These rules limit advertising in programming targeted to viewers 12 years old and under to no more than 10 1/2 min an hour on weekends and 12 min per hour on weekdays. Program-length children's commercials, defined as programs associated with a product in which commercials for that product are aired, were barred. Licensees also must serve the educational and information needs of children 16 years old and under and maintain a summary reflecting the most significant children's programming aired (Policies, 1991).

FCC rules concerning ownership underwent change during the 1980s and 1990s. The number of television stations a group could own nationally changed from 7 to 12 during the mid-1980s, and the number of FM and AM radio stations a group could own increased from 12 and 12 to 18 and 18 in 1992. Broadcast managers are well advised to keep tabs on FCC ownership rules as political power shifts from party to party.

The Public Broadcasting Act of 1967 established the Corporation for Public Broadcasting (CPB), whose functions include channeling federal funds to qualified noncommercial licensees and helping to develop high-quality educational programming. The Public Broadcasting Service (PBS) provides programming and interconnection to public television stations, and National Public Radio (NPR) does the same for public radio stations ("ABC's," 1990; Gillmor et al., 1990). Noncommercial broadcasters must meet many of the same FCC requirements as commercial broadcasters.

The Cable Communications Policy Act of 1984 established the basic system local franchising authorities use to grant franchises. Cable operators receive their franchises from local authorities and often are governed by local and state utility regulations. The local franchising authority describes the general conditions under which a cable system operates. Franchise renewals also are handled locally. Thus, managers of cable operations must concern themselves with serving community needs and responding to local reactions to service.

The act limited the authority local franchisers have over programming. Franchisers cannot take programming into account when granting franchises; they only can ask that broad categories of programming be provided without specifying which services must be used. Franchisers may ask systems to designate channels for public, educational, and governmental access. Local franchisers only may regulate basic service rates in communities where a local cable system has no effective competition. For competition to be effective, at least six broadcast television signals or an alternative multichannel television service must be available to viewers in a market. Premium services like HBO and Showtime are exempt from rate regulation (Andrews, 1991; Gillmor et al., 1990).

There is no limit on the number of systems multiple systems operators may own nationally. Owners of local full-power television stations may not own cable systems serving the same locality. Generally speaking, telephone companies are not allowed to own cable systems (Gillmor et al., 1990).

Cable systems operators also must be concerned with obscenity. Operators with over 36 channels may lease some channels, as long as the leased access service is not lewd or obscene. They also must sell or lease lock boxes to enable subscribers to prevent viewing of certain channels by children or others. Transmitting obscene material over a cable system could result in fines and imprisonment under both state and federal law. In 1988 the FCC again required cable operators to block out syndicated programming at a local broadcaster's request if exclusive rights to that program had been purchased. And sponsorship identification is required for cable and broadcast programming (Gillmor et al., 1990).

It should be obvious that broadcast and cable regulation evolves constantly and often takes new directions ("Broadcasters Win," 1991; "Going to the Mat," 1991). By late 1992, Congress was actively considering regulating cable prices and some services. Future broadcast regulation will increase in complexity as regulations for new technologies are developed and revised. And telephony is expected to come more under the rubric of mass communications law. Telephones are used more and more for one-to-many communications such as 900 telephone number services for stock information and potential "romantic" partners. In the future, phone systems may be unable to eschew responsibility for the content they transmit (See Gillmor et al., 1990, pp. 700-713, for a discussion of emerging broadcast technologies).

Advertising

Ideally, advertising provides information to help consumers make rational purchase decisions and adds to the free flow of marketplace information. But if ad content is misleading or omits important information, advertising's marketplace function is usurped. Sections 5 and 12 of the Federal Trade Commission Act of 1914 give the FTC the power to regulate deceptive advertising and other unfair acts or practices. And if an advertiser is injured by a competitor's misleading ad, he may sue under Section 43(1) of The Lanham Act, which provides protection for trademarks. Deception under the Lanham Act is defined as any false or misleading description or representation of fact (Gillmor et al., 1990; Preston, 1990; Rosden & Rosden, 1990;). Readers interested in advertising regulation should review Preston (1975, 1986, 1987, 1990), Richards (1990), and Rosden & Rosden (1990).

Originally, the FTC Act was interpreted to shield consumers from deceptive advertising. However, in *FTC v. Raladam Co.* (1931), the Supreme Court held that the FTC could not ban false advertising unless it were shown to be an unfair method of competition, essentially eliminating deceptive advertising from the FTC's scope. The 1938 Wheeler-Lea Amendment enabled the FTC again to protect consumers as well as competitors (Richards, 1990). The current FTC definition of deception is composed of three elements: (a) There must be a representation, omission or practice that is likely to mislead the consumer; (b) the representation, omission or practice is examined from the perspective of a consumer acting reasonably in the circumstances, to the consumer's detriment; and (c) the representation, omission or practice must be a material one (Policy Statement of Deception, 1983). Richards (1990) noted that "regulable deceptiveness results only if purchase behavior of a substantial number of people is likely to be affected" (p. 24).

Past FTC decisions and actions illuminate these three elements. First, practices found deceptive include false verbal or written statements, misleading price claims, selling dangerous or defective products without adequate disclosures, not delivering promised services, and failing to meet warranty obligations. Even though all claims made in an ad are technically true, if the general impression of the ad is false, it still may be deceptive. That is because the FTC considers whether the entire ad is likely to mislead consumers acting reasonably; it is not necessary for the ad actually to deceive. Nor is it necessary to prove that the advertiser intended the deception (Policy Statement on Deception, 1983; Preston, 1990).

Both express claims (i.e., representations that are directly stated) and implied claims can be deceptive. The statement or representation itself establishes the meaning of an express claim. For an implied claim, the FTC examines the representation, evaluates the entire ad as well as the placement of its elements, considers the nature of the claim, and reviews the transaction itself (Policy Statement on Deception, 1983).

With the second element, the FTC evaluates whether the consumer was acting reasonably, the test being whether the interpretation is reasonable, given the claim. If the ad was targeted to a specific audience, the FTC evaluates the ad's effect on a reasonable audience member from that group. So if an ad is directed to the elderly, the FTC discerns the effect of the practice on, and any special susceptibility of, an elderly person acting reasonably (Policy Statement on Deception, 1983).

Advertising managers should ensure that an ad's headline and visual convey an accurate meaning. The FTC has noted that reasonable consumers may only glance at the headline; thus copy correcting an inaccurate headline may not be relied upon as a remedy. Also, any qualifying disclosures made in an ad should be clear and conspicuous.

The FTC stated that certain practices are not likely to deceive reasonable consumers. For example, the FTC noted its reluctance to find deceptive some misrepresentations regarding inexpensive products that are evaluated easily and purchased frequently by consumers. Such advertisers are less likely to deceive consumers intentionally because they depend on repeat sales for survival. In addition, as long as consumers understand the sources and limitations of such ads, the FTC usually does not pursue cases based on correctly stated and honestly held opinions about a product, or obvious exaggerations about the product or its qualities (e.g., the best or greatest) (Policy Statement on Deception, 1983; Richards, 1990). These exaggerations, known as puffery, are defined as "advertising or other sales representations which praise the item to be sold with subjective opinions, superlatives, or exaggerations, vaguely and generally, stating no specific facts" (Preston, 1975, p. 17—see this source for more information about puffery).

For the third element, the FTC considers whether a representation is material in determining deception. A material practice is one that is likely to affect consumer choice or conduct. Express claims are presumed to be material ones. Claims or omissions concerning a product or service's purpose, cost, safety, usefulness, durability, performance, quality or warranty, as well as areas of concern to the reasonable consumer such as health and safety, are likely to be material (Policy Statement on Deception, 1983). Advertisers must review carefully for accuracy any ad content that pertains to primary product or service attributes, is important to consumers, and/or may affect their buying decisions.

If the Commission finds a claim or omission to be material, then injury is likely to exist. In other words, consumers would have selected a different product or service had the deception not occurred. Consequently, "injury and materiality are different names for the same concept" (Policy Statement on Deception, 1983, p. 18).

Extrinsic evidence may be needed in certain deceptive advertising actions. Extrinsic evidence is any evidence apart from an ad itself regarding the meaning conveyed by that ad. Commonly used examples are consumer surveys and expert testimony about how an ad may be interpreted. Intrinsic evidence is the ad or sales communication itself (Preston, 1986, 1987).

Extrinsic evidence is not required for express claims or obvious implied claims (Preston, 1986). Express statements are identified by examining the ad itself. Instead, extrinsic evidence is needed when methodologically sound evidence which must stand up under scrutiny is needed to establish the meaning of a subtle implied claim. However, the FTC will "carefully consider any extrinsic evidence that is introduced" (Policy Statement on Deception, 1983, p. 5).

Consumer surveys or observations reported directly from consumers themselves are considered the best type of extrinsic evidence. Expert testimony (in which experts present opinions about consumer responses to ads that may or may not be consistent with actual consumer responses to similar ads) is the next best type. Other forms, such as dictionary definitions and textbook statements, are used rarely because they are considered less valuable (Preston, 1986, 1987, 1989).

Managers must anticipate that the quality of extrinsic evidence will be challenged. Experimental research is considered superior for determining advertising deceptiveness because it enables regulators to determine an ad's potential for conveying to consumers the challenged claim. Forced-choice questions are viewed as potentially superior to open-ended questions because they are posed about the specific claim in question and thus obtain a response about it. Managers should ensure that such questions are not leading, do not fail to include all options that consumers might perceive reasonably, or force one answer when consumers might perceive reasonably two or more to apply (Preston, 1987, 1989).

Samples must be representative, although they need not always be random or confined to the product's target market. Using control ads may be problematic because it is difficult to find subjects who have not seen the ad beforehand and/or find control ads that vary only in the specified way. The FTC considers evidence like consumer product evaluations and consumer responses to one part of the ad irrelevant. Other pitfalls to avoid include failing to provide verbatim responses to questions, failing to code such responses in an appropriate manner, and using responses from focus groups based on sources other than the ad in question (Preston, 1987, 1989).

The Federal Trade Commission adopted its advertising substantiation program in 1971. Advertisers and ad agencies must have a reasonable basis for advertising claims before they are disseminated. What constitutes a reasonable basis depends on a number of factors, including: the product, the type of claim, the benefits of a truthful claim, the consequences of a false claim, the cost of developing substantiation for the claim, and the amount of substantiation experts in the field believe is reasonable (Policy Statement Regarding Advertising Substantiation, 1984). In various substantiation cases, the FTC has held manufacturers, advertising agencies that produced ads, retailers who ran ads, and celebrities who endorsed products responsible (Aaker & Myers, 1987).

Both express and implied claims must be substantiated. When express claims are made (e.g., doctors recommend, tests prove), the FTC requires the firm to have at least the advertised level, as well as amount and type, of substantiation the ad actually conveys to consumers. Advertisers also should be aware how consumers reasonably might interpret their ads and have the appropriate prior substantiation (Policy Statement Regarding Advertising Substantiation, 1984).

Surveys about consumer responses to products and tests examining products themselves are considered the best extrinsic substantiation evidence because they utilize methodological procedures designed to minimize bias. Yet there is no guarantee the FTC will find a test or survey acceptable. For example, a survey must provide evidence about the claim in question, tests must be controlled suitably, and any medical practitioners involved must be unaware of which is the control and treatment group. Managers also should ensure that sample sizes are large enough, tests represent reasonable conditions under which products perform, a sufficient number of clinical tests are conducted, statistically significant differences are found, survey response rates are sufficient, and parties conducting tests or surveys have the proper expertise. The FTC, at its discretion and only in certain circumstances, also may consider supporting evidence developed after an ad is disseminated (Policy Statement Regarding Advertising Substantiation, 1984; Preston, 1989).

Remedies available to the FTC include consent orders, cease-and-desist orders, restitution, affirmative disclosure, and corrective advertising. The FTC may stop an ad or practice without the advertiser admitting guilt by negotiating a consent agreement. Consent orders carry the force of law and violations may result in a civil penalty of up to $10,000 per violation per day. A cease-and-desist order prohibits the advertiser from engaging in the deceptive practice any longer. A problem is that several years pass between the time the FTC files the initial complaint and the order is finally issued, because a cease-and-desist order is not final until all appropriate legal avenues are exhausted. Restitution means that consumers are compensated for damages. Affirmative disclosure orders may be issued if an ad does not include sufficient information. Such disclosures must be clear and conspicuous. Corrective advertising is used to correct a past deception by including the appropriate information in future advertising. For example, Listerine advertised for years that its mouthwash helped to prevent colds and sore throats by killing germs. The Warner-Lambert Company was required to include the following statement in ads until $10 million was spent: "Listerine will not help prevent colds or sore throats or lessen their severity" (Warner-Lambert Co., 1975). More recently, corrective advertising has not been used as a remedy. (Aaker & Myers, 1987; Gillmor et al., 1990).

Public Relations

Public relations professionals publicize information about corporations and their products and services, as well corporate positions on various issues of concern to society. Corporations are freer to express views on issues since First National Bank of Boston v. Bellotti (1978), in which the Supreme Court held that speech should be protected without reference to the identity of the speaker. Although the case did not discuss directly whether the free speech rights of corporations are protected, it invalidated a Massachusetts law prohibiting companies from attempting to influence referendum proposal votes on important matters of public interest that materially affect their assets, property, or business (Gillmor et al., 1990).

However, corporations face limits on their communication rights just as other media organizations do. Public relations employees must screen press releases and other corporate communications with an eye for potential libel, slander, copyright, and privacy infringements. For example, instruct employees not to copy or plagiarize a story that has been covered before. The sources publicized in these stories may be contacted and new interviews conducted. Just be sure a story or release contains original material and writing. And if a free-lance writer or photographer is used, be sure to obtain a written agreement, as described earlier (Joffe, 1989).

Those providing free-lance public relations services should remember that these agreements typically protect publishers' rights. The American Society of Journalists and Authors (ASJA) encourages writers to include certain clauses in their contracts to protect their rights. If the company asks a writer to sign a contract containing libel and privacy indemnification clauses, the writer ought to insist that the clause apply only to actual breaches sustained by a court judgment, not alleged ones. Ask that the company and/or publisher be compensated for actual and reasonable attorney's fees. Finally, retain the right to choose a lawyer in the event any action is brought to avoid paying expensive hourly rates charged by a company's high-powered firm (Joffe, 1989).

Public relations professionals also can ask clients to enter into contracts to avoid unethical or illegal conduct. Contracts could include the tasks the client wants completed such as conducting a survey, preparing press releases, and/or planning and coordinating a grand opening of a branch office. In return, the public relations free-lancer insists that lying and deception be prohibited in all communications prepared or disseminated on behalf of the company. If the company balks, this is a signal that it is unwise to accept the work. It also allows the free-lancer to avoid subsequent personal legal liability and damage to one's professional reputation (Crable & Vibbert, 1986).

Public relations professionals also must review corporate ads for deceptive content and report financial information properly. The Securities Acts of 1933 and 1934 and the Investment Company Act of 1940 require that adequate and accurate information be provided about a company and its securities in connection with the sale of those securities to the public. Certain promotional activities are banned by the Security and Exchange Commission (SEC), including releasing overly optimistic sales reports, earning reports and projections, and placing undue emphasis on favorable news and developments in publicity. Public relations professionals should familiarize themselves with these and other SEC requirements (Grunig & Hunt, 1984).

The best way to avoid problems in reporting financial information is to ensure that press releases and ads are truthful and disclose all appropriate information. Corporate communications always should be reviewed carefully for content before dissemination, as well as for the effect they may create in light of other previously publicized information. Truthful statements in a press release may be misleading when taken in context with other corporate communications. It is in the best interest of the public, as well as public relations firms and their clients, to report information truthfully. Courts have held public relations firms, companies, and their officers accountable when news releases are found to contain false and misleading information (Rubin, 1991).

SELF-REGULATION OF MEDIA COMPANIES

Legal and ethical concerns must be of primary importance to media managers for both moral and practical reasons. An industry that provides information to society bears a special responsibility to assure its accuracy and fairness. And an industry that reports on the mistakes and flaws of public officials and other citizens must practice ethical principles. Otherwise, those criticized by the media legitimately may point out its hypocrisy.

Media managers also must guard against personal hypocrisy. First, resist the temptation to point to other types of media companies as "ethical sinners" as a way of avoiding honest scrutiny of one's own field. All types of media organizations have been guilty of ethics violations. A responsible manager turns the gaze of honest, critical scrutiny to her own media field, as well as others. Second, remember that employees look to managers to set an example. So if you do not practice ethical behavior, can you credibly insist that your employees do? And can you expect them to respect you?

Each media profession develops codes and standards of behavior to help guide ethical behavior. Many questionable practices are not technically illegal; they are simply "wrong" by generally accepted moral standards. Although the American Newspaper Publishers Association has not adopted its own code and believes such matters are best left to individual newspapers, it does recognize the American Society of Newspaper Editors and the Society of Professional Journalists (SPJ) Codes. The SPJ Code states that it is the duty of journalists to serve the truth and be free of obligation to any interest other than the public's right to know. In addition, inaccuracies or lack of thoroughness are inexcusable and journalists should show respect for the dignity, privacy, and rights of people encountered when gathering and presenting news (SPJ Code, 1987).

The Magazine Publisher's Association has not promulgated ethical guidelines either. However, some magazines have their own written codes or rely upon the codes of various professional associations for advice. For example, the Direct Marketing Association, Better Business Bureau and American Advertising Federation have promulgated guidelines regarding advertising acceptance and screening that magazines use (Rotfeld & Parsons, 1989).

The broadcast industry relied on the NAB's Radio and Television Codes for many years for guidance regarding programming and advertising practices. Although the codes were abandoned, many stations still refer to them for advice. The national television networks have standards and clearance departments that review ads and programming. Many individual radio and television station also have formal or informal guidelines and use various advertising screening procedures (Rotfeld, Abernethy & Parsons, 1990; Rotfeld & Abernethy, 1992; Wicks, 1991a, 1991b).

The Radio-Television News Directors Association (RTNDA) Code of Broadcast News Ethics provides advice for broadcast news managers. The code states that broadcast journalists must gather and report information impartially, honestly, and accurately. The code also requires that news be presented in a balanced way, gifts that may influence or appear to influence news judgment be declined, and confidential sources be protected (RTNDA Code, 1991).

The advertising industry has developed codes and a self-regulatory body to review national advertising. The American Association of Advertising Agencies (AAAA) developed the *Creative Code, Agency Service Standards,* and *Standards of Practice* to guide advertisers and advertising agencies (AAAA, 1956, 1962a, 1962b). The advertising industry and the Council of Better Business Bureaus (CBBB) established the National Advertising Division (NAD) and the National Advertising Review Board (NARB) in 1971 to help promote truth and accuracy in national advertising. The Children's Advertising Review Unit (CARU) of the Council of Better

Business Bureaus was established in 1974 to advance responsible children's advertising and has published children's advertising guidelines (NAD, 1983; Rosden & Rosden, 1990).

The NAD opens inquiries, determines the issues, collects and evaluates data, and makes an initial decision whether a claim made in a challenged ad is substantiated. Cases may be brought by the NAD itself, by competitors, by referrals from local Better Business Bureaus, and by consumer complaints. Advertisers usually are asked to submit substantiation for claims made in challenged ads. Following an investigation, the NAD may dismiss the complaint because the ad is substantiated or decide that the complaint is justified. The NAD asks advertisers to modify or stop running ads that are found to be unsubstantiated.

NAD decisions can be appealed to the NARB, composed of 50 individuals representing national advertisers (30), advertising agencies (10), and the public (10). NARB's chairperson selects an impartial panel of five members for each appeal. Advertiser compliance with NAD/NARB decisions is voluntary. However, failure to comply could result in a case being referred to the appropriate government agency. NAD/NARB decisions are publicized in the NAD Case Reports. Local Advertising Review Committees, which function as local appeals boards for local BBBs, also have been established in some major cities (NAD, 1983; Rosden & Rosden, 1990).

The Public Relations Society of America (PRSA) adopted its *Code of Professional Standards for the Practice of Public Relations* in 1977. PRSA members pledge to conduct themselves professionally and serve the public with truth, accuracy, fairness, and responsibility. Provisions note that members should conduct their professional lives in accord with the public interest, not engage in any practice that tends to corrupt the integrity of channels of communication, and sever relations with any party requiring conduct contrary to the code's provisions. The code also encourages continuing research and education to improve member competence (PRSA, 1977).

Codes of conduct and self-regulatory bodies are useful to managers seeking advice on fair and ethical conduct. However, critics argue that codes are developed to prevent government regulation. Critics assert industry members are not critical enough of their colleagues and often have ethical standards that are different than the public they are supposed to serve. Critics also complain that ethical violations typically result in a minor "slap on the wrist"; thus, such codes and bodies do not represent a meaningful front against unethical behavior.

SUMMARY

Media law and regulation is obviously very complex. The reader is reminded that media law involves much more than what was discussed in this chapter. For example, Zuckman et al. (1988) and Gillmor et al. (1990)

reviewed the topics covered in this chapter as well as others like restraint of the press for national security reasons, free press-fair trial conflict, freedom to gather news and information, and newspersons' privilege in more depth. Prudent media managers review these and other appropriate sources to keep abreast of the law and retain good counsel to protect themselves, their employees, and their firms.

CHAPTER 5 CASES

Case 5.1

The Case of A Father's Dilemma: Sell or Pass On?

Steve Simpson, 58 years old, owner and publisher of the *Bloomfield Banner*, was in a quandary. Yesterday, a major newspaper chain made a handsome offer to buy the *Banner*. Although unexpected, the offer was not a total surprise. He had run the *Banner* carefully and kept debts at a minimum. The owner of the newspaper chain had given Steve a month to make his decision. If he accepted, he and his wife would have an extremely comfortable retirement. But he had always planned to pass the paper on to his youngest son, Eric, and/or his daughter, Chris.

For as long as Steve could remember, Eric wanted to take over the paper. Eric had graduated from college with a degree in journalism the year before. He was working as the police beat reporter for the *Banner* and doing a good job. Steve felt confident about Eric's reporting skills; he was a good writer and had a nose for news. However, Steve had reservations about whether Eric could handle the business side of the newspaper. He'd earned only average grades in his business minor and had remarked a few times how he disliked accounting and finance. Eric often privately criticized the advertising staff, especially the ad manager, and felt very strongly that advertising and editorial interests be kept separate. Steve agreed that editorial and advertising interests should be separated but was concerned that Eric's negative attitude toward business in general might cloud his judgment on personnel matters. Steve wondered if Eric could deal with advertising staffers effectively and fairly. Eric had always found it difficult to compromise and to respect opinions that differed from his own. But Eric was only 22 years old and certainly could change.

James Axsom, who had been his advertising manager for 18 years and a good friend for even longer, had sensed Eric's attitude and expressed his concerns about it. Axsom said: "Look, I can understand why Eric is uncomfortable with advertising. And I agree that advertising and editorial decisions should be made separately—you know that. I've turned down a lot of ads over the years because I didn't like what they said and how they said it. And I've had my ear burned off with complaints about stories and threats to cancel ads. That's why I'm worried. If Eric can't see that I'm on his side now, what's he going to be like if he takes over?" Steve generally agreed that James had been a good and fair ad manager. However, there had been a couple of times when he'd questioned James' judgment regarding the proper balance between advertising and editorial interests. His circulation manager of 2 years, Anne Hendricks, also appeared to have concerns about Eric. Steve wasn't sure whether this was true or what they were because she'd never talked to him about it.

Steve also wondered how his other two children would feel if he turned down the offer. His eldest son, David was 33 years old and had no interest in working for the paper. He had just been fired again, this time at the Ford truck factory. David and his wife were contemplating a move to Lansing, Michigan, so he could take a job with Oldsmobile. Steve hated to see his grandchildren move away, but personally felt it would be a relief if David left. He was always trying to borrow money, even though Steve had turned him down repeatedly for never repaying his first loan of $5,000.

His daughter, Chris, was a vice-president of software development for Pear Computers at age 31. He thought highly of Chris and her abilities. She was bright, got along well with people, and was able to handle responsibility, although she was impatient and sometimes did not follow through on things as well as she should. She had helped Steve pick a computer system for the paper, which streamlined the production process, improved the quality of color reproduction, and saved the paper a good bit of money each year. He was especially impressed by the fact that the system Chris chose was not produced by Pear. Steve thought Chris would do a fine job of running the paper, but he was not sure if she wanted to leave the San Francisco area. And he wondered whether Eric would like the idea of sharing responsibility with her.

Steve also felt pulled by his wife's desires. Kathy urged him to accept the offer. They had been careful about saving, but really did not have that much set aside for retirement. "What if one of us gets sick? Would our insurance cover it? Could we afford it if one of us has to go into a nursing home?" Steve thought so, but things would be tight. Kathy also said, "You always promised to take me to Japan. You know that we'll never even have a chance to contemplate a trip like that unless you accept this offer. We'll never be able to do the things we've always wanted to do. I know Eric wants to run the paper, and Chris might, too, but what about me? I sacrificed for 35 years so the kids could go to college and so you could keep the paper afloat. I love you, the kids, and the paper and was happy to put things off to make it all work. I gladly sacrificed so all of you could have what you wanted and needed. But the kids are adults now and you've had the chance to run a paper. When will I get my chance to fulfill my dreams? Will my needs ever come first? Will I ever get the chance to do what I want, too?"

Steve closed the door to his office and asked his secretary to hold his calls. He thought about how much he really liked the idea of leaving his paper to his children. He thought about how much he liked the idea of having a comfortable retirement. He also thought about all of the sacrifices his wife had made, how gracious she had been about them, and how much he truly wanted to give her the things she deserved. He knew that he felt more confused than he ever had in his life. "What should I do?" he whispered to himself.

Assignment

1. How should Steve go about deciding whether to sell the paper?
2. Should he involve his family in the deliberations? Why or why not? If yes, who should he involve?
3. Should he involve any of his employees in the deliberations? Why or why not? If yes, who should he involve?
4. Should Steve sell the paper? Why or why not? If yes, what steps should he take? If no, what steps should he take?

Case 5.2

The Case of Who's Protecting the Patients?

Jenny Baston, a reporter at *Peoria Herald-Leader* for 6 months, had the makings of a great story. She had been contacted by a registered nurse from the Greenwood Nursing Home, Sally Ratchet, who asserted that conditions had gone from bad to worse there. Although contracts specified that patients would be fed three times and bathed once daily, some were not being fed regularly. Others were only bathed on days when family members were expected to visit. These patients were bedridden, paralyzed, and unable to speak, often the victims of strokes. So they lay in filth for days and could not tell their families about it. Finally, patients who tended to make trouble or misbehave were given drugs, without authorization from family or doctors, to keep them quiet. Sally offered to give Jenny medical records and let her into the home to photograph the deplorable conditions. Exposing corruption like this certainly would help the neglected patients, Jenny thought. Photographs of such problems would cause a public outcry and lead to change. People would be justifiably angry at how these poor people were being treated.

Jenny did some background work and found out that Sally had been fired from the Barker Farm Retirement Community about 7 years ago. At Barker Farm, elderly clients could live in private condos and apartments but have nurses on call for 24 hr. Patients who could not care for themselves lived in the main building, where constant care and feeding were given. There was also an on-site clinic to deal with medical emergencies. Barker Farm had a reputation for excellent care and concern for its patients. Jenny's grandfather had lived there for a few years before his death and she felt that its reputation was well deserved. Sally confirmed that she had been fired when confronted, saying that she had just started her nursing career and accidentally gave the wrong medication to a patient. She asserted that she had made no such errors since then.

Jenny heard rumors that corroborated Sally's assertions. Nurses at Barker Farm and other facilities she had visited told her that patients were not fed and bathed adequately and promised social activities were not held. However, she couldn't convince any of them to go on the record with their accusations. All of this was complicated by the fact that the cousin of the *Herald-Leader*'s publisher owned about 20% of Greenwood's stock.

Jenny thought about asking Sally for the names of some of the abused patients. She could try contacting the families to get permission for interviews. Or she could pose as a relative to get into the nursing home. Once inside, she could check out conditions for herself and decide whether to write the story. She had a small, fully automatic camera she could hide in her purse. If the staff is as negligent and unavailable as Sally asserted, she could easily pull it out and snap a few shots of the neglected patients. She could visit on Sally's day off, so even she would not know Jenny had been there.

Jenny was afraid to tell her editor, Eddie Castor, about the possible scandal. He was a nice guy and seemed trustworthy, but nothing like this had ever come up before in the newsroom. She was not sure whether he would give her permission to pursue the story, for fear of retribution from the publisher. She was afraid he would assign the story to a more experienced reporter. And she was scared of looking dumb if the story did not pan out. But if she gave him photographs and a finished story, she'd have proof and could demonstrate to Eddie that she was a good investigative reporter. And if she went to Greenwood on her own and found nothing, she would not look dumb, because nobody would know.

Assignment

1. Should Jenny talk to Eddie before deciding to go? Why or why not?
2. If Jenny goes, should she take any pictures of the patients? Why or why not?
3. If Jenny goes, should she give her editor a finished story? Why or why not?
4. What kinds of legal problems may occur if Jenny visits the Greenwood Nursing Home under an assumed name with a camera hidden in her purse?

5. What kinds of legal problems may occur if Jenny actually takes photographs during her visit to the Greenwood Nursing Home under an assumed name with the camera she hid in her purse?
6. What do you think Jenny should do? Why?

Case 5.3

The Case of the Frustrated Copywriter

Peter Burton was in a quandary. He had been a copywriter at Wenthe & Butler Advertising for almost 2 years. Wenthe & Butler was a small creative boutique that specialized in developing highly creative and effective advertising. In one way, he was happy to have his job—Wenthe & Butler was a great place to work and a lot of his friends at other agencies had been laid off during these hard economic times. Peter knew that the reason he had not lost his own job was because his bosses considered him one of the best up-and-coming young copywriters in Atlanta.

The problem was that he never seemed to get credit for his own ideas. Peter worked under the best creative director in Atlanta, Eve Wenthe. He also worked with the most respected art director, Kevin Butler. So the ad community in Atlanta just assumed that the good work coming out of Wenthe & Butler for the past 2 years was primarily theirs. Eve and Kevin were not the problem; they had always credited Peter as copywriter on all entries in the local and national Addy advertising award competitions. And Eve always noted the individual contributions of Kevin and Peter when she accepted the awards for their creative team. People just seemed to assume that Eve and Kevin were responsible for the team's success, because they had been around longer.

And Peter wanted more than recognition. His salary was a bit above average for the Atlanta market, but the benefits were not that great at Wenthe & Butler. He also needed to start saving for two college educations because his son was entering kindergarten and his daughter was 2 years behind. Although it was still early, he knew that the earlier he started saving, the better. His wife worked as a sales representative for IBM, with a good salary and generous benefits, but things were awfully expensive these days. Prices were pretty high in major cities like Atlanta. Peter cringed when he thought about how outrageous his mortgage payment was. Even though he and his wife had pretty good jobs, they just barely were breaking even. How was he going to save for his kids' futures and prepare for retirement unless he got a break?

Peter thought he may have found a way to get the recognition he wanted, which would allow him to bargain for a better salary and benefits or a better job at another agency. Peter was considering entering this year's Atlanta Addy Awards on his own by developing a print campaign for a fictitious client. That way, if he won, nobody else would get the recognition he deserved. And he finally would get to accept an award himself because he could list himself as creative director, art director, and copywriter. This might make the Atlanta advertising community sit up and take notice. It also might lead to a better job at Wenthe & Butler or elsewhere.

Peter had also considered approaching a local nonprofit organization and offering to develop a campaign for free. His only "payment" would be permission to enter the campaign in the local Addy Awards. That way, everybody would win. Some strapped nonprofit organization would get a great campaign for free. And Peter would have samples of his own work to enter. The problem was, many creative people thought developing public service advertising was easier than developing ads for commercial clients.

However, Peter had some concerns about both ideas. How would his employers take it? Would they see it as trying to upstage them? He did not think so—he felt that if he explained to Eve and Kevin that he only wanted to see how well he would do on his own, they would understand. In fact, they might even let him accept the Addy for campaigns he developed in the future, rather than sticking to tradition and letting the creative director accept.

Peter wondered how the ad community in Atlanta would react. No one had ever entered a campaign for a fictitious client or entered a "donated" campaign before. There was nothing in the rules prohibiting either action. Perhaps people would admire his gumption. Or perhaps they might see him as a prima donna who wanted attention. Peter really did not know how the ad community would respond. He certainly would be taking a risk if he tried either idea.

Peter wondered what he should do on the drive home. What would the long-term implications for his career be if he tried either idea?

Assignment

1. Where might Peter turn for advice on how to act in this situation?
2. Should Peter discuss his plans with his employers? Why or why not?
3. Should Peter discuss his feelings about not getting enough individual recognition and compensation with his employers before entering his work? Why or why not?
4. If Peter decides to develop a campaign for a fictitious client, should he tell his employers? Why or why not?
5. If Peter decides to develop a campaign for a nonprofit organization, should he tell his employers? Why or why not?

6. How do you think the Atlanta ad community would react if Peter's entry for a fictitious client won?
7. How do you think the Atlanta ad community would react if Peter's entry for the nonprofit organization won?
8. What do you think Peter should do? Why?

Case 5.4

The Case of the Rent-A-Wreck Trade Out

Janie Parker had been working as the media buyer for Barker Advertising for about 2 months. She was scared and did not know what to do. She suspected that her boss, agency owner and namesake Vic Barker, had been pocketing money for airtime that should be going to Rent-A-Wreck or its owner, a major national car rental company. Julie inadvertently had stumbled onto the scheme when she found a copy of Rent-A-Wreck's contract in the Loveman Furniture file in her desk. She thought nothing of it until she examined the monthly billing reports from the local newspaper and broadcast stations showing the times and dates when commercials for the agency's clients ran. Commercials for other advertisers were sometimes running in times and spaces supposedly reserved for Rent-A-Wreck. These other advertisers were also Barker clients. The local newspaper and broadcast stations had been given the free use of Rent-A-Wreck cars in return for running the commercials in certain desirable time slots or positions.

Janie had asked for and reviewed the last month's accounting books when she noticed that Rent-A-Wreck's bill for print space and airtime was less than the monthly total for car rentals to local print and broadcast salespersons. She did not mention to anyone that this was why she was reviewing the books. These amounts were supposed to be equal every month, based on the contract between Barker and the major national car rental agency that owned Rent-A-Wreck. By comparing the monthly accounts with monthly billings, she noticed that ads for four other Barker clients had aired in positions and times promised to Rent-A-Wreck.

Janie was apparently the only person at the agency who knew about this discrepancy. It was standard procedure for her to review the monthly billing and accounting reports, so there was no reason for her boss to suspect her. She had made a point of behaving normally. And because she was fairly new on the job, no one would really know what was "abnormal" for her anyway. There was no reason for her to suspect the local newspaper or broadcast stations: They listed ad times and positions correctly. There was apparently no effort to hide the fact that other ads ran when Rent-A-Wreck ads were supposed to. Because the agency was privately owned, no outside stockholders or other parties regularly reviewed the books. Vic Barker's wife, Annie, was an accountant so she handled the bookkeeping for the agency. It appeared that no one knew the terms of the contract except Vic Barker.

The only reason Janie had seen a copy of the Rent-A-Wreck contract was because she had found it stapled to a monthly bill. Both were filed in the Loveman's Furniture file in her desk. She did not think anything was amiss at first; she figured her predecessor simply had filed the documents in the wrong place. Now she was not so sure. She was glad she had not told anyone that she had found the Rent-A-Wreck contract and bill. She made copies of these documents and brought them home. She figured she'd better have some evidence if this blew up in her face before she decided what to do.

But the bill was what really frightened her. It showed that the monthly contract totals were the same. In fact, it appeared to her that the bills from the newspaper and local broadcast stations may have been altered. She decided to make a copy of next month's reports before forwarding them to Annie. That way, she could tell for sure whether next month's bills were altered.

Janie's predecessor had moved on to another agency in town. She tried to contact him at first, but he never returned her calls. It was just as well, she thought; he may have been involved and it was probably best to keep all of this to herself until she decided what to do. And that was the real problem. What should she do? Should she contact the police? Should she contact Rent-A-Wreck? Should she confront Vic Barker? What if she was wrong? What if Rent-A-Wreck had given permission for other companies to use their airtime? What if Mr. Barker was giving the money back to Rent-A-Wreck? But then why was there no record of payments to Rent-A-Wreck in the books?

Janie knew she could not go on like this for long. She thought about looking for another job and keeping everything to herself. She also thought about secretly making copies of next month's billing reports from the media and the agency's bill to Rent-A-Wreck, and then secretly bringing them to Rent-A-Wreck's president. She also thought about confronting the Barker's or going to the police. She was afraid to confront Vic or Annie first, because she was afraid of being fired. She was terrified because she had never faced anything like this. She laughed when she remembered how proud she had been to land this job. "I never thought my first job in advertising would be like this!"

Assignment:

1. What steps should Janie take to protect herself? Explain your answer.

2. Should Janie secretly make copies of company documents and bring them home? Why or why not?
3. Should Janie confront her employer with the evidence she has obtained? Why or why not?
4. Should Janie show the evidence she has obtained to the president of Rent-A-Wreck? Why or why not?
5. Should Janie show the evidence she has obtained to the police? Why or why not?
6. Should Janie keep all of this a secret and look for another job? Why or why not?
7. What do you think Janie should do? Explain your answer.

Case 5.5

Assignment: Monitoring Advertising for Children

Many critics of television and advertising have expressed concern about television advertising for children. As a result, the FCC treats children as a special group of viewers with special rules about advertising. These rules limit the number of minutes per hour of advertising and the connection between program and advertising content. Your text gives more specific information about these rules. The purpose of this assignment is to examine advertising content aimed at children to see if it meets these standards.

Assignment:

Please complete the following steps:

1. Check to see if the FCC rules governing children's advertising have changed recently.
2. Using the most recent rules, watch 2 hr of a network's Saturday morning children's programming and 2 hr of an independent's weekday afternoon children's programming.
3. Answer the following questions:
   A. Did the two stations follow the FCC standards about advertising time and content?
   B. How did the two stations compare and contrast? Was one better or worse than the other?
   C. Did you notice any types of advertising that were legal but raised ethical concerns? Where any of the advertisement particularly offensive? Did any of the advertising seem to be misleading? Did any of the advertisements seem particularly manipulative?

6
Market Analysis

Market analysis is an effort to understand the process of selling a media commodity to those who use it. Such a process is extremely complex. It starts with the media company and involves consumers, competitors, government regulation, and the general nature of the economy. The complexity multiplies because every action by a firm, government, or group of consumers affects every other group in the market. A change in the commodity, a new commodity, a price change, a new media company all change the market, and such changes affect the entire market. Market analysis allows managers to understand the market so changes can be predicted and action can be taken. Failure to conduct adequate market analysis can result in loss of revenue and even the closing of the business.

At its simplest level, a market is a place where goods and services are bought and sold. This selling process requires demand by consumers and supply by businesses. Every market is defined geographically by the area in which a company sells its product or service. For example, a newspaper's market is defined by the area in which copies of the newspaper can be obtained by home delivery or newsstand and newsrack sales. A television station's market is determined by the ability of viewers to receive the signal.

Media organizations are unusual because they participate in more than one type of market with the same commodity. An automobile dealership sells cars to people and is, therefore, in the automobile market. However, a magazine company can sell copies of magazines to readers and space in the magazines to advertisers. The multimarket nature of many media firms creates a complexity that makes media management an especially difficult challenge.

In order for media managers to meet the challenge, they must be able to analyze demand and supply in the various markets. Such an analysis is necessary, but it does not guarantee success. The complexity of the market process, the difficulty of generating accurate data, and the nature of the decision process make many managerial decisions risky. However, market analysis reduces this risk, by yielding information and analysis that fits into the hub of the decision-making wheel in chapter 1. Because information and analysis are central to decisions, market analysis is central to any major changes in the nature or price of media commodities.

This chapter provides an overview of the nature of media markets, the economic environment in the markets, and how factors that affect firms in these markets can be analyzed.

STEPS IN MARKET ANALYSIS

Market analysis has five steps: (a) The type of market must be identified; (b) the general goals of a manager's organization should be understood; (c) the nature of demand for a firm's commodity must be specified; (d) the market structure needs to be identified; and (e) the economic environment must be examined.

Types of Markets

Media firms function in one or more of three types of markets (Lacy & Simon, 1992): advertising, information, and intellectual. The *information market* is where readers, viewers, and listeners seek nonadvertising information. In exchange for this information, they pay money or make their attention available for advertisers. The *advertising market* is where advertisers buy space or time from media organizations to present their products and services to the viewers, readers, and listeners. The *intellectual market* is where individuals and social groups seek ideas and information that will help the groups pursue their goals within the society. This market is the equivalent to the marketplace of ideas developed by John Milton and amplified by John Stuart Mill.

These three markets are connected for some media because the same physical product will serve all the markets. This type of connection involves a *joint commodity*, which means two or more markets are served with a single production process. For example, a newspaper firm prints newspaper copies with information that can be sold to readers and advertising space that can be sold to advertisers. The connection is even stronger because readers use advertising as information.

All three types of markets are important for news media. The information and advertising markets generate revenue for business survival, but it is the intellectual market that gives news media their special place in society. Yet this market is the most difficult to examine because there is no direct exchange of money for a product. This difficulty does not mean the market can be ignored. It is the supply and demand interaction in the intellectual market that the First Amendment protects. The Hutchins Commission warned in 1947 that if media organizations ignore their responsibilities in this market, the special protection offered by the First Amendment could be revoked by society (Commission on Freedom of the Press, 1947). In a more direct relationship, the regulation of broadcast television by the federal government carries with it an obligation to serve this market.

One last problem in dealing with these three markets is their interrelationship. People use what they learn in the information market for decision making in the intellectual market, and they buy newspapers for advertising as well as news. Because people use content in ways that it may not have been intended, it is difficult to predict the demand behavior of readers, listeners, and viewers.

Despite the complexity of identifying and separating business behavior in markets, it is necessary to do so. Managers need to be aware that decisions affecting one market have an impact on the other markets. Lack of awareness about the interrelation can increase government intervention into their affairs.

Goals

The term *goals* means the object of some behavior. Goals tend to be connected to particular behaviors. Before this term is applied specifically to media management, it is worthwhile to step back from the individual goals and examine the origins of organizational goals. Goals flow from the basic philosophy of an organization. This basic philosophy is usually a reflection of the nature of society. For example, capitalistic-oriented companies generally perform better in capitalistic societies rather than in socialist societies. A company's basic philosophy is expressed in the general purposes of the organization. The following section starts with general purposes and then defines goals for media organizations.

General purposes refer to the reasons that media organizations exist. A company may want to make a profit or change society, but whatever it seeks to do, its goals will reflect the financing that media organizations receive. Altschull (1984) listed four patterns of financing media: official, commercial, interest, and informal. The *official pattern* involves government control of media content through rules, regulations, and decrees. The purpose is to promote the goals of the government entity controlling information. The *commercial pattern* presents content that reflects the view of advertisers and their "commercial allies, who are found among owners and publishers" (Altschull, 1984, p. 254). The purpose is to make profit for the owners. The *interest pattern* generates content that reflects the goals of the special interest group that produces the content. The purpose is to promote the aims and ideology of the interest group. The *informal pattern* produces content that reflects the goals of the relatives and acquaintances who provide money to produce the content (Shoemaker, 1987). The purpose of the media organizations becomes the achievement of the goals of the individuals and groups who finance these organizations.

As Altschull (1984) pointed out, no communication system is pure, but some forms of financing patterns are more prevalent than others within social systems. The United States tends to have a commercial pattern, whereas China has an official pattern. However, the emphasis of Altschull's discussion of the commercial pattern is on the advertising market rather than the information market. He assumed the former dominates the latter. Whether this is true is a matter of debate, but for purposes of this book, it is assumed that the media readers, viewers, and listeners have influence over the content of the media they use. Without the media user, the advertisers will not buy space or time.

Although U.S. media markets involve a commercial pattern of financing, the official pattern is also important. In the U.S. hybrid system, the commercial pattern is affected by government regulation. The extent of regulation and its impact varies with changes in political power. Government also influences commercial media by serving as a source of news.

General purposes are useful in understanding a communication system, but particular goals of individual media organizations show a great deal of variance. Goals are the planned results of behavior by the organization. The variation of goals among commercial enterprises has not always been considered an important factor in market analysis. The assumption of traditional economic theory is that companies attempt to maximize profit. This rather simple assumption allows economists to use calculus for generating theories, but it also limits their ability to explain some variations in economic behavior. In reality, firms often pursue goals other than the maximization of profit.

Just as the "rational man" assumption of traditional decision theory (see chapter 1) has come under criticism as unrealistic, so the assumed goal of profit maximizing has been attacked (Greer, 1980). As a result of the debate concerning business goals, several theories emerged during the 1960s that start with alternative goal assumptions. Williamson (1964) said managers maximize their own utility because the separation of management from ownership means strict profit maximizing need not be observed. Managers spend some profits to enhance their utility through staff, expense accounts, office suites, executive services, and other perks. The staff helps to reduce insecurity and expand power, whereas the perks enhance status and prestige.

Baumol (1967) said some firms in markets with few competitors would maximize sales revenue, as long as profits reached an acceptable level. Sales revenue can be a main concern in these markets because declining sales can result in banks being less likely to loan money; it can cause suppliers of raw materials to go to other firms; and it can result in consumers buying substitutes because of a perceived decrease in popularity.

Cyert and March (1963) rejected the assumptions of profit maximizing because people within an organization pursue many goals and because managers tend to seek satisfactory profits rather than maximum profits. They also said firms do not have perfect knowledge, a traditional assumption for rational decision making and profit maximizing.

In place of maximization, Cyert and March (1963) postulated a coalition theory of behavior based on three areas of behavior inside the firm—goals, expectations, and choice. These areas of behavior involve interaction among people in an organization to determine how that firm will behave in the marketplace.

Behavioral theories have received research support, which indicates that organizational behavior is complex and that goals vary from organization to organization and with time. The important point is that the goals of an organization must be understood at the time a market analysis is undertaken. A daily newspaper facing intense competition from another local daily might lose money purposefully in an effort to increase its circulation. Management sees this as a necessity because of the tendency of only one daily in a city to survive. A similar daily newspaper without direct competition might try to gain the largest profit margin it can. In both cases the goals are neither right nor wrong; they are simply the goals that have been adopted.

The process by which goals are established and changed fall within the realm of earlier chapters, but market analysis begins with the goals of all firms in the market. Managers must clearly understand their firm's goals in order to pursue them. Managers also need to understand as best they can the goals of competitors in order to react to their behavior. Such reactions can be crucial to success in an intensely competitive market.

Nature of Demand

Demand in a market is measured by the number of people, households, or firms wishing to buy a product or service. For example, if the number of minutes of advertising sold by a radio station is greater this year than last, demand is said to have increased. The theory of perfect competition states that demand is related to four factors: the price of a commodity, the price of the commodity's substitutes and complements, the income of consumers, and the taste of the consumers (Stigler, 1952). *Price of a commodity* means the amount of money it cost to get one unit of that commodity. The *price of substitutes* is the unit price of another commodity that might be used in lieu of your company's commodity. For example, *Time* and *Newsweek* are considered by many readers to be acceptable substitutes. So the price of one can affect the demand for the other. The *price of a complement* is the price paid for a commodity that is used with the one your company produces. For example, dip is a complement for chips. For some people, a television set and a VCR are complements. *Consumer taste* is a catchall term for the wants and needs that individual buyers have for various commodities. The impact of consumer taste on demand is related to the quality, or perceived quality, of media commodities.

Price. Price is related negatively to demand for most products and services. As the price of a product goes up, the demand for that product will go down, and vice versa. The degree to which demand changes when prices changes is called *elasticity of demand*. If a 1% increase in price results in a decrease in demand that is greater than 1%, demand is *elastic*. If a 1% increase in price results in a decrease in demand less than 1%, demand is *inelastic*. If a 1% decrease in price results in a 1% drop in demand, the result is *unit elasticity*.

Price elasticity is a measure of how sensitive demand is to price changes. Inelastic demand means a product is not very sensitive, whereas elastic demand means it is. With inelastic demand, an increase in price often can result in an increase in revenue because the decline in demand can be offset by the increase in revenue. For example, a city magazine entitled *Downtown* has a circulation of 100,000 per month. With a price of $1 per copy, *Downtown* has a monthly circulation revenue of $100,000. If this magazine has inelastic demand, an increase in price to $1.25 may cause circulation to drop to 90,000, but the company actually will increase its monthly revenue to $112,500. The percentage drop in circulation was less than the percentage increase in price.

The price increase may seem like a good idea, but the fact that advertisers buy space based on the number of readers means a reduction in circulation could cause advertising revenues to drop. If a 10% drop in circulation for *Downtown* caused a 10% decline in advertising, the circulation revenue increase would not make up the decrease in ad revenue. The connection between the advertising and circulation markets means the elasticity in both markets must be considered when changing price in one.

Companies with elastic demand curves must be careful with price increases because demand may drop so much that the revenue increase generated from a price increase will not offset the loss from declining customers. Continuing the previous example, *Downtown* might have an elastic demand. In such a situation, the price increase to $1.25 could cause in a drop in circulation to 70,000. The monthly profit would then be only $87,500. Combine this decline with the loss in advertising revenue from losing 30,000 readers and the price cut would be disastrous. Elasticity usually is related to the number of acceptable substitutes. The greater the number, the greater the elasticity.

Price of Substitutes and Complements.   The price of substitutes also is important in determining demand. The ability to substitute one service or good for another gives consumers power because it allows them to shop around for a better buy. Whether a substitute will be used depends on its price relative to the commodity being considered. As the price of a substitute decreases, the demand for the original commodity will decrease because buyers will get a better deal buying the substitute.

The relationship between the price of a commodity and its substitute is called the *cross-elasticity of demand.* If a 1% decrease in the price of a substitute causes a 1% drop in the demand for a commodity, the cross-elasticity of demand is *unitary.* If a 1% decrease in the price of a substitute causes a greater than 1% drop in the demand of a commodity, the cross-elasticity of demand is *elastic.* If a 1% drop in the price of a substitute results in a less than 1% drop in demand for a commodity, the cross-elasticity of demand is *inelastic.* In effect, the cross-elasticity of demand is a measure of how well one commodity substitutes for another. The more elastic the demand, the greater the substitutability.

For example, if a competitor for the city magazine *Downtown*, which sells 100,000 copies per month, increases its price to $1.25, the cross-elasticity will be elastic if *Downtown* gains more than 25,000 readers. The cross-elasticity will be inelastic if the gain in readers is less than 25,000. The important managerial consideration is not whether the demand is strictly elastic or inelastic but the degree of elasticity. An inelastic relationship between magazines still can benefit the firm that holds its price when a competitor has a price increase.

Demand for a commodity is related negatively to the price of complements. As the price of complements increases, the demand for the commodity decreases because it is more expensive to use the two in conjunction. For example, if the price of coffee increases, the demand for sugar decreases because less coffee is being consumed. It is difficult to establish a relationship among media complements based on price. However, one could say that public relations releases are complements for news content. As the amount of news content declines, the demand for press releases will decline, all else being equal.

Income.   As a person's income increases, his overall demand for products and services will increase because he has more money to spend. The proportion of income spent on a given commodity, such as information, does not necessarily remain constant for all incomes. The percentage of a person's income spent on a type of good or service depends on that person's needs and the price of the various products. A person who makes $30,000 may spent 20% a year on food. The same person making $50,000 might spent 12% if she ate the same type of food after the increase in income, or she might spend 21% if she decides only to eat at the most expensive restaurants.

People vary in their demands for information. People who make a living by selling or using information, such as a stockbroker or writer, tend to spend a higher percentage of income on information because it becomes an investment for future income growth. However, most people will spend less of their higher income on information because much of their media use is for entertainment. As income increases, these people are more likely to substitute travel or live entertainment for information as entertainment.

Overall, an increase in income will result in increased expenditures on media, but the increase may not be proportionate to the income gain. This is where individual taste comes into play.

Consumer Taste.   Consumer taste is an umbrella term for the reasons people want and need goods and services. Unlike the role of price and income in demand, little theory exists to explain how changes in consumer taste affect demand. This results from the difficulty in measuring taste. At best, it can be said that as taste changes, demand changes.

When examining markets for media organizations, it is worthwhile to understand how people use information. Table 6.1 shows a two-dimensional classification for information use (Lacy & Simon, 1992), based on research about the uses and gratification of media content (Severin & Tankard, 1992) The two dimensions are type of use and timing of use. Type of use includes surveillance, decision making, entertainment, and social-cultural interaction. Timing of use includes short-, medium-, and long-term use.

Surveillance means people use information to keep up with what is happening around them. *Decision making* involves the use of information for selecting among various options. *Entertainment* is used broadly to mean the use of information for diversion and enjoyment. *Social-cultural interaction* is the process of using information to establish and promote group membership and survival.

Information use is affected by time. *Short-term use* means the information is used as it is acquired. For example, a cartoon provides enjoyment as it is being read. *Medium-term use* involves a delay in the use of information. A person might read a sports story and use that information during a discussion at work later that morning. *Long-term use* involves the purposeful commitment of the information to long-term memory and a later recall. Information about a presidential race is retained and combined with other information across time to develop an opinion about the candidates.

Consumer taste is important in understanding the markets for media

TABLE 6.1
Dimensions of Information Use

I. Type of Use

A. *Surveillance*—People use information to check the environment to see what issues and events might interest them. This monitoring can identify new information about old issues and events of interest, or it can identify new areas of interest.

B. *Decision Making*—This is the purposeful use of information to decide on a course of action or to form an opinion or belief. Information that a person encounters usually is judged to be relevant or not relevant to the decisions. This use involves seeking specific information about a specific decision.

C. *Entertainment*—Information used for entertainment may include, but is not limited to, material that is enjoyable, such as movies, television shows, books and feature articles. This type of information provides utility to a user from the material itself. The benefits flow just from the acquiring and understanding of the information and not from its application to another process. The entertainment need not be pleasant. For example, a well-written feature on a person or an account of a crime might both fit in this category. This use has emotional effects on the user.

D. *Social-Cultural Interaction*—Communication is a central part of group membership. Social and cultural groups share information in a process that allows members to identify common ground on which they can establish interaction. The exchange may be about serious issues, such as the goals and processes of the group, or about less serious matters, such as shared interest in sports. Such group communication will take many forms. All such communication that helps either to bond members or to separate members from groups fits under this heading.

II. Timing of Use

A. *Short-Term*—Information can be used immediately in the four ways listed previously. In one sense it is consumed because the majority of bits of information we receive is used and then forgotten. However, all is not forgotten. Some is retained. Information becomes short-term when it serves its use as it is taken in by the user. Examples are the sports scores and many of the comics in newspapers. It is difficult to define when the short-term ends, but as a rule the term means the time period during which a user is acquiring information from the source of the information. This could be during a television show or during the 20 min in the morning a person allots to reading the newspaper.

B. *Medium-Term*—Information that is used at times other than following its acquisition but before it enters long-term memory is considered medium-term in nature. This means information that does not fit into the short-term time frame. A person might read a story about a political campaign. Recalling that information during a discussion later in the day fits this category.

C. *Long-Term*—This information is committed to long-term memory and used at periods more than 48 hr after its acquisition. This type of information is usually used more than once. It includes the type of information used in performing one's work, as well as general information about such things as laws and even spelling. This type of information is crucial to social and cultural interaction.

Note. From Lacy and Simon (1992, p. 27). Copyright 1992 by Ablex Publishing. Reprinted by Permission.

183

commodities because price usually is not as important as content in determining demand. In other words, demand for media content is less elastic with respect to price than with respect to content (Lacy, 1989). Consider the use of local television news for weather information. If a newscast cuts back the time spent on weather and adds this to time spent on sports, people who want weather information will turn elsewhere, whereas people who want sports information will watch the newscast.

The use of information is related to the content of the information provided by a media organization. Information used for decision making tends to be very concrete, whereas information used for entertainment need not be detailed and may even be inaccurate. Timing plays a role in content demand. Breaking news of worldwide importance, such as war news, becomes of primary concern during the crisis period. However, in noncrisis periods, different people may use the same information at different times.

Although the use of information is important in determining content, the lack of theory concerning demand for media commodities makes demand by particular types of individuals difficult to predict. Research is helpful, but without theory it is difficult to generalize about the complex nature of consumer taste for information.

Market Structure

The nature of demand is a separate issue with market analysis, but it is also a crucial part of market structure because it affects the nature of the media commodity. *Market structure* is the way the market is organized. This structure comes from the collective behavior of all firms and in turn affects the individual behavior of all firms. The market structure faced by a media company begins with the geographic limitations of the market. After the geographic limits are defined, structure depends on the nature of the media commodity, the number of competitors, and the barriers to entry in the market.

Geographic Limits. Geographic limits establish who will have access to a commodity by determining the area in which buyers and sellers interact. Several factors come into play in determining geographic boundaries of markets, but they fall into the areas of *cost* and *revenues*. If a geographic area costs more to serve than the revenue it generates, most businesses will not serve that area. The costs include production, distribution, and selling costs. *Production costs* are the expenses a company has from creating its product or service. *Distribution costs* are the expenses from delivering a product or service to the consumer. *Selling costs* are the costs of getting people to buy the product or service, which include promotion, advertising, and commission expenses.

Revenue is classified as circulation and advertising revenue. *Advertising revenue* comes from transactions in the advertising market, such as selling time or space to advertisers or selling classified ads to local readers. *Circulation revenue* comes from transactions in the information market, such as selling magazines or newspapers to readers or cable service to viewers.

The interaction of costs and revenues that determine geographic market varies from company to company and from medium to medium. A newspaper, for example, will circulate primarily in areas where it attracts advertising. Thus, the farther away a person lives from the businesses that advertise in a newspaper, the less likely that person is to be in the newspaper's geographic market. But this observation varies with the newspaper. Some large daily newspapers circulate in areas distant from their primary advertisers because they feel it is part of their responsibility to the intellectual market to provide news across a wide geographic area. Some newspaper groups have been criticized for not fulfilling this public service obligation when they cut back distribution in high-costs areas (Blankenburg, 1982).

Television faces a different type of geographic limit. The range of broadcast signals traditionally has determined a television station's geographic market. The signal fades as one moves away from the transmission point. The development of cable has reduced the impact of this limitation. Stations, such as WTBS in Atlanta, have the ability to distribute programming around the county by satellite and cable. The dependence on advertising revenue tends to limit the geographic market, but the tendency of U.S. businesses to select television for national advertising means some national stations can be supported.

Nature of Commodity. Once the geographic limits of a market are defined, the commodity must be examined. A *commodity* is simply the physical good or the service provided by a company. The term commodity is used because media content has the physical aspect associated with a product, while at the same time providing a service. The analysis of media commodities starts with the uses of information mentioned earlier. In addition to types of use, the content of media can fall into several categories based on four dimensions (Lacy & Simon, 1992): geographic emphasis, nature of information, information format, and topic of information. These four dimensions and their subdivisions are presented in Table 6.2.

Geographic emphasis concerns the geographic location addressed in the content. The emphasis may involve events at the local, state, regional, national, or international levels. It may also be nonspecific with regard to geography. The definitions of geographic emphasis given in Table 6.2 are ones that have been used in media research, but specific definitions may vary from firm to firm.

TABLE 6.2
Dimensions of Media Content

I. Geographic

A. *Local*—Information about the county, city, or neighborhood in which a reader lives.
B. *State*—Information about events and issues affecting the state in which a reader lives.
C. *Regional*—Information about the region of the country in which a reader lives (the Great Lakes region, e.g.)
D. *National*—Information about the U. S. government and other events affecting the country or a part of the country outside the region.
E. *International*—Information about countries outside of the United States.
F. *Nonspecific*—Information that has no geographic connection, such as personal advice.

II. Nature of Information

A. *Advertising*—Information put in the newspaper by a group or individuals in order to influence the reader to take some action or to make the reader aware of an issue, event, product, or service.
   1. Awareness Advertising—Information that attempts to bring an event, issue, product or service to the readers' attention.
   2. Price Advertising—Information about the price of a product or service.
   3. Quality Advertising—Information about the quality or reliability of a product or service.
   4. Identity Advertising—Information that is designed to create a positive image of a product or service in the minds of the readers.
B. *News*—Information that is prepared by the newspaper's staff or by another news-gathering organization. The news organization does not receive pay for printing this information.
   1. Hard News—Information that deals with disaster and physical or ideological conflict. The emphasis is on a specific event or series of events.
   2. Features—Information that does not involve conflict and disaster. The emphasis is usually on people and interaction among people.
   3. Analysis—Information that is meant to improve understanding of an event, trend, or issue by providing context.
   4. Opinion—Information about someone's or some organization's position concerning events, trends and issues. This includes editorials, some columns, and letters.

III. Information Format

A. *Written*—Information conveyed with words.
B. *Visual*—Information conveyed primarily with visual images and symbols other than words and letters.
C. *Audio*

IV. Topic Area

A. *Government*—Information concerning an official governing body, members of a government body, or people seeking to become a member of a government body.
B. *Business*—Information concerning groups and individuals involved in commerce or trade.
C. *Sports*—Information about athletic efforts and athletes.
D. *Science*—Information concerning the natural, applied, and social sciences.
E. *Schools*—Information about systems of education and members of those systems.

(continued)

TABLE 6.2 (*Continued*)

F. *Crime*—Information about people or groups who violate laws and about people and groups who enforce the laws.

G. *Leisure Activities*—Information about things people do for entertainment and those who provide entertainment.

H. *Social-Cultural Activities*—Information about actions that affect the society and culture in which the readers live. This includes information about marriages, deaths, and activities of noncommercial organizations.

Note. From Lacy and Simon (1992, p. 32-33). Copyright by Ablex Publishing. Reprinted by permission.

The second dimension addresses the *nature of information*, which has two main subdivisions. The information can be *advertising*, which is information placed in space or time bought by an organization in an effort to influence attitudes and behavior. This involves advertisements designed to make people aware of a product or service, to give price information, to give information about quality, or to create a positive image of a product or service.

The other subdivision is *news*, which is information that is prepared by a media organization's news staff and placed in space not bought by an advertiser. This news generally falls into four categories: hard news, which emphasizes conflict and violence; features, which emphasize information and people; analysis, which is an effort to give context about an event, trend, or issue; and opinion, which is someone's or some organization's position about an event, issue, or trend.

The third dimension is *information format*, which can be written, visual, or audio. Written information is conveyed with words on paper or a screen. Visual information is presented with still and moving photographs or graphics. Audio information is received by a person's ears. The three can be combined in various forms, and various media have different degrees of these three formats. For example, most printed matter is written and visual; radio uses audio; and television uses visual, audio, and sometimes written formats.

The fourth dimension is *topic area*, which deals with particular topics covered in the information content. The eight subcategories presented in Table 6.2 are used often, but they are not the only possible categories. These categories have been used because they have meaning to media users and the media people who create content.

These four dimensions allow a manager to develop a profile of media content. This profile is important because the nature of a commodity determines whether it will meet the demand of the readers, listeners, and viewers in a market. For example, a large segment of people in a city may be interested in getting hard news about local government, schools, and sports because they play a role in the social-cultural interaction in the community. A media commodity that does not contain a high degree of information in these areas may not meet the demand of this segment.

Number of Competitors. Firms compete when their products or services can be substituted. The greater the cross-elasticity of demand, the greater the competition. As the number of competitors increases, the probability increases that a buyer can and will substitute commodities for one another.

Economic theory can be categorized on the basis of the number of sellers in a market and the nature of the commodity. Perfect competition theory assumes many sellers and homogeneous products that are perfect substitutes. Monopolistic competition assumes many sellers and heterogeneous products that are differentiated into submarkets by location, advertising, and the nature of the product. Oligopoly theory assumes few sellers and either heterogeneous or homogeneous products. Monopoly theory assumes one seller and one product serving a market (Litman, 1988). Identifying the number of competitors in media markets is not always easy because the commodities produced by various forms of media are not good substitutes in all markets. For example, television news and newspapers are different in many ways. They are not good substitutes for many people, but others find them to be acceptable substitutes. An additional complicating factor is that television stations do not charge users for content, whereas newspapers do. This makes a measure of cross-elasticity of demand between newspapers and local TV newscasts difficult or impossible to determine.

As a practical tool, however, managers can classify other media commodities as excellent, good, adequate, and poor substitutes for their commodities. Two daily newspapers headquartered in the same city usually are excellent substitutes in the information and advertising markets. A daily produced in the next county that covers a wide area may be a good substitute for the local daily in the information market, but only an adequate substitute in the advertising market, and a poor substitute in the local intellectual market. A local television newscast might be an adequate substitute for a local newspaper in the information market but a poor substitute for supermarket advertising. A better substitute for supermarkets' advertisements would be direct mail.

Despite the difficulties, identification of competitors is crucial to decision making in the market. In addition to identifying competitors, their behavior must be monitored across time because the nature of a commodity can change.

Barriers to Entry. The last factor in market structure involves the barriers confronting a company that wants to start a firm in a market.

Types of barriers to entry vary from industry to industry and even from market to market. Three important barriers to media organizations are high fixed costs, regulation, and the market power of existing firms.

High fixed costs play a major role in keeping firms from entering some markets. The term *high fixed costs* means the firm faces a great deal of expense just to operate. These fixed costs do not vary no matter how many pages a magazine or newspaper has or how many minutes a broadcast program contains. The high fixed costs of running a daily newspaper come from the expense of having printing presses, computer systems, and a large staff to collect news. Television news has high fixed costs, but they are not as high as those at daily newspapers. Magazines have low fixed costs because they can hire printers and free-lancers for writing.

In addition to fixed costs, media organizations also have *variable costs*, which are those that increase with each additional unit. For example, adding another page to a newspaper increases variable cost because that extra page uses more ink and paper.

Table 6.3 shows how fixed and variable costs change as production increases for a newspaper. The cost of owning a printing press is $1,000 per day, whereas the cost of ink and paper is 25¢ per copy. Producing one copy, the average fixed cost is $1,000. But the average fixed cost drops to $1 with a circulation of 1,000 and to 5¢ with a circulation of 20,000. This rapidly declining average fixed cost contrasts greatly with the stable average variable cost of 25¢. The rapid decline in average fixed cost contributes to the rapid decline in average total cost, which equals fixed plus variable costs divided by number of units produced.

High fixed costs are related to the cycle of the publication or broadcast. Daily media firms have higher costs than do weekly or monthly ones, because daily media must own more equipment to reduce the uncertainty of having someone else produce their commodity. These high fixed costs generate *economies of scale*, which means the more units that are produced,

TABLE 6.3
Costs of Producing a Newspaper

Circulation	Fixed Cost Per Day	Average Fixed Cost Per Copy	Cost of Paper & Ink Per Copy	Total Cost	Total Cost Per Copy
1	$1,000	$1,000.00	$.25	$1,000.25	$1,000.25
500	$1,000	$ 2.00	$.25	$1,125.00	$ 2.25
1,000	$1,000	$ 1.00	$.25	$1,250.00	$ 1.25
5,000	$1,000	$ .20	$.25	$2,250.00	$ .45
10,000	$1,000	$ .10	$.25	$3,500.00	$ .35
20,000	$1,000	$ .05	$.25	$6,000.00	$ .30

the lower the average cost per unit. This is shown in Table 6.3 by the declining average fixed cost. Thus, each additional reader or viewer adds nothing to fixed cost. Additional expense comes only through the variable cost.

High fixed costs work as a barrier to entry because they require a large investment of money to start a business. This money usually is borrowed. Paying interest increases operating costs, which means the price of a commodity will be higher and demand will be reduced. In addition, established firms with high fixed costs enjoy the economies of scale to a greater extent than will new firms. Established firms sell more units, which lowers their average cost. This means the older firms will have either a higher profit per unit or lower unit price because their costs per unit will be lower. Either way, a new firm entering an industry with high fixed costs is at a disadvantage.

Technology development is connected to fixed costs. Efficient technology, such as high-speed offset presses, can add to economies of scale. At the same time, less expensive technology, such as personal computers, can lower barriers to entry by providing low-cost quality products. During the 20th century, technology has increased barriers to daily newspaper markets. However, technology has lowered entry cost for weekly newspaper markets during the past decade.

Regulation can be a strong barrier because government can exclude companies through a licensing procedure. Historically, regulation has played a key role in the broadcast industry. Regulation of radio declined during the 1980s, as did the regulation of television to a lesser degree. Originally, broadcast was regulated to reduce chaos in markets from overlapping radio bands and to control the public airwaves. The argument goes that companies are licensed to operate and in return they owe service to the public in the intellectual market. The ability to enforce this public service aspect has been curtailed, but the assumption of television service remains an important public policy issue.

Regulation also plays a role in determining the number of competitors. Antitrust law was developed to counteract efforts by large organizations to use their market power to exclude unfairly other firms and keep new firms from entering a market. The assumption underlying antitrust law is that people are best served by many sellers, which keeps price down and improves efficiency.

Antitrust laws are applicable to newspapers, although they were used rarely during the 1980s (Busterna, 1988a). The main antitrust laws and the issues they address are presented in chapter 5. The impact of these laws on market structure is to limit behavior that might reduce the number of firms in a market. The behavior most dealt with in the newspaper industry involves pricing.

Although antitrust is applicable to newspapers in general, some newspapers were given a special exemption to these laws by the 1970 Newspaper Preservation Act (NPA). This act is a limited exemption that allows two daily newspapers in the same city to combine their business, advertising, circulation, and production departments. Their editorial departments must remain separate. The effect of the NPA is to give two newspaper companies greater monopoly power in the advertising market, while maintaining two separately operated news-editorial voices in the information market. The argument is that the two voices better serve the information and intellectual market than would one voice. These combinations are called *joint operating agreements* (JOAs).

Justification for the NPA came from the decline in the number of cities that had separately owned and operated daily newspapers. The number of such cities fell from 43% of all cities with dailies in 1920 to less than 2% in 1986 (Busterna, 1988b). Originators of the NPA argued that daily newspaper markets were natural monopolies because of economies of scale. The economies were such that only one daily could survive (Lacy, 1988). This argument was partially correct, but an equally important contributor to the death of daily competition is the connection between the information and advertising markets, which creates the circulation spiral.

Circulation spirals occur because advertisers within a market tend to advertise in the daily with the largest circulation. This lowers the advertising rate per thousand readers. Because readers also want advertising information, they tend to read the newspaper with more advertising space. As a newspaper gets more readers, it will attract more advertising. As it attracts more advertising, it will attract more readers. The leading circulation newspaper in a market will have a disproportionate amount of advertising space considering its circulation lead. A newspaper with 40% of the circulation will have 65% to 75% of the advertising. Because advertising accounts for 70% or more of the revenue at most daily newspapers, the result of the spiral is to run the trailing paper out of business.

Evidence indicates that JOA papers tend to spend more on their content quality than monopoly papers, but not as much as competitive newspapers (Lacy, 1988). However the NPA has not really saved newspaper competition. In April 1991, there were 21 JOAs, which equaled the number when the law was passed in 1970. JOAs allow newspaper firms to share the economies of scale but do not end the circulation spiral (Lacy, 1990).

Regulation is a response to the illegal accumulation and application of market power, which is the third main barrier to entry. *Market power* simply means a firm can influence the factors that affect demand. The more market power a firm has, the more influence it has over price and quality decisions. A company with a great deal of market power that wants to maximize profit will increase prices to increase revenue and lower quality to cut costs.

Whether market power, or its use, is illegal depends on how that power was accumulated and how it is used. Market power that comes from economies of scale and the circulation spiral is not illegal, per se. However, if that power is used to further increase power by fixing prices or excluding competition, antitrust laws can be applied.

Competition is related conversely to concentration. As the number of firms in a market increases, consumers have more potential substitutes. The availability of substitutes moves power from companies to consumers. This consumer power keeps prices down and improves quality, but it also reduces profits. From a manager's viewpoint, competition limits her power and increases uncertainty. But in the long run, competition can be beneficial to a firm because it forces it to react to consumer demand. These reactions will reduce the chance of the company producing inferior commodities that lowers demand across time.

Although competition increases as concentration decreases, the relationship is not perfect. An information market with four television stations may not be as competitive as a market with two newspapers. This could happen if one of the four televisions stations is dominant in the ratings for local television news. If two daily newspapers are about equal in their shares of circulation in the market, the competition can be extremely intense, with both newspapers losing money to avoid the circulation spiral.

The variation of competition within equal levels of concentration can be demonstrated by three concepts. *Market share* is the proportion of the geographic and product market one media firm serves. If a newspaper company sells 80,000 copies out of 100,000 sold in the market, its market share is 80%. Market share is important in measuring concentration and competition.

Market concentration means the extent to which a few firms have a high percentage of market share. A commonly used measure of concentration is the Herfindahl-Hirschman Index (HHI), which is determined by adding the squared market shares of all firms in the market (Sherer, 1970). The HHI equals one in a monopoly and zero in a perfectly competitive market. This measure is used by the U.S. Justice Department in antitrust cases.

Market concentration is not the same as the *competition intensity level*. Two firms that are close in market share may be very competitive toward each other despite the low shares of the other stations. In such cases, a competition index (CI) is useful. This index subtracts the market share of the second largest firm from the share of the most dominant firm and runs from zero, which would be equal market shares, to 100, which would be a monopoly.

The difference between the HHI and CI can be illustrated by comparing the measures in two markets. The first has four local television newscasts with shares of 30, 30, 20, and 20. As determined previously, the HHI would equal .26 and the CI would equal zero. A second market with four stations may have a shares distribution of 45, 45, 5, and 5. This would have an HHI of .41 and a CI of zero. Looking at just the HHI, one would assume the second market is less competitive, but the battle over shares between the two top stations would be equally intense, according to the CI.

Both measures are useful for evaluating competition. One includes all local stations, whereas the other emphasizes head-to-head competition that can occur in such markets.

Market structure is an important aspect of market analysis. The structure constrains firms in the market and those wanting to enter that market. Managing in a market without understanding the structure is similar to driving across the United States for the first time without a map. You may get to your destination, but only if you are lucky.

Economic Environment

The first four steps in market analysis have concerned the actual markets in which the media firms operate. The final one is more general and it influences all businesses. It is called the *economic environment*, and it covers general business conditions. As with all businesses, media companies take inputs in the form of raw materials and people's skills and turn them into a commodity they can sell. These inputs include products, such as paper, and skills, such as the writing and reporting ability of journalists. The "production" processes use capital equipment, such as television cameras and printing presses, and require financing.

The process and acquisition of inputs and financing are influenced by general economic conditions within and outside the particular market. This section deals with three of these conditions: availability and price of inputs, availability and cost of financing and investment, and general economic conditions in the market.

Availability and Prices of Inputs. People in the computer industry use the acronym GIGO to explain poor performance. It stands for "garbage in, garbage out." This applies to media organizations as well. If inferior journalists, salespeople, and managers are used, the commodity produced will not be of high enough quality to retain readers, viewers, and listeners. The same can be said of raw materials.

The flip side of high quality inputs is price. Just as media firms serve markets as sellers, they also enter markets as buyers. The quality of the inputs is a matter of availability and price of *intermediate goods and services*, which are goods and services used to produce other goods and services. The most important input for media firms is labor, which is used here to mean all people who contribute to the production process. The price that the media organizations will pay for raw material and labor depends on supply and demand. As the price paid for labor increases, the number and quality of people available will increase. As the price paid decreases, the number and quality of people available will decline. Many news organizations are notorious about underpaying journalists. This has resulted in many good journalists leaving the field (Weaver & Wilhoit, 1986).

In the long run, price and other factors determine availability of inputs. If a media organization is located in a geographic area that is not attractive to people, it becomes more difficult to hire quality labor. Thus, the price the firm pays either will increase, or the firm will accept lower quality labor. Similarly, the expense of raw material increases with geographic features such as mountains and large bodies of water. The closer a firm is to the location of production of intermediate goods, or the easier a supplier can reach a firm, the lower will be the costs of these raw materials.

Availability and Cost of Financing and Investing.   As with all business, managing media firms involves financing the operations. This means long-term costs must be paid for as well as the expenses of day-to-day operations. Firms have three basic ways of financing: revenue, borrowing, and expanding ownership. *Revenue financing* means firms pay for goods and services from the revenue they generate in day-to-day operations. *Borrowing* means they pay for the use of money from financial institutions or investors. *Expanding ownership* involves selling part, or all, of the control of an organization either to a person, firm, or the public through the issuance of stock in the company.

Most business expenses, which accrue from day-to-day operations, are paid with revenue. Borrowing money to pay for operating expenses is a sign that a company may be in trouble. If this behavior extends over a long period, the company most likely will fail.

Borrowing and expanding ownership are used more for long-term financing. For example, a company that produces several magazines may want to move to larger offices. This will be financed most likely through borrowing. On the other hand, a newspaper group that wants to expand and buy more newspapers can either borrow the money or sell stock in the company. The advantage of the former is that the current owners retain control. The advantage of the latter is that the newspaper group does not have to pay interest on that money at a prescribed rate. Stockholders, however, will be paid dividends, but management has more flexibility with this form of financing.

An important aspect of financing is long-term investment. Investment can take the form of better technology, such as improved printing facilities, but equally important is investment in human capital. *Human capital* includes the skills, knowledge, and talent of the people who work in an organization. This human capital is generated through education and training. Long-term standing in the market is related to investing in the people within an organization. This type of investment often is overlooked because of the expense involved, but it is just as important as investment in equipment.

The long-term success of a media firm is related to its investment, which is related in turn to the availability and costs of financing that investment. If interest rates are high, the expense of borrowing can be a long-term burden. An example is the Ingersoll newspaper group, which financed expansion in the 1980s with money borrowed at high interest rates. As a result, the company had to sell all of its American newspapers because it could not pay off the debt with revenues.

Expanding ownership also can have high costs. Public trading of stock requires that the management be aware of the price of the company's stock. The price is related primarily to profit performance, although other factors can come into play. This means managers at public corporation often must cut costs during economic downturns to keep profits up. This cost cutting can have a long-term impact by lowering the quality of the commodity and services, which result in declining demand.

General Economic Conditions. *General economic conditions* are the third aspect of the economic environment. This refers to how well the economy is performing and is reflected in the employment rate, inflation rate, and the cost of borrowing money. Media organizations, like most businesses, perform better when the economy is prospering. However, when consumer disposable income and business advertising budgets decline, profits and quality of commodity tend to fall. Economic conditions tend to be cyclical, with expansions being followed by recessions.

If revenues decline because of deteriorating economic conditions, management can react by cutting expenses, cutting profit margins, or both. *Profit margin* refers to the percentage of revenue that goes to the company as profit. It is determined by dividing the profit, which is what is left over after expenses are subtracted from revenue, by the total revenue. If a company is not willing to lower its margin during economic hard times, it must cut expenses. This means firing people and accepting inferior raw material. However, if it will lower its margin, the company may be able to get through the bad economic conditions with little drop in quality. The long-term impact of quality reduction is difficult to measure, but it does occur.

Whether a company can reduce profit margins is often dependent on the type of ownership. As discussed earlier, publicly owned companies tend to be less likely to lower profit margins. However, private ownership is no guarantee of how managers will react to poor economic conditions. Again, the reaction of a given firm to economic conditions is a function of the organizational goals and the nature of the mangers and owners.

One special area of concern during difficult economic times is the intellectual market. The tendency to cut costs at news organizations often results in canceling expensive investigative projects. Sometimes news organizations will tend to be less aggressive in covering businesses because they fear loss of advertising. This tendency is unfortunate because readers, viewers, and listeners continue to need and expect the ideas and information news organizations can provide. Recessions create a great deal of uncertainty, and uncertainty increases the need for information. During a recession, this need increases just as information companies are cutting back on quality and quantity of information.

Poor economic conditions may offer long-term growth opportunities for media organizations. A newspaper, magazine, or television news organization that can provide useful information during uncertain times may be able to capture a larger market share. This strategy, of course, means that a firm would improve its commodity when economic conditions suggest cutting costs. Such a strategy is risky but should be considered. At the very least, media managers must be aware of the long-run implications of cutting their contributions to the intellectual market.

Overall, the economic conditions work as constraints on decisions and actions by a media firm. During good times, they offer opportunity for expansion and growth. During bad times, the economic conditions test the flexibility of a company to contract without reducing its commitment to its readers, viewers, and listeners.

ANALYZING THE MARKETS

Managers need to analyze their markets for two reasons. First, market analysis is needed for specific projects, such as changing the nature of the commodity or starting a new media company. Second, periodic analysis is useful to monitor the firm's market position. The first type of market analysis is part of strategic planning and is discussed in chapter 7. This section discusses how a manager might conduct a periodic analysis of markets.

The analysis includes the examination of market structure, organizational goals, the nature of demand, and the economic environment. The information and advertising markets are addressed together. The analysis of the intellectual market is discussed separately.

Information and Advertising Markets

The general questions that follow are applicable to both the advertising and information markets.

Market Structure. The first step is to understand the market structure. This involves asking seven questions:

1. *What is our firm's geographic market?* The answer to this question is relatively simple. It is determined primarily by management decisions as to where material will be available. However, all firms within an industry or market cannot and do not choose to cover the same area. Even though the answer is simple, the question is important. The geographic market affects the answers to the other questions.

2. *What is the nature of our firm's commodity?* This question addresses the content of the media commodity and is related to the breakdown of information content in Table 6.2. Most managers have a sense of the nature of their commodity, but an explicit content analysis will provide more accurate data.

3. *Who are the competitor's for our firm?*

4. *How do our competitors' commodities compare to ours?* The third and fourth questions should be examined together. Both questions are related to the cross-elasticity of demand and should be approached from a consumer's viewpoint. No media commodity can be everything to everyone. People sometimes will substitute one media commodity for another even when the two do not appear to be good substitutes. The manager must deal with the majority of users, and he needs to realize this is a matter of degree. So, market analysis must determine which commodities are potential substitutes and to what extent this substitution might take effect.

Although content is most important in considering substitutablility, price also plays a role. If a media commodity becomes too expensive, people will use another commodity that would have been less acceptable at a lower price.

5. *How difficult is it for new firms to enter our market?* This question deals with barriers to entry. If it is difficult for a new firm to start in a market, your company has more discretionary power. This question addresses whether fixed costs are high and whether there is extensive regulation in the industry. One way of answering this question is to examine how many new firms have started and survived in your market and similar markets during the past 10 years. The higher the start-up and survival rate, the easier it is to enter.

6. *What barriers contribute to this difficulty?* This question is an extension of the fifth and deals with the future of these barriers. Cost barriers to entry are a function of technology. Being aware of technology trends and uses will help answer this question.

Regulation changes require legislative and administrative activity. Much of the activity here has to do with which political party is in power. Traditionally, Democrats have had more of a regulatory tendency than Republicans. Keeping up with the political environment is important.

7. *Will the structure of our market change in the immediate future?* The answer to this question comes from the answers to the other six. Are new commodities coming out that can be substitutes for yours? Will government policy change? Will technology lower the barriers to entry? The more volatile the market structure, the more uncertainty a manager faces. The less concentrated the market structure, the less control a manager has in implementing decisions.

Organization's Goals. The second step is to examine the firm's goals. In strategic planning this means goals of specific actions. In a general market analysis, the manager must ask five questions:

1. *What are our firm's specific short-term and long-term financial goals?*
2. *What are our firms' specific short-term and long-term quality goals?* These two questions may seem obvious. But it is relatively common to find organizations that have no explicitly stated goals. And in the cases where an organization has explicit goals, only the short-term profit goals may be listed. It is difficult to achieve vague or unspecified goals because people cannot share a common aim.

Financial goals involve profit goals and revenue goals. Once revenue goals and profit goals are determined, the roles of expenses can be determined. All goals should be obtainable.

Quality goals are related to financial goals. First, quality is related to expenses. All else being equal, a media firm that spends more will have higher quality. Of course, all else is never equal. The individuals who work within an organization also affect quality. But, in general, the greater the expenditure, the more likely quality will increase. Second, the quality of the media commodity is related to revenue through price and demand. Higher quality results in higher price, but it also can result in greater demand.

3. *How well are we achieving these goals?* The answer to this question rests on the ability to measure performance. Financial performance is relatively easy to measure. Quality performance is more difficult. Managers usually measure quality with their sense of what makes quality, content analyses, and surveys of readers, viewers, and listeners.

4. *If we are not achieving the goals, is it because the goals are inappropriate for this market?* If goals are not being met, the reason is important. Such failure can be because the goals are set too high, or the firm simply is not performing well, or the market is too competitive, or economic conditions are creating problems, or the prices are too high, or some combination of these factors. Price usually plays a lesser role in the information market. Television and radio do not charge directly for their content, and newspaper firms often undercharge for newspapers (Picard, 1989). The answer to this question lies in the other steps of market analysis.

5. *Should we consider changing, adding, or dropping any of the firm's goals during the immediate future?* The answer to this question comes from the entire market analysis. Other factors contribute greatly to this decision. For example, as new media developed, some newspaper companies diversified by buying television and radio stations. The acquisition of new forms of media resulted in redefining the organizations' goals. As market structure changes, competition can decrease or increase. Either one can affect specific performance goals for a given period.

The Nature of Demand. In this third step, the manager can ask three questions:

1. *Has demand for the firm's product increased, decreased or remained constant since the last analysis?* Change in demand is relatively easy to determine. In newspaper and magazine markets, this means circulation and penetration, which is the percentage of households in a market subscribing to a publication. In the television and radio markets, demand is measured by ratings and share of audience. In book, movie, and recording markets, demand means the number of units or tickets sold.

2. *If demand has changed, was it because of changes in price, price of substitutes and complements, consumer income, consumer taste, or quality of product?* The answer to this question is difficult to determine because more than one cause underlies changes in demand. The answer to this question is related to the evaluation of competitors in the section about market structure. Variations in pricing are easiest to address because price is easy to measure. Changes in consumer taste and substitutability are more difficult because they involve content, which is not easy to quantify. However, these two factors often tend to be the most important in determining changes in demand.

The best approach is to analyze the nature of your commodity and the nature of possible substitutes across time to see if the patterns of commodity change mirror the trends in demand. Care must be taken, however, because many factors come into play.

3. *Are there any indications that demand will change in the immediate future?* This question is even more difficult than the first two because it requires prediction of future trends. It may be that trends of increasing or decreasing demand will continue or level off. This question becomes crucial because it is the basis for most long-term planning. If the answer about direction of future trends is wrong, a great deal of resources can be misallocated.

Economic Environment. Analyzing the economic environment is also important. This area of analysis deals primarily with the amount of resources that will be available to a firm and to the users of its commodity. Three questions should be answered here:

1. *Will unemployment in your market increase or decrease in the near future?* This question concerns demand for information and is related closely to question one in the nature of demand section. If unemployment increases, people in the market will have less money to spend and demand for some media products will drop. Demand for others may grow. For example, broadcast television viewing might increase if people have less money for other forms of entertainment. Any effort to estimate future demand must take employment trends into consideration.

2. *Will business activity in your market increase or decrease in the near future?* This question deals primarily with demand in the advertising market. If unemployment increases, business activities in many areas will decrease. Not all business activities are affected equally, however. Decline in purchasing power affects the purchase of larger items, such as houses and cars, more than the demand for food. But even food demand can be affected because people will buy cheaper types of food as income drops.

If business activity decreases in a market, advertising will decline for many businesses, although not necessarily all. Advertising is looked upon as less important for many businesses than providing a good product or good service.

3. *What will happen to the interest rate in the near future?* This question addresses the long-term operations of a media organization. Plans to expand the number of media outlets or improve equipment usually are related to the ability to borrow money. The higher the interest rate, the more such an expansion will cost in the long run. If the interest goes up, more future revenue must go toward paying off the debt.

Intellectual Market

The purpose of the analysis is to determine whether the social contract implicit in the First Amendment is being met by news organizations. As mentioned, this market is served by information acquired through the information market and even through advertising. However, some news organizations, especially newspapers, have sections that are designed specifically to address public policy issues. These are the editorial and op-ed pages.

The analysis of the intellectual market involves four questions. These questions are not exhaustive, but they will help managers explore how well their companies are serving this market.

1. *How much of the content carried in our commodity deals with the context surrounding issues and events?* Traditionally, news media have concentrated on events, often of a fast-breaking nature. The needs of a complex society extend beyond this type of coverage. Just as important is why and how events unfold and issues develop in society. This is the context that is

needed for individuals to have informed opinions about policy issues.

The percentage of content developed to context is one way of answering this question. But the amount of content alone will not answer this question. A standard for adequate performance would be useful because no optimum standard exists.

2. *How balanced is content concerning controversial issues?* News organizations usually assume a responsibility to present several sides to a controversy. This approach lies behind the development of op-ed pages, which carry opinions that contrast with those expressed in the newspaper's editorials.

In most markets, adequate performance in the intellectual market requires diversity of opinion in the editorial and op-ed pages. News coverage also should be balanced. This is determined by examining content related to important issues across time.

3. *How well are events and issues covered across time?* One criticism of news organizations is that they tend to be erratic in coverage. A great deal of time and space will be spent on topics that grab attention, but these topics fade from attention after a few weeks. This tendency results in sensational stories dominating news, whereas more complex and subtle stories are neglected. Serving the intellectual market requires a news organization to be aware of the long time frame associated with some important issues and trends.

4. *Do our goals include serving the intellectual market?* If a news organization does not address this market explicitly in its statement of goals, it probably is not serving the intellectual market well. Goals are the basis for decisions. If no goals exist concerning this market, few decisions will address issues associated with meeting demand.

News media managers may be aware of these types of goals, but it is easy to neglect them in the everyday operation of a news organization. Explicit goals will help managers avoid overlooking the types of behavior that underlie the special treatment of their organizations by society.

SUMMARY

The analysis of a market is part science and part art. Quantitative research is crucial to analyzing markets, but measurement problems limit the accuracy of some research. Managers need to be able to identify the limits of particular research and be able to fill in holes in that research with their own judgment and experience.

Market analysis plays two important roles. First, it allows for better day-to-day decisions. You make better decisions about where to go when you know where you are. Second, market analysis is the central part of long-term strategic planning. Going back to the decision wheel presented in chapter 1, market analysis is part of that wheel's hub. This analysis provides information basic to decisions within the organization.

The analysis of the information and advertising markets addresses four areas: market structure, organizational goals, nature of demand, and the economic environment. The analysis of the intellectual market deals with the way news media organizations fulfill their responsibility to members of the society in which they operate.

CHAPTER 6 CASES

Case 6.1

Assignment: Determining Radio Market Structure

The purpose of this case is to analyze the structure of radio markets. The idea is to select the five largest radio markets in your state. Your analysis of the structure of these markets should determine the best market in which to buy a station. The analysis should cover the past 5 years.

Data for this case can be found in several locations. (See the section entitled Broadcast Research Sources in chapter 8 and the radio formats listed in Case 8.5.) Using these resources in your library answer the following questions:

Market Concentration

1. Which of the five markets is most concentrated, based on the Herfindahl-Hirschman Index?
2. Has the concentration increased or decreased during the past 5 years?
3. Which of the five markets has the smallest competition index between the top two stations in the market?

Listener Demand

1. What has been the trend in total listenership during the past 5 years?
2. Has a particular format dominated the market during the past 5 years?
3. Are any of the formats present in some markets but missing from the other markets?
4. What are the population and listener trends among ages 18 to 25 years during the past 5 years?
5. What are the population and listener trends among ages 25 to 35 years during the past 5 years?

6. What are the population and listener trends among ages 35 to 45 years during the past 5 years?
7. What is the unemployment trends in these five markets during the past 5 years?

Based on your findings, rank the markets in order of preferred location to buy a radio station. Explain why you ranked the markets in the order you did. What format would you pick for a radio station in the top-ranked market? Why?

Case 6.2

The Case of Examining a Local Television News Market

You are the news director at WWWB, which has 165,000 households in its area of dominant influence (ADI). Of these households, 95% have television, 50% have multiple television sets, 57% are cable subscribers, and 60% have VCRs. The metro area, which is part of the ADI, has 110,000 households with the same percentages for multiple TV sets, cable penetration, and VCR penetration.

Your station is an ABC affiliate. WBBB is the NBC affiliate and WPPR is the CBS affiliate. The market has one independent station, WXZX. The cable system carries a Public Broadcast Station, one commercial station from a large metro area 100 miles away (WERE), three super stations, two specialized channels, and three premium channels.

All of the network affiliates and the distant metro station have local newscasts at 6 pm. The winter ratings period just ended. The average weekly ratings and shares for the 6 pm time slot for the past four ratings periods were:

| | Shares | | | |
	Spring	Summer	Autumn	Winter
WWWB	20	22	22	25
WBBB	45	45	43	43
WPPR	6	6	7	8
WXZX	8	7	7	4
WERE	4	4	3	3
All other uses & stations	17	16	18	17
	Ratings			
WWWB	10	11	12	13
WBBB	23	22	23	23
WPPR	3	3	4	4
WXZX	4	3	4	2
WERE	2	2	2	2
All other uses & stations	9	8	10	9

Each of the newscasts lasts 22 min. The geographic breakdown of numbers of stories for news and sports for the three local evening newscasts for the four periods were:

	Spring	Summer	Autumn	Winter
WWWB				
ADI	10	11	12	13
State	3	2	2	2
National	3	3	3	2
International	3	2	1	1
WBBB				
ADI	11	10	10	10
State	2	4	4	3
National	3	3	3	4
International	3	2	3	3
WPPR	Spring	Summer	Autumn	Winter
ADI	8	7	7	8
State	3	3	4	3
National	5	5	4	4
International	3	4	4	4

The following table gives the stories by the type of presentation for the four periods:

	Spring	Summer	Autumn	Winter
WWWB				
Anchor read with no video	9	8	7	6
Anchor read with video	6	6	5	6
Reporter package with video and reporter taped before newscast	4	5	6	6
WBBB				
Anchor read with no video	9	10	9	10
Anchor read with video	5	5	6	5
Reporter package	5	4	5	5
WPPR				
Anchor read with no video	10	11	10	11
Anchor read with video	6	4	6	5
Reporter package	3	4	3	3

Assignment

Using the data given in the previous tables, answer the following questions:

1. What is the nature of your product?
2. How has that product changed across the four periods?
3. How does your product compare to those of your competitors?
4. Has the demand for your newscast increased or decreased during the four periods? By how much?
5. What reason for the change in demand is suggested by these data?
6. If you wanted to continue the trend, what would you suggest for the content of the newscast? Why?

Case 6.3

Assignment: Assessing Quality of Newspaper Content

Media commodities can be evaluated in several ways. One approach is to determine if a newspaper has "quality" content. However, quality is a term that has different meanings to different people. Some research indicates that a newspaper with high standards of journalism attracts readers. The problem is developing accurate measures of quality. Leo Bogart published the results of a survey of editors as to what makes a good newspaper in his book *Press and Public*. The top 10 characteristics are listed below. The purpose of this assignment is to evaluate the content of newspapers as to quality of the news product.

Using these characteristics, take two newspapers of equivalent circulation size and analyze the content. Which of the newspapers has the best quality based on the survey results? Did the newspaper that was more consistent with the editors' standards also have the best penetration in its market? If yes, what does this suggest about analyzing newspaper content as a manager? If no, what other factors might affect penetration and what implications does this have for newspaper editors?

Characteristics	Editors' Rank
High ratio of staff-written to wire and feature service copy	1
Total amount of nonadvertising content	2
High ratio of news interpretations & backgrounders to spot news reports	3
Number of letters to the editor per issue	4
Diversity of political columnists	5

Characteristics	Editors' Rank
High "readability" on Flesch or similar scoring systems	6
High ratio of illustration to text	7
High ratio of nonadvertising content to advertising	8
High ratio of news to features	9
Number of staff-by-lined features	10

This survey included 746 editors and was taken in 1977. From *Press and Public* (2nd ed., pp. 253-265) by Leo Bogart, 1989, Hillsdale, NJ: Lawrence Erlbaum Associates.

Case 6.4

The Case of Starting a City Magazine

You have been hired as a consultant for a corporation that produces magazines–Caine's Publications. This corporation currently has business magazines in 10 large cities across the United States. It also publishes several other special interest magazines. Management plans to enter the field of city magazines. However, the company wants to begin in one city before expanding into others. For reasons involving costs, Caine's will start a city magazine in one of the following three markets: Denver, Pittsburgh, or the Tampa-St. Petersburg area. You have been hired to analyze the markets in these three metropolitan areas.

Plans call for the monthly magazine to be a general-circulation magazine primarily carrying articles about cultural, social, and entertainment activities in the metropolitan area. However, it also will carry some in-depth articles about local government and business. The magazine will be aimed at the entire metropolitan area and not just the central city.

The audience will be primarily middle- to upper-income households. These are the people with discretionary income to spend on social and cultural activities. The advertising market will be those companies that attract these types of people.

The competitive environments for these markets are as follows:

Denver has two separately owned and operated general circulation daily newspapers. The suburbs have an extensive newspaper market, with about two dozen weeklies, most of which are group owned. The Denver market has nine television stations and 33 radio stations.

Each of the three central cities in the *Tampa-St. Petersburg-Clearwater* metro area has a daily general circulation newspaper. About a dozen weekly newspapers can be found in the smaller cities and towns in this area. The metropolitan area also has eight television stations and 31 radio stations.

Pittsburgh has two newspapers that have a joint operating agreement. This allows the combination of the business, circulation, advertising, and production departments of the two newspapers under the Newspaper Preservation Act. However, the two editorial departments must remain separate. There are about 18 weekly newspapers in the metropolitan area. The Pittsburgh area has six television stations and 33 radio stations.

Each of these markets also has one monthly magazine. In *Denver*, the magazine is called *Denver Today*. It has been in existence for about 4 years and is owned by a family that has no other media interest in the area, although the company owns 10 small daily newspapers throughout the Mountain region of the country. The magazine contains cultural and entertainment information with an emphasis on feature articles about people in these areas. Additional material includes articles about the Denver art scene, the local symphony orchestra, local theater productions, and movies. It is a slick monthly that averages 40 pages and uses a moderate amount of color and graphics. It carries about 10 pages of advertising. It is rumored to be have lost about $250,000 last year. Paid circulation was about 25,000 last year.

The Tampa area monthly is called *Florida West* and is in its second year of existence. It is a news-oriented magazine with long stories about business, government, and other organizations in the Tampa Bay area. It tends to have aggressive reporting, especially about business. It averages about 36 pages a month, of which 20% are in advertising. It carries some entertainment and cultural information, but these tend to be short reviews and reports that account for about 10% of the news space. The first-year losses were well over $1 million, but this included the start-up cost. The magazine has been praised by media critics in the local newspapers and has a circulation of about 20,000. The magazine is owned by a company with similar successful magazines in Los Angeles and Phoenix. The company also has several national specialty magazines.

Pittsburgh has a magazine entitled *Pittsburgh*. It is only in its 6th month of operation and is owned by a company that also owns a local network affiliated television station. The magazine emphasizes entertainment and contains a great deal of graphics and color. It averages about 32 pages a month and always has a long piece about a local figure connected to the entertainment world. The remaining articles tend to be short, much like the articles in *USA Today*. Its paid circulation is about 15,000. It has an average of 10 pages of advertising a month, with the majority of ads coming from television, movies, and book companies. No figures are available about profits.

Assignment

Despite the presence of an existing magazine, these three cities have costs savings related to production facilities and none of the existing magazines is well established. These markets are the most favorable for starting a city magazine. Your job is to use the aforementioned information, the attached data from secondary sources (Tables 6.4–6.9), and the focus-group data collected by Caine's to suggest which market would be best for starting a city magazine. Explain the basis for your recommendation, including a discussion of market demographics, the validity of research conducted by

TABLE 6.4
Retail Sales Data for Tampa/St. Petersburg, Denver, and Pittsburgh Metro Areas

	Tampa/St. Pete	*Denver*	*Pittsburgh*
Year 1: Total Retail Sales	11,750	10,936	11,891
Year 2: Total Retail Sales	14,910	14,327	13,525
Year 1: Lumber/Hardware Sales	489	518	449
Year 2: Lumber/Hardware Sales	841	880	634
Year 1: General Merchandise Sales	1,582	1,493	1,851
Year 2: General Merchandise Sales	1,734	1,526	1,982
Year 1: Food Sales	2,918	2,279	2,700
Year 2: Food Sales	3,302	2,783	2,817
Year 1: Auto Sales	2,129	2,149	2,286
Year 2: Auto Sales	3,765	3,641	3,114
Year 1: Gasoline Sales	963	805	1,051
Year 2: Gasoline Sales	862	811	793
Year 1: Apparel Sales	383	482	512
Year 2: Apparel Sales	533	676	673
Year 1: Furniture Sales	477	507	479
Year 2: Furniture Sales	900	921	652
Year 1: Eating and Drinking	1,335	1,296	1,149
Year 2: Eating and Drinking	1,557	1,622	1,297
Year 1: Drugs	411	287	377
Year 2: Drugs	496	290	452

Note. Figure are in millions of dollars. The data are from *Editor & Publisher Market Guide*, 1984/1988, New York: Author. Copyright 1984. Adapted by permission.

TABLE 6.5

Income, Household and Farm Product Data for Tampa/St. Petersburg, Denver, and Pittsburgh Metro Areas

	Tampa/St. Pete	Denver	Pittsburgh
Year 1: Population	1,623,781	1,434,304	2,218,645
Year 2: Population	2,014,319	1,739,385	2,198,649
Change in Population Year 1 to Year 2	24.1%	21.3%	−0.9%
Year 1: Number of Households	749,244	595,881	839,647
Year 2: Number of Households	837,308	690,096	842,377
Year 1: Estimated Disposable Personal Income	13,436,745 (Thousands)	13,434,752 (Thousands)	20,195,981 (Thousands)
Year 2: Estimated Disposable Personal Income	28,033,994 (Thousands)	26,722,404 (Thousands)	31,096,000 (Thousands)
Year 1: Income Per Capita	10,070	12,681	10,955
Year 2: Income Per Capita	13,917	15,363	14,143
Year 1: Income Per Household	24,172	32,880	29,211
Year 2: Income Per Household	33,481	38,723	36,915
Year 1: Number of Farms	4,302	1,830	4,366
Year 2: Number of Farms	4,505	1,976	4,378
Year 1: Value of Crops	131,857 (Thousands)	55,995 (Thousands)	23,334 (Thousands)
Year 2: Value of Crops	175,215 (Thousands)	71,286 (Thousands)	26,908 (Thousands)
Year 1: Value of Livestock	92,103 (Thousands)	48,738 (Thousands)	35,365 (Thousands)
Year 2: Value of Livestock	164,164 (Thousands)	70,758 (Thousands)	56,537 (Thousands)

Note. The data are from *Editor & Publisher Market Guide*, 1984/1988, New York: Author. Copyright 1984. Adapted by permission.

Caine's, and an analysis of the extent and nature of competition in the market. Feel free to recommend further action by Caine's to determine the best market for starting a city magazine.

Focus Groups

Caine's hired a researcher to conduct focus groups in the three cities. They ran an add in the local dailies asking for people who were interested in entertainment and the arts to volunteer for research about their reading habits. Caine's was trying to keep their intentions a secret. In each city, the research had five focus groups of 10 people each. The following data were collected for the three markets:

TABLE 6.6

Retail Sales Data per Household for Tampa/St. Petersburg, Denver, and Pittsburgh Metro Areas

	Tampa/St. Pete	Denver	Pittsburgh
Year 1: Total Retail Sales	18.40	22.30	15.20
Year 2: Total Retail Sales	17.80	20.80	16.10
Year 1: Lumber/Hardware Sales	.65	.87	.53
Year 2: Lumber/Hardware Sales	1.00	1.28	.75
Year 1: General Merchandise Sales	2.11	2.50	2.20
Year 2: General Merchandise Sales	2.07	2.21	2.35
Year 1: Food Sales	3.89	3.82	3.22
Year 2: Food Sales	3.94	4.03	3.34
Year 1: Auto Sales	2.84	3.61	2.72
Year 2: Auto Sales	4.50	5.28	3.70
Year 1: Gasoline Sales	1.30	1.35	1.25
Year 2: Gasoline Sales	1.03	1.18	.94
Year 1: Apparel Sales	.51	.81	.61
Year 2: Apparel Sales	.64	.98	.80
Year 1: Furniture Sales	.64	.85	.57
Year 2: Furniture Sales	1.07	1.33	.77
Year 1: Eating and Drinking	1.78	2.17	1.37
Year 2: Eating and Drinking	1.86	2.35	1.53
Year 1: Drugs	.55	.48	.44
Year 2: Drugs	.59	.42	.53

Note. The figures are in thousands of dollars and are based on data from *Editor & Publisher Market Guide*, 1984/1988, New York: Author. Copyright 1984. Adapted by permission.

1. Would you like to have a monthly magazine about entertainment and the arts in your city?

Denver		Tampa/St. Pete		Pittsburgh	
yes	no	yes	no	yes	no
92%	8%	96%	4%	90%	10%

2. What sort of stories would you like to see in the magazine? Following are percentages that said yes.

	Denver	Tampa/St. Pete	Pittsburgh
Live theater	25%	20%	35%
Movie & Stars	45%	50%	40%
Orchestra	33%	35%	40%
Art Galleries	37%	45%	33%
Opera	15%	18%	24%
Museums	11%	15%	20%
Craft Shows	20%	21%	14%
Other	70%	60%	49%

3. What is your average household income?

Denver	Tampa/St. Pete	Pittsburgh
$69,500	$54,000	$42,000

TABLE 6.7

Percentage Change in Retail Sales per Household for Tampa/St. Petersburg, Denver, and Pittsburgh Metro Areas

	Tampa/St. Pete	Denver	Pittsburgh
Year 1: Total Retail Sales			
Year 2: Total Retail Sales	−3.3	−6.7	+5.8
Year 1: Lumber/Hardware Sales			
Year 2: Lumber/Hardware Sales	+53.0	+47.0	+42.0
Year 1: General Merchandise Sales			
Year 2: General Merchandise Sales	−1.8	−11.6	+6.8
Year 1: Food Sales			
Year 2: Food Sales	+1.3	+5.5	+3.7
Year 1: Auto Sales			
Year 2: Auto Sales	+58.0	+46.0	+36.0
Year 1: Gasoline Sales			
Year 2: Gasoline Sales	−21.0	+1.3	−25.0
Year 1: Apparel Sales			
Year 2: Apparel Sales	+25.0	+21.0	+31.0
Year 1: Furniture Sales			
Year 2: Furniture Sales	+67.0	+56.0	+35.0
Year 1: Eating and Drinking			
Year 2: Eating and Drinking	+4.5	+8.2	+11.7
Year 1: Drugs			
Year 2: Drugs	+7.3	+1.0	+20.0

Note. The numbers are based on data from *Editor & Publisher Market Guide,* 1984/1988, New York: Author. Copyright 1984. Adapted by permission.

TABLE 6.8

Percentage Change in Retail Sales for Tampa/St. Petersburg, Denver, and Pittsburgh Metro Areas

	Tampa/St. Pete	Denver	Pittsburgh
Year 1: Total Retail Sales			
Year 2: Total Retail Sales	+7.8	+7.9	+6.2
Year 1: Lumber/Hardware Sales			
Year 2: Lumber/Hardware Sales	+72.0	+70.0	+41.0
Year 1: General Merchandise Sales			
Year 2: General Merchandise Sales	+9.6	+2.2	+7.0
Year 1: Food Sales			
Year 2: Food Sales	+13.2	+22.0	+4.3
Year 1: Auto Sales			
Year 2: Auto Sales	+77.0	+69.0	+36.0
Year 1: Gasoline Sales			
Year 2: Gasoline Sales	−10.0	+1.0	−25.0
Year 1: Apparel Sales			
Year 2: Apparel Sales	+29.0	+40.0	+31.0
Year 1: Furniture Sales			
Year 2: Furniture Sales	+89.0	+82.0	+36.0
Year 1: Eating and Drinking			
Year 2: Eating and Drinking	+17.0	+25.0	+13.0
Year 1: Drugs			
Year 2: Drugs	+21.0	+1.0	+20.0

Note. The numbers are based on data from *Editor & Publisher Market Guide,* 1984/1988, New York: Author. Copyright 1984. Adapted by permission.

TABLE 6.9
Additional Demographic Data about Tampa/St. Petersburg, Denver, and Pittsburgh

| | Age Distribution Year 2 | | |
	Tampa/St. Pete	Denver	Pittsburgh
Under 5 year	5.2%	7.4%	5.8%
5–17 years	17.1	20.5	19.1
18–24 years	10.6	14.2	12.2
25–44 years	23.4	34.9	25.6
45–64 years	22.2	14.2	23.9
More than 65 years	21.5	8.8	13.4
Median Age	38.6	28.9	33.4

| | Education Attainment and Unemployment | | |
	Tampa/St. Pete	Denver	Pittsburgh
Percentage that finished 12 years or more of school (Year 2)	65.5	80.5	67.3
Percentage that finished 16 years or more of school (Year 2)	13.4	24.6	14.1
Percentage of work force unemployed in Year 2	5.2	4.7	11.6

Note.   Data are from U.S. Bureau of Census documents.

Case 6.5

The Case of Analyzing a Suburban Newspaper Market

Molly McLane has always liked a challenge, but the new one she has is as big a problem as she ever will want to face. Her latest assignment from Howard-Slipps Newspaper Corp. is to take six weekly newspapers in the suburbs around Detroit and make them into a viable group that can compete in a media-rich environment.

Howard-Slipps is a well-established group of about 30 daily newspapers and six television stations. This project will be their first expansion into the weekly newspaper industry. Howard-Slipps just acquired six independent weeklies in six Detroit suburbs, all within Oakland County. The cities in which the weeklies are located are: Pontiac, Southfield, Troy, Novi, West Bloomfield and Birmingham. The Detroit metropolitan area includes three counties: Oakland, which is north and northwest of Detroit; McComb, which is north of Detroit; and Wayne, which includes Detroit and other suburbs.

McLane has worked for Howard-Slipps for 7 years. For 6 years she was publisher of a medium-size daily in Ohio. About a year ago, she was appointed head of the Nondaily Division of Howard-Slipps. She came to Howard-Slipps from a job as publisher of a group of 14 weeklies in Ohio. Her assignment as head of the NonDaily Division is to develop a long-term strategy for acquiring Midwest weekly newspapers, primarily in metropolitan areas. As part of this plan, Howard-Slipps has decided to buy existing independent newspapers rather than start new newspapers or buy existing groups. The cost of starting new newspapers or of buying existing groups is seen as being higher than buying independents and reshaping them into competitive groups in the information and the advertising markets.

The Detroit area has been selected by McLane as the test market for three reasons:

1. Many advertisers in the Detroit metropolitan area still hold bad feelings toward the metro dailies, *The Detroit News* and the *Detroit Free Press*, about the big increase in advertising prices following the creation of a joint operating agreement between the two newspapers in 1990.

2. The main competition for the newspapers in the area is a group of 11 twice-weekly newspapers called the Times & Sentinel Newspapers. McLane thinks these newspapers are not doing an adequate job serving the readers.

3. The six independent newspapers were available at good prices.

The exact strategy for the Detroit suburban market is now being formulated. McLane has put together a task force to examine the markets and come up with a plan. You have been hired as a consultant to analyze the market based on the following data.

Market Data

The 11 Times & Sentinel (T & S) newspapers are published on Wednesdays and Sundays. Six of these newspapers are located in the cities where Howard-Slipps has bought newspapers. In all six cases, the T & S newspapers have a circulation lead over the Howard-Slipps papers. Three of the T & S newspapers are located in McComb County and the other three in western suburbs of Wayne County, where the printing plant and corporate headquarters are located.

The T & S papers are the only other newspapers with editorial offices in the six cities in which Howard-Slipps has newspapers. The two Detroit dailies have Oakland County bureaus that serve these cities. The cities also are served by a total market coverage shopper that covers all of Oakland County. The T & S newspaper sell at the newsstand for 50¢ a copy ($1 a week) or for 75¢ a week for home delivery.

The six T & S newspapers average about 36 pages per edition, of which

17 pages are news hole. The following are average percentages of the news-editorial pages in T & S newspapers filled with the various types of news about the hometown suburb:

Hometown government	6.5%
Hometown law enforcement	1.8%
Hometown sports	6.0%
Hometown business	1.0%
Hometown societal news	14.4%
Editorials about the hometown	3.3%
Total hometown copy	33.0%

Of the remaining 67% of the news hole, 35% is about other suburbs in Oakland County, which is taken from the other T & S newspapers, 10% is about the county in general, 10% is about other happenings in the Detroit three-county area, and 12% involves information about events outside the Detroit metropolitan area or information that has no geographic emphasis, such as syndicated material. Of this 67% 3.5 percentage points are nonhometown editorials and opinion pieces.

The variations in percentages among cities is only slight. The T & S newspapers draw from each other extensively. The T & S newspapers have three news-editorial offices. One is at the printing facility in Pontiac. It contains the news staffs for Pontiac and West Bloomfield papers. The office at Southfield houses the staffs for Southfield and Novi, whereas the office in Troy contains the news-editorial staff for Troy and Birmingham.

The number of households in each city and the circulation of the T & S newspaper in that city are:

City	Households	T & S Circulation
Pontiac	30,769	15,922
Southfield	27,963	13,175
Troy	26,075	14,645
Novi	11,428	5,999
West Bloomfield	51,111	23,599
Birmingham	9,258	5,396
Total	156,604	78,736

The circulation of the other six T & S newspapers equals 32,921 for a total of 111,657 circulation for the entire group.

The penetration of the morning *Detroit Free Press* in Oakland County is 36%, whereas the circulation of *The Detroit News*, which is the afternoon newspaper, is 29%.

The six suburbs fall into two types. Pontiac, West Bloomfield, and Troy include a relatively large amount of business and/or industry. Each has a distinct downtown shopping area. Southfield, Birmingham, and Novi are primarily commuter cities with the residents working in other parts of the metro area. The shopping areas for these three cities are located primarily in malls within the city limits.

All six cities have fairly high average incomes and education levels. With a few exceptions, most of the neighborhoods would be classified as middle to upper middle income. The exceptions include some very wealthy and lower middle-income neighborhoods.

Assignment

Using the aforementioned data and the concepts in this chapter answer the following questions:

1. How would you describe the geographic market for the T & S newspapers you will compete against?
2. How should Howard-Slipps set up its geographic markets?
3. What should be the nature of the Howard-Slipps newspaper commodities in the Detroit Market? Why?
4. How will this commodity compare with those of the T & S group?
5. How well is the T & S group serving the intellectual market?
6. How can the Howard-Slipps newspapers serve the readers better than the T & S newspapers?

7
Planning

If a manager wants to make effective decisions, she must plan. If a manager wants to plan adequately, he must make effective decisions. This chicken and egg relationship between decision making and planning is illustrated by the closeness of the processes. In many ways, the decision wheel presented in chapter 1 easily could be retitled a planning wheel. Many of the steps are basically the same.

Despite the similarities, planning and decision making do differ, although these differences tend to be more practical than theoretical. Before these differences are explored, a working definition of planning might help. Cass (1978) said, "a plan is a statement by a person that he intends to do a certain thing by a certain means. Planning is the process by which he develops that statement" (p. 250).

The planning process differs from the decision-making process in its concreteness. Although the decision wheel can be applied to most any decision, business planning takes three forms: (a) strategic planning, (b) intermediate planning, and (c) short-run planning (Fink, 1988; Kreitner, 1986). *Strategic planning* involves allocating resources to achieve the long-run goals of an organization. These plans cover anywhere from 1 to 10 years, but they usually are developed for a 3- to 5-year period. *Intermediate planning* usually covers 6 months to 2 years and serves as a contributing process to strategic plans. This process determines how organizational departments contribute to the strategic goals of an organization. *Short-run planning* involves plans that cover a couple of weeks to a year. This process allocates resources on a day-to-day and month-to-month basis.

Figure 7.1 shows how the three plans fit together. The strategic plan is the overall plan for fulfilling the firm's missions and obtaining the general goals. The intermediate plan involves the general way in which the strategic plan will be pursued, and the short-run plan is how the strategic plan will work on a day-to-day basis.

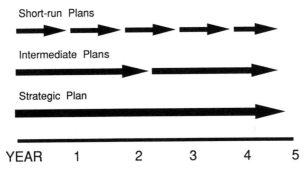

FIG. 7.1. Relationship among strategic, intermediate, and short-run planning.

Planning is much like taking a long trip by car. The goal is to reach the destination. A route is drawn on a map and estimates are made of the time and money the trip will require. This is a strategic plan. As part of the plan, cities and towns are selected where the traveler will sleep, based on how much driving per day seems reasonable. Motels are chosen and reservations are made on the basis of cost and convenience. These are the intermediate plans. Each day of the trip, certain decisions have to be made, such as where to eat and buy gasoline. This involves short-run planning. The daily plan is flexible because unanticipated problems always arise. For example, the traveler will plan on stopping at certain service stations based on the types of credit cards she has. If those stations are not available when needed, other stations will do. As with all plans, how well the trip goes depends on the planning. Poor planning can cause the traveler to reach the destination late and at a higher expense than she would have liked.

COMMON CHARACTERISTICS OF PLANNING

All three types of planning have common characteristics even though the time period to which they apply, who plans, and actual steps vary. The common characteristics fall into four categories: (a) goals, (b) preparation, (c) tools for planning, and (d) the plan.

As Cass' (1978) definition points out, all plans aim at accomplishing certain things. These things are *goals*. Organizations have three types of goals. *General organizational goals* are fairly abstract statements of what a firm hopes to achieve within given areas of performance. These goals are derived from the organization's mission. Smith, Arnold, and Bizzell (1985) defined an organization's mission as its business domain. It often will include statements about the firm's role outside its primary business markets. For example, a newspaper's mission might be to provide its readers with a complete and accurate report on the events and issues of concern to its community. The goals associated with this might include:

1. Cover all important issues confronting civic organizations, such as the city council, police and fire departments, and school board.
2. Cover noncivic issues that relate to individual reader's health and welfare.
3. Cover events and issues that relate to the community's culture and social background.
4. Cover recreational events that are of interest to members of the community.
5. Provide a forum for the exchange of information about goods and services available to members of the community.

The planning goals must match the mission of the organization because the mission reflects the expertise within that organization. It would make little sense for a television network news department to pursue a goal of developing an inexpensive but powerful personal computer.

The other two types of goals are related more specifically to the planning process. *Planning goals* are general goals associated with particular plans. These are general in that they have no specific measurement associated with them. For example, a plan aimed at viewership of a television newscast might have as its goals an increase in viewership among long-term residents of the community and an increase in viewership among those in the 30- to 40-year age group.

In order to measure these planning goals, an organization must have *operational goals*. These define the planning goals in terms that can be measured with research. For example, the goal of increasing viewership among long-term residents of the community could be operationalized as increasing ratings by 2 points during the next 6 months among audience members who have lived in the area of dominance influence (ADI) for more than 10 years. The operational definition must define in measurable terms the group to be affected (people who have lived in the ADI for more than 10 years), a time period during which the change is expected (next 6 months), and a measurable level of performance that is being sought (2 ratings points).

Just as the general goals follow from the mission of the organization, the planning goals must be consistent with the general goals. The role of the operational goals is to translate the planning goals into something that can be measured. Properly defining goals is the essence of good planning. Planning without well-defined goals is like starting a trip without a destination. The traveler may wind up somewhere she likes, but it will be by chance.

Managers should select goals that can be reached. Setting goals that cannot be reached guarantees a plan's failure and can have dire consequences for employee motivation. Frustration from trying to accomplish what cannot be done always will have a negative effect on a work force. Goals should be placed high enough that they require effort, but not so high that they cannot be achieved.

Every plan must involve preparation. This characteristic is analogous to the collecting and analyzing of information in the decision wheel presented in chapter 1. The better the preparation, the greater the chances of reaching the goals. A newspaper publisher who embarks on a plan to increase circulation will have little success unless she has some idea during the planning process why people do or do not read her newspaper.

Preparation is simply the collection of information about the goals and possible alternatives for achieving those goals. Preparing for the planning goals involves identifying the goals that fit with the mission of the organization and developing operational goals that can be achieved. Preparation also is crucial in defining the ways of achieving those goals. A goal may be obtainable, but without an adequate understanding of options, it may not be reached efficiently.

All planning has tools that can help develop an appropriate plan and be used for carrying out the plan. The *tools* are mechanisms for analysis, information collection, and monitoring that assist in developing and executing plans. The analysis tools discussed in chapter 1, financial documents discussed in chapter 9, and the market analysis discussed in chapter 6 are all tools that can be used for planning. Of course, knowing what tools are available for use in planning is not the same as knowing how to apply those tools. The application of tools is learned through experience, practice, and reflection.

Finally, all planning involves a plan, which is the tangible result of the process. This *plan*, as defined by Cass (1978), is the way that the goals will be achieved. It should be explicit and detailed. It should set forward the specific steps in achieving the goals and a time frame for carrying out these steps.

The probability that a plan will result in attaining its goals depends on the skills of the planner. The planning process, with its preparation and application of tools, must be understood by management if a workable plan is to be developed. The remainder of the chapter is aimed at increasing the understanding of the three types of planning.

STRATEGIC PLANNING

Strategic planning is the long-term process by which an organization pursues its mission and hopes to reach its goals. If a media organization participates in two or more of the three markets—information, advertising, and intellectual—the strategic plan must address explicitly these markets and explain the relationship among them. A television station cannot make plans for the advertising market without including the information market where they will attract viewers. A newspaper cannot plan for the information market without examining the role it will play in the intellectual market. All strategic plans should be divided into sections based on these markets.

Writers have proposed various models for planning. Schoell and Guiltinan (1990) said strategic planning has four steps: situation analysis, organization mission, organization objectives, and organization strategies. Cass (1978) said planning takes six steps:

1. Decide in general terms what you want to accomplish.
2. Take a look at what you have to work with.
3. Determine what will happen if no exceptional action is taken.
4. Decide very specifically what you want to accomplish.
5. Figure out very specifically how you can get these planned results.
6. Follow up with an effective program of reporting and analysis of performance.

Smith et al. (1985) used the term *strategic management* in lieu of strategic planning because the traditional concept of strategic planning did not include control of the plan as it was implemented. They said strategic management has six steps and a feedback loop. The steps are: (a) analyze the environment, (b) determine objectives, (c) analyze strategic alternatives, (d) select strategy alternatives, (e) implement the strategies, and (f) evaluate and control performance.

Combining these approaches with the decision wheel in chapter 1 and adding control to planning results in eight steps of strategic planning:

1. Examine the business environment and past performance.
2. Evaluate available resources.
3. Identify, select, prioritize, and operationalize planning goals.
4. Identify alternative approaches for obtaining goals.
5. Select from among the alternative approaches.
6. Implement the plan.
7. Monitor implementation.
8. Evaluate plan's progress and adjust the plan.

As with decision making, the collection and analysis of information is a part of all eight steps in strategic planning. The process is shown in Fig. 7.2

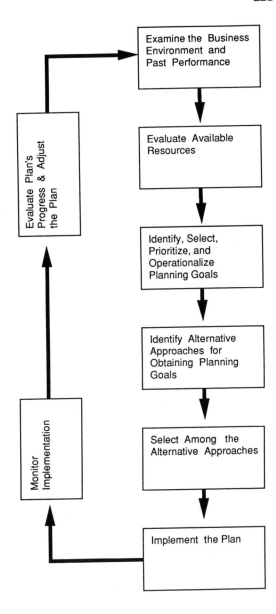

FIG. 7.2. Steps in strategic planning.

Examine the Business Environment and Past Performance

Plans for the future must be grounded in experience and an understanding of current market conditions. This starting point for strategic plans involves looking both inside and outside the organization. The market analysis is the primary method of evaluating the business environment. This analysis will allow management a basis for estimating the impact of external factors on accomplishing the plan. A strategic plan that starts without a thorough market analysis will fail more often than not.

The internal examination involves how well the firm accomplished its goals in the past and why. Failure to reach goals could have resulted from any number of problems inside the firm, including inappropriate goals, goals set to high, poor analysis of data, inadequate resources, and poor performance.

Both types of problems, internal and external, can be classified in two ways. First, the problems could have been foreseeable or unforeseeable. A foreseeable problem means that the planning system failed to work properly. An unforeseeable problem that interferes with achieving planning goals comes from a change that could not have been predicted. Second, the problems could have been controllable or uncontrollable. A controllable problem could have been corrected if it had been detected. An uncontrollable problem could not have been corrected even if it was known.

These two dimensions of problems are shown in Table 7.1, along with examples of the types of problems they represent. A foreseeable problem that could have been controlled would be a lack of adequate market analysis before adopting the last strategic plan. If this was a problem, it was because of a management failure. It should not have occurred. A foreseeable problem that could not have been controlled would be how far a current recession extends into the future. Management knows a recession will affect their plans, but there is nothing they can do except develop contingency plans. An unforeseeable problem that could not have been controlled would be the surprise closing of a large business in a community. In these situations, managers can react only to the problem. An

TABLE 7.1
Dimensions of Management Problems

	Foreseeable	Unforseeable
Controllable	Poor analysis Incomplete planning Inadequate research Unskilled employees	Changes in group dynamics Inadequate inventories due to underestimated demand Employee changes
Uncontrollable	Increased in costs of raw materials Extension of economic recession Retirement of top executives	Some changes in regulations New economic recessions Natural disasters

unforeseeable problem that could be controlled would be changes in personnel.

Because of the inherent uncertainty in planning, managers prefer to have problems they can foresee and control, but that does not always happen. Yet, many problems are not foreseen because of poor planning. Many problems, especially ones in the business environment, cannot be controlled. But if they are foreseen, alternative strategies can be developed to lessen the impact.

It is important to evaluate the environment and past performance and to identify which types of problems arose. In doing so, managers can anticipate better these types of problems in the next plan and can evaluate better whether their planning and operational goals are appropriate.

Evaluate Available Resources

In order to make sure the planning goals can be obtained and the strategies for reaching the goals can be pursued, a manager must evaluate available resources. The types of resources at hand include human resources, plant and equipment, and financial resources. *At hand* means the resources either are held currently by the firm or can be borrowed easily. Thus, financial resources include an organization's credit.

In mass media organizations, human resources are crucial because they create the commodity that attracts the audience that is sold to advertisers. The quality of the commodity is important, and that quality depends on the people who produce the commodity.

Although resources take three forms, interchangeability is possible among these forms. If a magazine does not have the writers and editors necessary to prepare the content, it can try to hire writers and editors using financial resources. If a newspaper needs more money, it can try to sell the information it generates in a subsidiary market, such as computer data bases.

Evaluating available resources is important because resources will determine whether a goal can be achieved, and although resources can be changed from one form to another, the process does not always occur as quickly as management would like. If a large metropolitan newspaper needs a top-notch columnist, she usually will come from another newspaper, and it can take a long time to woo a writer. The uncertainty of time necessitates good resource planning based on accurate evaluation.

As the strategic plan develops, an evaluation of available resources will tell the planner whether the resources needed to achieve the plan's goals are currently available in the form necessary. When the organization does not have the resources needed by the plan in the appropriate form, the plan must include the ways of getting or converting these resources. If the needed resources are not and cannot be made available, then the goals associated with those resources should be reconsidered or not pursued.

Identify, Select, Prioritize, and Operationalize Planning Goals

This step actually begins the planning process, but it must be based on the first two steps. *Identify* the planning goals means listing the goals that the firm might pursue. *Select* means choosing the ones from this list that can be reached. In media organizations, it is important that goals be identified within all three markets—information, advertising, and intellectual.

No guidelines exist for how many goals a firm needs to identify or select, but all of the selected goals should be obtainable and consistent with the general goals and mission of the firm. The more goals an organization pursues, the greater the probability that all of them will not be reached. Each goal requires resources, which are relatively fixed. The more goals a firm pursues, the more competition will exist within the organization for resources. For example, a smaller Ohio newspaper group might select the following goals:

1. Add daily newspapers until the group has papers in markets that make up 20% of the circulation in Ohio (Information market goal).
2. Increase significantly the penetration of existing markets (information market goal).
3. Increase revenue from national advertising (advertising market goal).
4. Increase the column inches of display advertising that are run in the paper (advertising market goal).
5. Increase the column inches and percentage of the news hole devoted to letters to the editor and guest columns (intellectual market goal).

The two goals listed for the information and advertising markets conceivably could compete for resources. The acquisition of newspapers will cost money, as will efforts to increase penetration. The penetration goal will involve additional spending for the circulation and news departments, as well as money for promoting the changes from the increased spending.

All five goals will consume resources and initially would compete. However, as the plan is placed into effect, the achievement of the goals will generate more revenue, which then can be put back into reaching the goals. Timing is important to consider because not all goals have to be reached at the same time. Some can be set for the second or third year of the plan, and some can be made contingent upon reaching others.

After identifying and selecting the goals, they need to be prioritized. Even though the plan has a manageable number of goals, there is no guarantee that they all will be reached. By listing the goals in order of importance, controlling the plan becomes easier. If the manager realizes that not all goals will be reached, efforts can be directed toward achieving the ones that are within reach.

The final part of this step is to operationalize the goals. This means defining a measurable goal and a time period during which this would be obtained. Goals 1 and 3 listed previously could be operationalized as follows:

Goal 1. The group will own daily newspapers that have 20% of all of the daily circulation within Ohio by the end of this 5-year plan.

Goal 3. The revenue gained from selling national advertising in the group's newspapers will increase by $500,000 during each of the 5 years covered by this plan.

Often management can operationalize a planning goal several ways. For example, the second goal listed earlier was to increase penetration significantly. Just what percentage increase in households taking the newspaper would be significant is up to management to decide based on Steps 1 and 2 of the planning process. Significant could mean 1 percentage point a year, or 2 percentage points in year 1 through 3 and 1 percentage point the last 2 years of the 5-year plan.

Identify Alternative Approaches for Obtaining Goals

Almost all long-term goals can be reached with more than one approach, and they often require multiple approaches. For example, a radio station that wants to increase its share of listeners can do so by altering its music format and promoting itself in a number of ways. The aim is to select the most efficient and effective way of reaching or surpassing the goals. The ability to select the "best" approach depends on this approach being recognized, which requires that the identification process be as exhaustive as possible. Often management settles for a less than optimal plan for achieving a goal because not all ideas were identified.

The process of identifying alternative approaches has three steps: (a) list all possible approaches, (b) eliminate the impractical and improbable, and (c) develop the probable approaches. What level of probability is acceptable is a function of several factors, including the amount of risk that management is comfortable with, the completeness of the information collection and analysis process, resources available to the firm, and the uncertainty of the environment.

The first step is a matter of creative thinking. Brainstorming is a commonly used technique for generating ideas. It accepts two basic principles of creative thinking techniques: A positive attitude is established, which means criticism is withheld until after ideas are developed; and unusual ideas are encouraged, even if they seem impractical (Whiting, 1955).

The second part of identifying approaches involves assessing the alternatives and eliminating the ones that are impractical or improbable for whatever reason. Improbability and impracticality can be based on any number of characteristics, including approaches with high risk, high environmental uncertainty, and high resource needs. The list of approaches should be pared to a manageable number of good alternatives for achieving the goals. This usually would range from three to six methods.

The number of approaches should be limited because the more alternatives that remain after Step 2, the more resources that must be expended on the next step, which is to develop the probable approaches. Development means creating rough preliminary plans for the approaches that might work. These plans should include: (a) operationalized goals for each department as well as the overall organization's operationalized goals; (b) the role of each department in placing the plan into effect; (c) the resources, both type and amount, needed by each department to achieve the goals; (d) a timetable for the plan, complete with intermediate goals by year for each department; (e) a statement of how this plan will interact with and react to the environment; and (f) probability estimates for obtaining needed resources, of environmental change occurring, and achieving expected results.

An example of generating approach ideas would be to take the goal of increasing penetration by 5 percentage points in 5 years. Because penetration is the percentage of households taking the newspaper, this means the newspaper must increase circulation at a rate higher than the growth in number of households. The areas that need to be addressed are the nature of content, quality of delivery, and promotion of newspaper. Changes in content could include adding more coverage in areas such as sports, neighborhood news, health care, business, or religion. Improving delivery could involve hiring older carriers, hiring more carriers, increasing pay for carriers, redesigning the distribution system for getting newspaper copies to carriers, changing the printing schedule, providing more incentives for carriers, or guaranteeing 1-hr delivery if a house is missed. Better promotion might include using more radio advertising, giving away 3-month subscriptions to new residents in the market, giving away prizes, using telemarketing, or using billboard advertising. All of the approaches and more could come from a brainstorming session and should be considered.

Selecting from the Alternative Approaches

Once preliminary plans are developed for the probable approaches identified in step 4, the one approach that will accomplish the goals best is selected. This selection process involves three steps: (a) Compare alternative approaches; (b) prioritize the approaches; and (c) further develop the top ranking approach.

The comparison of the alternative plans can be as formal or informal as management likes. Formal methods for comparison are those discussed in chapter 1 and include cost-benefit analysis, decision trees, and utility theory. From these comparisons, the methods can be listed by priority of effectiveness and efficiency, with the top-ranked method being the one selected. *Effectiveness* is the probability that the approaches will achieve the goals of the plan. *Efficiency* is the amount of resources needed to reach the given goal. The most efficient approach is the one that will achieve the goal with the least cost.

Managers should remember that it is not too late to rethink the approach at this stage. Managers might realize from the comparison that a combination of approaches would work best. This means coming up with a preliminary plan for the hybrid approach. This will require more time, but if the hybrid is the best approach, the time will be spent well.

Listing all the alternatives by priority is important because if the selected approach does not work properly a rejected method might be used. During a 5-year period, any number of changes can occur inside and outside the organization. The final step of the strategic planning process involves evaluating and adjusting the plan's progress. This adjustment is made easier if the alternative approaches have been prioritized.

The final part of the fifth step in strategic planning is to develop the top-ranked approach. The first requirement is to develop a more detailed strategic plan from the preliminary plan that ranked at the top of the priority list. This means adding enough detail to the plan that it can be implemented. Part of this detail is creating the first intermediate plan that goes into the strategic plan. The intermediate plan includes three types of plans: a marketing plan, a financial plan, and a human resources plan. These are detailed in the next section of the chapter.

Implementing the Strategic Plan

Implementing the strategic plan is a matter of following the steps it contains. Because a strategic plan involves several years, implementing also involves the implementation of intermediate plans and short-run plans. In effect, if the intermediate and short-run plans are drawn up and implemented properly, the strategic plan should reach its goals.

Success at this stage is related directly to the plan's quality. Failure at this stage can occur even if the plan was well developed because unforeseeable and uncontrollable problems do arise. It is the function of the next step to deal with such problems.

Two important aspects of the organization come into play in the implementation. First, the structure of the organization must be consistent with the plan; second, the communication system must allow the plan to be implemented. As discussed in chapter 2, structure affects communication. Because structure defines the authority and responsibility relationships in an organization, it also defines the formal communication network. The impact of structure and communication must be considered at the planning and implementation stages.

Monitor Implementation

Monitoring the implementation of a plan is a feedback mechanism that helps to control the entire process. Monitoring occurs primarily through intermediate and short-run plans. These are the data sources for checking the progress of the strategic plan against the goals. Part of the plan is establishing medium-range goals in the timetable that then serve as goals for the intermediate and short-run plans. These intermediate goals must be operationalized, in a form consistent with the data generated by the budget and the three types of intermediate plans. The monitoring step generates the data to be analyzed by people who are in positions to affect the strategic plan. The data then are used in the final step of the strategic planning process.

Evaluate Plan's Progress and Adjust the Plan

The data generated in the monitoring stage are used to evaluate how the plan is proceeding, whether adjustments are needed, and what types of adjustments will work. The test of a strategic plan is whether the intermediate and short-run plan goals are reached. If so, the plan is proceeding and few or no adjustments are needed. If the intermediate and short-range goals are not reached, then the plan must be adjusted.

The first question in making adjustments is: Why were intermediate and short-run goals not reached? This question is answered by examining past performance and the business environment. In effect the need for adjustment takes management back to the first step and the process becomes a loop. This examination can fall into the categories given in Table 7.1. Particular solutions will vary with the type of business and individual situations, but generally the following adjustments can be made:

1. If the problem was unforeseeable and uncontrollable, try to determine the probability that a similar event will occur during the reminder of the strategic plan and alter the plan accordingly. For example, if an unanticipated recession in advertising revenue will continue for another year and make it impossible to reach profit goals of the strategic plan, lower the goals.

2. If the problem was unforeseeable and controllable, make the appropriate adjustments in the marketing, financial, and human resources plans.

For example, a plan might involve hiring another camera crew to improve the local television newscast and increase ratings. If the one crew does not increase the quality of the newscast, management must determine whether the problem is with the particular crew members or with hiring only one crew.

3. If a problem was foreseeable and uncontrollable, it is difficult to handle. This could occur when some change in the economic environment is anticipated but the firm is powerless to do anything about it. Usually the firm will take this type of trend or event into consideration in planning, but such a problem sometimes can have a greater negative impact than anticipated. For example, an anticipated recession can be deeper than predicted. In such a case, the plan and goals must be adjusted to a greater degree than first was believed necessary.

4. A foreseeable and controllable problem that needs adjustment means the planning was not done properly. This often can occur through a miscalculation of probability or the extent of an event's impact. If a newspaper changes its format significantly, it can anticipate an initial negative reaction and compensate with promotions to help people accept the new format. When the negative reaction is underestimated or the promotions prove to be inadequate, the managers have a foreseeable and controllable problem. This type of problem is usually easier to fix because control is possible.

Adjustments can be made in many ways. The actual strategic plan may be changed in the cases of uncontrollable problems; the goals and/or steps can be altered. In cases where the firm exercises control, the intermediate and short-run plans are usually changed to try to achieve the existing long-run strategic goals.

The nature of the required changes will determine which steps of the strategic planning model in Fig. 7.1 must be repeated. The more extensive the needed overhaul of the plan, the more steps that need repeating. If the economy has entered a long-term recession, the goals and actual plan may need revising, which would include most of the steps. If a controllable problem within the organization is found, the process of adjustment might move from Step 1 to Step 4, where some of the other approaches are adapted to help correct the problems that have occurred. It is important to realize that strategic planning is not creating a plan every 5 years and then sitting back to watch. The plan should be adjusted as necessary. This adjustment procedure not only will help accomplish the goals of the plan being executed, but it will help management better prepare the next strategic plan.

INTERMEDIATE PLANNING

Intermediate planning requires three plans: a marketing plan, a financial plan, and a human resources plan. The three must be coordinated with each other as well as with the strategic plan. Together, these three plans should cover all aspects of the firm.

Marketing Plan

Marketing books have a variety of models for marketing plans (Berkowitz, Kerin & Rudelius, 1989; Schoell & Guiltinan, 1990). The steps given in Fig. 7.1 for strategic planning also can be applied to marketing planning. The main difference between strategic and intermediate planning is the plan itself. A marketing plan must deal with the market mix, which includes product, place, price, and promotion (the four *P*s). The marketing mix would fit into Steps 4 and 5 of the strategic planning model, which involve identifying and selecting alternative approaches for obtaining goals. The various options and combinations of the four *P*s become the alternative methods.

The marketing mix is applicable to the information, advertising, and intellectual markets. Although they are interrelated, each should have a marketing plan of its own, while acknowledging the role of the other markets.

Product. The product is simply the thing that is sold or given to a consumer in exchange for time or money. In the information and intellectual markets, the product is information and ideas, with their various subdivisions given in chapter 6 under the nature of the commodity. In the advertising market, it is the potential attention of consumers to advertising information. The value of the advertising attention depends on the the number of viewers, readers, or listeners and the types of people paying the attention.

When developing a marketing plan, management must look at two product decisions: whether and how to change the old product; and whether to add and what to add as a new product. In most organizations, the product decision is based on the location of older products in their life cycle. Buzzell and Cook (1969) discussed five stages of a *product's life cycle*:

1. Infancy is when a product enters the market. Sales are low.
2. Growth occurs when the product matures as to who and where it will sell. Sales grow rapidly if the product finds its niche in the marketplace.
3. Approaching maturity is when the established product begins to battle competitors over market share. Sales continue to grow, but at a slower rate than in the growth stage.
4. Maturity occurs when a product finds its place in its segment. Competition continues and sales grow much more slowly than earlier stages.

5. Decline is the final stage when consumers lose interest in the product for whatever reason and sales begin to decline.

Although the product cycle is applicable to many media products, confusion exists about its applicability to particular media industries or products. For example, it has become fashionable to say newspapers are dead, or that they are in decline. Yet, many newspapers continue to gain circulation, especially weekly newspapers. Industries do go through cycles, and those cycles affect individual products. Part of the confusion comes from identifying a product with an industry. It can be assumed that all products, just as all people, will die, but there is no inherent length to any of these periods of the cycle. The key to survival is using strategic and intermediate planning to continually change the media commodity to elongate the life cycle. Because most media products change with each publication or broadcast, it should be easier for media commodities to adjust. This will depend, however, on the management skills of the people running the media organizations.

Using the product life cycle and a market analysis should put management in a position to develop the product portion of the marketing plan. This must be a detailed explanation of what product changes will take place or the nature of any new products. A time frame for making the changes or introducing the new product is also necessary.

Place.   With most media products, place is an important part of product. News commodities, such as newspapers and newscasts, are aimed at specific geographic areas. The content reflects this aim. The size, geography, social aspects, cultural characteristics, and political nature of a society affect the places for which news products are designed. Place is also related to price in the United States. Some parts of the country have higher and lower standards of living than others. The same book, for example, would face a lower demand due to price in one region than in another region.

Place also affects the process and cost of distributing the media product. The cost of delivering a newspaper increases as one moves away from the production site. The cost of distributing a broadcast television program is basically the same within the range of the signal. If the station wants to distribute the program elsewhere, it must use either microwave or satellite transmission, which increases costs.

In setting up the marketing mix, it is crucial that the place be defined carefully and particularly for media commodities. This definition establishes the geographic market in which the commodity will be distributed and, therefore, the very nature of the information.

Price.   As explained in the market analysis chapter, price will affect demand, but it also determines how much revenue is taken in by the firm.

Pricing is a difficult process for many media firms because the joint commodity nature of most media commodities creates extreme uncertainty. Managers are afraid to overprice in one type of market because it will reduce demand in another. Increasing the subscription price for a magazine will reduce circulation, which can affect the price charged to advertisers. Research indicates that newspaper mangers often charge less for their advertising and circulation than they could (Picard, 1988).

In the case of most radio and television information markets, a consumer pays only her attention to receive the information. However, an indirect cost to consumers is the increased price for products that advertise. Companies with high advertising budgets charge higher prices for their products than those with small ad budgets. This indirect system of paying for information hides price as a part of the product mix for radio and television, but this is misleading. If the firm producing the information assumes the consumer is paying no price, it may not invest in the quality of that information because its managers assume that free information needs less quality to attract users. As a result, people with several substitute information sources may be less willing to pay attention to get the information with less quality.

The traditional way of pricing existing products is to look at inflation, examine competitors' prices, add on additional expenses that have developed, estimate the impact of price on demand, and set the price with a profit goal in mind. Then management looks for the reaction of consumers and competitors. If demand is driven down more than expected, management usually will try to increase it to previous levels with promotion. Rarely is price reduced.

The traditional way of pricing new products is to calculate the costs of production and distribution and add a desired profit margin. Then, of course, it becomes an old product and adjustments are made in the ways mentioned earlier.

Promotion. The final P in the marketing mix is promotion, which involves persuading people to use the product. Promotion includes advertising, public relations, and promotional activities. Advertising includes all paid communication between a firm and potential users. Public relations involves using news media and interpersonal communication to reach the potential users of the product. Promotional activities involves all efforts to promote a product or company that do not fall under advertising or public relations. For example, placement of a product in a prominent place within a store would be a promotional activity.

Media organizations have an advantage in both advertising and public relations because they are communication companies. Self-promoting advertisements are common. However, journalists object to public relations self-promotion in the news portion of media commodities. It is considered unethical. Self-promoting advertisements may work for current users of a media commodity, but they usually will not develop many new users.

Once the marketing mix is determined, a detailed plan is developed for applying the marketing mix decisions. This means detailed instructions for each of the departments involved in the organization. For example, an increase in the price of a magazine will affect the circulation, promotions, and advertising departments. The members of the circulation department will have to deal with complaints and dropped subscriptions. The sales-people in the advertising department will have to justify the change in circulation to advertisers, and the promotions department will have to come up with ways of retaining readers despite the price increase. All these changes, and more, that flow from a price increase must be included in the plan.

Just as structure and communication are related to the strategic planning, they also affect marketing. Any permanent variations in structure should be in the strategic plan, but marketing plans also may involve temporary changes in structure and communication.

Human Resources Plan

A human resources plan concerns the acquisition and development of people needed to accomplish the marketing and financial plans. This plan is crucial to most media organizations because of their labor intensive nature. People are needed to create the information content, and people are needed to sell advertising space and time. Lack of a human resources plan can hamper the implementation of the marketing and financial plans.

The process of human resources planning is similar to strategic and marketing planning and involves eight steps: (a) Identify human resource needs based on marketing plan; (b) evaluate current human resources; (c) determine needs for new resources based on first two steps; (d) determine methods for obtaining resources—either training or hiring; (e) develop plan for training and hiring; (f) implement plan; (g) monitor plan; and (h) adjust plan.

The first step flows from the market plan. For example, if a magazine company plans to start a local business magazine, it will need business writers and editors. This step involves figuring out how many and what types of business writers and editor will be needed. The second step means first looking within the company for the needed resources. Perhaps the magazine company already has writers and editors at other magazines who have the skills and interests needed for the new business magazine.

After the first two steps, managers can decide how many and what types of people they will need to hire or train. Managers can obtain the expertise they need either by hiring someone who already has that expertise or by training someone on staff. This training can take place at workshops, colleges and universities, and on the job. Which method is best will depend on the particular situation, but each method has its advantages and disadvantages. Hiring someone with a specialty is likely to be expensive because that person spent more time in school developing expertise and will be in greater demand. Sending someone to school and workshops to develop expertise also can be expensive because management not only pays for the training but they lose that person as a staff member during the training period. Advanced training also can make an employee more attractive to other organizations that might try to hire her. This can mean an increase in salary to keep her.

Once it has been determined to train and/or hire, a plan for proceeding is developed. The larger the number of hires and the greater the need for training, the more elaborate the plan will be. But all strategic and intermediate plans that involve significant staff changes should have an explicit plan for making those changes.

The sixth step is to implement that plan. For example, a new computer system with several uses is being introduced into a public relations firm. The entire staff will need some training on the system. The plan calls for a priority of uses and a system of training parts of the staff at different times. Implementing means someone has to be in charge of seeing that the training takes place. The level of manager who is in charge depends on the number and nature of departments involved. Every department should have someone who is responsible for that department, whereas interdepartmental human resource plans must have someone at the next managerial level to coordinate the change.

The final two steps are feedback and control processes. They involve collecting information about the change and adjusting the process if and when needed. If the plan called for 6 hrs of training on the new computer system but employees continue to make a number of mistakes after 6 hrs of training, management must decide how much additional training employees need.

Because marketing is an ongoing process with a series of plans across time, human resource planning has the same steps for each plan. The eight steps given here form a circular process that continues with each set of marketing and financial plans.

Financial Plan

The financial plan deals with how money will be acquired and how it will be spent. The marketing and human resources plans must be financed, and the financial plan should explain how. In addition, decisions must be made about how the profit from the intermediate plans will be used in the short run and with the strategic plan. Both types of decisions follow from the strategic plan and must reflect the mission and goals of the firm.

Money can be raised from the various income-producing ventures the firm has, such as selling copies of magazines or selling time to advertisers during the radio broadcasts. However, money also can be raised by selling assets. If a newspaper group decides it wants to get into the broadcasting business, one source of financing would be to sell less profitable newspapers and use the money to buy television stations.

In addition, organizations can raise money by borrowing from some other organization, such as a bank, by borrowing from the public by selling bonds and other securities, or by selling part of the ownership, usually through the sale of stock. Borrowing requires paying interest on the money, whereas selling part of ownership means giving up more of the control over decisions about the business. The particular need for money, especially the amount, and the conditions in the environment will affect which process is used in the financial plan. In the case of major changes in the firm, several methods may be used.

The disposal of profits must be included in the plan. Generally speaking, profits can be distributed to owners or they can be reinvested into the business. Reinvesting means using the operating profits to advance the marketing, human resources, and strategic plans. Just what is done with profits depends on the particular management running the organization, the long-term and intermediate planning, the happenings in the economic environment, and the inclination of the owners. It is important that the disposition of profits, as well as the acquisition of money, be included in the financial plan.

As with other plans, financial planning is a decision-making process that follows stages similar to the decision wheel and the steps mentioned for strategic, marketing, and human resource planning. Financial planning, however, has a large amount of data available from the accounting practices of the firm. Planning is aided greatly by using the profit/loss statements, budgets, balance sheets, and other documents mentioned in chapter 9.

SHORT-RUN PLANNING

Just as the intermediate plans are maps of reaching the goals of the strategic plan, so short-run plans are ways of meeting the goals of the intermediate plans. Three types of short-run planning are important: budgets, employee planning, and management by objective (MBO).

Budgets are the yearly plan of the organization. They cover how to spend money and the expected sources of money. As such, they are the essential short-run element of the financial plan. The budget must reflect the priorities of the intermediate and strategic plans or the mission of the organization will not be accomplished. Thus, budgeting must be pursued with an eye on the long-range goals.

Employee planning involves the development of the talents, skills, and aspirations of people within an organization. People do not work just for money. Employees spend as much time at work as they do pursuing any other single activity. For employees to be productive and successful they must achieve, which means planning is involved. To pursue employee development without a plan for doing so is to believe in magic.

Employee planning occurs through the evaluation process. This process succeeds only to the degree that it addresses the future plans, hopes, and aspirations of employees. Evaluation is not just about the past; it should address employee progress in relation to some plan. This plan, which can be relatively informal, should be part of every employee's file. It is determined when a manager asks the employee what he would like to accomplish in the future and when the manager tells the employee what she would like him to contribute to the organization.

The plans should involve more than just how much money the person wants to make. It should include career goals, plans for developing employee knowledge and training, and even personal goals that may be related to the firm. Media organizations are usually labor intensive, and as such, media managers must develop their human resources through employee training.

Management by objective is where the budget and the employee planning intersect. MBO is an explicit way of setting up objectives and evaluating employees' progress toward those objectives. It usually is done on an annual basis, which is why it fits as a short-run planning device. The idea is to make the evaluation process more detached from the idiosyncrasies of individual managers (Sohn et al., 1986). The process can have variations from company to company, and it can be abused if not properly instituted. But the idea of explicitly setting up standards of work and a process for evaluating the performance with that work is a worthwhile approach toward short-run planning.

The keys to successful use of MBO are: (a) employees accept the standards and evaluation process; (b) the standards are related to the intermediate and strategic plans; (c) the evaluation procedures are carried out consistently; and (d) the standards are consistent with the individual employee's plans.

WHO PLANS

Who carries out the planning process is as important as the process itself. This will vary with organizations, but two general rules make sense: (a)

Whoever has responsibility for performance should have input into and control over the planning process; and (b) people who carry out plans at the lowest level should provide information for the planning process.

Management falls into three types: upper level, middle level, and lower level. Planning has three approaches: top-down, which means all plans are made by upper level managers; bottom-up, which means all decisions are made by lower level managers; or a combination of the first two approaches (Lavine & Wackman, 1988). The first is limited because the upper level managers are not as familiar with day-to-day operations as are the lower level managers. The second approach is limited because the lower level managers do not have the overall organizational perspective found at the top. It would seem then that a combination of the two is a good approach for two reasons: (a) strengths of the various levels of management are taken advantage of; and (b) employees and managers who participate in planning are more likely to be committed to those plans (Giles, 1988).

A further complicating matter in selecting who plans is the variation in managerial skills. The fact that a person at a particular level of management should participate does not mean that person has planning skills. Table 7.2 lists important planning skills. They include the ability to function well in group decision making, the ability to be nonjudgmental in early planning stages, the ability to handle criticism of ideas and decisions well, the ability to think abstractly, and the ability to understand and analyze large amounts of information in various forms. If a given manager who normally would be in the planning process does not have the necessary skills, two approaches are available. An assistant can be involved in the planning process and report back to the manager, or the manager can be trained to acquire skills relevant to planning.

Determining the role of employees in planning is also a must. The people who do the work are the ones who are in the best position for providing information and often making decisions about the work process. Planning should take advantage of the experience and knowledge of the employees. This participation can come in the form of informational input

TABLE 7.2
Types of Planning Skills

Planning Skills
Group Decision Making
Reserving Judgement During Early Stages of Planning
Handle Criticism Well
Abstract Thinking
Analytical Skills with Many Forms of Data

or in actual planning through task forces and quality circles; both are a good idea. But because employee participation in planning is not standard in information firms, each media organization should develop procedures for getting the employees involved. This is especially true of news organizations because autonomy is an important job characteristic for journalists. Top-down planning that ignores input from workers will do little to encourage these journalists to stay in the organization.

SUMMARY

Planning is the essence of good management. The process is much like that of decision making, and its success depends on the adequate collection and analysis of information. The processes of planning should involve people from all levels of the organization.

Planning takes three basic forms: strategic, intermediate, and short-run. Strategic is long-range planning, usually involving 3 to 5 years. Intermediate planning usually involves periods of 6 months to 2 years. Short-run planning can involve a period of a week to a year. The marketing plan, human resources plan, and financial plan make up the intermediate plan. The most common form of short-run plan is the yearly budget.

Strategic plans must start with a market analysis and an audit of internal resources. The three types of intermediate plans are drawn from the organization's mission and goals. Each type of planning must build on the other and fit into the overall strategic plan. Coordination of plans is the key to successful goal attainment.

The types of people who actually make the planning decisions will vary from organization to organization, but in media firms, people from all levels of the organization should participate. This participation means using skilled employees and allowing them to make meaningful decisions about the organization.

CHAPTER 7 CASES

Case 7.1

The Case of Planning Human Resources at WXPT

WXPT is a network affiliate television station in a Southern city with a population of 300,000. It is the center of a metro area of 500,000 people and 216,000 households. As general manager of the station, your investment in the local television news department during your 3 years has paid off with growing ratings and shares for both the evening and late-night newscasts.

Your evening newscast has a 28 rating, which means about 59,000 households watch the news, and a share of 42, which means 42% of all TV sets in the market turned on at 5:30 pm are tuned to your newscast. The next closest station has a share of 27.

You credit your success to the heavy emphasis of local coverage in your newscast. In your 3 years as station manager, the news budget has grown by 50%. Your newsroom now has 1 news director, 3 producers, 6 news reporters, 2 anchors, 1 sports anchor and 1 sports reporter, 2 weather reporters, and 10 camera people.

Despite your success, you never have been one to be satisfied. As part of your 5-year strategic plan, you have decided to expand the early evening newscast to 1 hour from its current 30-min format. The news will run from 5:30 pm to 6:30 pm, with the network newscast moved from the 6 to 6:30 pm slot.

The move of the network news will not be a problem because your network newscast is a distant second in the market. Your hope is that the increased local news will draw more viewers than the other networks' newscasts. This type of programming has been successful in some of the very large markets, but it has not been tried in a medium-size market in your part of the country.

The change is scheduled to take place in 6 months, so it is important that you and the news director develop a human resource plan for the change. The current staff is as follows:

Jim Williams is a 61-year-old White man. He has been anchor at the station for 12 years and was a reporter there for 20 years before that. He also holds the title of managing editor. He is perceived by viewers as a steady, fatherly type who can be trusted. He is considered the "dean" of local television journalists in your state.

Sandy Denson is a 29-year-old White woman, who has been working with Williams for 2 years. Recent research indicates that both men and women in the market think she is beautiful. Her presentation is flawless, but she is not a strong reporter because she spent only 1 year as a reporter before moving to a small-market anchor. She came to WXPT from that small-market anchor spot 3 years ago.

The number-one weather person, *David Matson*, is a 62-year-old White man, who has been in the market for 30 years. He is a trained meteorologist and is considered to be an expert in weather prediction. He has been making sounds about retiring, but you are not sure if he really wants to, or if it is just a negotiation ploy because his 5-year contract is up at the end of the year.

The number-two weather person, *Janice Markham*, is a 30-year-old African American, who was born and raised in the area. She has been at the station for 4 years, after working as the weather person at a smaller station in the Midwest for 2 years. She is not a certified meteorologist but is quite knowledgeable about weather prediction. She credits Matson with teaching her most of what she knows. She handles the weekend weather assignment.

The number-one sports anchor is *Harve Johnson,* a 50-year-old White man, who is relatively new at the station. He came to WXPT 14 months ago from the second-place station in the market. He replaced Fred Benson, who retired at age 60. He has done a creditable job, but he has had a few conflicts with Williams over treatment of sports news. Williams thinks he should deal more with social issues and sports, whereas Johnson wants to just give the highlights and scores.

Susan Melissa is the number-two sports anchor. She came to the station a year ago from a sports-writing job at the local newspaper. Her leaving the newspaper created quite a local controversy. She resigned after a member of the local minor league baseball team cursed at her while standing naked in the locker room after a game. Melissa demanded an apology from the player and team manager, but her male publisher said this demand was inappropriate because "boys will be boys." WXPT hired her because of her expertise in baseball and car racing, both important sports in the area. The station received a large amount of positive mail from viewers for hiring her. In addition to anchoring the weekend sports spot, she also reports during the week. She has received good, but not glowing, evaluations during her first year on the air. Her weak points have been coordinating film with words, although her evaluations acknowledge her outstanding writing.

Of the six reporters, two stand out. *Leslie Thompson* is by far the star of the reporting crew. She is a 34-year-old African American who grew up in the area. She has worked at the station for 6 years. She came to the station immediately after receiving her degree in journalism from the local university. She has been named the "Outstanding Broadcast Journalist" in the state the past 2 years for her in-depth reporting on problems facing cities. She has a monthly five-min segment where she deals with a particular urban problem. As many people have pointed out, she could be working at a network or in a much larger market. In fact, she has had offers from larger stations in other parts of the country, but she stays at WXPT because of her family commitment.

Henry Peterson is another outstanding reporter. He was named "Out-standing Broadcast Journalist" in the state 4 years ago. He is a 31-year-old White man who has been with the station for the 9 years since he graduated from college. He covers government and is knowledgeable in all areas of local and state government. He is solid in every way, but in his last evaluation, he seemed to be tiring of the reporting work. He said he would like to move into either anchor work or management.

The other four reporters are all relatively new in the business. None has more than 5 years' experience, and two are in their first year at the station. They are all White, and three of the four are men.

Assignment

It is your job to develop plans regarding your newsroom staff as you increase the time given to the news. Answer the following questions:

1. How many new reporters will you hire for the expanded newscast?
2. What level of training will you look for?
3. Will you look to hire specific types of reporters based on gender and race? If so, why? Discuss the gender and racial breakdown of the new reporters.
4. Who would you like to be your weekday and weekend news anchors, weather anchors, and sports anchors a year from now? Why?
5. Who would you like to be your weekend and daily news anchors, weather anchors, and sports anchors 3 years from now? Why?
6. Will any of these changes during the next year to 3 years require additional training? If so, how and where will this training come from?

Case 7.2

Assignment: Evaluating Human Resources

One of the essential ingredients in evaluating human resources for planning is reliable information about the people who work in a media organization. This information is accumulated over a period of time through the evaluation process. This process involves an appraisal of past performance and a discussion of future goals. Media organizations vary as to the nature and extent of their evaluation processes. This assignment involves interviewing mangers at media organizations in order to determine the nature of their evaluation process. Recommended reading before conducting this assignment is chapter 10 in Robert H. Giles' *Newsroom Management* (1988).

Assignment

Select a media organization in order to examine its evaluation process. It can be any type of media organization. Set up an interview with a manager at the departmental level or higher. The interview subject is employee evaluation. Questions asked in the interview should include, but not be limited to the following:

1. Who conducts the evaluation process?
2. How often does the process take place?

3. What type of behaviors are evaluated?
4. What type of form is used for the evaluation?
5. How does the evaluation process address the goals of the employees?
6. How is the employee allowed to respond to the evaluation?
7. How long has the evaluation process been in effect?
8. What are the uses of the evaluation process?

After the interview, prepare a report of the media organization's evaluation process. This report should address the following issues:

1. Describe the evaluation process, using the answers to the aforementioned questions.
2. How adequate is the time and effort that goes into the evaluation process?
3. How well does this evaluation process work in providing information that can be used in planning for the future? Why?
4. How would you change the evaluation process to make it a more effective tool for planning in the organization?

Case 7.3

The Case of Planning at a Journalism Magazine

Lucinda Simpson is publisher of *News Magazine*, which is a monthly professional magazine that covers the news business in all its forms. It is a mixture of media criticism, media business and economics analysis, media ethics, and profiles about businesses and journalists. The magazine is one of four national publications designed to serve this market, although several others that specialize in particular media also cover the news business to a degree. However, most of these magazines also deal with entertainment issues.

Simpson has been publisher since the magazine's inception 5 years ago. The magazine broke even for the first time last year, a year ahead of schedule. The 5-year strategic plan is considered a success. During this period, the magazine saw its circulation go from zero to 12,050, which exceeded the 10,000 5-year goal.

The magazine, which is located in Washington, DC, covers all areas of the news business. It emphasizes news organizations' performances as businesses and as social institutions. Its promotional slogan over the past 5 years was "News Magazine, where Business and Community Commitment Merge." The motto on the magazine masthead is "Good Journalism Makes Good Business." The result of this approach has been some hard-hitting stories about specific companies and their performances in the business market and in helping their communities.

The magazine has three staff writers, but it also takes free-lance work. Its main features, other than the articles and book reviews, are a summary of federal regulatory activities and a section called "Winners and Losers." This section divides the country into six regions and has one example of bad journalism and one example of good journalism from each region. The magazine averages about 56 pages an issue, with 35% advertising.

News Magazine (NM) faces three other magazines that fit its market niche. Two of these are associated with educational institutions, and one is the publication of the Association for Professional Journalism. The following is a brief description of these magazines:

National Journalism Review (NJR) is a monthly publication associated with a large East Coast university's journalism department. It was started originally as a business and later donated to the journalism school at this institution. It covers all aspects of the journalism business, although it has a special emphasis on the business, economics, and technology of these media organizations. It has several columns covering the individual media: newspapers, television, magazines, and radio news. Its editorial staff is composed of editors, and almost all writing work is free lance, often on a commission basis. About a dozen writers work with the publication on a regular basis, excluding columnists. It averages about 64 pages, with 35% advertising, and is located in Boston.

American Journalism Review (AJR), also a monthly publication, is associated with a large Midwest university's school of journalism. This magazine covers the entire range of news media with an emphasis on evaluating the performance and ethics of these organizations. It has several standard features, including a section of short pieces addressing what its editors see as good and bad performance by the news media. It is called "Bullets and Bouquets." It also reviews books about news media and reports on academic research in the area. It is similar to the *NJR* in that almost all writing is done by free-lance writers. It averages about 60 pages, with 38% advertising, and is located in Chicago.

Journalists (J) is the every-other month magazine of the Association for Professional Journalism. It addresses all areas that might be of interest to journalists and journalism students. It encourages articles from scholars about their research and essays about the future and the role of journalism in society. It is entirely written by freelancers and averages about 36 pages an issue, with 28% advertising. It is located in New York.

Tables 7.3–7.7 give data about subscription price, ad prices, and circulation.

Assignment

Based on the information you have been given, develop a 3-year marketing plan for the *News Magazine*. The plan should address both the advertising

TABLE 7.3
Price for Readers

	Subscription Price per Year	Single Copy
NM	$20.00	$2.00
NJR	$24.00	$2.95
AJR	$22.00	$2.50
J	$10.00	$2.00

TABLE 7.4
Circulation Figures for 4 Years (in Thousands)

	Last Year		Year 1		Year 2		Year 3	
	Sub.	Single	Sub.	Single	Sub.	Single	Sub.	Single
NM	11.1	1.0	9.9	0.9	7.5	0.8	4.5	0.5
NJR	22.5	1.5	21.7	1.2	22.3	1.3	21.8	1.5
AJR	18.5	2.6	19.4	2.2	19.7	2.2	19.9	1.9
J	19.4	– –	19.6	– –	20.4	– –	21.7	– –

Note. Sub. means subscription and single means single-copy sales. *Journalists* sells only through subscriptions.

TABLE 7.5
Sales Broken Down by Region of the Country (in Thousands)

	New England	Middle Atlantic	Southeast	Midwest	Southwest	Mountain & Far West
NM	2.2	4.3	0.9	2.1	0.8	1.8
NJR	6.1	5.8	2.1	4.1	1.4	4.5
AJR	3.7	3.8	3.4	6.1	2.0	2.1
J	3.7	4.5	1.0	3.7	2.8	3.7

TABLE 7.6
Advertising Rates for One-Time Ad

	Full Page	2/3 Page	1/2 Page	1/3 Page	1/6 Page
NM	$1,500	$ 750	$ 600	$ 400	$225
NJR	$4,400	$3,200	$2,400	$1,650	$870
AJR	$3,400	$2,300	$1,500	$1,100	$700
J	$2,200	$1,400	$1,100	$ 700	$450

TABLE 7.7
Advertising Rates for Three-Time Ad

	Full Page	2/3 Page	1/2 Page	1/3 Page	1/6 Page
NM	$1,400	$ 700	$ 540	$ 375	$210
NJR	$4,225	$3,075	$2,300	$1,600	$825
AJR	$3,175	$2,225	$1,450	$1,050	$875
J	$2,100	$1,325	$1,050	$ 650	$425

and circulation markets and include the four Ps: product, price, place, and promotion. Suggestions in the plan need not be exact because data are missing, but they should address the following questions:

1. Should changes be made in the product? If so, what types of changes?
2. What types of pricing should be pursued in the advertising and circulation markets?
3. What types of promotion and advertising would help increase circulation?
4. Should certain geographic areas be emphasized in promotion? If so, where?

Case 7.4

The Case of Setting Goals in a Suburban Market

Case 6.5 asked for a market analysis of the six cities in which Howard-Slipps Newspaper Corp. bought newspapers. The purpose of this case is to develop strategic planning goals and a brief summary of plans to reach those goals for the six Howard-Slipps newspapers. Combine the information in Case 6.5 with the material that follows to answer the case questions.

Molly McLane has just received the information given in Tables 7.8–7.11) about advertising space in the T & S Publications and in the weeklies recently purchased by Howard-Slipps.

The newspapers recently purchased by Howard–Slipps had the financial data given in Table 7.12 for last year.

Circulation figures for the Howard-Slipps newspapers are: Pontiac, 10,345; West Bloomfield, 11,890; and Birmingham, 3,245. The other three are free distribution papers, which means all of the households listed in Case 6.5 receive a copy.

TABLE 7.8
Percentage of Ad Space in the T & S Newspapers for Last Year

| | City | | | | | |
	Pontiac	Southfield	Troy	Novi	West Bloomfield	Birmingham
Local Retail	52%	47%	57%	45%	51%	60%
Local Real Estate	15%	18%	12%	12%	19%	17%
National	3%	2%	5%	5%	6%	3%
Inserts	2%	5%	3%	5%	3%	3%
Legal	8%	7%	6%	4%	6%	6%
Classified	20%	21%	17%	29%	15%	11%

TABLE 7.9
Percentage of Ad Space in the Howard-Slipps Newspapers for Last Year

| | City | | | | | |
	Pontiac	Southfield	Troy	Novi	West Bloomfield	Birmingham
Local Retail	43%	40%	51%	43%	42%	52%
Local Real Estate	12%	13%	9%	15%	12%	14%
National	4%	3%	5%	5%	5%	5%
Inserts	5%	4%	4%	5%	3%	3%
Legal	9%	7%	7%	5%	7%	5%
Classified	27%	33%	24%	27%	31%	21%

TABLE 7.10
News, Editorial/Op-Ed & Advertising Space in T & S Newspapers (Pages per Week)

	Pontiac	Southfield	Troy	Novi	West Bloomfield	Birmingham
News	16	15	16	11	18	14
Editorial/Op-Ed	2	1	1	1	2	1
Advertising	22	20	19	16	28	17

Assignment

With these data and the material in Case 6.5, your assignment is to help Molly McLane answer the following questions:

1. What 5-year circulation goals should be set for each Howard-Slipps newspaper? Briefly explain how you would proceed in trying to reach these goals.

TABLE 7.11

News, Editorial/Op Ed & Advertising Space in Howard-Slipps Newspapers (Pages per Week)

	Pontiac	Southfield	Troy	Novi	West Bloomfield	Birmingham
News	15	14	13	10	18	12
Editorial/Op-Ed	1	0	1	1	0	1
Advertising	16	14	14	13	14	11

TABLE 7.12

Last Year's Financial Data for Newspapers Recently Purchased by Howard-Slipps (in Thousands)

	Circulation Revenue	Advertising Revenue	Newsroom Expense	Other Expense	Profit
Pontiac	122	1,059	181	991	9
Southfield	0[a]	971	151	810	10
Troy	0[a]	892	143	746	3
Novi	0[a]	787	120	669	−2
West Bloomfield	135	1,023	201	985	−28
Birmingham	29	664	112	587	−6
Total	289	5,393	908	4,788	−14

[a]These are free distribution newspapers.

2. What 5-year goals for distribution of pages among advertising, news, and editorial/op-ed sections should be set for each Howard-Slipps newspaper? Briefly explain how you would proceed in trying to reach these goals.

3. What 5-year profit goals should be set for the six newspapers? Briefly explain how you would proceed in trying to reach these goals.

Case 7.5

The Case of Setting Goals for a Radio Station

The third step in strategic planning is setting up planning goals. This assignment involves identifying realistic goals for a 3-year strategic plan for a radio station. Using the information given next, answer the case questions concerning goals for station WKYZ.

Station Background

WKYZ is a 50,000-watt station located in a Midwest city with a metropolitan population of 1.4 million in 540,000 households. The radio format is all news and talk. It has a strong local news orientation, although state, national, and international news are carried. The station has a one-person bureau in the state capital, and all of the metro news is staff produced. The remainder of the news comes from networks and syndicated services.

The station carries a local and state 2-hr news show from 6:30 am to 8:30 am and from 4:30 pm to 6:30 pm. During the remainder of the day, it carries a 15-min newscast every hour, which contains a mixture of local, state, national, and international news. The time in between is filled with interview and call-in programs. Several local celebrities participate in these shows.

The station was founded in 1925 and is the top-rated news and talk station in the market. It has a newsroom of about 15 full-time journalists, and it uses another 10 part-time people.

Net profit has declined for each of the last four quarters. The net profit for the quarters were: spring $125,000; summer $130,000; fall 153,000; winter $161,000. The overall profit for these four periods was $569,000, which was down from $711,000 the year before.

The Market

The market contains 20 radio stations. Table 7.13 contains the stations, their format, and the target audience.

Table 7.14 has the average estimated number of people who listen to a given station a minimum of 5 minutes in a quarter hour and the average share, a percentage of all metro listeners, for four ratings periods. The figures are limited to the top 10 stations in the market. The spring period was the most recent.

Table 7.15 has the average number of people in the target age groups for WKYZ for the past four periods.

The Economy

Economic conditions in the market are good. Unemployment dropped to 7.1% this year from 7.6% at the same time last year. Economists predict that the economic expansion will continue for about 2 years and turn down again in 3 years. Unemployment is predicted to be about 6.5% next year and about 6% in 2 years. Interest rates also are dropping and consumer spending is on the increase.

TABLE 7.13
The Market

Station	Format	Target Audience[a]
WKYZ (FM)	News and Talk	Adults 25–64
WEEK	Adult Contemporary	Adults 18–49
WASR (FM)	Middle of the Road	Adults 18 +
WWRT-FM	Middle of the Road	Adults 18 +
WWWP	All Talk	Adults 25–64
WPOY (FM)	Contemporary Hits	Adults 18 +
WZTY	Album-Oriented Rock	Adults 18–44
WASP	Golden Oldies	Adults 18–54
WOPE (FM)	Black	Adults 18–49
WQQI	Country	Adults 18–54
WEEP (FM)	Country	Adults 18–54
WLLT (FM)	Classic Rock	Adults 25–44
WSRU	News and Talk	Adults 25–64
WHHY (FM)	Black	Adults 18–34
WDTR	Album-Oriented Rock	Adults 18–44
WNNM	Golden Oldies	Adults 25–54
WAAK (FM)	Jazz	Adults 18–54
WLLK	Country	Adults 18–64
WOYT (FM)	Middle of the Road	Adults 25 +
WFGO (FM)	Religious	No report

[a]Ages are in years.

TABLE 7.14
Average Estimated Number of People Who Listen a Minimum of 5 Min per Quarter Hour and Average Share for Top 10 Stations in the Market (in Hundreds)

Station	Spring		Summer		Autumn		Winter	
	People	Share	People	Share	People	Share	People	Share
WPOY	288	9.6	276	9.5	290	9.7	291	9.7
WASR	276	9.2	281	9.7	286	9.5	289	9.6
WKYZ	254	8.5	264	9.1	272	9.1	287	9.5
WEEP	253	8.4	253	8.7	247	8.2	245	8.1
WNNM	251	8.4	250	8.6	243	8.1	239	7.9
WSRU	193	6.4	196	6.8	182	6.1	181	6.0
WHHY	188	6.3	196	6.7	194	6.5	191	6.4
WOYT	167	5.6	161	5.6	162	5.4	159	5.3
WZTY	155	5.2	160	5.5	165	5.5	168	5.6
WWWP	150	5.0	144	5.0	141	4.7	136	4.5

TABLE 7.15
Average Number of People In Target Age Groups for WKYZ (in Hundreds)

| | Ages (in Years) | | | | | | |
	18–24	25–34	35–44	45–54	55–64	64+	Total
Spring	25	55	71	59	34	10	254
Summer	25	60	73	60	33	13	264
Fall	23	62	75	58	34	20	272
Winter	24	69	77	59	36	22	287

Assignment

1. What should be the general 3-year ratings and share goals of WKYZ?
2. How should these general goals be operationalized (actual ratings and share figures) for each of the next 3 years? These operational goals should include overall goals and goals for specific age groupings.
3. Explain why and how these goals could be reached.

8
Marketing and Research

Managers in all types of media companies need to obtain a statistical profile of consumers for various reasons. A broadcast manager might use research to determine whether viewers like and trust the local news anchor. A newspaper publisher might use research to determine the types of stories readers enjoy. A brand manager for a large advertiser company or a manager at an advertising agency might use research to select among various advertising campaigns. Thus, a familiarity with the techniques and uses of marketing and research is important, regardless of the branch of the media in which a manager works.

The goal of the chapter is to allow the reader to develop a broad perspective on marketing and research. Many research techniques and uses are common to the various media organizations. The basic types of research used by different kinds of media organizations are presented. The similarities between the kinds of research different media organizations use also are discussed. References are provided throughout the chapter to enable the reader to find more information on a topic of interest.

BACKGROUND ON MARKETING AND RESEARCH

Marketing is the "process of planning and executing the conception, pricing, promotion, and distribution of ideas, goods, and services to create exchanges that satisfy individual and organizational objectives" (AMA Board, 1985, p. 1). The underlying "marketing concept" is that the company that is best at determining what consumers want, and then meeting those desires more effectively than competitors, will be successful (Kotler, 1980). Marketing research provides a way for media managers to discover the needs and wants of their readers, viewers, and listeners and determine how best to meet them.

Research is the systematic and controlled investigation of relationships among observable phenomena. All research begins with a basic question about a particular problem, such as: Why do consumers buy one product rather than another? Which newspaper design do readers prefer? A researcher reviews the available information on a topic of interest; states the research problem to be solved; develops a plan for collecting the appropriate data; collects the data, analyzes, and interprets it; and then presents the results in verbal and/or written form (Wimmer & Dominick, 1991).

The type of research problem suggests which method to use. When the factors affecting a research problem need to be closely observed and controlled, such as when advertising researchers track eye movements to determine which parts of an ad layout readers look at, experimental designs are used. Survey research is used to describe or document current attitudes or conditions, or to attempt to explain why certain situations exist in the general public. For example, A. C. Nielsen conducts surveys that provide current data on television audience size and composition.

Field research methods are used to solve a problem in a natural setting. For example, two versions of a newspaper lifestyle section are tested by delivering one version to residents in one geographic region of a city and a second version in another market region. Reader reactions are monitored in both regions to determine which section was preferred. A *longitudinal study* is appropriate when data collected at more than one point in time are needed to evaluate the research question. For example, National Purchase Diary, Inc., analyzes market share trends for brands by collecting purchase diaries monthly from respondents. Finally, *content analysis* provides a means of objectively investigating media content. Content analysis often is used to examine typography, layout, and makeup in newspapers and magazines. (See Wimmer & Dominick, 1991, for more information about research methods.)

Media managers need to understand the basic kinds of research in order to select the appropriate technique for answering questions and solving problems. This understanding enables managers to decide between competing research proposals submitted by outside suppliers (including evaluating the research design, methods, questionnaire, and sampling techniques used) or to design and implement research in-house. Managers also must be able to understand and interpret research findings in order to use the results effectively.

DEVELOPING A BROAD UNDERSTANDING
OF MEDIA RESEARCH TECHNIQUES

It is also becoming increasingly important for managers to understand how and why their counterparts at other media organizations use marketing and research. Even advertisers in small markets ask for audience size and composition data. The newspaper or broadcast advertising sales manager who understands how an advertiser and/or its advertising agency uses audience data to select the appropriate vehicle (e.g., individual publication or broadcast program) can prepare better materials. A manager or media representative who has a broad perspective on the relative strengths and weaknesses of all of the competing media in a market can explain intelligently, and in detail, why her media vehicle is the appropriate buy. This knowledge results in more effective sales calls and the development of more effective media kits.

A media kit should be aimed at current and potential advertisers, and should demonstrate that the medium in question delivers the appropriate reading or viewing audience. Such a kit should use color and provide reliable and credible primary data (e.g., results of a survey conducted by the newspaper's or station's employees) and secondary data (e.g., information about the market found in *Editor and Publishers Market Guide* or other published sources). A kit also should present readable data in a form that is useful to advertisers and media buyers. Information about the advantages of the particular medium should be featured. Finally, sales personnel should ask advertisers and ad agency media planners (who evaluate audience data) and media buyers (who negotiate and purchase time and space) for their honest opinions about the kit (Willis, 1988).

The importance of understanding the strengths and weaknesses of each medium is underscored by the fact that advertisers and agencies make relative comparisons of the cost efficiency of various media vehicles when deciding to buy time and space. Comparisons of cost effectiveness between vehicles are determined using the cost per thousand (CPM) formula. Advertisers and ad agency personnel use CPMs to identify the vehicles that reach the largest appropriate audience segment at the lowest unit cost. CPMs, which may be used for intramedia or intermedia comparisons, allow comparisons of one medium or vehicle with another to find those that are the most cost efficient.

The basic CPM formulas are as follows (Sissors & Surmanek, 1982):

For Print Vehicles:

$$CPM = \frac{\text{Cost of 1 page black \& white (or appropriate size and color)} \times 1000}{\text{Circulation or Number of Prospects Reached}}$$

For Broadcast Vehicles:

$$CPM = \frac{\text{Cost of 1 unit of time} \times 1000}{\text{Number of Homes or Prospects Reached by a Given Program or in a Specific Time Period}}$$

Here is how the CPM formulas are used. Assume that a media planner is trying to decide which newspaper to buy in a particular major market. The cost of a full-page, black and white ad in Newspaper A, with a circulation of 540,000, is $23,562. The cost of a full-page, black and white ad in Newspaper B, with a circulation of 750,000, is $36,162. The audience composition of both newspapers is similar. The cost-per-thousand for each newspaper is:

$$\text{CPM for Newspaper A} = \frac{\$23,562 \times 1,000}{540,000} = \$43.63$$

$$\text{CPM for Newspaper B} = \frac{\$36,162 \times 1,000}{750,000} = \$48.21$$

Although Newspaper B's circulation is larger, Newspaper A is more cost efficient for reaching readers in this hypothetical market because the audience composition is similar for both newspapers. In other words, it costs $42.63 per thousand impressions using Newspaper A and $48.21 to reach 1,000 readers in Newspaper B.

Media managers also need to understand research from a broad perspective because the methods used in one type of media organization often are used by others. For example, newspapers use psychographic research to identify segments of readers and develop news and feature articles for these segments, whereas advertisers and advertising agencies use psychographic data to identify consumer segments based on underlying purchase motives. All media managers use some combination of demographic data including age and income, psychographic data including lifestyle characteristics, geographic data about trends in the various regions of the country, media use, and/or purchase behavior statistics to create a profile of readers, viewers, or consumers (Francese, 1988). Understanding these basic uses can make a manager more effective at using, obtaining, and compiling the appropriate information for organizational decision making and advertising sales.

Demographic data provide information about the subject's age, sex, race, income, education, occupation, and household structure. However, demographic information is not enough, as two men, both 45 years old with household incomes of $75,000 per year, buy different products based upon their personal values and lifestyles. Psychographic data explain why one man buys a BMW and the other a Ford Explorer. As Francese (1988) explained, both cars will provide transportation, but the BMW fulfills a desire for status and the Explorer provides recreation. Psychographics include information about how people view themselves, their families, social institutions, and the future. The goal is to use psychographics to design "products" (either toothpaste or a newspaper lifestyle section) or promotional messages to fulfill consumer desires (Graham, 1989).

Geographic information might reveal that one man also may purchase the Ford Explorer because he lives near national parks or other recreational areas. Media usage or preference data reveal information about what these two men watch on TV, which radio stations and programs they listen to, and the newspapers and magazines they read. Purchasing behavior provides information about the actual purchases these men make (Francese, 1988).

The combination of demographic, psychographic, geographic, media usage, and purchase behavior data provides a fuller picture of readers, viewers, and consumers for media managers, depending on the information need or situation. Demographics in combination with psychographics reveals which features or story types readers want a newspaper to provide. Demographics combined with purchase and media usage data can inform a local men's clothing retailer about how customers obtain information about the store, who shops there, why, and when and how often they buy a particular suit style. A local radio station sales manager uses that same combination of information to explain specifically why her station reaches the kind of suit buyer the retailer is targeting.

However, media managers must realize that certain responsibilities affect how the marketing concept and research should be used by media companies. The local newspaper, magazine, radio station, and television station are not the same as a tube of toothpaste. Local media companies are responsible for providing news, information, and opinions on local, state, regional, national, and international issues. Media managers are responsible for providing fair, unbiased information to the public. Managers also must remember this special responsibility when deciding how to promote media organizations to the public and to advertisers. The need to make a profit must be tempered by professional standards and ethics.

Again, it is useful for a media manager to have a basic understanding of marketing and research, and how both are used by media organizations. The rest of this chapter describes the types of research media managers use, the problems to consider when utilizing research results, and some of the sources of available research. References are provided throughout the chapter to enable the interested reader to find more information about a topic of interest.

TYPES OF RESEARCH USED BY ADVERTISERS AND ADVERTISING AGENCIES

A discussion of the research techniques used by advertisers and advertising agencies provides insight into the unique characteristics of advertising research. It also educates print and broadcast managers about the kinds of information advertisers desire. Advertising research is discussed first so readers may see later how these same techniques are used by print and broadcast organizations. These techniques are divided into four, broad-based categories for discussion: situational or market analysis, consumer research, product research, and research to evaluate the effectiveness of advertising. A number of sources are available (besides textbooks dealing specifically with advertising and marketing research) that discuss the various aspects of advertising research (e.g., see Burton, 1990; Dunn, Barban, Krugman, & Reid, 1990; Lancaster & Katz, 1989; Sandage, Fryburger, & Rotzoll, 1989; Schultz, 1990; Wells, Burnett, & Moriarty, 1989).

Generally speaking, advertising and marketing research assists advertisers and agencies in developing advertising, media, and marketing strategies. Marketing strategy defines the basic objectives (e.g., increasing market share or sales) of the brand or product and the strategies planned to achieve it, including advertising and media strategies. Advertising or message strategy incorporates the decisions involved in determining what an advertisement should say, whereas message tactics involve how the ad should say it. Media strategies explain how the media objectives of an advertising campaign will be met, including the which media were selected and why, and the money allocated to each medium and geographic region (Schultz, 1990).

Marketing research is conducted to obtain information about the marketing mix, including the product itself, its price, its distribution, the market, and competitors. Advertising research is conducted to develop, test, place, and evaluate the ads in a campaign (Schultz, 1990). Advertising and marketing research are also useful for developing a competitive position for a product or brand. Positioning describes how an advertiser wants consumers to perceive its product and should represent a product attribute that is meaningful to consumers. The strengths and weaknesses of the product or brand, as well as those of its competitors, are considered in order to identify which position is most effective. This comparison should identify a product or brand's primary advantage or benefit. The advertiser then expresses that benefit clearly, convincingly, and creatively in an ad (Ries & Trout, 1986). For example, Avis positioned itself as follows: "Avis—We're Number 2, So We Try Harder." Media managers might use this same approach to develop images or positions for their publications or broadcast stations.

Advertisers also want to know whether their ads conveyed the appropriate message or position to the appropriate segment. Consequently, they must be able to express a measurable communication objective before the campaign begins in order to have a "signpost" for evaluation. These advertising objectives are typically of three basic categories: learning (e.g., becoming aware of the product or comprehending the ad's message), feeling (e.g., developing attitudes, preferences, and/or beliefs or convictions about the product or brand), and behavioral (e.g., inquiries about, an expressed intention to, or actual purchase of the product). Advertising objectives are different from marketing objectives, which involve increasing sales or market share (Aaker & Myers, 1987).

Moriarty (1986) suggested using the formula "to do—what—to whom—how many—by when" and to be as specific as possible when writing advertising objectives. Specifically identifying the goals of a campaign is important. But stating those strategic message goals more precisely, stating a specific communication task to be accomplished, and stating the time frame in which to do so make it easier to decide whether the campaign was a success after it runs. Here is an example of an advertising objective that the Maytag company might develop for an upcoming 6-month campaign:

> To convince 30% of appliance owners who do not own our brand that Maytag sells the most dependable washers you can buy in 6 months.

Here is the same advertising objective with each component of the formula identified:

> To convince (TO DO) 30% (HOW MANY) of appliance owners who do not own our brand (TO WHOM) that Maytag sells the most dependable washers you can buy (WHAT) in 6 months (BY WHEN).

After the campaign completes its run, appliance owners who do not own Maytags can be polled to discover whether they are convinced that Maytag sells the most dependable washing machines. If 30% or more are convinced, then Maytag can conclude that its campaign successfully communicated the intended message strategy. Broadcast or print managers also may develop advertising objectives to evaluate the success of their own promotion campaigns.

Situation or Market Analysis

A market or situation analysis, the first step in developing advertising and marketing strategies, involves an in-depth examination of an advertiser's existing market situation. It is basically the planning process described in chapter 7, with those principles applied to marketing and research. The relevant history of the product or brand, including past advertising budgets and themes, is examined. The product or brand itself also is evaluated, considering such factors as how the product compares to its competition, how it has been changed in the past few years, and consumer perceptions of the product. The target market is evaluated and defined in terms of demographic, psychographic, geographic, and benefit segments. The strengths and weaknesses, current and past ad themes and expenditures, and market share and sales data of direct and indirect competitors also are examined.

An advertiser or agency conducts a situation or market analysis in order to suggest new advertising approaches, based on opportunities identified from the analysis. It enables advertisers to define the primary target market and/or identify new segments based on new social trends or the identification of new consumer desires. The situation analysis enables advertisers to develop effective and realistic advertising, media, and marketing strategies. This approach could be used by print and broadcast managers to discover new reader, listener, or viewer segments.

Consumer Research

Consumer research, which is included in a market or situation analysis, basically includes demographic, psychographic, and geographic data. Commonly used psychographic services include Yankelovich Clancy Shulman's Monitor and the Stanford Research Institute's VALS 2 (Values & Lifestyles). The Monitor surveys respondents' values and attitudes, tracks trends and uses this information to segment respondents into groups (Wickham, 1988). The VALS 2 typology emphasizes the psychological underpinnings of behavior. It categorizes consumers into three overall categories of self-orientation and presumes they are motivated by principle, status or action. VALS 2 is based on the idea that consumers buy products that provide satisfaction and give meaning to their identities (Graham, 1989).

Understanding consumer desires and the factors that influence them is of primary importance to advertisers. An advertiser selling microwave dinners who knows that convenience and good taste are important to consumers can develop more effective media strategies. The media planner can select, and the media buyer can purchase, time and space in the vehicles that the convenience segment prefers. Creative strategy can be tailored more effectively, too, by developing a message that stresses convenience and good taste. The prudent print or broadcast advertising sales manager provides the planner or advertiser with audience data that demonstrate why his vehicle should be included in a media buy. Or he could use consumer research to develop a promotional campaign touting his newspaper, magazine, broadcast station, or cable channel.

Product Research

Product research, also a component of a situation or market analysis, focuses on the perceptions consumers have about a product. Its purpose is to discover the product's unique attribute (or combination of attributes) and stress this difference in advertising. It includes other factors such as how a product compares to similar competitive offerings, present and potential new uses, and the product's relationship to other aspects of the marketing mix (e.g., price, promotion, and distribution channels).

Product research is important because it reveals what consumers do and do not know about the product. If consumers are unaware of a positive product attribute, product research identifies this opportunity and the advertiser can exploit it in advertising. It also is used to pinpoint negative perceptions and identify ways to counter them. Again, one can imagine how this kind of research might be used by other media managers to develop promotional campaigns for "products" like newspapers, magazines, broadcast stations, or cable channels or identify potential problems and opportunities.

Evaluating Advertising Effectiveness

Conducting a situation analysis, which includes product and consumer research, assists the advertiser in determining what message to convey in an ad. Before and after the ad runs, its effectiveness may be evaluated. A type of pretest of advertising effectiveness would be evaluating alternative message strategies before the general public sees the ad in order to select the most effective creative approach. A posttest might determine whether the appropriate message (e.g., that a new microwave dinner is convenient and tastes good) was conveyed to a predetermined number of the target market after the campaign completed its run (e.g., whether the advertising objective was accomplished).

Media managers can take advantage of this knowledge to explain why their vehicles help advertisers to attain effectiveness goals. For example, a newspaper advertising sales manager might explain to a retail advertiser who has a great deal of information to convey about a product (and has an objective of increasing comprehension or knowledge about the product) why a newspaper is best suited for that communication task. People can spend as much time as they need with an ad and can reread it. Thus, it is a good medium to use when conveying "knowledge" is an objective.

Sources of Advertising Research

Obviously, advertisers use many different kinds of data for many different kinds of advertising problems and questions. There are many companies, listed in Table 8.1, that provide information about consumers and their product and media usage habits to advertisers and advertising agencies (Broadcasting/Cablecasting Yearbook, 1991; Solomon, 1989). Interestingly, print and broadcast managers also use some of these same sources.

TABLE 8.1
Sources of Advertising Research

Sales and Marketing Management's Survey of Buying Power: Provides data for buying power, household income, and retail sales by type of store and merchandise.

Standard Rate and Data Service (SRDS): Provides data on consumer spendable income, retail sales and the number of households. Also publishes *The Lifestyle Market Analyst*, which breaks down the population geographically, demographically, and psychographically.

Simmons Market Research Bureau (SMRB): Provides demographic and media usage information for light, medium, and heavy users of over 500 product categories.

Mediamark Research Inc. (MRI): Provides demographic and media usage information for light, medium and heavy users of many product categories.

Selling Areas - Marketing, Inc. (SAMI): Provides data on market share and dollar volume for food and related products on a continuing basis.

National Scantrack (Nielsen) and Behavior Scan (IRI): These two companies provide retail sales data obtained using supermarket scanners.

National Purchase Diary, Inc. (NPD): Provides demographic, geographic, and media usage data obtained from a nationally representative panel that reports purchases for certain consumer product categories.

Broadcast Advertising Reports: Provides data on competitive expenditures in the broadcast medium.

Leading National Advertisers: Provides data for magazine and outdoor advertising expenditures.

Media Records: Provides data on newspaper advertising expenditures.

Radio Expenditure Reports: Provides spot radio advertising expenditure data.

Nielsen Retail Index: Provides data regarding consumer sales and retail prices and relates them to competitors.

Starch INRA Hooper: Provides media and cable radio audience measurement, radio station programming and image studies, and customized marketing and advertising impact studies.

National Yellow Pages Service: Provides reports on yellow pages advertising.

Institute of Outdoor Advertising: Provides case studies and reports on uses of outdoor advertising.

Traffic Audit Bureau: Audits outdoor circulation.

Point of Purchase Advertising Institute: Provides research reports and a newsletter.

TYPES OF RESEARCH USED BY NEWSPAPERS

A newspaper manager uses research to understand the marketing environment in which her newspaper operates. For example, a manager who is aware of changing readership and market conditions can capitalize on an opportunity to attract new readers to help offset other declining readership segments. On the other hand, if she does not know that the demographic composition of a neighborhood that traditionally has provided large numbers of readers is changing, she suddenly may be trying to increase circulation without understanding why it is declining. Thus, the prudent manager regularly conducts or contracts for research studies to keep abreast of market changes. The major types of research used by newspaper managers include circulation, readership, and advertising studies.

Circulation Studies

"Newspapers are almost always defined by geography—in their names, their local news and advertising, and their distribution" (Sohn, et al., 1986, p. 99). Geography is important to local newspaper managers because it defines the area in which readers are attracted. Circulation studies reveal the newspaper's market share, the market share of competing media, existing circulation patterns, and areas of potential circulation growth (Mauro, 1980). A newspaper manager then can conduct a situation or market analysis to determine which areas to target for increasing circulation.

Readership Studies

Readership studies help a manager to describe the people who live in those target areas. Although demographic studies are the most common type (Willis, 1988), psychographic and media usage questions also may be included in readership studies. Studies that include demographic, psychographic, and media usage questions reveal who reads the newspaper, why, which sections particular reader segments prefer, and the benefits they accrue from reading the paper. Results suggest ways to attract new readers. For example, a large metropolitan newspaper might develop a special lifestyle section to appeal to upper income city residents who are moving to a particular zip code zone. A small town newspaper might increase soccer coverage in the sports section when research shows that it is becoming an important activity for children and their parents.

Studies incorporating demographics, psychographics, and media usage may be used to measure the characteristics of audiences for competing media. Information about who exclusively reads each local daily, weekly, and shopper, who reads a combination of these publications and why, and how these and other publications are used may reveal untapped readership segments.

Using a combination of demographic, psychographic, and media usage data with content analysis reveals which segments prefer local, regional, or national news. This information helps the editor to tailor stories to the segments most likely to read them. A readership study also might test a "new" newspaper, revised to appeal to new reader segments. Finally, a readership study might determine which typeface is the most readable for all reader segments (Francese, 1988).

The prudent media manager also realizes that research is an ongoing, not a one-time, process. Cities and towns are not static. People move into or out of a region; people move to different neighborhoods; and the importance of various social, economic, and community issues changes. How can a manager tell which segments are moving in or out of a town or neighborhood if he only conducts one readership study? And how can a manager keep tabs on whether the well-educated, upper income segment that prefers international news is increasing or decreasing? Obviously, research must be conducted on a regular basis to answer these kinds of questions. Small- to middle-size papers might conduct annual surveys of readers. But larger metropolitan newspapers may find it necessary to conduct readership studies three or four times a year (Sohn, et al., 1986).

However, managers must remember that research results provide direction, not answers. Readership studies may suggest problems or opportunities. How well those problems are solved or those opportunities are exploited depends on the creativity of the individual manager using the data. In addition, managers must realize that they cannot meet all of the needs of all of their readers. Individual judgment and common sense must be used to determine which segments are large enough, and attractive enough to advertisers, to justify the development of new features or sections.

Most important, research should be viewed as an aid to making editorial decisions, not as justification for changing content. Managers always must remember that they bear the responsibility of informing the local community. This means that managers and editors must be able to make editorial judgments independent of financial concerns. Managers of media organizations understand that their responsibility to inform readers and viewers sometimes will mandate decisions about editorial content that will not be the most attractive financially.

Advertising

With this responsibility in mind, let us now consider the kinds of information advertisers and advertising agencies want from newspaper managers and sales personnel. As the advertising section explained, advertisers and agencies want information about demographics, psychographics, and media usage before buying newspaper space. The smart media manager provides accurate and honest data about the merits of his newspaper in a form that is useful to media buyers and advertisers. For example, media kits should provide the information needed for calculating and making cost per thousand comparisons. Newspapers also should include credible data, such as providing circulation estimates developed by the Audit Bureau of Circulation rather than the newspaper itself. And managers should train their sales personnel to explain why certain sections or features are useful for reaching certain reader segments. Not all segments of readers are equally attractive to advertisers. For example, well-educated readers earning higher incomes will be more attractive to advertisers selling expensive products. Although the newspaper's total proportion of these readers may not be high, research may reveal that they read certain features or sections. Media representatives should be armed with this knowledge.

The importance of providing accurate and honest information about your own medium, as well as being familiar with the competing media's advantages and disadvantages, cannot be overstated. Local, regional, and national advertisers and their agencies constantly are approached about purchasing everything from time or space to a specialty item like personalized ink pens. The typical media planner, buyer, and advertiser is familiar with the relative merits of newspapers, weeklies, shoppers, magazines, radio stations, television stations, cable channels, outdoor, direct mail, direct marketing, point-of-purchase, and specialty items. All types of media compete for a bigger share of the advertiser's dollar. And all of these media representatives are aware of the advantages and disadvantages of their own and other media. A media representative who tries to use "enhanced" data quickly is identified and countered by competing reps and ultimately loses the trust of the advertiser, media buyer, and/or planner. More important, the ethical reputation of that salesperson and vehicle is damaged, often permanently.

Media managers at smaller newspapers, radio stations or cable channels with small budgets might use published data to develop a media kit. Census data, Sales and Marketing Management's *Survey of Buying Power, Editor and Publishers Market Guide* and Standard Rate and Data Service's various publications on newspapers, magazines, radio station,s and TV stations might be found at the local library and consulted for market information. Local, state, or national trade associations also may provide data about industry trends. All of these sources can be used to discover which retailers are experiencing sales increases or decreases. The media representative then can suggest the appropriate advertising strategy. For example, if the newspaper ad manager discovers an increase in specialty store sales in her market over the past few years, she might recommend promotions or special advertising sections be developed to accommodate this trend.

Sources of Newspaper Research

Various sources are available to newspaper managers seeking any kind of information (see Table 8.2). Managers should consult local organizations like the Chamber of Commerce or other local economic development offices for market information. State agencies concerned with economic development also may provide information. State or regional press asso-

TABLE 8.2
Sources of Newspaper Research

Newspaper Association of America (NAA): Provides data about the attractiveness of newspapers as an advertising medium. Also publishes the annual *Facts About Newspapers* report.

Magazine Publishers of America (MPA): Conducts studies comparing print and TV every few years. Also publishes the *MPA Newsletter of Research*, which includes an annual statistical report on magazines.

Media Records Inc.: Measures and reports newspaper advertising lineage for over 200 daily and Sunday papers. Also provides compilations of national brands and products in news and trade publications.

Starch INRA Hooper Inc.: Conducts newspaper and magazine advertising readership studies. Provides local, national and international advertising and public opinion research.

Pulse Research: Conducts market research for small newspapers. Designs studies that analyze readership demographics, the relative strengths of media, shopping patterns, purchase data for the retail market and so forth.

Editor & Publisher's Market Guide: Provides facts and figures about all U.S. daily newspaper markets, including estimates of number of households, local population estimates, estimates of disposable personal income, kinds of industries, important shopping centers, and the number of banks and deposits.

Sales & Marketing Management Survey of Buying Power: Provides information on the population, retail sales, and buying power of U.S. markets.

Standard Rate and Data Service Newspaper Rates and Data: Provides rankings in descending order of U.S. markets based on gross household income, total household expenditures, and expenditures for food, drug, general merchandise, and automotive stores. Includes a consumer market data summary that provides totals of 18 market data categories by state, census divisions of the United States and total United States. Also provides metro demographic characteristics, as well as rates charged by daily, weekly, Black, and college and university newspapers.

Audit Bureau of Circulation (ABC): Audits the circulation of paid newspapers, consumer, and trade magazines. Provides individual publication circulation and trend data, and specialty analyses.

Business Publications Audit (BPA): Provides roughly the same services ABC does, except for trade publications.

U.S. Bureau of the Census: Publishes data and indexes providing the demographic, social, and economic characteristics of U.S. markets, as well as annual Census updates in the Statistical Abstracts.

---

ciations sometimes compile primary and secondary market information. The creative manager consults these and other sources when developing a market kit (*Broadcasting/Cablecasting Yearbook*, 1991; Solomon, 1989).

TYPES OF RESEARCH USED BY BROADCASTERS

Broadcasters also use the same kinds of information that newspaper managers, advertising managers, and ad agency managers use. However, as with the other groups, this research is tailored to the special needs of the broadcast media.

There are few basic concepts that all broadcast managers must understand. A rating refers to the estimated percentage of the universe of TV households (or some other specified group) that is tuned to a program at one time. A share refers to the estimated percentage of households using television (HUT) that is watching a program. Advertisers and agencies compare the ratings and shares of different programs on different stations and channels to decide which ones to buy. The term reach refers to the percentage of the audience that is exposed to a vehicle, ad or program in a given period. Frequency refers to how often that audience is reached. An advertiser may select a particular medium, or combination of media, based on whether he sells his product to the public at large or a specialized segment (such as basketball fans). Generally, one might expect to reach more viewers using television, because this medium typically attracts larger audiences. One might achieve higher frequency using radio, because spots are cheaper and an advertiser can purchase more of them (Lancaster & Katz, 1989).

Managers should be aware of the different kinds of broadcast research in order to use these techniques to compete effectively. These research types include audience, programming, and sales.

Audience

Audience research is the lifeblood of the broadcasting industry. Broadcast managers want to know which programs attract the highest number of viewers or listeners, and the characteristics of those attracted, in order to make programming decisions. Advertisers and agency media planners scrutinize audience data to find the appropriate audience for their products. Some advertisers who sell products to the general public (e.g., laundry detergent) may desire large, heterogeneous audiences, whereas others who sell more specialized types of products (e.g., tennis rackets) may seek smaller and specialized, homogeneous audiences. Broadcast managers must keep abreast of audience demographics, psychographics, and media usage habits in order to sell the station's time to advertisers (Beville, 1988).

Audience research may become even more important in the future because of the continued segmentation of broadcast audiences. With increasing competition from pay cable, pay-per-view, subscription TV, satellites, and VCRs, managers expect that the competition for broadcast audiences will intensify. This means that the competition for advertising dollars will intensify as well. Broadcast managers must also understand the advantages and disadvantages of their own, as well as other, media vehicles in order to select the programs viewers prefer and thus remain attractive to advertisers.

Arbitron and Nielsen provide estimates of the size and characteristics of broadcast audiences. Both Nielsen and Arbitron provide audience measurement data for television and cable and Arbitron reports audience data for radio. These services also offer specialized and customized reports, in either printed or computer-ready form.

Both Arbitron and Nielsen assign stations nationwide to only one viewing region based on whether they are the stations primarily tuned to by viewers in a given metropolitan area. These nonduplicated, mutually exclusive market areas establish by county the area to which viewers tune. Nielsen calls them Designated Market Areas (DMA), whereas Arbitron calls them Areas of Dominant Influence (ADI). Arbitron defines an ADI "as a geographic survey area created and defined by Arbitron based on measurable patterns of television viewing" (Guide, 1987, p. 37). Each county in the continental United States is assigned only to one DMA or ADI. Another commonly-used market definition is the Total Survey Area (TSA) or the total market area in which viewing or listening takes place. The Metro Survey Area (MSA), which generally corresponds to the U.S. Government's Office of Management and Budget's Standard Metropolitan Statistical Area (SMSA), is a geographic area that includes a city and the area nearest to the station's transmitter (Guide, 1987).

Listening and viewing habits typically are measured by using diaries, meters, or telephone surveys (Beville, 1988). Diaries are booklets in which viewers and listeners record the stations they watch or listen to and when. Meters automatically record when each set in a home is turned on and off and to which station each is tuned. One of the commonly-used telephone survey methods is day-after recall, in which respondents are called to determine their listening and viewing activities from the previous day. The coincidental method also is used commonly. Here, households are called at random during the time period of interest and respondents are asked what they are watching or listening to at that time (Wimmer & Dominick, 1991).

Managers must keep a few of limitations in mind when evaluating audience data. Respondents may not be careful, or honest, when reporting their viewing and listening habits. A meter only records which channel is tuned in and when by the respondent pushing the appropriate button(s) — it does not record whether anyone stayed in the room to watch. In addition, diary reports tend to underestimate the audiences of independent stations; such stations typically earn higher ratings in reports based on meters. The three major national TV networks (ABC, CBS, and NBC) have raised concerns over the reliability of data based on people meter estimates. Questions about improving the cooperation rate of households in the Nielsen sample, metering more households, and developing ways of dealing with respondents who become tired of pushing buttons to indicate what they are watching have been raised (Walley, 1990).

Concerns have been raised about radio audience data. Arbitron's diary method favors stations using formats like news/talk and easy listening that target audiences 35 years old and over ("Katz Study Says," 1988). A manager must consider these and other limitations when evaluating audience data for radio, TV, and cable. Specifically, managers must be aware that all ratings are estimates and there is no perfect system for obtaining and developing those estimates. And managers must remember the paradox that ratings and shares measure past performance yet are used to predict future performance (Beville, 1988).

Programming

Audience data are also used by radio, television, and cable managers to aid in programming decision making. A ratings decline for a syndicated television program (e.g., Wheel of Fortune) over a few sweeps (or ratings periods) signals the need for obtaining a new show for that particular time period. A decline in shares during morning drive time (6–10 am) may force a manager to consider firing the morning on-air personality. Audience data are very important to radio, television, and cable managers to assist in planning and changing program schedules.

Radio programming research is developed to discover the audience's favorite music, formats, and on-air personalities. A random telephone survey might ask potential listeners about the kinds of music they like to hear and the artists and on-air personalities they prefer. Radio programmers also must find out whether their listeners are familiar with, like, and/or are tiring of their musical offerings and on-air personalities. Commonly used techniques for answering these questions include focus groups and call-outs (Sherman, 1987).

Focus groups, led by a trained moderator and composed of about 10-12 listeners from the appropriate target audience, discuss for a few hours the pluses and minuses of the programming, promotions, on-air personalities, and commercials aired by a station. Focus groups are used to discover the preferences of present and potential listeners. Samples of the station's musical and on-air sound are played to focus group members, who are encourage to express candid opinions about what they hear.

Managers must keep a few limitations in mind when evaluating focus group results. The insights based on in-depth comments may not represent listeners' feelings as a whole, because only a few were interviewed. Managers also must look at results with an eye for determining whether the moderator actually encouraged honest group discussion and how carefully the group itself was selected.

Call-out research is used to evaluate the popularity of the station's present and future musical offerings. "Hooks," which are representative 10- to 30-sec song excerpts, are played over the phone to respondents of a one-shot study or members of an ongoing listener panel. Both types of respondents report whether they like or dislike each hook. A manager must discern whether the sample is representative of listeners' demographic and psychographic characteristics when evaluating call-out results. If the sample is not representative of the appropriate audience segment, results will hamper future programming decisions (Rich & Martin, 1981).

Television managers also are concerned with determining how popular their programs and on-air personalities are. A manager might conduct a mail or telephone survey, focus group, or personal interviews to determine whether his news talent and newscast is favored by the local community. Results may be used to determine whether the local news anchor should be replaced.

Image studies are used to find out how the public perceives a local TV station or cable system. Such studies are used to find out whether promotions featuring new on-air personalities and remote news equipment succeeded in changing local perceptions of the station. Image studies should be conducted regularly to keep tabs on whether changes in programming and talent have altered station image positively or negatively. That way, a manager can take advantage of certain changes or correct others before they become a problem.

A station must also ascertain community views about programming, including how well it is covering local issues and problems. The Federal Communications Commission notes that licensees should try to discover local broadcasting "tastes, needs and desires" (*Ascertainment*, 1976; En banc, 1960, p. 2312; *Primer*, 1971). It evaluates licensee performance in this regard by considering how responsive programming is to local needs rather than how a licensee arrives at programming decisions (*Revision*, 1984).

Test marketing is another research technique used for television and cable. For example, a program might be shown in one market before it is shown nationally in order to project what its national rating might be. Programs might be shown in two different markets or on a two-way cable system in one city, with subscribers in one part of the city seeing one version of a program or commercial whereas those living in another area might see a second version. Results of a random telephone survey would reveal which program version earned higher ratings or which commercial spurred more sales.

Concept testing is used to test the popularity of a program before it is viewed by the general public. A program concept might be tested by having respondents read a one-page written summary or showing them a mock-up of a commercial made using slides and an audiotape. In a third type of concept test, respondents are invited to a theater to view a pilot program. After viewing, they report their feelings about the program to help network executives determine how popular various characters and endings might be (Fletcher, 1981).

Advertising Sales

Audience estimates also are used to sell station, cable channel, or network time to advertisers. Advertisers are interested in information regarding audience size and composition. They want assurances that their ads reach customers who buy, or are likely to buy, their products and services. Broadcast managers must provide such information in order to compete effectively in a market.

Advertisers buy individual spots as well as total packages. Advertisers, media planners, and/or media buyers use Gross Rating Points (GRPs) to obtain a rough estimate of audience potential. GRPs are simply the sum of the rating points delivered by an advertising schedule (Lancaster & Katz, 1989). Broadcast managers and sales personnel must be able to discuss their stations' offerings to national, regional, and local advertisers in terms of individual programs as well as the ability of a group of programs or daypart to reach a particular audience segment in appropriate numbers.

One way of providing advertisers with useful information is to develop a case study (Warner, 1989). Case studies describe in detail how a station helped an advertiser solve marketing and advertising problems. Salespersons use case studies to demonstrate the kind of advertising assistance and expertise a station offers. A manager first must obtain permission from the client and/or ad agency, who may fear that competitors will try to duplicate their success. However, the identity of the advertiser and agency may be changed to avoid this problem.

Warner (1989) explained the elements to include in a successful case study: (Note the similarities between a case study, a market or situation analysis, and the planning process discussed in chapter 7.)

1. *The marketing environment*: This section describes the short-and long-term developments and trends in the market. It might include changes in demographics, regulation, and/or the economy.

2. *The competition*: This section evaluates current and potential direct and indirect competitors. The primary strategies and market shares of competitors are discussed, as well as major strengths and weaknesses. Advertising strategies and positioning statements also should be reviewed.

3. *The marketing objectives*: This section describes the advertiser's measurable marketing goals, such as "increasing market share by 3 points."

4. *The marketing strategy*: This section reviews how well the advertiser's primary marketing strategy is executed.

5. *The advertising objectives*: This section describes the measurable communication goals that the advertiser wants the advertising to accomplish.

6. *The advertiser's competitive positioning statement*: This section describes the advertiser's expression of how she wants consumers to perceive or think of her product or service or store. A positioning statement must make a promise to consumers and define "who" the product or service or store is.

7. *The problems that advertising can solve*: This section describes the problems from the advertiser's point of view in an objective and unbiased way.

8. *The solutions to the advertising problems*: This section provides details about the solutions the station and its salesperson provided. These include creative solutions, such as the advertising idea, strategy and execution, and media strategies, plans and executions, such as promotions, research, and copy testing. This section provides details about the actual schedule purchased, as well as reach and frequency estimates.

9. *The results*: This section summarizes the results in measurable and specific terms. Discussion should include how well the campaign worked, whether and how the objectives were met, and whether any or all of the campaign's success was attributable to the station.

Broadcast Research Sources

Various industry groups provide assistance for developing case studies and sales kits, as well as market or industry data (Solomon, 1989). A number of companies provide research services for radio, television, and/or cable broadcasters (Broadcasting/Cablecasting Yearbook, 1991). Again, note that some of these companies provide information also used by print and advertising managers (see Table 8.3).

SUMMARY

All media managers must understand research from a broad perspective in order to use it effectively. Advertising, brand, print, and broadcast managers use similar kinds of data and research techniques in different ways and obtain information from the same research sources. Managers also should understand the research data and techniques their counterparts use. Hopefully, managers will use this knowledge to serve their own media organizations, clients, and especially their audiences more effectively.

TABLE 8.3

Sources of Broadcast Research

National Association of Broadcasters (NAB): Industry organization that works on broadcast issues. Provides research advice and assistance to members.

Television Bureau of Advertising (TVB): Publishes *TvBasics* annually, which contains a wide variety of statistics.

Association of Independent Television Stations (INTV): Provides studies about viewing habits and commercial effectiveness for independent TV stations.

Advertiser Syndicated Television Association (ASTA): Provides reports and sponsors workshops to improve understanding of use of syndication.

Cabletelevision Advertising Bureau: Provides reports on cable audiences and advertising and produces *Cable TV Facts*, a compilation of cable information.

Cable Television Information Center: Advises local governments on cable TV legal, financial, and programming matters.

Radio Advertising Bureau (RAB): Provides information about radio advertising and publishes *Radio Facts and RAB Instant Background Report*, which includes marketing data on 50 industries.

FMR Associates, Inc.: Provides perceptual and programming studies, weekly call-outs, format opportunity, and vulnerability positioning studies. Also provides testing of TV commercials and programming simulation tests.

The Research Group: Provides marketing research for radio.

Radio Expenditure Reports: Provides national spot radio expenditures on a monthly and quarterly basis by advertiser and market.

Frank N. Magid Associates, Inc.: Provides consulting and research services for broadcast, cable, and programming. Methods for local and national studies include personal and telephone interviews, opinions polls, focus groups, and in-studio groups.

Reymer & Gersin Associates Inc.: Provides marketing, programming, and promotions research for broadcasting and cable based on attitudinal, psychographic, and segmentation analysis.

Arbitron: Provides estimates of radio and TV audiences for specific dayparts and programs. Audiences are broken down demographically and geographically. Data are available in print or computer form. Also provides *Broadcast Advertisers Reports*, which _____ ___mercials, and SAMI product tracking services.

Nielsen Media Research. Provides _____ ___ ___ ____ ____ services for television and cable.

Electronic Media Rating Council: Reviews rating services' methodology to ensure users of credible data. Also has developed Minimum Standards for Electronic Media Rating Research.

Starch INRA Hooper: Measures media and cable radio audiences, provides radio station programming and image studies.

Market Opinion Research: Provides market and viewer satisfaction research for television stations. Also assists in strategic planning.

SRI Research Center Inc.: Provides news, promotion effectiveness, image studies, positioning, and programming research.

TVQ Inc.: Provides national syndicated rating services for TV performers, cartoon characters, companies, products, brand names, sports personalities, and athletes.

Mediamark Research Inc.: Provides product usage data and demographics for radio, TV, and cable.

Simmons Market Research Bureau (SMRB): Provides broadcast and related intermedia data, including demographics and geographics.

CHAPTER 8 CASES

Case 8.1

The Case of WZZY's Dilemma: Do We Need A New Format?

Todd Backer was thrilled—he'd finally been appointed programming manager at a major market radio station. However, he had a big job on his hands. WZZY had been ranked either tenth or eleventh in the Dallas market for years. A succession of program managers had tried to improve WZZY'S record, with limited success. Part of the problem was that the top four stations had been successful at maintaining their high rankings for years. Two reasons were that their formats, musical selections, and on-air personalities were popular and their station images were well developed. WKCK and WCTY cornered the market on country, so to speak. WKCK, otherwise known as Kickin' Country, had been a strong number one for years. WKCK relied on its traditional country format, playing the music of "old" artists, such as Charley Pride and Loretta Lynn, coupled with new traditionalists like Randy Travis. Kickin' Country also had a strong news department, known for live, on-the-spot coverage of breaking news.

WCTY was content with its third place ranking in the market, because it used the contemporary country format that appealed to younger, more prosperous, country fans (who were attractive to advertisers because of their buying power). WCLS, the second-ranked station using a middle-of-the-road format, attracted the 25 to 45 year olds and was known as the local sports leader (because it carried high school and college football and basketball broadcasts). Finally, the fourth-ranked WTOP played contemporary top 40 hits, appealing to the lucrative 18- to 24-year-old market. WTOP was very successful at promoting itself with this segment, sponsoring local music festivals and college events.

Todd's mandate was to improve WZZY's standing—or else. WZZY's format was presently album-oriented rock (AOR), featuring artists like the Rolling Stones, Eric Clapton, and ZZ Top. Todd's "gut feeling" was that this format was a major part of the problem. WRCK, another station in the market that had been ranked about sixth for years, also used an AOR format. Todd felt there just was not enough interest to support two AOR stations.

Todd discussed this problem with the general manager and owner, Bob Curtis, and suggested that the station conduct research to determine if his suspicion was correct. He also wanted to discover what other formats the station might adopt. Curtis agreed, but also wanted the research project to suggest which audience segment (or segments) to target. He wanted to be certain that this new format would attract listeners advertisers wanted to reach. Curtis directed Todd to recommend a research project which would accomplish all of these goals.

Assignment

1. How can Todd determine whether the album rock format is the problem? What kind of research project should he recommend?
2. Should Todd recommend more than one study? If so, which research project should be conducted first and why? Which aspect of the problem should be researched second, and so forth.
3. How can Todd determine which audience segments might be good potential listener targets before the research project begins?

Background on Radio Formats

The Broadcasting/Cablecasting Yearbook (1991) provides a breakdown of the radio programming formats used in the United States and Canada. McCavitt and Pringle (1986) and Head and Stirling (1990) provided descriptions of the major formats, including:

> Adult Contemporary/Hit Music—appeals to persons age 18 to 34 years. Emphasizes currently popular songs and artists and uses a broad array of current and classic hits to appeal to a wide range of adults.
>
> Album-Oriented Rock (AOR)—appeals to persons, especially men, age 18 to 34 years and includes current hits and oldies, with a strong emphasis on artists. Album cuts, and occasionally the entire side of an album or CD, are played. Mixes less popular songs from successful albums with classic rock hits.
>
> Beautiful Music—known as good or easy listening; traditionally background, instrumental versions of slower tempo hit songs and oldies.
>
> Big Band/Nostalgia—appeals to persons age 35+ years, who prefer the music of the 1930s, 1940s and 1950s (nonrock only).
>
> Black—features Black artists and music. Playlist may include gospel, soul, and other traditional Black recordings.
>
> Contemporary Hit Radio (CHR)/Top-40—appeals primarily to 18 to 24 year olds, but also attracts listeners age 12 to 34 years. Playlist consists of top-selling pop and rock singles. Oldies are played occasionally.
>
> Classic Rock/Oldies—appeals mostly to listeners over 30 years old. Features hits from the 1950s and 1960s.

Classical—plays recorded classical music, as well as live opera, symphony, and chamber music performances. Appeals to better educated and higher socioeconomic categories.

Country—appeals to men and women ages 25 to 64 years in all socioeconomic categories. Specialized versions of this format include traditional and contemporary country/country-rock (music appealing to both country and rock audiences).

Jazz—appeals mostly to persons in the higher socioeconomic categories. Usually has limited appeal.

Middle-of-the-Road (MOR)—appeals to adults 25 to 45 years old. Includes vocal and instrumental versions of contemporary, nonrock popular music and standard hits and makes extensive use of on-air announcers. Typically a heavy emphasis on news, sports, weather, traffic, sports events, and broadcast talk and interviews.

News—appeals to adults 25 to 54 years old, mostly to better educated men. Consists of local, regional, national and international news, features, analysis, commentary and editorials. Program cycles of 20 or 30 min are developed, because it is assumed audiences will tune in only for short periods of time.

Urban Contemporary—appeals to Black 18–49-year-old group, but also attracts many Whites. Basically a combination of jazz, disco, and dance-beat rock and roll. Format varies widely by station and market.

Talk—appeals to adults age 35 to 65. Features interviews and audience call-ins about many different subjects. May also feature psychologists, marriage counselors, and sex therapists who encourage listeners to talk about their personal problems.

Case 8.2

Assignment: Analyzing A Media Market

You have just been hired as the head of the media department at Acme Advertising Agency. (Assume Acme is located in the largest major city nearest you.) You are the top media planner for the agency, as well as department head. Acme is a small agency with only 10 employees in its media department. Acme's clients are mostly local, but the agency has begun to attract a few national clients because of its outstanding creative reputation. Your predecessor worked for the agency for over 20 years, but left because these national, and some local, clients were complaining that they did not understand why certain media buys were made. They also complained that they did not receive adequate justification for the media buys that were made.

As you sift through your predecessor's desk and files, you note a woeful lack of information about the local media, and essentially none about the national media. Basically, the files contained rate cards and recent copies of syndicated radio and television ratings reports. You call your predecessor, who says that he simply "knew the market by heart" and did not need much documentation for the various media. He tells you that he thought it was a big mistake for the agency to solicit national clients. They were too demanding and were always nitpicking about details. You quickly realize that you do not have the information on hand that you need to do your job.

You report your impressions to your boss, the agency's owner, who agrees with your assessment and directs you to develop the data base you need. "We don't have any big media projects due right now. Unless something comes up, spend the next 2 weeks putting together the information we need to bring our media department into the twenty-first century. Develop an analysis of the local media market that we can use and suggest what outside sources of data we might buy. As you know, we serve local and national clients in a number of different areas: a major local bank, a national manufacturer of packaged goods, a major national wine producer, a major local grocery chain, a major local automobile dealership, a national catalog selling men's and women's clothing and household goods, a major local department store, and a prominent local restaurant, to name a few. Keep these clients in mind when you develop your analysis, but also consider that we're going to try to attract other major local and national accounts over the next few years. We need to be 'up to snuff' with the big agencies, if possible. But remember: We're a small agency. So prioritize what you need so I can figure out a way to buy the essentials for you now and buy other materials as funds become available."

Develop a market report for your boss that evaluates and compares the major local media outlets. Compare the merits and demerits of the major local print, broadcast, outdoor and direct mail outlets. Also include any other important local media vehicles that are unique to the major city nearest you. Provide a basic description of each vehicle and its audience, providing information about its most popular features or programs, as well as audience composition data. Avoid the tendency to rely solely on information provided by each vehicle. Also seek out information that describes the demographic and psychographic composition of the market, as well as purchasing habits and the level of local discretionary income. Also find out as much as you can about local media usage habits.

Review the *Gale Directory of Publications & Broadcast Media* and the *Broadcasting Yearbook* to find out what the major media vehicles are in your city. Examine Census data, Sales & Marketing Management's annual *Survey of Buying Power, Editor & Publisher Market Guide*, and any Standard Rate and Data Service publication for market and consumer information. Also review SRDS's *The Lifestyle Market Analyst*, which breaks down the American population geographically and demographically and includes lifestyle information on the popular interests, hobbies, and activities in each market. Also review other appropriate sources of information about your market, its residents, and their buying patterns.

Consider what other syndicated research reports you might need for your agency besides syndicated ratings reports for broadcast. For example, consider whether your agency should purchase the *Simmons* and/or *Mediamark* reports, as well as other local, regional, or national sources of syndicated research. Also consider any other sources of information that might be appropriate for the agency to purchase. Evaluate the merits of these sources and recommend which ones your agency should buy. Prioritize and explain your choices.

Finally, develop a report for your boss that includes all of these elements:

1. An analysis of the consumers in your market and any major segments that may be good targets for your clients. Provide any data tables that support your analysis.

2. An analysis of the various major media vehicles in your market. The strengths and weaknesses of each vehicle should be discussed and cost efficiencies compared.

3. An analysis of the national and/or local sources of syndicated research that should be purchased by the agency. Review the merits and demerits of each and rank each source in order of importance to the agency.

4. An analysis of any other sources you recommend for purchase. Review the advantages and disadvantages of these sources and rank each source in order of importance to the agency.

5. An analysis of how all of this information will be used by the agency. For example, describe how your local market and media analyses can be used now in developing media plans. Discuss how each syndicated research source can be used to develop media plans for current clients. Also discuss how each source might be used for potential clients.

6. Recommendations on the sources of information that must be purchased right away. Present a timetable for purchasing other sources of information. Justify your decisions.

Case 8.3

Assignment: Conducting a Situation Analysis and Developing Advertising and Media Recommendations

Mediamark Research Inc. (MRI) publishes 20 volumes every spring that cross-tabulate product/service data by demographic characteristics and media audiences. Three types of tables are presented for the majority of

products and services included in the reports: summary, detailed product/
service, and brand tables. The summary tables provide data about users,
including users by brand, users by type and kind of product, and share of
total volume by brand. The detailed product/service tables cross-tabulate
heavy, medium, and light users by demographic and media usage information, including magazines, newspaper readership, TV by daypart, and
radio by daypart. The brand tables are cross-tabulated by demographics.
(MRI has developed a guide entitled "How to Read and Use the Mediamark Product Reports," which explains how to read and interpret these
tables.)

Select a brand of a product or service that is found in the *Mediamark
Product Reports*. (Note that the Simmons Market Research Bureau reports
also may be used.) Review the tables, as well as advertising trade and
academic publications for information about the brand you have picked. (It
is a good idea to use the *Business Periodical Index* to start your search. Also
review the sources of advertising research listed in the chapter and see if
any are available at your local campus or community library.) Try writing
to the company for information about the brand. Examine the brand itself
and its advertising. Analyze competitive products/services and advertisements as well. Also consult any other sources or publications you can think
of that provide information about your brand, the product or service
category in which it competes, and its competitors.

Then write a situation analysis and make advertising and media
recommendations for the brand. (Use the case study example described in
this chapter, as well as the market analysis chapter, as a guide. Also review
Schultz, 1990, chapter 4.) Your situation analysis should include a relevant
history of the brand and an evaluation of how it compares to its competitors on important attributes. Include a consumer evaluation that provides
a demographic and psychographic description of present and potential
users, as well as an analysis of present customers' behaviors. Evaluate your
brand's direct and indirect competitors as well in a competitive analysis
section, by analyzing their strengths and weaknesses and advertising
campaigns and themes.

After completing your situation analysis, make advertising recommendations for the brand. Identify who the primary and secondary target
markets should be and why. Write an advertising objective that states what
future advertising for the brand should accomplish. Explain the creative
strategy, or "what" should be said in your proposed ad campaign. Make
any suggestions you can about ad layout and copy, the tone or manner to
be used in ads, and any other content or production ideas that explain your
campaign more clearly.

Then, make media recommendations. Explain as clearly and concisely as
you can which media the ads should run in and why. For example,
recommend newspaper(s), magazines(s), radio station(s) or network(s),

television station(s) or network(s), and/or cable channel(s) or network(s) in which your ads should appear. (Also review the appropriate Standard Rate and Data Service books for more information about media.) Calculate and provide CPM figures if the appropriate data are available.

Case 8.4

Assignment: Measuring Newspaper Quality

Assume you are the director of marketing research for the local or national newspaper of your choice. The publisher of this paper is concerned about a research trend that suggests circulation is beginning to decline. The publisher wants you to develop a study to test editorial, as well as reader, assessments of the quality of your paper. The goal is to identify the paper's strengths and weaknesses in order to find out what actions are needed to stem a circulation decline. She suggests that you consider the criteria found in Leo Bogart's book *Press and Public: Who Reads What, When, Where and Why in American Newspapers* (1989, see pp. 258-265). (See Wimmer & Dominick, 1991, chapter 2, for more information about how to write a research proposal.)

Assignment

Write a preliminary research proposal for the publisher that includes the following:

1. Suggest an appropriate method for conducting research regarding newspaper quality. Describe the type of research, appropriate subjects, sample size, and so forth. that you think will assess quality best. Decide whether separate studies are needed to examine editorial and reader perceptions of quality. Describe the appropriate methodology for both, if you think separate studies are needed.

2. Provide a preliminary list of questions or a questionnaire that demonstrates how you think quality should be measured for each study you propose.

3. Provide a rationale for why you chose the quality measures you did for each study you propose. Explain how the questions or questionnaire items will measure assessments of quality from both an editor's and reader's standpoint.

4. Provide a timetable. Explain when you think the research project(s) should be conducted and why. Discuss how long you think it will take to complete the study or studies and provide information regarding when each stage in development and implementation will take place. Also state when you expect to present the results.

Case 8.5

Assignment: Should the News Anchor Be Fired?

Jane Smithies, news director at KDTV, summoned the station's marketing and research director, Jack Johansen, in for a meeting. It seemed that the ratings for the early and late evening newscasts were slipping. "Walter Dobson may no longer be the news institution he once was," Jane told Jack. "It's your job to find out. We have to find out why ratings are slipping and take action. Otherwise, we'll quickly slip from number two to number three in this market. And we can't afford that."

Jack was well aware how competitive the market was. A loss of just a few ratings points usually meant thousands of dollars of lost advertising revenue. The station had to be very careful in taking any action, whether trying something new or resolving a problem. Any change that resulted in even a minor ratings loss was usually felt in the pocketbook.

"Jack, you've got to find out whether Dobson is the problem or whether changes are needed in the format and content of our newscasts." Jane also told Jack that he needed to present a brief summary of the kind of research the station could conduct to solve this problem, or whether it would make better sense to hire an outside company to evaluate the problem and propose solutions.

Pretend that you are Jack Johansen. Prepare a report that explains whether the stations should conduct research itself or hire an outside consultant to evaluate the news programs. Explain the rationale for your decision. Consult your local library for information about broadcast research and broadcast consultants. Also interview a local broadcast manager (or invite one to speak in class). Pretend that KDTV is located in your home market and make suggestions accordingly. Prepare a report that includes the following information:

1. Suggest the type of research that might be conducted. Prepare questions that would assess fairly whether the anchor or the program is the problem. Suggest the best methodology for finding this out. Explain why this methodology is the best one for solving this problem.

2. Evaluate the advantages and disadvantages of conducting research in-house versus hiring an outside consultant. Is it better to have an independent party plan the research and make a judgment in this case? Why or why not?

3. Suggest which local research company, national research company, local consultant, and national consultant might be suited best for solving this problem. Present the advantages and disadvantages of using each.

4. Recommend the best way to address this problem. Explain why the station itself should conduct the research, or who should be hired. Be sure to justify your answer.

Case 8.6

Assignment: Starting a Local Magazine

Pretend that you work for a research company in your own or the nearest major city. You have been contacted by Brown Publishing, a major national publishing firm based in that city. Brown wants to expand into magazine publishing, ideally in the same market where it is based. The company would prefer to learn about magazine publishing by trying it locally first. If successful, it would try introducing a national magazine.

You have been assigned the Brown account. Your job is to prepare a report that states whether it is advisable to start a new magazine locally. Sources of available data should be examined to discern if there are any demographic, psychographic, special interest, or other segments in the community that could support a magazine. You might start by reviewing the Standard Rate and Data Service's publications, *Consumer Magazine & Agri-Media Rates & Data* and *Business Publication Rates & Data*, to see what the major magazine categories are and the many types of magazines that are published. These books also include data on metropolitan statistical areas, as well as consumer market data. The *Gale Directory of Publications & Broadcast Media* could be reviewed to see what publications already exist in your city. The *Editor & Publisher Market Guide* could also be reviewed for a description of your city, as well as population, income, and retail sales tables. *The Lifestyle Market Analyst* also could be reviewed for demographic and psychographic information. Use your imagination and do some digging to locate other sources of information. Your report should include the following:

1. Suggest a magazine title and theme. Describe what the editorial mission of the magazine might be. Suggest possible features, columns, and other contents.

2. Identify and describe the possible segment(s) in your community that could support this magazine. Discuss the size and composition of these segment(s). Provide as much information as you can about the segment(s).

3. Propose a brief research plan that would reveal whether the segment(s) would support the proposed magazine and its contents. Tell which research method would be suited best for this research problem and why. Explain how the research should be conducted and the kinds of questions that should be included in the questionnaire.

4. Present a timetable and brief outline of the entire research project. Briefly outline what each stage of the research project will be and estimate how long each stage will take to complete each stage.

5. Describe the criteria that should be used, based on the research findings, to determine whether the magazine should be launched.

Case 8.7

Assignment: Dealing With Cable Customer Dissatisfaction

You are the manager of the cable system in your city (or the nearest city). You are concerned about the constant complaints from customers regarding service. You received 20 letters this week alone; you shudder to think how many complaints the receptionist received by phone. You also are concerned because the local city government is beginning to make noise about the poor level of service the cable company provides.

You have decided to conduct a survey of subscribers to identify what the major problems are and how they might be solved. You have never conducted a survey before and you really cannot afford to hire a research firm. You must find a way to design a study that can be conducted by you and your employees.

Prepare a report describing how you could design and conduct such a survey from scratch, using only company employees and resources. This report should include the following:

1. Identify and describe the appropriate method to use to conduct the survey and how it can be handled in-house. In other words, what kind of a survey can be handled by local cable employees and why?

2. Discuss which sources of free or low-cost information might be consulted for developing your consumer survey. Explain how these sources can be used and why they are appropriate for this situation.

3. Explain how questions for the questionnaire will be developed. In other words, how can you find out what the major problems probably are before you conduct the survey? How can you decide which questions to include in the survey and why? How can you allow for employee input on which questions should be included? How can you allow for community input on which questions should be included?

4. Provide examples of the types of questions that will measure accurately what your major service problems are.

5. Suggest other questions that should be included, if any, besides questions regarding the problems and their solutions? Describe the other types of questions that might be included and explain why they are/are not needed.

6. Make a decision regarding the kind of survey you should conduct. Explain and support your decision.

9
Budgeting and Decision Making

Managers use a variety of types of information in the process of making decisions. This chapter discusses how media managers use accounting information for making decisions, planning the future, and controlling organizational behavior. Most people think of accounting as indecipherable and sometimes meaningless columns of numbers representing debits and credits. Indeed, accounting information often is presented in annual reports and budgets as rows and columns of dollars and cents. Despite the financial emphasis, accounting also provides meaningful, nonfinancial information describing the past, present, and future status of an organization. Without accounting information, managers would not have the necessary information for planning, decision making, and evaluating performance; organizations would have poorly defined goals, if they were to have goals at all; and managerial learning and organizational growth might never occur. Consequently, accounting provides essential information for the day-to-day activities and long-term growth and survival of organizations.

A manager is faced with a wide range of accounting information. The information a manager chooses to use in making a decision depends on several factors, including the manager's level in the organization, the long- or short-term nature of the decision, the organization's size and complexity, and the nature of the firm. Regardless of the variety of types and forms of accounting information available to managers, one form of information managers use extensively is the budget. Thus, the focus of this chapter is on how managers develop and use budgets in planning and controlling the functions of a media organization.

TYPES OF ACCOUNTING INFORMATION

Based on the intended use of the information, accounting activities and the types of information they generate generally are divided into financial accounting and managerial accounting. Financial accounting provides information about an organization's health to outsiders. Managerial accounting provides information about the day-to-day operation of the company for managers to use in planning and budgeting. Although both are related to managing an organization, this chapter concentrates primarily on managerial accounting.

Financial Accounting Information

Financial accounting refers to the preparation of materials for use primarily by individuals external to the organization. Materials such as annual reports are products of financial accounting and are intended for a variety of users including the general public, regulatory agencies, owners, investors, creditors, taxing authorities, and industry associations. A primary component of financial accounting reports is the balance sheet. An example of a balance sheet for a newspaper corporation with six twice-weekly newspapers is provided in Table 9.1.

A balance sheet reflects the financial status of a corporation by listing its assets and liabilities. It serves as a stop-action photograph of a company on a given date. When a series of balance sheets are examined together, the stopped action begins to move, showing how the company behaved across time.

The balance sheet is divided into two main sections: assets and liabilities and shareholder's equity. *Assets* are resources that a company owns or that are owed to a company. *Liabilities* are amounts of money that are owed by the company in some form to a person or organization. Both assets and liabilities take many forms, but the total assets minus the total liabilities reveals how well off the company is. The difference between assets and liabilities is *shareholder's equity*, which represents the value of the company that belongs to the owners.

The balance sheet gets its name from the fact that assets always must equal liabilities and shareholder's equity. In other words, the balance sheets tells you how the assets are related to the liabilities and owner's equity.

Several of the terms in the balance sheet shown in Table 9.1 need defining:

Assets

Current assets include money or other resources that are converted easily to money. For example, accounts receivable includes money owed the company for services or products rendered. Inventories are those objects that can be sold readily for cash.

Investments and other assets are any resource that comes from investing other resources. For example, a daily newspaper that has bought part

TABLE 9.1
Balance Sheet for Weekly Newspaper Group

		Year	
Assets	This Year	Last Year	2 Years Previous
CURRENT ASSETS			
Cash	782,090	954,000	449,870
Accounts receivable	2,086,650	1,956,530	1,600,840
Inventories	699,260	687,790	511,000
Other current assets	237,090	193,780	168,680
Total current assets	3,805,090	3,792,100	2,730,390
INVESTMENTS AND OTHER ASSETS			
Equity in joint ventures	998,780	1,081,980	976,730
Other	454,750	399,720	440,380
Total investments and other assets	1,453,530	1,481,700	1,417,110
PROPERTY, PLANT AND EQUIPMENT			
Land and improvements	334,080	309,580	298,200
Buildings and improvements	2,017,770	1,887,630	1,679,240
Equipment	6,042,850	5,015,280	4,619,540
Construction and equipment installations in progress	388,360	337,490	369,370
Total	8,783,060	7,549,980	6,966,350
Less accumulated depreciation	3,310,520	2,724,490	2,716,870
Net property, plant, and equipment	5,472,540	4,825,490	4,249,480
GOODWILL, PUBLICATION AND BROADCAST RIGHTS			
Less accumulated amortization	3,033,920	3,160,680	3,048,430
TOTAL ASSETS	13,765,080	13,259,970	11,445,410

Liabilities and Shareholders' Equity

CURRENT LIABILITIES			
Accounts payable	650,870	598,760	472,990
Accrued expenses and other liabilities	648,760	578,590	459,870
Accrued compensation and amounts withheld from employees	473,380	482,900	398,760
Federal and state income taxes	229,870	308,350	317,780
Deferred revenue	238,870	197,780	179,780
Dividends payable	112,340	113,670	91,310
Short-term borrowing and current portion of long-term debt	437,680	13,560	57,860
Total current liabilities	2,791,770	2,293,610	1,978,350

(continued)

TABLE 9.1 (Continued)

	Year		
Liabilities	This Year	Last Year	2 Years Previous
NONCURRENT LIABILITIES			
Long-term debt	2,653,660	764,450	763,380
Deferred federal and state income taxes	969,800	765,670	678,650
Employment benefits and other noncurrent liabilities	394,650	297,650	196,430
Total noncurrent liabilities	4,018,110	1,827,770	1,638,460
SHAREHOLDERS' EQUITY			
Common stock	38,120	57,890	54,330
Additional capital	323,440	362,880	429,760
Retained earnings	6,656,620	9,089,970	7,853,750
	7,018,180	9,510,740	8,337,840
Less common stock held in treasury at cost	62,980	372,150	509,240
Total shareholders' equity	6,955,200	9,138,590	7,828,600
TOTAL	13,765,080	13,259,970	11,445,410

ownership of a nearby weekly newspaper would record that as "equity in a joint venture."

Property, plant, and equipment include land, buildings, and equipment owned by the company. Because some media organizations, such as daily newspapers and television stations, require a large fixed investment, this category is often a large portion of assets for these firms. This is less likely to be true for magazines and weekly newspapers, where printing typically is done by outside companies.

Accumulated depreciation represents the value of property, plant, and equipment that has been used up in the operation of the organization. If a newspaper buys a computer system, a certain percentage of the cost of that system becomes depreciation each year until the value reaches zero. One can look at property, plant, and equipment as investments in future production. As that investment is used for production, it declines in value, which must be represented on the balance sheet.

Goodwill, publication, and broadcast rights represent the value of any legal rights a company has to publish or broadcast and the value of how people feel about the company. Goodwill is the value of the company's reputation. A problem with these categories is that they are hard to measure. Quite often, a company will figure its liabilities and owner equity and the difference between these two and its assets will be goodwill. Just as equipment depreciates, goodwill has a limited life. People who read newspapers die and move away, so goodwill for these people ends. This loss of goodwill is amortized across the line and is placed in the balance sheet to show this loss of this asset.

Liabilities and Shareholder's Equity

Current liabilities are debts that are due within a relatively short period of time. For example, dividends payable listed in Table 9.1 represent dividends owed to stockholders on a quarterly basis. Accounts payable usually must be paid within 30 to 60 days.

Noncurrent liabilities are those that extend for a year or more. For example, if a company sells bonds, the amount owed the bond holders would be noncurrent liabilities.

Shareholder's equity represents the resources of the company that belong to the owners in one way or another. For example, retained earnings is the amount of profit that remains in the control of the managers of the company. In the case of the newspaper company in Table 9.1, ownership is distributed through common stock, some of which has not been sold and remains in the company. This is held in the "treasury."

Although a balance sheet generally is used by outsiders to evaluate the financial position of the company, a series of balance sheets also can help managers. They are not so much generators of information for decision making as they are a warning signal. By monitoring the balance sheets across time, one can get a sense of whether the company's financial position is improving or deteriorating. If the ratio of assets to liabilities is increasing, the company is doing well. If the ratio is declining, it could be doing better.

Managerial Accounting Information

Managerial accounting emphasizes the accounting information needs of the manager for decision making. Budgets and income statements are developed to aid managers in assessing whether organizational goals are being met. Budgets and income statements are the accounting information formats most frequently used by managers.

BUDGETS AND INCOME STATEMENTS

A *budget* is a statement of the planned use and acquisition of financial resources for meeting specific goals during a particular period of time. Budgets quantify the objectives and specific goals of the manager's department or company. Budgets also provide direction for decision making, and are an integral part of the planning process. Consequently, budgets are used as detailed and coordinated plans for the future.

Budgets also set performance standards or criteria for evaluation. At the end of the budgeted time period, an income statement is generated. The *income statement* reflects the actual expenditures and revenues for each category listed in the budget for the time period. A comparison of the budget and income statement for the same time period allows the manager to evaluate the unit's performance and provides necessary information for controlling the functions of the department.

Annual budgets are prepared for the business and each of its departments, and each budget is subdivided into 12 monthly periods. The budget for the business is called the *profit plan* or *master budget plan*; departmental budgets are known as *operating budgets*. Long-range budgets also are developed, but typically only at the level of the business as a whole. Table 9.2 illustrates a master budget plan for radio station WNJR. WNJR is a hard rock music station serving a geographic area with a population of about 200,000. The summarized master budget plan displayed in Table 9.2 reflects the budget for the business as a whole. The actual profit plan would include operating budgets from each department,

The budget is comprised of expenses, which are the costs associated

TABLE 9.2
Annual Budget for Radio Station WNJR

Station Revenue & Expense Items	Dollars
Revenues	
National/regional advertising	150,000
Local advertising	685,000
Total projected sales	835,000
Agency and rep commissions	(66,800)
Other revenue	30,000
Total projected net revenue	798,200
Expenses	
Departmental operating expenses	
Engineering	27,000
Program production	115,000
News	25,000
Sales	171,000
Advertising and promotion	40,000
General administration	283,200
Nonoperating expenses	
Depreciation	42,123
Interest	15,400
Total expenses	718,723
Pretax profit	79,477

with running the radio station, and revenues, which are the sources of income for the station. Table 9.2 shows the proposed allocation of financial resources to the various departments in the radio station as expenses, as well as the revenues expected from specific sources for the coming year.

The major source of revenue is generated from the selling of air time for advertising. The advertising revenue is categorized by geographic source; local advertising accounts for 82% of the station's revenues, and national/regional advertising accounts for 18% of revenues. Total expected revenue is calculated by subtracting the sales representatives' commissions, which depend on the amount of sales. Miscellaneous additional revenue is added to calculate the projected total revenue for the coming year.

Projected operating expenses are itemized by department and indicate each department's forecasted financial needs. The two types of expenses itemized in the budget are operating and nonoperating expenses. *Operating expenses* include the day-to-day costs of running the radio station. The operating expenses of a radio station might include the cost of using an outside news service, music license fees, subscribing to an audience ratings service, and the compensation of employees. *Nonoperating expenses* include other costs that are not incurred from operating the station, such as the depreciation of equipment and interest to be paid on any outstanding loans. Depreciation is a common nonoperating expense because equipment loses its value and eventually needs to be replaced.

The departmental operating and nonoperating expenses are summed to calculate the projected total expenditures for the coming year. Total expenses are subtracted from total net revenues to calculate the projected business profit before paying taxes. For radio station WNJR, the expected profit for the coming year is $79,477.

Table 9.3 displays this year's budget in comparison to the previous year's income statement for radio station WNJR. A comparison of the previous year's actual expenses and revenues with the projected figures for the coming year shows some small but significant differences. The major differences can be seen in the revenue expected from local advertising and other revenue and in the expenditures planned for program production and advertising and promotion. These figures reflect the planning and decision-making activities of several key figures at WNJR.

The budget for the coming year was developed by the sales manager, general manager, and programming director over the course of 3 months of discussions, data gathering, and decision making. The sales manager noted what he thought could be a problem for the coming year. His salespeople had been reporting that many of their clients were expressing reservations about committing to the same level of advertising time purchases for the coming year. Indeed, the entire country had been experiencing a recession for more than a year. Many local businesses had gone bankrupt. Most of the smaller local business owners expressed deep

TABLE 9.3

Comparison of Annual Budget with Last Year's Income Statement for Radio Station WNJR

Station Revenue & Expense Items	Dollars This Year	Dollars Last Year Actual
Revenues		
National/regional advertising	150,000	148,000
Local advertising	685,000	693,567
Total projected sales	835,000	841,567
Agency and rep commissions	(66,800)	(67,325)
Other revenue	30,000	–
Total projected net revenue	798,200	774,242
Expenses		
Departmental operating expenses		
Engineering	27,000	26,543
Program production	115,000	123,987
News	25,000	23,676
Sales	171,000	165,999
Advertising and promotion	40,000	30,000
General administration	283,200	278,006
Nonoperating expenses		
Depreciation	42,123	40,000
Interest	15,400	10,050
Total expenses	718,723	698,261
Pretax profit	79,477	75,981

concerns that their decreasing sales revenues would not be enough to cover their essential costs, let alone their advertising. (Many small-business owners believe that advertising is not an essential expenditure.)

The sales manager reassured the general manager that his sales staff would exert the extra effort necessary to convince clients that their businesses would only suffer greater losses should their advertising budgets be cut. Nonetheless, the sales and general managers agreed that revenue from advertising sales most probably would be lower for the coming year. The general manager stated that the station could not stand to suffer the advertising losses and that some strategy had to be developed to prevent the coming year's profits from plummeting. In fact, the station owner recently had expressed her dissatisfaction with the performance of the station. She had informed the general manager of her expectations for an increase in the profits for the coming year, and she said the general manager would be held personally responsible for meeting her expectations.

Given the situation at hand, the general manager reviewed some general strategies for achieving the goal of maintaining or increasing profits. The strategies fell into three types: The staff could work harder to maintain existing revenues, costs could be cut, and/or other types of revenues could be sought.

Because the main threat to reaching the profit goal was the possible loss of advertising dollars, persuading the station's local advertisers not to cut their advertising would solve the problem. This would be difficult, however. Many local small-business owners feared that they would not have enough money for advertising and that their advertising dollars would not generate enough revenue to pay for the advertising.

The second solution of cost cutting would improve the situation in the short-run, but the long-run consequences could affect the station's ratings negatively, thereby reducing their advertising revenues in the future. The station manager felt that the only area that might sustain cuts, without jeopardizing the integrity of the station, was program production.

The programming head developed an idea he thought would promote the station while generating additional revenue. He proposed that the station buy T-shirts displaying the station call letters and slogan and then sell them at local establishments who advertise with the station. The added cost for advertising and promotion would be approximately $10,000, but the programming head and sales manager agreed that they might expect to generate an additional $30,000 from the sales. In addition, the station could attract business for their advertisers by selling T-shirts in their stores. Indeed, any advertising for the T-shirt promotion also would be advertising for their participating clients.

In addition to generating additional revenues, such a promotion might help persuade advertisers to maintain their advertising spending with WNJR. So, the management team decided to pursue the T-shirt promotion.

The budget developed for WNJR's coming year represents the desired future status of the radio station based on the decisions of the management team that prepared the budget. The budget provides spending guidelines for the department heads spending and sets performance expectations for the sales staff. In particular, this budget sets a criterion for evaluating the short-range decision to promote the station through the local sale of T-shirts. If T-shirt sales generate additional revenues of at least $30,000, thus minimizing local advertising revenue losses, then the radio station might choose to repeat the promotion the next year. If the outlined expectations are not met, then radio station probably would not choose the same strategy for the coming year.

The example of radio station WNJR illustrates how annual budgets are developed and used for short-range planning and routine decision making. Long-range budgets are used for plans of 5 or more years and cover more nonroutine decisions. Whether a manager is making a fairly routine, short-range decision or a nonroutine, long-range decision is often a function of the manager's level in the organization. Indeed, the types of budget information a manager needs and uses for decision making are affected by the long- or short-term nature of the decision itself.

The steps in the decision-making process are reviewed in order to explain how managers use budgets. Two important aspects of the process also are discussed: how short-range versus long-range decisions affect the use of information and how the different organizational levels affect managerial decision making.

MANAGERIAL DECISION MAKING

Managerial decision making, like most decision making, is a process that consists of six stages, as shown by the decision-making wheel in chapter 1. Collecting and analyzing information plays the central role in the this process. But managers at different organizational levels collect and use information differently.

The case of WNJR illustrates this process. The sales manager identified the problem of expected losses in advertising revenue through discussions with sales personnel and advertisers. Other pertinent information came from reviewing information about the local economy. He viewed the problem from the perspective of how it would affect his department during the coming year. The general manager, on the other hand, specified the overall organizational goal of maintaining or increasing profits in comparison to last year. The sales manager informed the general manager of the threat to reaching that goal. The general, sales, and program managers reviewed several strategies and selected the T-shirt promotion because it appeared to be the best solution for the impending problem. But all managers were involved in that decision to ensure that the overall organizational and departmental perspectives were considered.

This example also demonstrates how the budget is used for implementing the solution. The income statement will be used to monitor the solution because it provides information about the performance of the solution. Both can be reviewed to refine the solution in future years.

Long-Range Versus Short-Range Decisions

Short-range decisions are often routine decisions, the type that a manager has some degree of experience in making on a regular basis. Because of the manager's experience with a routine decision, he accumulates information about alternative strategies and the results of the those strategies. As a result, routine decisions usually involve less risk and the decision outcomes are more predictable in comparison to nonroutine decisions.

Routine decisions also are evaluated within some short period of time. Consequently, if short-range decisions have unexpected negative consequences or just do not produce the expected results, changes can be made quickly in an effort to minimize the impact of the undesired outcomes.

Nonroutine decisions are made infrequently and have long-range impact. Such impacts are difficult to anticipate. For example, the decision to invest resources in new equipment, such as a new system of computers for a newspaper, has a short-range consequence of increasing costs during the fiscal year of the purchase. However, the long-range consequences may be more difficult to determine and forecast. For example, desired long-range outcomes would be increased writer productivity and efficiency in the production of the paper itself. Background research is needed to evaluate the likelihood of those outcomes, and to predict the value added to the paper in the long run.

Even more difficult to predict than expected positive long-range outcomes are long-run negative, unexpected results of decisions. A prime example is the repetitive strain injury (RSI) many newspaper journalists have developed from using video display terminals. RSI problems were not anticipated by the managers who first adopted computer technology in the 1970s. As a result, many newspapers have lost services of talented journalists. Had its impact been predicted, several techniques of curtailing or alleviating RSI could have been incorporated into the VDT systems as they were adopted.

The fact that future outcomes must be predicted makes long-range decision making more risky than short-range decision making. Long-range decisions often involve some large investment of capital, making the decision even riskier: The company has more to lose if the decision does not produce the desired outcomes. The decision also is evaluated over a longer period of time. For example, it will take a year or more before newspaper management will notice all the effects of purchasing a new computer system.

Long-range decisions most often occur at higher levels in organizations, and shorter range decisions occur at middle and lower levels. Higher level management makes the riskier decisions and takes responsibility for decisions that affect the entire organization. Middle and lower level management make decisions that are more routine, are less risky, and result in consequences that directly influence their departments. Obviously, the level of decision making and the nature of the decision affect the type of information the manager needs for the decision-making process. Indeed, the type of budget information managers use and evaluate varies based on these same factors.

Levels of Planning and Decision Making and Information Needs

The nature of planning and decision making varies with the organization level at which each process occurs. At the highest levels of management, decisions are made determining the firm's policies and general guidelines for evaluating the company's performance. The information top management uses is often summarized and future oriented. For example, information about future market share, economic indicators, and other market performance measures are forecasted and then used by upper level management to predict revenue and profit goals for the coming year.

Middle-level management often deals with semistructured problems about using resources efficiently and effectively. At this level, managers need information to develop operating budgets. Often decisions need to be made about investing in new equipment, services, or people. For example, WNJR's sales manager might hire a consultant to teach account executives ways of effective selling during economic downturns. A newspaper's managing editor might decide to buy a new health advice column.

Lower level management deals with more structured, routine tasks and uses information from inside the organization. Decision rules are well known and the information used is very detailed and typically accurate. At this managerial level, information is not necessarily forecasted or very future oriented. For example, the city editor at a newspaper must decide when to assign a reporter to work overtime.

Consider an "oldies" format radio station in a large metropolitan area. The greater metropolitan area has a population of approximately 6 million. The head of programming and the station manager notice a seasonal trend in the ratings during the last few years. Unlike most other music radio stations in the area, their station had been experiencing a smaller summer audience in comparison to other times of the year. The summer dip in the ratings had been a consistent phenomenon during the past 3 years. The programming head suggests that the station sponsor a series of summer concerts featuring music groups from the 1960s. Such concerts would appeal to their target audience of men and women age 25 to 54 years. The primary goal of this strategy would be to increase their summer audience by reminding the target audience of the radio station.

The sales manager believes that she could get some of the station's large advertisers to cosponsor the concerts, thereby reducing the station's expenses. The general manager agrees that this strategy sounds appealing, but he is concerned about the cost of the concerts and whether they would add significantly to the station's ratings. The key question is whether the concerts will produce enough revenue to cover the costs. The programming head suggests that the long-run effects would be positive, but she cannot predict the magnitude of the effect. However, she is quite sure that as a result of the concerts the first summer's ratings would be higher than those in previous years.

Table 9.4 shows the budgets the station manager and programming head might develop for the next 2 years, as well as this year's budget. The new budgets reflect the estimated investment associated with sponsoring

TABLE 9.4
3-Year Budget Plan for Radio Station KOLD

Station Revenue & Expense Items	Dollars Year 2	Dollars Year 1	Dollars This Year
Revenues			
National/regional advertising	1,867,954	1,705,632	1,639,012
Local advertising	1,891,632	1,710,098	1,650,836
Total projected sales	3,759,586	3,415,730	3,289,848
Agency and rep commissions	(300,766)	(273,258)	(263,187)
Other revenue	– –	– –	– –
Total projected net revenue	3,458,820	3,142,472	3,026,661
Expenses			
Operating departmental expenses			
Engineering	170,236	168,457	130,534
Program production	254,913	251,932	234,149
News	51,325	50,943	48,923
Sales	710,821	708,205	700,451
Advertising and promotion	551,867	544,723	498,264
General administration	479,034	471,947	465,297
Nonoperating expenses			
Depreciation	343,974	376,321	388,923
Interest	65,932	67,461	70,432
Total expenses	2,628,102	2,639,989	2,536,973
Pretax profit	830,718	502,483	489,688

the concerts for two summers and the expected gain in advertising revenues. The expected gain in advertising revenues was predicted based on market research.

In Table 9.4, the impact of the summer promotion is felt greatest in the second year, although the station expects to reap some benefit the next year. The assumption is that the first year will help establish the summer concerts and the second year will show even greater ratings increases.

The expense of the concerts would come from a small increase in engineering cost for setting up the concerts and a larger increase in the cost of advertising and promotion. The important questions that need addressing are how accurate the assumed ratings increases will be and whether they will translate into the advertising sales anticipated. The programming head estimates an increase in total projected net revenue of $432,159 during the next 2 years, compared to an estimated increase in total expenses of $101,129. The difference becomes profit for the station.

DEVELOPING THE MASTER BUDGET PLAN AND DEPARTMENTAL BUDGETS

Developing budgets is one part of the planning process where decisions are made about the available resources for achieving goals. Generating the master budget plan for the entire business can take some time, usually 3 to 6 months, depending on the size, nature, and complexity of the organization. Managers at all levels of the organization participate in the effective development of the master budget plan. At the highest level, a budget committee in most organizations would consist of the company president, the controller, vice president of sales, and vice president in charge of production. In a media organization, the top manager, the controller, and all department heads would make up the budget committee. This committee establishes budget goals for the company that directly affect the budgeting at the departmental level. The budget committee also reviews and approves departmental budgets.

A budget director, who reports directly to the controller, coordinates the budget at the departmental level. The budget director prepares a timetable for the development and approval of all the operating budgets and works with unit managers in the development of each departmental budget. The master budget plan then is assembled and submitted to the budget committee and then the board of directors for approval. Finally, the budget director is responsible for preparing and distributing performance reports, based on the previous year's budget, to the budget committee and unit managers.

Forecasting

A key element of generating budgets is forecasting. *Forecasting* is an effort to predict future events and trends and to anticipate their implications for the company. Granger (1980) listed three types of forecasting: event outcome forecasts, event-timing forecasts, and time series forecasts. *Event outcome forecasts* try to predict the consequences of an event. For example, how will the closing of a manufacturing plant in a town affect a newspaper? *Event-timing forecasts* attempt to predict when a specific event will take place. For example, if a growing city has only one network-affiliated television station, that station's management would be interested in knowing when a second network affiliate might enter the market. *Times series forecasting* is an effort to predict the impact of a series of phenomena on the business. For example, what impact will continued declining employment have on a newspaper's classified ad linage?

The benefits of accurate forecasting seem obvious, given the central role of information in decision making. As with most valuable things, accurate forecasting is not easy. So many factors can change and the possibility of measurement errors is so great, that accurate long-range forecasting is as much an art as a science.

Despite the limitations, however, budgeting requires some forecasting. Kreitner (1986) listed three types of forecasting: informed judgment, surveys, and trend analysis. *Informed judgment* involves the forecasting of events and trends by an individual or group, based on a knowledge of the topic being forecast. Informed judgment is used extensively in the creation of most short-term budgets. *Surveys* are efforts to anticipate the future by asking questions of a sample of people that represent a larger group. The idea is to draw conclusions about the future of the larger group based on comments from a small percentage of that group.

Trend analysis extends historical trends found in data about the past into the future, with some alterations based on assumptions of change. Because everything changes to a degree, all trend analysis must address key factors that shape the event being forecast. For example, if an advertising staff at a radio station is extending trends in advertising sales, the staff needs to specify assumptions about changes in overall business sales. The staff might assume, based on predictions by government economists, that retail sales in their market would increase 5% during the next year. Using this figure, the staff could come up with an estimate of retail sales. From this figure, they could estimate their revenue during the next year by applying the percentage of local retail sales that they have received as advertising revenue during the past 5 years.

It is important to deal explicitly with assumptions about the changing economic environment. Otherwise, a station will underestimate revenues during a booming economy and overestimate revenues during an economic downturn.

All budgeting requires some forecasting. Two principles tend to hold true: The longer the range a budget covers the more important forecasting becomes; and the longer the range a budget covers, the harder it is to forecast accurately. This in effect is the forecasting dilemma. The only solution is to invest in several methods of forecasting for the long range and to hire competent forecasters.

Departmental Operating Budgets

Although forecasting plays a role in the annual departmental budget, the need for extensive forecasting is minimized by the data from previous years' income statements and budgets and from the expertise of the people within the departments. Informed judgment plays a key role, although this should be bolstered by available data about the marketplace.

The department budget is the central document for controlling the finances of an organization, and it plays a direct or indirect role in most decisions. Table 9.5 shows the newsroom budget for a daily newspaper of about 40,000 circulation. The departmental operating budget is set up on an annual basis, with at least monthly updates on past spending and resources that remain available.

All budgets are broken down into categories of expenses considered to be important in running the business. Which expense categories are important varies from medium to medium and from company to company.

TABLE 9.5
Operating Budget and Income Statement for the News/Editorial Department of a 40,000-
Circulation Daily Newspaper

Item	This Year	Last Year
Payroll		
Salaries	956,000	920,000
Overtime	19,120	18,500
Correspondents and free lancers	36,700	35,700
Office supplies	15,000	14,500
Research material		
Computer time	4,000	3,000
Books, magazines, papers	5,000	5,500
Travel	50,000	48,000
Photography supplies	15,000	14,000
News services	75,000	70,000
Syndicated material	60,000	58,000
Other news/editorial	75,000	75,000
TOTAL	1,310,820	1,262,200

At the newspaper represented in Table 9.5, payroll is divided into salaries for full-time employees, overtime paid to full-time employees, and money used to pay part-time employees, called correspondents and free lancers. A larger newspaper might list photography salaries separately from those of writers and editors. It also might differentiate between regular part-time employees (correspondents) and irregular part-time employees (free lancers). The important consideration is that budget categories and subcategories reveal how the money is being spent within the department in a way that allows for decision making.

The amount of money allocated to a budget category reflects its relative importance to reaching the goals of a department. For example, management at the newspaper represented in Table 9.5 decided to spend more on wire services this year than on syndicated material. Resources also were cut for books, magazines, and newspapers this year compared to last, whereas the money spent on computer time increased. This represents an increased use of data bases instead of printed material. The importance of budget items can change across time to reflect the long-term plans of the organization. A plan that would increase profit by controlling cost at the newspaper would be shown by a series of budgets that cut payrolls or kept them stable as revenues increase.

The operating budget can be thought of as an ideal for the year's spending. But with news media, the ideal rarely happens. This is why managers often end up shifting money from one category to another, and may even get additional resources from the top management of the media organization. If the Soviet Union dissolves, as it did in 1991, news organizations will ignore the operating budget to a degree. Money will have to be shifted and new resources found. A budget is a map; it is not reality. A quality news operation often will require deviations from the budget.

Budgeting Methods

The department heads are usually in charge of generating their department operating budgets. They are most familiar with their department's needs. But they are not as familiar with the business environment as the employees who maintain contact with those outside the organization. The reporters, camera crews, salespeople, and receptionists are the ones who deal with news sources, readers, listeners, viewers, and advertisers. For this reason, the informed judgment of the department heads must reflect the experience of their workers.

Budgeting methods involve two considerations: the flow of information and the assumed starting point of the budget. Both play a role in how well the budget will serve the goals of the department and, therefore, the organization.

The flow of information can be either upward, downward, or both. *Upward flow* means the information goes from employees to the managers. *Downward flow* is the reverse, and *both* means a two-way flow occurs. In the departmental budgeting process, information must flow both ways to generate an effective budget. Managers need to get information from employees in order to understand what they need to do their jobs effectively. At the same time, workers need to understand the budgetary constraints that face their organization so they do not squander resources.

Although this flow of information will be greatest during the budgeting period, it should continue all year long. The budget is a starting point. Actual expenditures must be compared to the budget throughout the year. Employees need to know how expenditures compare to the budget process throughout the year. This is especially true of journalists. A journalist who understands the budget and can argue for a big story within its constraints is more likely to have management's support than one who does not understand what a particular story request means to the department's budget.

The second consideration is the assumed starting point of the budget. Typically, it is assumed that last year's operating budget reflects the needs of the department. The previous year's funding levels become the starting point for this year's budget. This approach is similar to trend analysis because it assumes the trend represents what is needed. The shortcoming is that it perpetuates any miscalculations or errors from previous budgets.

An alternative starting point is called *zero-based budgeting*, which assumes that every budget starts at zero and managers must justify whatever

they put into the budget. It is easier to identify inefficiencies or wasteful-
ness using this method, but the process is far more time consuming than
the first approach.

An example of how the two might come into play can be found in Table
9.5. Suppose the editor finds in the income statement that she spent only
$30,000 last year on correspondents and free lancers, which was $5,700 less
than budgeted. In creating the new budget, she could start with the
$35,700 in last year's budget, even though she does not need that amount
based on last year's performance. She then can add an inflation figure of
$1,000. Using this method, her request for $36,700 is probably more than
she will need. If zero-based budgeting is used, she would have to justify
the $36,700, which would be hard to do based on last year's performance.
Most likely, the amount she would need for correspondents would be the
same as the previous year, plus the $1,000 inflation figure, which would
equal $31,000. This assumes no major change in the use of correspondents
and that their payment will increase at the inflation rate from the previous
year.

Despite the seeming appeal of zero-based budgeting to the overall
organization, it is not a commonly used process in media organizations.
First, the increased demand on time is a problem for many managers who
already have too many responsibilities or who do not enjoy dealing with
numbers. This latter problem is especially true in newsrooms where many
people consider themselves to be "word" and not "number" people.
Second, this approach takes power away from departmental managers.
Money is power, and if you have to justify your money in a changing
environment, organizations will see shifts in power from department to
department. Many of those who have power do not like to risk giving it up,
which is what zero-based budgeting can do. In effect, the goals of the
individual managers can interfere with what is best for the organization.

Some compromise between the two assumptions is best. Justifying
budget items is an important process in identifying areas that no longer
need as many resources; this allows the shifting of resources to new areas.
However, the time requirements to justify all budget items would over-
burden many smaller organizations. If the budget director actively identifies areas that are waning in importance within departments, the department heads can deal with these categories without having to justify totally
all budget items.

SUMMARY

Accounting practices fall into two categories: financial and managerial.
Financial accounting is used primarily by those outside the organization
and is typified by the balance sheet. The balance sheet is a picture of the

assets and liabilities of an organization at a given point in time. It summarizes the financial well-being of that organization.

Managerial accounting is aimed at generating information for decision making. The most important forms of managerial accounting are budgets and income statements. A budget is the plan for how the organization will spend money during a given time period. The income statement is a summary of how money was spent in previous time periods. The master budget plan covers the entire organization, whereas the departmental operating budget deals with the plans for the individual departments within the organization.

Forecasting plays an important role in budgeting. The longer the period covered by a budget, the more important and difficult accurate forecasting becomes.

The information flow for budgeting within an organization should be upward and downward through the organization structure. It is also important in budgeting to consider whether last year's budgeted expenses are the appropriate starting point for creating next year's budget, or whether all managers should start at zero in making up their budgets. Usually, a compromise between the two approaches is best.

CHAPTER 9 CASES

Case 9.1

The Case of Cutting the Budget at *Metro Monthly*

Metro Monthly is a city magazine in a Midwest city of 1 million, with about 2.5 million people in the metropolitan area. The magazine has been in business for 15 years and has shown a profit every year except the first 3 years. Recently, however, profits have declined.

The magazine was started by five people who had worked at the local newspaper. During the first 12 years or so, the magazine content had emphasized hard-hitting journalism, humorous features, and personality profiles of important community members. The magazine won several national awards during the first 10 years.

Of the original group, three sold their shares to the other two after the 11th year. The group had a falling out about content. The two remaining owners recently sold the magazine to Phillips Publishing, a company that publishes city magazines throughout the county. The new owners said they expected a higher profit than the magazine had delivered during the past 3 years.

The decline in profits can be traced to several factors. First, several local business people started a new city magazine, *Metro Magazine*, 4 years ago.

The magazine was started as a reaction to the "negative" stories in *Metro Monthly*. It has never made a profit, but it is close enough to breaking even that it continues to publish. It is a free publication that contains what the business people define as "good news," which means it is primarily a public relations tool for local businesses. However, its existence has affected both the circulation and advertising linage of *Metro Monthly*. In addition, *Metro Magazine* has taken away some advertising accounts.

A second problem has been the increasing cost of printing. Paper and ink prices have continued to rise more rapidly than the inflation rate during the past 4 years.

Finally, advertising has dropped off recently due to an economic recession. Three large factories have closed within the past 5 years, laying off about 25,000 workers. Several retail businesses have closed, and others have cut back advertising budgets. The area economy is expected to continue in a recession for about a year.

Martha Myers was the general manager of *Metro Monthly* under the previous owners. Phillips Publishing appointed her publisher of *Metro Monthly*. The first directive from Phillips was to prepare a budget that would increase profits by 10% over the estimated level for the current year's budget.

Assignment

Your assignment is to become a consultant for Myers. First, create a budget for next year that will meet the requirements of the new ownership. This process will require that you set prices for subscriptions, single copies, and advertising. Use the magazine data and income statements in Tables 9.6, 9.7, and 9.8. The budget for next year should follow the budget form in Table 9.9.

Second, explain in a statement the process you followed in creating the budget. Third, explain the possible impact of any price changes or budget cuts that you suggest. If the impact is negative, explain why this negative impact is more acceptable than cutting other areas of the budget.

TABLE 9.6
Circulation and Price Figures for *Metro Monthly*

| Year | Circulation | | Single Copy Price | Subscription Price |
	Subscription	Single		
Current	91,500	10,500	1.95	14.00
Last year	94,500	10,800	1.75	14.00
2 years ago	98,400	11,000	1.75	13.00
3 years ago	98,000	10,500	1.75	13.00
4 years ago	98,200	10,700	1.50	13.00

TABLE 9.7
Advertising Prices

	Current Year	Last Year	2 Years Ago	3 Years Ago	4 Years Ago
Full Page					
1 time	5,000	4,900	4,750	4,500	4,300
6 times	4,125	4,000	3,750	3,500	3,300
12 times	3,760	3,500	3,250	3,000	2,800
Half Page					
1 time	2,940	2,900	2,750	2,500	2,300
6 times	2,540	2,440	2,300	2,100	1,900
12 times	2,320	2,220	2,150	2,000	1,800
Quarter Page					
1 time	1,950	1,860	1,770	1,700	1,500
6 times	1,650	1,600	1,550	1,500	1,300
12 times	1,500	1,450	1,400	1,350	1,250

TABLE 9.8
Total Pages and Advertising Pages

	Advertising Pages	Total Pages
Current year (Estimate)	384	912
Last year	415	960
2 years ago	445	980
3 years ago	480	940
4 years ago	425	912

TABLE 9.9
The Current Year's Budget and Income Statements from Previous Years (in Thousands)

	Current Year	Last Year	2 Years Ago	3 Years Ago	4 Years Ago
Revenues					
Local advertising	1,604	1,721	1,812	1,798	1,613
National advertising	401	468	495	450	403
Circulation	1,527	1,550	1,510	1,495	1,469
Total Revenue	3,532	3,739	3,817	3,743	3,485
Expenses					
Production	1,603	1,579	1,543	1,489	1,334
Editorial					
Staff salaries	298	300	300	291	284
Free lancers	135	130	120	119	109
Other	47	45	37	35	30
Advertising					
Salaries & Commissions	462	490	511	452	421
Other	20	22	25	22	18
Administration	200	225	215	195	180
Circulation	612	632	656	651	653
Total expenses	3,377	3,441	3,407	3,254	3,029
Profit	155	298	410	489	456

Case 9.2

The Case of Budgeting at WARP

As general manager of WARP, it is your job to develop a preliminary budget for next year. You have completed the first step, which was to meet with the station owner. She said she would like a pretax profit margin of 10%, which is an increase of 2 percentage points over last year. She said she would like to see the station's ratings improve, but this was not as high a priority as the profit margin. Implicit in the discussion was the desire for ratings at least to remain stable. Using the background information and income statements given in the following section, prepare next year's budget.

Background

WARP is located in a city of about 250,000. It is one of 10 radio stations. It has an "easy listening" format and ranks third in the market with a share of 13. The top two stations have shares of 20 and 19. The top station has an oldies format, and the second-place station is an all-news and talk format.

Advertising revenue is expected to increase by 5% next year, all of which will be in local advertising. Inflation will be about 4%. The staff averaged raises of 3% in the last budget, although actual raises varied with the person.

The expected income statement for the current year and the income statement from last year are given in Table 9.10. The "other income" in Table 9.10 represents money earned from the sale of T-shirts and other memorabilia at promotional concerts sponsored by the station on a break-even basis. The station expects to make $17,000 next year from the sale of these items.

Assignment

Prepare a preliminary draft of next year's budget based on the revenue and inflation projections and profit expectations given above. The draft should be in the form found in Table 9.10. In addition, prepare a short report explaining your allocation of the expected increase in revenue.

Current Year's Expected Income Statement and Last Year's Income Statement for Station
WARP

Station Revenue & Expense Items	Dollars This Year	Dollars Last Year Actual
Revenues		
National/regional advertising	75,000	69,000
Local advertising	450,000	430,000
Total projected sales	525,000	499,000
Agency and rep commissions	(47,500)	(44,000)
Other revenue	15,000	10,000
Total projected net revenue	492,500	465,000
Expenses		
Operating departmental expenses		
Engineering	21,000	18,750
Program production	72,500	68,800
News	19,000	19,000
Sales	110,000	104,000
Advertising and promotion	22,000	20,000
General administration	177,600	170,575
Total operating expenses	422,100	401,125
Nonoperating expenses		
Depreciation	21,500	20,000
Interest	9,500	9,000
Total expenses	453,100	430,125
Pretax profit	39,400	34,875

Case 9.3

Assignment: Forecasting to Start a Radio Station

The key to budgeting is forecasting. Forecasting involves drawing conclusions about future phenomena based on past experience. This case involves developing a report forecasting economic conditions in a particular market for each of the next 3 years. The report needs to address at least the following types of economic activities: employment, manufacturing, retail sales, local taxes, housing sales, and expenditures on advertising. The purpose of the report is to decide whether the economy will be strong enough for Grant Communications to start a new radio station in that market during the next 2 years. The assignment should follow these steps:

First, select a market to study, preferably one about which you can find economic data in a nearby library.

Second, collect data from the library from the past 5 years for each of the areas listed previously. Look for trends in the data that might give you clues to the future.

Third, interview people who have knowledge of the economic conditions in the market. These would include, but not be limited to, economists, business people, the local government economic development staff, people from the advertising departments of local media companies, government officials, and business reporters.

Fourth, prepare a report of three to five pages that forecasts economic activity in the selected market. The report should touch on each of the six topics mentioned earlier for each of the next 3 years. At the end of the report, draw conclusions about the strength of the market's economy during the 3-year period and whether the economy will be strong enough to support a new radio station.

Case 9.4

The Case of Distributing the Wealth at KOOL

KOOL is a network affiliate television station in a market of about 500,000 people. Three years ago, it had the top-rated early evening and late night newscasts. It had a rating of 25 and a share of 42 for the evening newscast. Its next closest competitor was KAAP, with a rating of 18 and a share of 30. KOOL also led in the late night newscast competition, with a rating of 21 and a share of 39. KAAP was even further behind in the late night newscast race with a rating of 12 and a share of 21.

Things have changed. During the past 3 years, KAAP invested heavily in their news department. Three years ago, the station brought in a new team of coanchors, a new sports anchor, and a new meteorologist. Last year, KAAP bought a satellite news-gathering truck for about $1 million. Just recently, the evening newscast increased from 30 min to an hour. KOOL has stayed with a 30-min newscast.

All of this has paid off for KAAP. The latest ratings report shows KAAP and KOOL tied with shares of 38 for the early evening newscast. KOOL still leads the late evening newscast competition, but its share has dropped to 31, whereas KAAP has increased its share to 29.

As a result of the trends in ratings and shares, KOOL has lost advertising and is facing pressure to lower its advertising rates, which have remained stable during the past 2 years. The owners and general manager of KOOL have decided to fight back. The general manager has been given $1 million to invest in the station's news operations and related areas during the next year. The objective is to increase the revenue from the two newscasts by at least 5% this year and 20% during the next 3 years.

Table 9.11 lists the expenses for the advertising department, news department, and advertising and promoting the newscasts from the past 3 years. The advertising and promotion expenses represent those that are related to the newscasts and not all programming.

The assignment is to distribute the additional $1 million among the budget items given in Table 9.11 in order to reach the revenue goals mentioned earlier. This involves two steps: (a) present the allocations as a budget fragment, like the one in Table 9.11; (b) explain why the money was allocated as it was. This second step should include answering these questions:

1. What strategy for increasing revenues is represented by this allocation?
2. Why will this strategy work?
3. What are the potential drawbacks of this strategy?

Case 9.5

The Case of Toxic Waste in Carlyle

You are the editor of the *Carlyle County Advertiser*, a weekly in Carlyle, Michigan. Susan Jackson, the publisher, calls you in and says you have got

TABLE 9.11
Expenses for Selected Budget Items (in Thousands)

	Last Year	2 Years Ago	3 Years Ago
News Department			
Salaries	880	830	780
New equipment	200	175	140
Equipment repair	25	20	18
Travel	100	85	77
Miscellaneous	45	40	35
Total	1,250	1,150	1,050
Advertising department			
Salaries & commissions	520	485	439
Expenses	135	120	115
Misc.	33	31	24
Total	688	636	578
Advertising & promotion[a]	100	75	50
Total	2,038	1,861	1,678

[a]These figures represent the amount of money spent on promoting the newscasts.

to do something about John Callway, the newest of the three reporters on staff. Jackson tells you that he ran up a telephone bill of $200 last month and that the newspaper just got a bill from the Environmental Protection Agency for $300 in photocopying costs.

"I don't know what he's up to, but we couldn't afford this type of spending even in a good year, much less during a year when ad linage is down 30%," Jackson says.

You reply that you are sure the money was spent for a good reason, but you will talk with him about it.

"Listen," Jackson says, "we are in serious financial trouble. We may have to let some people go if things don't pick up. I know the guy is one of those State University go-getters, but we're just a county weekly. We're not the *Detroit Free Press*. Hell, we're not even the *Petosky News-Review*."

You tell the publisher that you will talk with Callway and see what is going on.

The next day you find out that Callway is working on a story about a dump south of town that may contain toxic materials that are known carcinogens.

"OK, I understand about the money," Callway says, "but this is a great story. The dump may be killing people, and no one seems to know anything about it."

When asked what he knows, he says that Congressman Bill Smith's brother owns the land and that the FOIA was used to get information from the EPA.

You ask what the EPA said. He replies that he has not finished collecting all the information he needs. So far, he explains, the records show that some small amount of noncarcinogenic waste was dumped there. But he adds that FOI only works when you know what you are looking for and now he thinks he knows the key.

When asked how much more money he will need, he says about $1,000.

You ask how he got wind of the story. He replies that District Attorney Jane Halford mentioned that there might be a problem with the dump.

You remind him that Halford is a Republican who is interested in running for Democrat Smith's House seat.

"Yeah, I know," Callway says, "but I have put in a lot of my own time on this. I want to finish it. Will you help me or not?"

Assignment

1. What do you tell him?
2. What do you tell the publisher?
3. Do you see any way of helping Callway and keeping the publisher happy?
4. What can be done with the story at this point?

10
Technology and the Future

Managers, occupying the authority positions within a company, often can determine single-handedly how well that company performs. Nowhere is this more evident than in the area of technology, that is, how well the company uses technology and the degree to which the technology affects the company's internal operations. Management's approach to the technology affects technology's performance, which, in turn, affects the company's performance.

In a media company, this is especially true. A newspaper editor, for example, sets the tone for how well reporters use their word-processing computer terminals. If the editor constantly complains about the computer's shortcomings, such behavior undermines staff trust in the technology. If, on the other hand, the editor consistently praises the machine's capabilities and helps staffers understand and master its capabilities and intricacies, then the editor enhances the staff's ability to write, report, and communicate effectively – in short, the editor enhances productivity.

Of course, the machine may have something to say about what approach the editor takes. If the machine is simple to operate and consistently performs its intended task, then the editor will see it as one of many tools to aid the reporting process. But if the machine is "cranky" – its performance is inconsistent at best – or if it is hard to master and operate, then the editor's attitude toward it will be antagonistic or, at the least, wary and cautious.

And then there is the question of management's expectations regarding the technology. If the editor expects the computer to do simple word processing and little more and if that is indeed what the computer is designed to do, then the editor's reaction most likely will be positive. But if the editor expects much more complex and sophisticated accomplishments and that is not within the computer's capabilities, a different, more negative reaction will occur.

Regardless of those expectations, a media manager's job is to turn the technology to the company's advantage. To do so, the manager must first analyze the organizational role and impact of technology on organizations and on management. This chapter will help you in that analysis by examining managerial approaches to technology, the process of how a company uses or "adopts" technology, and how technology may affect media organizations.

MANAGERIAL APPROACHES

There are three schools of thought as to how a company should approach and consider adopting a technology before—and sometimes during—the adoption process. These areas are the structural approach, the technological-task approach, and the sociotechnical approach.

Structural Approach

This area focuses on the management of change and the change in management via the impact on formal devices, such as rules and organizational hierarchy. In other words, this approach sees technology as a planned, controlled instrument of management, which makes conscious decisions concerning the implications of the technology. In this case, *structure* means considering technology as a tool for managing people (Leavitt, 1965).

A structuralist manager believes that employee behavior does not change by teaching employees new skills, but rather by changing the organization's structure. This manager sees behavioral and attitudinal change as best brought about by devices such as rules, role prescriptions, and reward structures, of which technology is a part. For example, one company adopted the latest in word-processing hardware primarily because company management believed the new technology would not change the structure of the work needing to be done—typing, in this case.

A study of other cases showed that senior management used new technology to attain strategic and operating objectives, indicating there are choices of work organization not determined by the technology (Buchanan, 1985).

In reality, of course, management does not always have such choices. Although computers have moved into many aspects of organizational life, it does not follow that supervisors and lower level managers have been prepared fully to cope. Sometimes management's computer preparation—how well management has been trained and how well it has planned for the new technology—often seriously lags behind installation of the technology or is narrowly conceived or even nonexistent (Burack & Sorensen,

1976). This is particularly true in media organizations where so much of the work cycle centers around daily deadlines, leaving precious little time for any planning, let alone planning for a new technology.

It also is difficult for media managers to be quite so calculating and control oriented in regard to structure because media businesses are people intensive. Subordinates are the ones who actually produce the product. Management relies heavily on employees' skills, talents, and judgment before and during the printing of the newspaper, prebroadcast, and on the air. In many respects, media managers are largely at the whim of their hired professionals, so sometimes it might be impractical to view the technology and not see the employee who's going to be using it.

Technological-Task Approach

This approach complements the structural school, albeit with slightly different focus. This school emphasizes that technology has a certain, observable, direct impact on the employee and on the organization. The technological-task manager sees technology as the variable that the manager controls and that determines a response in the organization.

When an organization decides to adopt a technology, there are some definite steps (Rogers, 1983) that precede and follow the decision.

Agenda-Setting.   This means there are general organizational problems that management defines as signifying a need for the technology. In this step, the manager surveys the industry, related publications, and technological experts for potential solutions to the problem.

Matching.   In this stage, the manager matches the problem with a technology and then plans and designs a solution.

Let us say a television station advertising department is having problems with advertising clients being able to reach account executives (AEs), who by and large spend a major portion of the day commuting from client to client. The AE is doing her job as best she can, but she cannot be expected to sit around waiting for phone calls; nor can she waste much time calling the office to check for messages.

The sales manager knows this is a relatively minor problem, but a pesky one that can cause the loss of certain accounts to whom time is of the essence. The manager calls an industry acquaintance, a sales manager in another market. Both have attended several seminars together. "What do you do," the manager asks her friend.

"Try beepers," the friend says, matter of factly.

So now the manager has an idea to mull over. It probably will not take long for her to realize this is the near-perfect match for the problem. But that's a mental match. Now she's got to implement the decision, which brings us to the next step.

Redefining/Restructuring. In this phase, our sales manager will want to modify or "reinvent" her friend's idea to fit her department's particular situation. She will ask herself whether the organization of her department's work process is directly relevant to adopting beepers.

At first glance, the beepers sound like the ideal solution. So she buys beepers for all her AEs. After a month, she discovers that AEs are now receiving all their messages—when they turn the beeper on, which some AEs regularly do. The problem is that not all AEs welcome the invasion of privacy brought on by the beepers; they complain the beepers sound at the most inopportune times, when they are with clients or in a restaurant or when they are not close to a phone.

So the sales manager makes some changes. She asks receptionists and secretaries to screen client calls more thoroughly, to attempt to service the client as much as possible at the time of the call and only to "beep" the AE when the client insists on talking to an AE. Thus the sales manager has "reinvented" the technology to some degree as well as "reinvented" the work routine of office personnel. But the process still is unfinished.

Clarifying. Another month passes, and the AEs still are not receiving all their messages. The sales manager checks with the receptionists to see if they have followed her orders. The check reveals they have. The fault, she discovers, lies with some AEs who still do not turn on their beepers the entire time they are out of the office. The sales manager talks individually with each AE, stressing the value of the beepers to them and emphasizing the beeper's role in the work process. "Keep them on," is her bottom line. The innovation has lost its newness and is embedded in the department's established routines. Then comes the final step.

Routinizing. In this phase, the technology is firmly in place and is part of work. Back at our TV ad department, new AEs now automatically get a beeper when they are hired. So in this approach, our sales manager has chosen a technology that controls work routines and dictates a certain, somewhat predictable outcome.

But as we have seen, how the adopters (the AEs, in our example) perceive the technology is a very important factor that this approach must consider. This adopter/employee perception can be categorized in the terms of *relative advantage* (the degree to which a technology is perceived as being better than the idea it supersedes), *compatibility* (the degree to which a technology is perceived as consistent with the existing values, past experiences and needs of potential adopters), *complexibility* (the degree to which a technology is perceived as relatively difficult to understand and use), *trialability* (the degree to which the technology may be experimented with on a limited basis before adoption needs to be confirmed), and *observability* (the degree to which the results of a technology are visible to nonadopters). Each perception or "attribute," then, can lead to good or bad consequences, depending on the organization (Rogers, 1986). All of which logically leads to the next school of thought.

Sociotechnical Approach

As you probably could predict, this approach lies somewhere between the first two. Here, the manager stresses or focuses on the needs and actions of those who will use the technology, in addition to examining the attributes and characteristics of the technology itself. A sociotechnical manager sees person and machine mutually interacting to the benefit or detriment of the organization. The technology is seen as dynamic and changing in purpose and use according to its perceived utility (Argyris, 1962).

At first glance, the sociotechnical manager seems to be the norm for today. It is not uncommon to find managers sensitive to employee needs and growth—managers who recognize that formal organizational values sometime infringe on a subordinate's personal values or skills. As a result, these managers realize that psychological and social planning play an important part in new technology introduction. They evaluate technology not simply according to objectives, but also according to the process of change the technology introduces and its impact on employees' motivations, skills, and organizational competence (Blackler & Brown, 1985).

These three approaches—structural, technological-task, and sociotechnical—illustrate that management has to have a basic orientation in dealing with technology. No action occurs in a vacuum and neither does a company's adoption of a new technology.

Media managers need to understand the initial orientation viewpoint they use when it comes to considering implementing any innovation. But once they understand it, they also have to know how to deal with it during the dynamic process known as adoption (and its opposite process, rejection). This means learning to anticipate and predict somewhat the impact of technology on management and, ultimately, its impact on behavior—of employees and in the market. To do so, we must first reexamine the process of technology adoption and place it in the proper context.

ADOPTION PROCESS

The managerial impact of technology can be predicted by using the adoptee's/employee's knowledge and perceptions of the organization's task and by considering the organizational and external contexts. Consider the following assumptions:

1. *For various reasons and objectives, a media organization's management chooses to introduce or adopt a technology.* The company believes it can use new technology to obtain some strategic, operating or control objective and management determines many choices of work and of work organization. Simply put, a worldwide cable news organization, such as Cable News Network (CNN), uses various means of satellite news gathering to give it a long-range toehold in the international television news market. CNN probably could not do as well without this technology. CNN then organizes its staff and work procedures, plans its budgets and markets its programs to take advantage of the technology. More often than not, this decision is an economics-based one, but that is just the beginning.

2. *The technology is introduced to organization members, who interact in various ways with the technology.* Consequences of this interaction can be viewed three ways (Rogers, 1986): (a) direct (changes that occur in immediate response) or indirect (changes resulting from immediate responses), (b) desirable (helps the user or system function more effectively) or undesirable (dysfunctional), and (c) anticipated (changes recognized and intended by management) or unanticipated (changes neither recognized nor intended).

For instance, when many newspaper copy editors were introduced to pagination, they were told the computerized process would mean they would be in total control of the page layout process: no more worrying about accommodating the production staff's idiosyncrasies and ignorance of good journalistic format, no more laying out pages by hand, no more rulers and pencils to use. But they later discovered that using pagination also meant shorter deadlines in some cases, computer delays/glitches, and reorganizing the work day because there were not enough computers to go around.

In addition, such employee-hardware interactions can be mental or physical, pleasant or unpleasant, work or play, and so on. All reactions are expected in a wide range of areas. Employees voluntarily or involuntarily respond positively or negatively. Regardless of the attitudes involved, a response/interaction occurs.

A media firm is likely to experience this response fairly quickly, partly because of the changing nature of the product, the sequential nature of the work, and the routinized nature of the work. Although journalists, for example, publish or broadcast new information daily, they gather that information in a highly structured, predictable way. Any editor or news director who implements a technology that interrupts that method will get immediate feedback, which the next assumption points out.

3. *The interaction is determined in part by the job and task characteristics and values of the user of the technology and in part by the technology's attributes.* This interaction is likely to be fed back to management in terms of costs and benefits. Job/task, values, and technological attributes come together to provide the context for the interaction—the user's judgment (a personal cost-benefit analysis of sorts) about how he will proceed with the specific task. This assessment is repeated as the task needs change.

Using CNN again as an example, its correspondents—most of them American citizens—routinely travel the globe in search of news. But being in another country, many of them also initially and normally referred to that country and other non-American countries as "foreign." Not any more. Senior management directed them to use the word "international" because, by virtue of its satellite-induced worldwide presence, CNN is an international news network and its audience not solely made up of Americans.

4. *The resulting interaction influences management's perceptions of the technology's usefulness and adaptability.* The organization gains experience that will lead it to update its ideas on employee use of the new technology. This, in turn, will lead the organization to modify the desired level of use of the technology. This "learning mechanism" self-adjusts at less-than-infinitely fast speed. Organizational capabilities, development risks, and other factors shape management's perceptions, which appear as corporate cost-benefit ratios or "project profitability." (Stoneman, 1983; Strassmann, 1976)

Suppose a local ad agency wants to save its account executives some telephone and travel time by having them send rough drafts of ads and other materials to clients via facsimile transmission (i.e., "fax"). The fax develops into such a popular machine that all the account executives are "faxing" first, traveling second, to the point that personal contact with clients is at an all-time low and fax costs are at an all-time high. The agency chief executive officer then probably would issue a directive to staffers to use the fax in moderation.

5. *Management's perceptions cause it to redefine its objectives and adjust or restructure the role of the technology to the organization.* Once the perceptions form, management uses various methods to reinforce or readjust its technological priorities. Relationships between technology and job content or between technology and organization structure may be mediated by management assumptions, deductions, and objectives. Such mediation may be drastic or gradual, depending on the circumstances (Child, 1972).

Reexamining the previous example, the ad agency then may want to gradually limit the operating times of the fax machine, or place a limit on pages to be faxed or, eventually, to set standards as to what is considered fax-worthy.

6. *These management actions lead to clarification of the technology's organizational meaning to employees/users.* "Clarification," as indicated earlier, means that as the technology becomes integrated into the day-to-day operations of the organization, its meaning gradually becomes clear to employees. The technology loses its newness and becomes embedded in company operations. The ad agency's fax machine, then, becomes "part of the furniture" instead of some new toy; it no longer represents a change in work. Now it is an accepted way of doing business.

7. *This reeducation of employees/users will mean a change in technology perceptions, which best explain job performance and technology interaction of the employees/users.* This does not mean teaching new skills, but rather a change of the organization's interactional structure. Most often devices such as rules, new job descriptions, or rewards of some kind can bring about these changes.

In the case of the copy editors and pagination, this may have meant staggering their work schedules (to make optimum use of the few pagination terminals), or laying out their pages on scratch paper so that if the computer "breaks down" they will at least have some idea of their original design plans. Or perhaps in the event of a particularly negative work experience with this technology, mastering the machine might mean a promotion, a bonus, or more responsibility, if that is what the copy editor desires.

8. *Management constantly must adjust to those job performances and, in this case, to the employee-technology interaction.* Management is, by nature, adjustment. Typical managerial functions often include planning, staffing, organizing, controlling and motivation. Introducing technology requires the use of one or all of these functions at some time in the adoption process. The key is when to perform which function.

9. *Finally, the organizational and external industrial environments interact with the technological, employee and managerial assumptions mentioned previously.* In short, the manager must not evaluate in a vacuum but, rather, look at the operating environment as well. The environment often indirectly shapes the technology via management perceptions about such issues as competition, market share, and legal regulations, as well as the organization's internal environment.

Suppose a magazine publisher decides to switch her editorial staff from its traditional word-processing equipment to a much more flexible, sophisticated and complex desktop publishing apparatus that will provide flashier graphics and enhance readability. Her concern, then, will probably not be so much about how reporters and subeditors react (because the computer software's forte is journalistically oriented) so much as it will be the impact on production capabilities, ads, and advertisers' concerns for quality.

Once the media manager examines the aforementioned assumptions, she is equipped to ask the appropriate questions regarding the technology, that is, to realize that technology has a definite impact on management. But what kind of impact? In what forms?

TECHNOLOGY'S IMPACT ON MANAGEMENT

To begin with, these impacts can be described in one word: change. But what kind of change? It differs with the situation.

Think back a minute. Remember earlier we said a company decides to implement a new technology for its own, various reasons—many having to do with profits or, at the least, cutting long-range costs.

If you take those managerial expectations and plant them in the technology, you usually have the seeds of organizational change. This change occurs in several areas.

Technology changes the nature of work for the manager.   Whereas the manager of a normal media operation—whether it be in an editorial, advertising, distribution, or production area—deals with change as a matter of routine, technology brings about a different change because its role is as basic to media as routine itself. That role is that of a tool—a way of doing things, the very basis of routine.

When a newspaper equips its reporters with laptop computers with which to write stories, that in effect changes the way the reporter does her job. Instead of phoning in a story or waiting until he returns to the office to write it, the reporter now can file the story electronically by means of hooking up the laptop to a telephone and transmitting the story to the newspaper's master computer. That reporter's editor, then, no longer has to worry about finding someone to take dictation or extending the copy deadline until the reporter comes into the office to write the story. The editor now simply awaits the story as he would any story that was being written from any computer terminal—in-house or not. This saves the editor time, which in turn allows him to do more with that time. Thus his work methods are changed—probably for the better.

Or consider when a local television station sends reporters to cover some national event—such as a political convention—via satellite transmission. The same thing that happened to the newspaper editor in the previous example happens to the TV reporter's boss. In addition, it also changes the scope of the station's coverage in that it now means it no longer reports only local news. The manager—whether it be the assignment editor, news director, the producer, or whoever must edit the story—now must become more familiar with national events and more sensitive to the effect those events have on the local market. The satellite capability will cause the manager to think twice when a reporter asks to be sent to cover an event outside the station's viewing area. No longer will "no" be an automatic response in that situation.

Or suppose a book publisher buys a failing local television station as a means of diversifying the publishing company's interests. This means the publisher will have to change her entire focus to include the business of running a broadcast operation—a technology probably foreign to her, with its own rules of operation, government regulations to consider, different set of egos to deal with and different types of audiences to please. In each of these examples, the manager obviously changes her way of doing work. But there is another managerial impact that many media managers find difficult to accept.

Technology Affects the Manager's Level of Control. Ironically, many companies adopt technologies to gain greater control over operations—control over the budget, or over employee behavior, or over the market, or over distribution of the product, among others. Managers often see the technology as a tool that will steer the process more toward short-term objectives or long-term goals. Certainly, technology does help those things to happen.

But it does not always work that way. Remember, we said technology has desirable or undesirable consequences. Just as laptops give the newspaper editor more time and thus more control over deadlines and copy editing, it also means he loses some control over what the reporter initially will say in the first draft. For just as before the laptop was adopted the reporter would come into the office to work on the story, the editor also would have had a chance to confer with the reporter and discuss a story angle, lead, and so on. Now with the laptop, the reporter has become her own editor, making decisions her editor alone would have made. True, the editor still will get the last word on how the story is edited, but the reporter now gets more of a say, albeit not the final, major authority of the editor.

In the case of the local TV station gaining satellite capability, a similar situation arises in that the producer no longer can package the material (if it is transmitted live on the broadcast) to her liking, at least not initially. She must record it and wait until the next broadcast to do so. That means she loses some control over content. Again, as in the newspaper reporter's case, the TV reporter benefits because she gains control via the questions she asks, the source she chooses, and so forth. Unless the producer (or the reporter, for that matter) has planned ahead, there may be no chance to get other sides of the story; some objectivity may be lost.

Finally, in the case of the book publisher's new acquisition, the publisher may retain ultimate authority but unless she has some television experience she must relinquish day-to-day operating authority to someone schooled in the ways of television administration—the TV general manager. To be sure, that person will have to report to the publisher, but that person also may be gaining more control because the publisher will view him as the "TV expert" and will be less likely to challenge his judgment than would another, more TV-savvy owner.

As these examples indicate, it is probably a short step from experiencing change via loss of control to experiencing change in other areas of management. Remember, management is, after all, a process of adjustment. That adjustment comes in other forms, as we discuss next.

Technology Makes the Manager a Better Intermediate-Range Planner. This is a polite way of saying that technology forces the manager to become more flexible in setting goals and objectives because inevitably adoption of the technology will be an eye-opening experience to the manager.

As we said earlier, management has a specific reason for changing to a new technology. Take, for example, the case of the small-time broadcast mogul who, seeing the steadily increasing numbers of subscribers many cable operations have, decides to purchase a cable franchise to add to his empire. He also may see it as a way to diversify his holdings and create new streams of revenue. So he buys franchises in three small, midwestern towns on the outskirts of major urban centers that he knows are steadily losing population.

But he forgot one thing. His knowledge of cable is not as good as his knowledge of broadcasting; he thinks cable is TV and that cable revenues work the same as TV revenues. As anybody in cable could have told him, that is not necessarily true. Cable TV does have advertising, but the franchise sees little of the money that pays for those ads. The franchises' revenues are hugely subscription based, with other revenues coming from fees paid by the stations it telecasts on its channels. Once our mogul realizes this, he also realizes it is time to rethink his strategy and plans concerning the purchase—fast!

The likelihood of such a scenario is probably remote, but the point is that a new technology—by virtue of being a new, unknown, untested, unobserved entity—creates unforeseen problems that require adjustment in planning. Why? Because managers are human, they see a glittering mass of hardware that they often believe will deliver an equally glittering mass of profits (or, at least, savings). Such near-sightedness (and there are degrees of this kind, too) can be avoided somewhat through proper, deliberate, and well-developed planning as well as through testing and observing the technology before it is adopted.

Not even the best manager can predict what will happen once the technology is put in place, although there is a positive side. Take the case of the newspaper newsroom that adopted new personal computers to perform word-processing (reporting and writing) tasks. Because of the computers' capabilities, the editors could maintain electronic files of stories to come in their computer directories. This file previously consisted of actual newspaper clippings and datebook-type notations. The computer also helped editors maintain a local sources file.

Each file was easily retrievable and facilitated story budgeting in that no more physical items—such as papers and pens—were necessary in such planning. Another editor in the newsroom maintained a list of reporters' regular assignments ("beats") and referred to that file whenever doubt existed about which reporter was to cover a certain topic. Still another editor maintained a writing stylebook for reporters' reference.

In General, Technology Forces the Manager to Functionally Adjust. This means that the same types of things discussed earlier (concerning managerial control and planning) occur in the other main managerial functions—staffing, organizing and motivation.

In staffing, a manager determines human resource needs: recruiting, selecting, and training employees. The new technology enforces this function in that it compels the manager to recruit, select, and train employees capable of effectively using the technology. The ease with which this is done depends on the technology and on the company's personnel.

Consider the editor of the newspaper that adopted the pagination terminals. He was not happy because he believed the technology enhanced the staff's editing abilities. But errors persisted. The editor saw such errors as stemming in part from staff members not taking full advantage of the terminals.

"I think [that] because of the old days in the paper newsroom, you had to take the [news] wire as it was; I think some of us have made the transition that 'Because it comes over the wire, I have to take it as it is.' Well, you don't. You're sitting here with this keyboard that will let you do anything you want to do with that copy [story] to make it better and we don't do it sometimes," he said, referring to his paper's obvious lack of proper employee training in use of the technology. On the positive side, having the latest editing equipment has made recruiting much easier because potential employees see the system as a potential benefit.

But the same editor also had problems in staff organization in regard to the pagination terminals, to which not all staffers had access. To resolve the shortage, the news desk reorganized. Previously, most copy editors arrived at work between 3 and 4 pm. It soon became obvious as the terminals were introduced that schedules would have to be shifted to control story flow and terminal use. "It's made us aware of the workload in that we can't all get here at one time and just shove stuff out. We have to put some thought, some work into making things work in the system," the assistant news editor said.

Such organizational change also took its toll in staff motivation. The terminal shortage resulted in their overuse and frequent system "crashes," in which no terminal would function properly. This system inefficiency lead to staff distrust, apprehension, and anxiety toward the technology. Newsroom managers had an uphill battle in restoring normal relations between users and their tools.

Why so much adjustment? Again, it is because of management's initial view of the technology. Most managers see the technology as basically a technical concern, that is, from the perspective of, "What can the machine do for us?" rather than, "What can the machine do to us?" The company's goals, objectives, and plans usually predate the purchase of the equipment and usually are based on economic considerations that include costs, labor savings, production efficiency, and continued company profits.

So far, we have discussed internal, organizational effects. As you will recall, we also said the technology also interacts with external, industrial environments. Let us see how one such external factor – markets and market behavior – are affected.

MARKET IMPACT

Remember, technology usually is viewed as a tool, a means toward some end. In the area of media markets, managers view technology basically as a means to change the market, hopefully for the better. But that change can take various forms.

Technology Can Expand Competition.   In this case, the technology effectively allows entry into a market that most would have thought closed.

For example, prior to 1982, there were only two newspapers considered national in scope – *The New York Times* and the *Wall Street Journal*. Both had a completely different focus, with the *Times* catering to upscale, affluent readers interested in general national and international news of importance and the *Journal* targeting business executives and professionals with economic orientations. Then along came *USA TODAY*, which used satellite technology to produce magazine-quality color and graphics and attract the busy, traveling professional with short, readable coverage and attractive summaries of state and regional news.

The effect was to expand the market that few thought expandable. True, Gannett Co. Inc. spent millions planning and researching the newspaper. But the technology made entry into the market much easier because not only could the content be electronically delivered to strategic regional printing plants, but the technology also allowed the printing of more than a million copies at a much lower cost than originally thought feasible. Before the coming of *USA TODAY*, the *Times* and *Journal* peacefully coexisted with largely different content and audience. Now there is increased competition for news as well as for advertisers, many of whom are attracted to the possibility of quality color ads in newspapers.

Another example of market expansion is cable television. With a technology that relies on transmitting signals via cable instead of by airwaves, it improved the quality of television reception and also allowed viewers more viewing alternatives. And during the latter part of the 1980s, it consistently eroded the market share of the big three television networks.

Technology Also Can Diminish Competition in Some Markets. It is possible for a technology to be so expensive that the price drives some companies out of business. Let us say two television stations compete for viewers in the same, basic market. Now, let us say the station leading in the ratings decides to enhance its product (and market share) by putting several million dollars into capital improvements—a new and renovated studio, new cameras, new sound equipment, a satellite news-gathering mobile van, to name a few.

The result is a clearer, crisper picture with better video footage, more colorful background graphics, not to mention better facilities with which to produce higher quality local commercials. The bottom line means more viewership, which in turn means more advertisers, higher advertising rates, and more prestige for the station. With those cards stacked against it, the competing station—unless it, too, has a large reserve fund or a good line of credit with local banks—may never recover.

Sound unlikely? Do not be so sure. The same thing happened in the 1970s in the newspaper industry (Compaine, 1985). When new production technology was introduced, it produced large cost reductions and higher profits for those who used it. In highly competitive newspaper cities, often one of the newspapers was owned by a local family, which could not afford to buy such technology. This caused some of those families to sell or close their newspapers.

Technology Can Blur Market Boundaries. During *USA TODAY's* first year or so of operation, analysts were trying to discern in which category it fell. Certainly it was printed on newsprint (regular newspaper stock), but its splashy graphics, somewhat breezy writing style, and its advertising strategies reminded some of a magazine. In fact, some viewed it as a magazine in newspaper format and, thus, a competitor of magazines.

The same phenomenon has occurred with the rise of cable TV. As mentioned earlier, cable and broadcast employ different technologies. But the end result—a television picture or program—is the same. Whereas the CBS, NBC, and ABC networks used to compete against each other for viewers, they now must also compete against anywhere from 15 to 75 other channels, thanks to cable technology.

And then there is the "electronic newspaper"—the initial label for videotext—which allows consumers to request information from a central computer. The computer then transmits the information to consumers via either telephone line or cable TV, for viewing on a video display screen (either a TV set or a computer screen). Consumers can read newspaper stories, do shopping or banking, make airline reservations—all without leaving home. This technology effectively merges print and electronics and obviously does not fit neatly into either the print or electronic industries. Such blurring directly leads to or is affected by to the next two effects: creating new markets and providing revenue alternatives.

Technology Creates New Markets. No one knew there was a market for videotext until the technology was mass-produced and introduced to the public. Using computers and combining them with telecommunication devices has enabled many media companies to become more flexible to the needs and wants of consumers.

Returning to the CNN case, when the company started there were no models to follow, no rules to guide its founders. The same is true for any new venture, of course, but when technology is involved, the venture becomes riskier because of the newness of the technology. For example, many newspapers have attempted to start a videotext service, most notably the efforts of Knight-Ridder and Times-Mirror media conglomerates. Both invested sizable amounts of money—$50 million and $30 million, respectively—in systems with grandscale ambitions (Friedman, 1986). But excessive consumer costs and still-developing transmission methods caused those efforts to fail. There remains some doubt as to whether the technology lends itself to a large market.

Technology Provides Revenue Alternatives for Media Companies. For too long, too many newspaper publishers viewed technology as a method to solely improve existing print production and distribution processes—better color photos, faster word processing, earlier deadlines, more efficient presses, and earlier delivery times. But in the 1980s and early 1990s, as newspapers' traditional stream of profits slowed as the American economy went into recession, publishers began to look at technology in a different light.

Newspapers began investing in such new technologies as cable TV, low power TV, videotext and audiotext services—not as ways to make printing more efficient, but as new sources of revenue. The idea of diversification is not new, of course, but the new technologies make the decision somewhat easier and more attractive.

Other media companies, most notably the major film studios, earlier recognized the wisdom in such a move. In the 1970s, video rental stores were an oddity because most people saw films in theaters and did not own videocassette recorders (VCRs) with which to view films. That all changed with the advent of the VCR, which prompted a booming increase in rental stores and provided an expanded market (and alternative revenue source) for film producers, all of which leads to discussion of another technological effect.

Technology Redefines or Changes Consumer Use and Behavior. As previously mentioned, VCRs changed film companies' ways of looking at revenue. It also transformed many film goers into stay-at-home film renters. After their purchase price declined in the early 1980s, VCRs were in 70% of all American homes. The VCR effectively eliminated many of the negatives associated with theater going: sticky floors, noisy audiences, expensive refreshments, costly admission prices, to name a few. It also meant the consumer could watch the film several times for a nominal, low charge before returning the videocassette to the rental store.

Other technologies have other, similar effects. Videotext, for instance, lets the consumer interact with the information—retrieving and sending messages. Previously, the consumer was simply a passive recipient of information. Cable and satellite technology, as indicated earlier, provide more viewing choices and thus, viewers are becoming more selective in what they watch. The result is evident in the types of channels available: HBO, Cinemax and Showtime (feature films); ESPN (sports); VH-1, TNN, and MTV (music); Lifetime (women's issues); Disney and Nickelodeon (children's programming); and Pay-TV (special events), to name a few. Audiotext services have changed the "letters to the editor" sections of many publications in that many readers no longer write their letters; they simply phone them.

As Technology Affects Consumer Behavior, It Also Indirectly Affects Advertising Strategies, Method, and Content. The example most of us are familiar with concerns, again, the VCR. Because the viewer is able to speed ("fast-forward") past commercials in programs the viewer has recorded, those commercials in effect lose their audience. This has caused some advertisers to alter their messages: shorter, more creative commercials that appear and attract the viewer's attention before the viewer can decide to fast-forward, for example. Other methods include increasing the volume and using current celebrities familiar to the viewer.

But if the new technologies force advertisers' hands, they also allow advertisers to be more selective about their audiences. Advertisers constantly are looking for ways to target specific messages to specific audiences. Many technologies make this easier.

For instance, selective binding allows magazines to reach individual subscribers via specialized issues that carry tailored ads to various targeted groups. Supposedly more efficient than the often used demographic/ geographic zoning method, selective binding gives the advertiser a chance to skim his target audience off the top of the magazine's readership. Other methods do the same thing: Computerized data-base marketing allows the advertiser to match products with their likely consumers; audiotext services offer advertisers a chance to sponsor a telephone message targeted to certain consumers; and television audience rating companies have developed an instrument to replace the traditional written diary technique of recording who's viewing which programs—a "meter" that allows the viewer to electronically register viewing habits.

Technology Often Develops Faster Than Attempts to Control It.   As was true with the development of television and radio, the U.S. government has been slow to regulate and license technology. Take the case of low power television, for which there were more applications in the 1980s than the government expected. Or take the case of satellite transmission: A consumer with a satellite dish often is able to directly get a network's transmission without the commercials. Another problem involves the VCR and its recording ability, especially when it records copyrighted material. How does the creator/author of the material preserve ownership?

SUMMARY

To summarize, technology has several market impacts but basically serves a two-fold marketing function from a media manager's point of view: to allow the company to enter new markets and to increase market share. The technology facilitates these tasks but also brings problems. For the manager, these problems appear in three forms:

1. If the technology helps the company enter a new market, this entry often is accompanied by an unfamiliarity or market unknowns. Any time a person visits a new place, there are new experiences. It is no different for the company that enters a new market. It may mean new regulations (for a newspaper entering broadcast waters) or new forms of revenue flow (going from an advertiser-based source to a subscriber-based source). Whatever the unknown factor, there is a catch-up period that the manager must deal with, either by researching the market thoroughly beforehand or learning on the job.

2. If the technology used is new to the manager or to the market, it introduces a volatility factor that may be hard to control. For instance, videotext in its early days was viewed as an extension of the printed page and several newspapers marketed it as such. They soon discovered, however, that consumers could read the newspaper just as easily on a printed page as from a television screen—in some ways the former was easier and more convenient to do. The videotext technology was meant to be interactive, not passive—a fact realized too late by some.

Managers have to understand that technology demands adjustment. To be sure, the know-how involved in managing does not change. But technology demands the manager be sensitive as to how to manage and when to manage.

3. Finally, because of this volatility factor, the unsuccessful or timid manager experiences a backlash of fear. This fear then causes conservative, reactionary management tendencies—precisely what some new technologies do not require. Obviously, when entering a new market a manager does not want to make a self-destructive decision. That should go without saying. But that is no reason for retrenching at the first hint of rough going.

As mentioned earlier, a media manager's job is to turn the technology to the company's advantage. In trying to show you how to do so, this chapter has examined managerial approaches to technology, the process of how a company uses or "adopts" technology, and how technology may affect media organizations and their markets.

There are three basic approaches: structural, technological-task, and sociotechnical. Each approach is rooted in a slightly different managerial orientation and each has its advantages and disadvantages. Most modern-day managers use some form of the sociotechnical approach.

A media company adopts a technology in much the same fashion as most companies. Each company has its own particular reasons. Then it introduces the technology to employees, who interact in various ways with the technology. Such interaction is determined by the employee and the nature of the task involved. Then management's perceptions and employee reactions prompt a period of adjustment, which ultimately leads to adoption or rejection of the technology.

As a result, the technology has a definite impact on managerial functions, including planning, organizing, staffing, motivating, and controlling operations. Also, there are market consequences to be considered. In all, technology causes a media manager to manage in an atmosphere of constant change and adjustment. How and when a manager acts has a great impact on the company's future.

CHAPTER 10 CASES

Case 10.1

The Case of So You Want to Be a Big Wheel, Huh?

It is 2 days after the start of the latest world crisis, this time in Korea, where Communist North Korean troops and U.N. allied peacekeeping forces have been embroiled in bloody clashes as the North Koreans invaded

South Korea. The president of the United States is closely monitoring the situation and is considering the deployment of 200,000 U.S. troops as well as adequate air support.

He has promised "severe retaliation" if any more Americans are killed or "if American interests are seriously threatened." There are reports of an all-out Communist offensive, as well as the usual carnage and pillaging accompanying war. Fifty American soldiers already have died in the surprise attacks and the North Korean dictator has promised to use atomic weapons, if necessary, to "unify" Korea.

You are president of World News Service, an all-news broadcast network and division of Wilson Television Systems Inc. Your broadcasts normally reach 1% of U.S. households on a normal day, but your operating income has risen steadily from $40 million 5 years ago to $140 million last year.

As you scramble to adjust to the war, you know you will have to add staff and pay other, new production costs. The challenge for you—in only your 7th month on the job (you previously were vice chairman of a newspaper conglomerate)—is to solidify the ratings blitz you have received (the last two nights your audience share has jumped to 11% of households) into steady viewership gains after the war ends.

But there is a problem: Up to now, your coverage has not vastly distinguished itself from that of your competitors—the major TV networks and another all-news network. You all have well-known anchors and satellite links and the Pentagon has tried its best to put a clamp on any aggressive coverage for fear of alienating public support of the American government's response to the situation.

And you get what you pay for when it comes to coverage. But WTS has big debts ($900 million) and those costs will have greater impact. Although your outfit accounts for a fourth of the company's $1.3 billion in overall revenues, you also are responsible for 40% of the company's $350 million in operating income before interest, dividends, and corporate expenses.

As of the last quarter, you are $6 million over budget. Complete yearly totals are not yet computed, but it is no secret WNS expenses exploded 25% in the last quarter and that operating profits fell to $20 million for the quarter—down $6 million from the same period a year earlier. Analysts say—even though it is early yet—you will probably spend anywhere from $250,000 to $1 million a day on any war coverage.

You have had ratings binges before, notably the string of nuclear reactor explosions in the Southeast last year and the assassination of the vice president 6 months ago. But neither event had a lasting ratings impact. You need a definite plan to grab viewers from regular network and cable programming. But things are too hectic now, with the outbreak of Korean hostilities, for you to fathom what that plan may be.

Still, there is always hope. Scott Nicols, your reporter from the front, has interviewed the North Korean prime minister numerous times and has made his way across the so-called demilitarized zone to P'yongyang, North Korea's capital. You talk to him—an unusual action for the top executive—and tell him the sad story.

"Listen, Scott," you say. "We've got to find a way to get something the other guys don't have. The bosses at corporate are breathing down my throat about our costs and 'Why don't we join the press pool and cut our expenses?'—that kind of crap. You got any ideas about how we can steal some thunder?"

"You know I don't do miracles," Scott says, half-joking.

"Well, the big boss is behind us, as always. But even ol' man Wilson himself has limits when it comes to money. He's told me he'll give us rave reviews in public but that he wants to see some sort of turnaround or it's curtains for the bottom line. He's talking about bringing you home."

"Look, I'm just a reporter," Scott shoots back. "I don't know anything about handling Wilson's money; the war's just 2 days old, for God's sake. But I do know about getting news, though."

"You got an angle up your sleeve?"

"More like angel in my pocket—one with wires for wings."

"What the heck are you talkin' about, Nicols?"

He tells you he's been talking with Kim, his Korean freelance photographer friend in P'yongyang. Kim has been trying to talk North Korean officials into letting him connect a dedicated phone line that operates outside the regular telephone system. But so far, they say he has no credibility (and no money to bypass the red tape it would take to clear the system for installation).

Kim says that with the phone line WNS could set up a direct communications link from P'yongyang to WNS headquarters in Denver and be prepared in case the allies start something militarily in the north. The cost: $12,000 to $15,000 a month, in addition to one-time "red tape expenses" not expected to exceed $250,000.

"Shall I tell Kim we're interested?" Nicols asks.

Assignment

1. As WNS president, how do you respond to the question Nicols has posed? Explain your response.
2. Should you consider the technology as a viable option? Why or why not? What would be the organizational impact of using the phone line?
3. How do you think the journalistic community will react if you purchase and eventually use the phone line?
4. What effect would a decision to use the phone line have initially on the market? Suppose the war escalates; what would be the marketing effect of that decision then?

5. How would the technology affect your coverage of the conflict?
6. What would you say to old man Wilson?

Case 10.2

The Case of The Ties That Bind You

You are the publisher of *Mirage,* one of the top four clothing magazines in the country in this, the last year of the decade. Your competitors are *Style Week* ($260.6 million in ad revenues last year), *Persona* ($157.7 million), and *DressUp* ($167.3 million). Your own ad revenues totaled $160 million.

But these are changing times, especially in advertiser markets. Each of the Top Four are looking for new opportunities as style-conscious consumers' personal affluence continues to grow. Your in-house marketing division has identified the following trends: (a) the increased need for information on travel, (b) an interest in corporate wear among your readers, (c) an increased awareness of global economic factors affecting style, and (d) the heightened sensitivity to diversity and multi-racial styles sweeping the country.

Industry analysts have noted that your competitors have started to position themselves for certain general ad categories: the office arena (*Style Week*), which recognizes the increase in consumer awareness of upscale workplace style; the lifestyle or consumer area (*Persona*), which tends to see the readers as people, not just clothes wearers; and the image area (*DressUp*), which attempts to position the typical style-conscious person within her proper social context.

But *Mirage* is still to find its niche. Part of your delay and consternation centers around a new technology that has gotten the attention of your production, advertising, marketing, and administrative branches: selective binding.

In a nutshell, selective binding offers magazine publishers a chance to reach individual subscribers via specialized issues that carry tailored advertising and editorial material to various groups. It sounds like a publisher's dream come true, but not more than one of every six publishers used it last year.

Price is a problem. As with any relatively new technology, the newness means few such binding systems have been built—demand is down, so price is up. It often is cheaper to do separate editions by simply stopping the press to create the second edition. As more printers begin to offer the service, the price will drop, but not in time for *Mirage* to benefit directly.

Also, up until recently, the technology has been available only for saddle-stitch magazines (those bound by stapling or stitching the pages in the center). *Mirage* is a perfect-bound publication, using glue (much like some paperback books) to bind its pages. *Mirage* has been told, however, that the technology is around the corner to selectively gather perfect-bound magazines.

Another problem involves the limit on the number of personalized ads per issue—until now, one. New revisions to the technology have allowed that number to increase, but most vendors say that there has not yet been a demand for this level of personalization, so the technology is largely untested.

Fulfillment houses (which service and maintain the subscription records of many magazines, including *Mirage*) also complain that they do not have a computer system to effectively use selective binding. The mail label-generating circulation file must know which subscribers will get what issue in order to inform the bindery's computer and create the necessary postal reports the process requires. Only one company—it does not service *Mirage*—has such a capability.

Even with such problems, you are intrigued enough by the potential advantages to give selective binding more than a passing thought. Some publishers have used the technology since 1986 with great success, with one magazine producing up to 180 versions a month.

A key to that performance has been the magazine's subscriber data base, which allows the publication to manipulate that data and offer ad packages to prospective clients. Although the technology provides the possibility to manipulate editorial content, some magazines contend that the technology should be driven by advertising—especially because there is no direct revenue flow from editorial matter. Still, formulation of a *Mirage* subscriber data base would be crucial to making selective binding work.

But imagine the possibilities: getting a list of the dozens of sportswear accessory manufacturers, running them against your list of subscribers, and offering them only those subscribers particularly interested in sportswear. Add various demographic categorical twists such as sex, age, or income and *Mirage* could gain unheard-of marketing potential, depending on its designated (and, as yet, undecided) niche of the next decade.

Selective binding has been compared to direct mail, meaning that instead of delivering run-of-press ads, the publisher using selective binding delivers target marketing but at much lower costs than direct mail. The magazine thereby competes with direct mail companies as well as with other magazines.

In the situation of *Mirage*, you are concerned about several things: the trade-off between what selective binding offers versus what you lose from run-of-press; the need to control costs and improve efficiencies in your printing; whether existing demographic or geographic/demographic edition technology would not suffice as well; nobody else in the Top Four has used selective binding; the small, anecdotal success reported by others using the technology; and, moreover, the technology's inherent dilemma of giving advertisers an option to advertise to only elite subscribers.

Add to that the fact that ad revenues for the Top Four as a group were down 7.5% for the year and ad pages through the first three quarters were down 1.5%.

Assignment

1. As publisher, in the long run do you think you would you adopt the selective binding technology? Why or why not? What criteria would you use for making your decision?
2. What would be your immediate response in this scenario? What are the basic issues? What poses the biggest problem?
3. What would you do as head of the *Mirage* marketing staff? Would you recommend adoption of the technology? Explain.
4. Suppose you adopt selective binding. What about your market niche? What would it be and how would selective binding help you attain it? How would your decision to adopt the technology affect your choice of market(s)? Explain.

Case 10.3

The Case of The Technology of Choice

You are the general manager of the *News*, the second-largest daily newspaper in Ryanna, second-largest city (population 150,000) in the state. Both papers are morning papers, so the competition is fierce, but not as intense as it could be.

Your rival, *The Daily Record*, has a circulation of slightly more than 72,000, compared to your 53,500 or so readers. But the differences do not stop there.

For years the *News* has been known as the feisty local-oriented paper, with hard-hitting investigative pieces, popular columnists and thorough sports coverage. You have served a mostly blue-collar readership. Two blocks down the street, *The Daily Record* has taken a different course.

As the most visible symbol of The Record Corp., a thriving statewide media empire (including the only paper in the state capital and the leading television station in the state's largest city), the *Record* is a rich paper with a more statewide outlook. It attempts to cover state and local issues with similar fervor. In addition, the *Record*'s advertising linage is 50% more than the *News*, thanks to the *Record*'s largely affluent suburban readership.

Your rival also considers itself a regional newspaper, offering home delivery in 20 outlying counties (including 2 in the closest neighboring state, 30 min to the west) and prompting its parent company to embark on an ambitious marketing plan linking the *Record*'s name to various upscale high school projects and Chamber of Commerce-type programs. The fact that the *Record* is seen as the more conservative newspaper seems to help.

Meanwhile, things are not as rosy for the *News*. In the last 5 years, your largely urban, middle-class circulation has dropped by more than 10,000— causing decreasing advertising linage and smaller-than-expected revenue. As you start your 2nd month on the job, you are the second general manager in 2 years, meaning leadership has been shaky at best.

The publisher has asked you to develop a plan to turn the newspaper's fortunes around. He wants you to find a market or markets that will position the *News* as a savvy, locally oriented alternative to the *Record*, which he calls "an old fogey rag for suits and Republicans." The *Record*, in fact, attempts to be the paper for everyone, even to the point of copying the *News* editor's idea of more and enhanced coverage of and for the city's growing (40,000) minority community.

In addition, the publisher wants your idea(s) to save money and/or generate more revenue. "Maybe we can trim some fat through technology," he says. You know the *News* is making more money than it ever has but the publisher has not mentioned how much he is willing to spend to help turn things around.

Some preliminary evaluation of the news staff shows it to be a lean, mean operation, with bright, aggressive, underpaid reporters. Advertising staffers are doing their best but advertisers say they are confident that core customers are more likely to see their ads in the *Record* than in the *News*. Production workers are doing their best to adapt to the new pagination system, which used computers to put page layout and composition duties in the hands of news copy editors; so you find no fat there.

It is becoming clear that the current operation needs a jolt from the outside, some means of improving the image of the newspaper without changing the paper itself. Readers are happy with the product; any content changes would alienate them and make circulation figures sag even more. Also, you do not want to copy the *Record*'s PR moves, for fear of seeming to affirm that strategy and also because your advertisers may worry and wonder about what audience you are after.

After reading industry publications and giving the problem much thought, you settle on these preliminary options:

1. A video version of the *News*, with the following sub-options:

   * *A daily half-hour information and entertainment program based on the News;* model the program on the newspaper's three sections—news, lifestyle, and sports and feature topical news with previews of stories from the paper's next-day edition, as well as interviews with reporters for behind-the-scenes perspectives on breaking news; this would be news that none of the local network affiliates offer; besides, none of them would go for

this, so you might want to make an offer to the local independent station, which has no local news show.

• *An 18-hr local news cable operation*; the local cable system is an almost nonexistent competitor in local news; this could be a way to take the *News'* resources and beat the *Record* at its own game; the local cable system reaches 65,000 homes and there is a niche forming for local news similar to that created when CNN started nationally; but the bulk of cable revenues would come from subscribers, rather than from advertising.

• *Buy and start a low-power television station (LPTV*, although still seen as a second-class service, the number of LPTVs continues to steadily increase; assigned to space left over from full-power stations, LPTVs can reach areas with radiuses between 5 and 25 miles in areas with topographies similar to Ryanna's; the majority of LPTVs are carried by local cable systems—90% at no cost; there are some regulatory problems, mostly due to having secondary status to the full-power stations; Ryanna currently has no LPTVs; the on-air look is clean, but not network-slick.

2. Database marketing:

• Micromarketing is now a fact of life and the *News* can help its customers better compete by building a data base; this means not only buying lists and demographic information, but also holding contests to yield consumer data, conducting surveys.

With an electronic data base, the *News* can locate good customers and prospects, determine their wants, and efficiently and effectively market programs toward them; advertisers and agencies will insist on knowing about subscribers and the *News* will have the answers.

If one store comes into the market and wants to sell specialty footwear, the *News* will be able to show the owner where those who wear such shoes live. The data typically are entered into a computer and cover such personal information as education and income level, family size, marital status, job, bill-paying behavior, and buying tendencies.

Price depends on the computer hardware, target-marketing software, and consultant costs, to name a few. But results are measurable and the *News* will be able to attribute circulation gains directly to specific campaigns. The idea is to build a body of knowledge about *News* home-delivery subscribers that will let the *News* be more effective in its circulation strategies.

3. Telecommunications, on two fronts:

• First, voice information services technology offers the *News* a chance for a fairly low-cost method to extend its publishing cycle, make it more distinctive, promote it, and better serve its customers.

The easiest and least-expensive method to enter the electronic information market is to offer one or more voice information services. For example, for between $30,000 and $200,000, the *News* can launch an advertiser-sponsored audiotext service, offering current and local information (stock reports, weather, sports, gardening tips, movie listings, TV programs) to readers as well as a 15-sec ad.

In addition, the *News* may want to combine audiotext and voice messaging. This means giving specific information as well as offering voice mailboxes to receive and store telephone messages for newspaper staff members or for receiving readers' called-in messages for possible publication. Then there are possible classified advertising applications (e.g., personals, trial ads, garage sale promotions, etc.).

- Also, there are voice service systems that charge on a per-call basis.

Evidence suggests readers will pay for data on various topics, depending on what is offered by the newspaper. Some newspapers hire a service bureau that has the technical capabilities and capacity to administer and market the service.

The *News* may want to get advertiser support for the system, but there need be no initial up-front investment for there to be modest revenue flow. The service will work better if newsroom cooperation can be obtained (and it can if you point out the advantages, such as gathering data for news stories).

4. Faxing the *News*

- Many experts consider this the lowest risk of today's technologies, although many newspapers have started and stopped such projects in relatively short periods.

Readers can scan a newspaper as an index for news by using a redesigned newspaper that provides news summaries and is delivered by facsimile machines. The paper also can use fax to send information regarding products and then charge advertisers for the service.

The *News*, however, might have to find a somewhat different audience for this, because most fax consumers are white-collar workers too busy to wade through a daily paper.

Assignment

1. Choose one of the aforementioned as your proposal for the publisher and make a convincing case for it. Why would the option you choose be a better alternative than the other options?

2. Which technology would cut most effectively into The *Record*'s market? Which would be least effective in that regard? Why?

3. Should a newspaper enter any nonprint market? Should technology drive or direct that entry? What would be some managerial challenges the paper's leadership should consider in making such a change?

Case 10.4

The Case of The Glittering SINS

For sale: Sports Information Network Systems (SINS), an all-day cable sports TV network offering the latest in round-the-clock sport news. Lost $36 million last year. Now under Chapter 11 bankruptcy protection.

Competition: other 24-hr cable operations with single-focus formats (one a financial news network, the other an all-news network with 47% and 38%, respectively, of the audience). Minimum price: $55 million. Audience: 18 million subscribers (about 15% of the market). Advertising revenue: $12 million. Staff size: 240 employees.

Why consider it: The competition, though good, is not great. Your company, a medium-size radio and magazine publishing conglomerate, wants to add to its radio holdings (none are in cable or TV). In addition, your previous cable ventures had been small-scale and you would like a cable outlet for your national sports magazine and an added medium for your sports information services (Sportsdata, a source of on-line sports statistics on any of the major sports).

As CEO of your company, you would like to tap into SINS' audience base, which reaches upscale viewers. SINS' competition boasts more polished reporting and slicker sets. SINS has advertisers, but its market share has slipped from the previous year's 18%. Industry experts think the market is already overcrowded.

You could think of millions of reasons to look the other way on this matter and go on with what you do best, but the board wants to try something "bold and innovative," as the board chairman said. Truth be told, your company could use SINS as an outlet for your sports-writing capability, but you are not sure how just yet. You have an award-winning staff, lead by some heads-up managers who know a story when they see it and who also know something about SINS' sports coverage.

But, there are SINS' considerable financial liabilities, including $60 million it owes to banks and lessors. You would have to get a federal bankruptcy judge to OK your offer.

And then there was the scandal one of its most visible anchors was involved in when he made seemingly racially tinted analytical remarks involving the most valuable player on the national collegiate champion basketball team. SINS has been trying to survive the controversy since last March.

In addition, you know that there may be other bidders for SINS, but you have the cash to match them. Besides, SINS looks like such a poor investment that you are 90% sure that you would be the lone bidder.

Your company has deep pockets, to be sure, thanks to conservative, sound fiscal management. But except for your national sports magazine, the company is invisible. SINS would eliminate that problem. But what about this cable industry? Your company has no expertise in that area.

Assignment

Persuade your board of directors to make the move to buy SINS, including some strategies on how your company can use SINS best, adapt to its new technology and, obviously, make a profit.

In your proposal, include a strategy for turning around the market situation, as well as dealing with SINS' debt situation. How would you handle each and in what way could you turn them to your advantage? Remember, your board want results, as well as glitter.

Discuss the pros and cons of this venture, answering in the process the following questions in your proposal:

1. What is the degree to which this new technology—as represented by SINS—could be managed by your management team, which is more comfortable managing radio and magazine properties? What adjustments in thought processes would be necessary?

2. How would the acquisition change the nature of work for your management structure? What new control mechanisms would this acquisition demand of your company? What would the acquisition do to your planning process? Your organizational structure?

3. How would the acquisition make your conglomerate operations seem more attractive to advertisers? What would be the potential market impact? Are new markets created? Will your advertising strategy change?

Appendix: Extended Case Studies

THE CASE OF FACING THE COMPETITION IN MOUNT PLEASANT

Mount Pleasant remains one of a handful of cities in the United States with separately owned and operated daily newspapers. Although *The Daily News* and the *Mount Pleasant Telegraph* have battled each other for 90 years, the war has intensified during the past 2 years, since the *Telegraph* was bought by Riddle Corporation. Riddle is a media conglomerate with 98 daily newspapers, 24 weeklies, and 7 television stations. Byrom Inc., a privately held corporation, has owned *The Daily News* for 15 years. In addition to *The Daily News*, Byrom Inc. owns four small dailies and 10 weeklies in the same state as Mount Pleasant.

You were contacted recently by James Severin, a lawyer for Byrom Inc. The recent drop in home-subscription price to $40 a year by the *Telegraph* has caused Byrom Inc. President Loyd Byrom to seek advice concerning long-range strategic planning in the market. Your job as a consultant will be to evaluate the market and competition and suggest possible strategies for *The Daily News* during the next 3 years.

The Market

Mount Pleasant is a city of 350,400 people in 125,591 households. The retail trade zone (RTZ) is Mount Pleasant County, which has a population of 698,560 in 265,612 households. Mount Pleasant County also includes 20 smaller cities and towns. The largest, Pleasant Valley, has 44,400 people and 18,122 households. The second largest is Townsen with 36,450 people and 14,019 households. Only 100,230 people do not live in an incorporated area.

The *Telegraph* and *The Daily News* are the only daily newspapers in the county. Mount Pleasant County has 10 weekly newspapers—1 each in

Pleasant Valley and Townsen. Six weeklies are owned by Suburb Corporation. These newspapers are zoned for the entire county. The papers average about 24 pages per week, of which half are common pages for all editions. They are free-distribution papers that circulate on Wednesday by mail. The other two weeklies are independently owned and serve other towns and cities in the county. One is located in the extreme southern part of the county and the other in the extreme north.

The market has five television stations: one each for the three major networks, a public broadcast station, and an independent station. The market also has 16 radio stations that play a variety of types of music. One station, which is publicly owned, is an all news and information station.

Other media in the county include a weekly financial newspaper, a Black weekly that circulates statewide, a monthly city magazine, and a college twice-weekly paper at the state university.

The county has two total market coverage publications. One covers just real estate, whereas the other is primarily classified advertising. Both are just breaking even.

Cable is relatively new to the county. The more affluent northern half of the county is wired. Wiring of the southern half is underway. The city has yet to be wired. Currently about 70,000 county homes have the potential for subscription, and 63% have signed up. The cable offers 32 channels, with 8 of these dedicated to public, government, and educational access. Local advertising can be carried by several of the free satellite networks.

Mount Pleasant is the capital of a western state that has a population of 3.1 million in 1.12 million households. The state is primarily agricultural, but there are also growing lumber, mining, and manufacturing industries. The state has a total of 26 daily and 72 weekly newspapers. The average gross household income in the state is $28,910.

The City of Mount Pleasant's primary businesses include state government, banking, insurance, distribution, and manufacturing. The average gross income per household in the county is $31,295. Unemployment has been stable at about 5.2% of the work force for 6 years. It is expected to remain at that level for the next few years.

The Newspaper War

The latest phase of the war between *The Daily News* and the *Telegraph* began with the purchase of the *Telegraph* by Riddle 2 years ago. The battle has included radical changes in news content and in subscription, newsstand, and advertising prices. The following sections review the history of the two newspapers, the current ownership, and the nature of the competition.

History of the *Mount Pleasant Telegraph*

The *Telegraph* was founded in 1834 by Judge Henry Talbot to promote Whig policies and to offer an alternative newspaper to the *Morning Intelligencer*, which closed in 1895. The *Telegraph* remained in the family until it sold to Riddle. During its history, the *Telegraph* became known as the "Voice of the State." It outlasted several competitors.

It had a tradition of being a very serious newspaper with an emphasis on international, national, and state news. Its editorial page varied during the years, but since the Great Depression it had taken a slightly liberal lean.

Until 1947, the *Telegraph* had been an afternoon newspaper. It became the first morning newspaper in Mount Pleasant that year. Since that time, it dominated the market, always having more than 50% of all circulation.

During the 13 years that the Talbot family competed with the Byrom family, the *Telegraph* lost market shares to *The Daily News*, although the losses occurred primarily during the last 10 years. This played a partial role in the selling of the newspaper to Riddle Corp., but it was probably not the main reason. As control of the company that owned the *Telegraph* became dispersed among descendants of Henry Talbot, it had become more difficult for one person or even a coalition to run the newspaper. Cliques within the family were almost constantly battling over editorial and news policy. Six years ago, the family ousted John H. Talbot, the great-great-grandson of the founder and replaced him with an outside publisher and editor. The resulting court battle became a segment on a national television news magazine.

The eroding market shares and the internal squabbling seemed to combine to make the family sell their shares to Riddle. Riddle paid $150 million for all shares. Riddle initially made few management changes, but there has been a distinct change in the appearance and news content of the *Telegraph*. After a year of Riddle ownership, several of the older employees left the paper.

Ownership of the *Mount Pleasant Telegraph*

Riddle Corporation, which is headquartered in New York, has been in the newspaper business for about 100 years. James M. Riddle started the group after he succeeded in establishing dailies in Cincinnati and Dallas. The group grew slowly at first. By 1920, Riddle Corp. owned 12 dailies. By 1940, this total reached 24, and 12 weeklies had been added. Riddle became a public corporation in 1965 and since that time has grown rapidly. After going public, the corporation moved quickly into broadcasting. It is now the largest U.S. media corporation. Its 98 daily newspapers have a combined daily circulation of 7.2 million copies and Sunday circulation of 7 million. Last year, Riddle's gross revenues exceeded $4 billion. The group's reputation is one of producing good, but not great newspapers. During the past 20 years, the group has won only 4 Pulitzer Prizes, despite owning newspapers in some of the largest cities in the United States.

Despite having 98 newspapers, Riddle does not have a history of running competitive newspapers. The *Telegraph* is the only newspaper it owns in a competitive market, although it owns four joint operating agreement (JOA) newspapers. All four were bought after the JOA was established.

Riddle has been a trend setter in the area of newspaper color and graphics. Its early adoption of computer systems designed for graphics resulted in an emphasis on information graphics among most of its newspapers. Along with the growing emphasis on graphics has come a deemphasis on lengthy stories. The average story in a Riddle newspaper tends to be about 30% shorter in length than the average story in other newspapers. This does not mean Riddle papers do not devote space to in-depth reporting. Several of the newspapers have won regional press association prizes for investigative reporting. However, these enterprise projects tend to be broken into several stories with a number of accompanying graphics.

History of *The Daily News*

The Daily News was founded 90 years ago by William Thompson. Thompson, who was active in the early labor movement, wanted the newspaper to be a voice for reform. He owned the newspaper for only 5 years before selling it to Charles Wilford. Wilford was not a reformer and ran the afternoon newspaper primarily as a business. It never had more than 30% of the circulation in the market and had dwindled to about 20% by the time it was bought by Byrom Inc. Wilford's relatives sold the paper to Byrom.

As a trailing newspaper in the market, *The Daily News* had a history of low pay and relatively small news holes. It had sometimes been called a training ground for *Telegraph* reporters. During the second half of the 20th century, its editorial page has ranged from conservative to reactionary. Since Byrom Inc. purchased the newspaper, the editorial stances have tended to be conservative.

Three years after Byrom bought *The Daily News*, it was still losing circulation market shares, but at a slower rate than before it changed hands. At this point, Byrom approached the Talbot family about joining the two newspapers in a JOA. Governed by the 1970 Newspaper Preservation Act, the JOA would have combined the business, advertising, production, and circulation departments of the two papers, but the newsrooms would have remained separate. John Talbot reportedly laughed at Loyd Byrom when he was approached with the idea.

Following the failed JOA request, Byrom decided to make a concerted effort to overtake the *Telegraph*. During the next 12 years, *The Daily News* switched to morning publication, increased its news hole, hired more staff at higher wages, and began to cut advertising and subscription prices to attract more readers and advertisers. The blitz worked, as *The Daily News* gained more than 40% of the circulation market within 10 years.

During the 2 years of Riddle ownership, the *Telegraph* has battled *The Daily News* on its own terms.

Ownership of *The Daily News*

Byrom Inc. is controlled by Loyd Byrom, who is a third-generation newspaperman. His grandfather, Donald Byrom, started the business in Smithville 75 years ago with a small daily. Loyd Byrom's father expanded the business by buying 3 other dailies and 10 weeklies. Loyd diversified the newspaper holding by buying into cable systems earlier in their development. Last year, Byrom, Inc. had gross revenues of $80 million.

Loyd Byrom also expanded the corporation by buying *The Daily News* 15 years ago for $5 million. At the time, the price almost equaled the equity of the newspaper. A local magazine article at the time said if Byrom had not bought *The Morning News* the paper would have closed within 6 months.

As President of Byrom, Inc., Loyd Byrom has developed a reputation for being an open but shrewd businessman. A former editor at *The Daily News* was quoted as saying: "Loyd is a nice guy but don't try to take advantage of him. He's got a long memory, and he can be as pigheaded as anyone I know."

A newspaper trade magazine article about the battle in Mount Pleasant quoted the same source as saying: "Loyd doesn't really care about making money in Mount Pleasant. The only quarter he made a profit he divided it among the staff. He just wants a newspaper in Mount Pleasant. He may be the last of a dying breed of independent newspaper owners."

Although Byrom has become somewhat of a hero among people who long for independent ownership in an increasing corporate industry, his heavy investment in *The Daily News* was not altruistic. It came after 3 years of continued circulation decline. For several years, salaries at the *The Daily News* were significantly lower than those at the *Telegraph*. A journalism professor at the state university pointed out that it was not until the last 5 years that *The Daily News* began to provide journalism anywhere near the quality of that traditionally provided by the *Telegraph*.

The History of Competition

- Fifteen years ago, Byrom, Inc. bought *The Daily News*.
- Twelve years ago, Byrom approached the owner of the *Telegraph* with a JOA proposal and was turned down.
- Following the failed JOA attempt, Byrom began to invest money in *The Daily News* in an effort to overtake the *Telegraph* in circulation and eventually advertising linage. This included hiring more reporters, photographers, and editors at higher salaries; holding down circulation and

advertising prices; and paying special interest to sports and local societal news. Six years ago, Byrom established a rule that *The Daily News* always would carry more news than the *Telegraph*.

The response of the *Telegraph* management to the measures was basically to ignore them. They did not match the price cuts and continued the same news policies.

• Nine years ago, as *The Daily News* began to make inroads into market shares of circulation and advertising linage, Byrom began aggressive editorial stances in favor of conservative causes. This was seen as a response to a swing toward conservative positions held by the state population. The editorial page always had been considered a weak part of the *News*. In addition, *The Daily News* began to do more enterprise reporting. This meant twice a month, the paper would devote two full pages or more to a single issue of importance.

The Daily News also began promotions of its changes in news and editorial policies. Its slogan was "People are changing to the better newspaper."

• The response of the *Telegraph* was guarded, at best. There was little effort to match the price discounting of the *News*, but there was an effort to beef up news coverage. The news hole was enlarged, but it still did not equal that of *The Daily News*. A half dozen more reporters were hired to cover new beats in the areas of business, environment, and science. During this period, the editorials tended to become more liberal on social issues as the *News* editorials became more conservative. Management of the *Telegraph* felt the "conservative movement" was a national fad. They argued that liberal social stances were more reflective of the state population's concern for other human beings.

• Six years ago, *The Daily News* decided to increase its activity in free distribution of its newspaper and in attracting classified advertising. The gap in circulation had continued to narrow between it and the *Telegraph*, but the advertising gap had not closed as much.

The Daily News was offered free to readers of the *Telegraph* for 1 week if the reader would show the circulation people of the *News* a paid receipt from the *Telegraph*. This offer was promoted on TV and radio as an effort to get the readers to compare. If the reader then took the *News*, they were given a year's circulation at half price.

The Daily News also offered free classified advertising for 3 days. A person could run a four-line classified for 3 days at no cost. This was done because classifieds were seen as a way of increasing circulation. This policy was promoted heavily on billboards.

• The *Telegraph* was more responsive this time. It began an advertising campaign with the slogan, "You get what you pay for." It offered guaranteed classifieds. If a person did not sell their advertised item within a week, they did not have to pay for classifieds and received a 2nd week free. This applied to all individual classifieds except garage sales.

The *Telegraph* began to editorialize against the free newspaper policy of the *News*, calling it predatory pricing and implying that the *Telegraph* might pursue an antitrust suit. In turn, the *News* said the editorials reflected the growing strength of its newspaper and the frustration of the *Telegraph* staff to being a second-rate newspaper.

• Part of the problem the *Telegraph* had in responding to the initiatives of the *News* was due to disagreements within ownership as to the proper response. It was shortly after the free classifieds and newspapers offers at the *News* that John Talbot was ousted as publisher of the *Telegraph* by family members who disagreed with his policies.

• During the 4 years after John Talbot left the *Telegraph* as publisher, the *News* continued to increase its market share of circulation and advertising. During this time, *The Daily News* had reached 42.5% of all the daily circulation in the city and retail trade zone and 49.7% of all the Sunday circulation in the city and retail trade zone. Its advertising linage had grown to 39% of all city and retail trade zone daily advertising and 41.9% of the Sunday linage. The *News* made a small quarterly profit of $25,000 during the last quarter of this period. It was at this point that the *Telegraph* was sold to Riddle.

• Riddle's reaction was quite different compared to the Talbot family's. Riddle CEO Jeffrey Newman was quoted in a trade publication as saying, "Cities aren't big enough any more to support two daily newspapers. Mount Pleasant is no exception. We ultimately will be the survivor in that city."

The results of this approach were seen immediately, as Riddle matched or beat any advertising discounts and held down subscription prices. Riddle also offered free classifieds. The new owners started a heavy advertising campaign emphasizing that the *Telegraph* was still the state newspaper. They started heavy telephone and door-to-door subscription solicitations.

The content of the *Telegraph* became more like other Riddle publications. It contained significantly more color and graphics and had a growing emphasis on feature and information types of stories. The news hole grew slightly, but the *News* continued to offer more space devoted to news and features. A new Sunday magazine was added and the Sunday TV guide was redesigned. The changes were designed to attract younger readers.

As a reaction to the changes at the *Telegraph*, some of the older reporters and editors left, either to join the *News* or to go to other markets. Lee Simpson, a sports columnist at the *Telegraph* for 20 years, moved to the *News*. His first column denounced Riddle as taking a television approach to newspapers. "The new *Telegraph* is like so many TV shows. It has become all form and no content," Simpson said.

• Despite the changes at the *Telegraph*, the *News* continued a slow gain in circulation and advertising share until a month ago. At that time, Riddle lowered the subscription price of the *Telegraph* to 75¢ a week, which was half of the already comparatively low price of $1.50 being charged by the *Telegraph*. Daily single-copy price was cut to 15¢ from 25¢. Sunday single-copy price was dropped to 50¢. At the same time, Riddle announced it would match or beat any advertising discounts by the *News*.

During the next month, the *News* saw a slight loss in circulation and advertising space, whereas the *Telegraph* saw a slight increase. This is the point at which Byrom called you to get your advice.

Current Content

The following appraisal of the two newspapers' content was performed by a journalism professor at the state university. The study covered a randomly constructed week from last year.

Overall. The *News* had more pages per weekday on average, 75 to 68. The difference represented the larger news hole of the *News*, which had 41.25 pages of news-editorial material, compared to the *Telegraph* with 31.75. The Sunday edition of the *News* had 120 pages with 60 pages of news-editorial material, whereas the *Telegraph* also carried 120 pages, with 45 pages of news-editorial material.

Front Page. Neither newspaper stood out as dominating the other. Each beat the other on various stories. The emphasis of the *News* was oriented a little more toward the suburbs and foreign news, whereas the *Telegraph* had a greater orientation toward state and city news. The *Telegraph* seemed more colorful, but the *News* also used color extensively.

Front Section. As with all sections, the *News* had a larger front-section news hole. Except for the front page, the newspapers were fairly consistent in their use of the front section. Both papers emphasized national and international news, although the *News* had more city and county stories mixed into the section. The *Telegraph* had shorter stories. Both papers had a second front page on page 3, and both ran color state weather maps on the back page of the first section.

Second Section. The *Telegraph* seemed to have more of a city orientation in this section. Its section heading was "Metro/State." The *News* heading just said "State." The *Telegraph*'s greater use of color and graphics made the first second-section page look more like a front page. This probably helped to create the impression of more local coverage.

In this section, the *Telegraph* had a slightly higher number of city and county stories, but the space devoted to these stories was greater in the *News*. State coverage was about equal in stories and space.

The big difference in local emphasis is impression. The *News* had more space and about equal number of stories, but the stories were scattered throughout the first two sections.

Editorial Section. The *Daily News* averaged three editorials a day, compared to two for the *Telegraph*, whose editorials where about 15% longer. The *News* had no advertisements on its two editorial/op-ed pages per day, whereas about half of one page of the *Telegraph* was devoted to ads. The *News* had 50% of their editorials devoted to state issues, 30% devoted to city/county issues and 20% to national issues. The *Telegraph* had 40% devoted to state issues, 40% devoted to city/county issues, and 10% devoted to national, and 10% devoted to international issues.

The op-ed page of the *News* carried significantly more letters to the editor, whereas the *Telegraph* tended to run more syndicated columns on its op-ed page.

Sports Section. The *Daily News* averaged 10 pages to the *Telegraph*'s 8 during the period of study. Both papers have strong columnists, who are controversial. The *News* columnist, who moved over from the *Telegraph*, has been in the market for 20 years, whereas the *Telegraph* columnist was recently hired from a newspaper in Atlanta. The *News* averaged a full page of outdoor sports, mostly hunting and fishing, with a designated page. The *Telegraph*'s outdoor coverage was slight, but its design and use of summary box scores for all sports was very good.

Business Section. Neither newspaper had an outstanding business page because of limited staff. The pages were mostly wire service stories and numbers, such as stock market and farm options reports. The *News* had more pages and emphasized farming slightly more.

Feature/Entertainment Sections. The *Telegraph* did a much better job with features and entertainment. There is more of an emphasis. For example, singer Roy Orbison, who had connections with the state, died during the period being analyzed. The *Telegraph* carried a lead story on the front of the feature section and a sidebar about his association with the state. The *News* just had a long obit on page 3A.

The *Telegraph* had two entertainment staff columnists, who cover the city and state, compared to one for the *News*. Space was about equal for the two papers, but the *Telegraph* had better design and more staff copy.

The *Telegraph* had better comics. It has three pages, one in color. The *News* had two pages in black and white. The *Telegraph* had the more popular comics among the 21 to 35 years age group.

Classified Advertising. The *News* averaged six more pages of classified, even though both had free classifieds. This included an advantage in real estate display classifieds. The *News* had a locator map for real estate and garage sales that was useful for readers.

The Population

The population of Mount Pleasant County is on average better educated than any other city in the state. Of the population, 75.2% have at least a high school diploma, and 22.6% have at least a bachelor's degree. Although the city's economy is primarily trade, professional, or service, the state's agricultural base still influences the nature of the population. A state university of almost 23,000 students is located within the county.

The vast majority of the population, 86%, are native to the state, and about 58% were born in Mount Pleasant County. As a large, agrarian western state, the population is somewhat provincial, but not unaware of issues outside the state. As one columnist put it, "It's not that we're hicks. It's just that this state has everything we need. Why go elsewhere when everything you want is next door."

The percentage of county households subscribing to national magazines in order of highest penetration are:

Readers Digest — 17%
TV Guide — 8%
Better Homes and Gardens — 8%
National Geographic — 8%
Southern Living — 7%
Family Circle — 6%
Ladies Home Journal — 5%
Time — 4%
Newsweek — 3%
U.S. News & World Report — 3%
Sports Illustrated — 3%

Assignments

The following assignments can be done separately or together.

Assignment 1

Your assignment is to conduct a market analysis for Byrom, Inc. using the material in chapter 6. It should be as complete as possible and cover the market structure, organization's goals, nature of demand, and intellectual market. The economic environment can be studied by assuming that the market is in your state and the current year is right now.

Assignment 2

Pick either the *Telegraph* or *The Daily News* and develop a 3-year marketing plan, based on the material in chapter 7. A variation would be to have the class divide into teams and have more than one team assigned to each of the two newspapers.

Assignment 3

Pick either the *Telegraph* or *The Daily News* and develop a 3-year strategic plan. This should include a marketing plan, a human resources plan, and a financial plan, based on the material in chapter 7. A variation would be to divide the class into teams and have more than one assigned to each newspaper.

Assignment 4:

As a consultant to Byrom, Inc., analyze the recent market actions of the *Telegraph* for possible antitrust violations. Using the material in chapter 5 and other references, determine if Byrom, Inc. might have a basis for an antitrust suit.

Assignment 5:

Using the information in chapter 8, design a plan for conducting research about the content and pricing of either newspaper. This would include the type of research and who would be the subjects of the research.

Assignment 6:

Pick a newspaper and write a report concerning possible new sources of revenue. This could involve new technology, or applying old technology in a new way. The new revenue sources could use old information in new ways, or they could develop entirely new information. The object is to come up with additional ways to generate revenue.

After suggesting the new revenue sources, explain the potential negative effects of any new technology on the existing organization. This would include a discussion of ways to avoid these potential negative effects.

Weekly Suburban Newspapers in Mount Pleasant County

The Pleasant Valley Mercury

This is the oldest weekly in the county, having been established in 1925. The current publisher/editor/owner is the daughter of the founder. It circulates only in Pleasant Valley, where it reaches 90% of the 18,122 homes. It publishes on Wednesdays and cost 35 cents a copy from a newsrack and $15 a year. It runs about 52% ads with 36 pages on average and is marginally profitable. Its penetration rate has been at about 90% for 30 years. Editorially, it is independent.

The newspaper has three times been named the best weekly in the state during the past 20 years by the state press association. The publisher/editor, who is 70 years old, often has said she has little use for money, except to turn out a good newspaper.

Pleasant Valley has turned from a rural town to a booming suburban bedroom community during the past 20 years. Its population has increased 150% during that period. The average gross income per household is $40,320, and the town has the highest average education level in the county. The town is 15 miles from downtown Mount Pleasant and 10 miles from the state university.

The Townsen Tattler

Townsen is similar to Pleasant Valley in its rapid growth, but the population is younger and not as well off. The *Tattler* was established 20 years ago as the boom began. It sells for 40 cents a copy or $20 a year. It reaches about 66% of the 14,019 households in Townsen. The paper averages about 60% ads a week with 24 pages.

The paper is run by a publisher, who has held the position for about a year. The owner is a real estate developer in the area. The paper is known for its prodevelopment stance. The content tends to emphasize entertainment, societal, and education news, and features, although the paper does carry police and city hall news.

Townsen is about 20 miles west of downtown Mount Pleasant. The city averages about $36,000 gross income per household a year. The residents are slightly above average in educational background.

Suburb Corporation

These six zoned weeklies are headquartered in Mount Pleasant but cover the entire county. They are called the Suburban Journals. Each has an area name attached to it. For example, the southern part of the county is served by the *Southeast Suburban Journal* and the *Southwest Suburban Journal*. The corporation also has similar groups of weeklies in seven other metro areas. The papers are distributed free to all homes in the county outside of Mount Pleasant city. The news-editorial content tends to be light, with 65% to 70% of the space taken up by advertising. They run about 24 pages a week, with half of the news-editorial pages taken up by common material for all editions. The remainder of the news-editorial material is assembled by one editor for each of the six newspapers. There is one reporter who covers county-wide news, and several part-time reporters are used to cover social and sports events. The papers carry no editorials or opinion material.

Suburb Corporation moved into the area 15 years ago and started these newspapers. They bought four independent weeklies to start the group. Initially, only four editions were published. The fifth and sixth were added 5 years ago.

The Mount Pleasant County Advertiser

This paper is located in the southern part of the county in Jonesboro. It is a free distribution paper with about 55% of its pages in advertising. It averages about 22 pages a week. It is primarily aimed at the more rural population of the county, although it circulates in some suburban bedroom communities. The paper is 33 years old. It has changed ownership three times and is marginally profitable.

The Weekly Call

The Weekly Call is located in north Mount Pleasant County, which is still the most undeveloped area in the county. It is 40 years old and still run by its founder. It carries about 18 pages a week on average, with 54% advertising. It emphasizes social news, education, sports, and city hall news for six smaller communities. The news-editorial sections are well written and the paper is known for its editorial stances against development. It appears that the paper breaks even.

TABLE 1
The Daily News Circulation Trends for the Past 15 Years

	City		Retail Trade Zone[a]		State	
	Daily	Sunday	Daily	Sunday	Daily	Sunday
Last year	44,189	68,661	46,115	76,549	14,546	16,992
Year 2	43,100	66,511	44,234	73,567	13,225	16,110
Year 3	40,221	59,233	43,345	72,932	13,200	15,899
Year 4	41,334	58,922	44,678	71,345	12,893	15,645
Year 5	39,334	59,344	42,398	70,400	12,001	15,890
Year 6	38,223	58,333	41,389	66,298	10,891	15,567
Year 7	35,566	56,271	39,899	61,888	10,556	14,678
Year 8	34,588	52,988	38,934	56,500	9,034	12,456
Year 9	32,987	49,356	35,789	49,345	8,967	12,090
Year 10	29,387	45,239	32,112	45,897	8,456	11,456
Year 11	28,356	40,899	29,129	40,999	8,345	11,230
Year 12	25,688	36,765	25,778	36,900	8,211	11,001
Year 13	22,178	32,222	22,600	33,290	6,456	8,912
Year 14	22,344	31,256	21,900	32,900	6,426	9,012
Year 15	22,567	30,899	21,789	32,456	5,789	9,213

[a]The retail trade zone does not include figures for the city zone.

TABLE 2

The Mount Pleasant Telegraph Circulation Trends for the Past 15 Years

	City		Retail Trade Zone[a]		State	
	Daily	Sunday	Daily	Sunday	Daily	Sunday
Last year	56,284	69,489	65,892	77,474	16,146	20,992
Year 2	56,521	70,551	65,911	78,911	15,912	20,101
Year 3	56,900	71,812	66,010	81,201	15,571	19,811
Year 4	57,511	73,211	66,402	83,811	15,881	19,011
Year 5	57,951	73,101	66,001	83,981	15,189	18,021
Year 6	58,201	74,901	66,201	85,210	15,111	17,557
Year 7	58,321	75,888	66,851	87,010	14,891	16,548
Year 8	60,011	77,401	65,900	88,541	14,257	16,189
Year 9	61,400	78,111	65,201	88,911	13,811	15,841
Year 10	63,500	78,215	64,500	89,757	13,621	14,251
Year 11	64,875	79,001	63,891	90,221	12,891	14,002
Year 12	64,921	79,751	65,011	90,911	12,511	13,891
Year 13	65,129	80,899	65,090	92,890	12,057	13,002
Year 14	64,444	80,256	63,990	91,780	11,826	12,812
Year 15	62,811	79,621	62,817	90,762	10,789	12,213

[a]The retail trade zone does not include figures for the city zone.

TABLE 3

Total Daily Advertising Pages

	The Daily News		Mount Pleasant Telegraph	
	Total Ad Pages	% of Total Newspaper	Total Ad Pages	% of Total Newspaper
Last Year	9,528	44.6	14,902	61.0
Year 2	9,389	45.0	14,884	60.8
Year 3	9,178	45.3	14,825	59.8
Year 4	8,439	45.0	14,326	60.2
Year 5	7,499	43.2	13,934	60.1
Year 6	6,658	43.1	12,918	60.8
Year 7	5,920	43.0	12,581	60.2
Year 8	5,478	43.1	12,441	60.7
Year 9	5,389	42.0	12,392	61.2
Year 10	5,268	41.2	12,900	62.0
Year 11	5,068	40.1	12,629	61.7
Year 12	4,981	40.0	13,205	63.0
Year 13	4,658	40.0	13,835	62.7
Year 14	4,505	40.0	13,928	63.2
Year 15	4,190	40.0	13,718	64.5

TABLE 4
Total Sunday Advertising Pages

	The Daily News		Mount Pleasant Telegraph	
	Total Ad Pages	% of Total Newspaper	Total Ad Pages	% of Total Newspaper
Last Year	3,476	49.6	4,814	62.0
Year 2	3,397	48.2	4,795	61.8
Year 3	3,259	49.3	4,941	62.0
Year 4	3,190	50.0	4,908	61.2
Year 5	2,806	47.2	4,599	62.1
Year 6	2,433	47.1	4,293	61.8
Year 7	2,181	47.0	4,421	61.2
Year 8	1,975	47.1	4,371	62.4
Year 9	1,640	46.0	4,242	62.2
Year 10	1,603	46.2	4,166	63.4
Year 11	1,472	46.1	4,188	62.7
Year 12	1,475	45.7	4,520	63.0
Year 13	1,342	45.0	4,527	63.7
Year 14	1,299	44.8	4,768	64.2
Year 15	1,210	44.5	4,695	65.0

TABLE 5
Advertising Rates for *The Daily News* and *Mount Pleasant Telegraph*—Open Rate for Column Inch (126 Column Inches Per Page)

	The Daily News		Telegraph	
	Daily	Sunday	Daily	Sunday
Last Year	$27.0	$31.5	$34.0	$38.0
Year 2	$27.0	$31.0	$38.5	$45.0
Year 3	$26.0	$30.0	$38.5	$45.0
Year 4	$26.0	$30.0	$37.9	$44.0
Year 5	$26.0	$30.0	$35.9	$43.0
Year 6	$24.4	$29.0	$34.4	$42.0
Year 7	$22.9	$27.0	$33.0	$41.0
Year 8	$21.4	$26.0	$32.5	$40.0
Year 9	$20.5	$25.0	$31.0	$40.0
Year 10	$19.5	$24.5	$30.0	$39.0
Year 11	$18.0	$23.5	$30.0	$38.0
Year 12	$17.5	$23.0	$29.0	$37.0
Year 13	$17.0	$23.0	$28.0	$36.0
Year 14	$17.0	$22.5	$28.0	$35.0
Year 15	$15.0	$21.0	$27.0	$34.0

TABLE 6
Percentage of Daily and Sunday Circulation Home Delivery

	The Daily News		Telegraph	
	City Zone	Outside City Zone	City Zone	Outside City Zone
Last Year	78	91	76	88
Year 2	77	90	74	88
Year 3	77	90	75	87
Year 4	75	88	75	87
Year 5	74	86	75	86
Year 6	74	85	75	87
Year 7	73	85	74	87
Year 8	73	84	75	86
Year 9	73	84	75	87
Year 10	72	83	74	87
Year 11	73	83	75	88
Year 12	72	82	74	88
Year 13	72	83	75	87
Year 14	71	82	74	87
Year 15	70	81	75	87

TABLE 7
Circulation Price for the Two Newspapers

	The Daily News			Telegraph		
	Subscription (Per Week)	Single Daily	Single Sunday	Subscription (Per Week)	Single Daily	Single Sunday
Last Year	$1.40	$.25	$.75	$1.50	$.25	$1.00
Year 2	$1.40	$.25	$.75	$1.50	$.30	$1.00
Year 3	$1.40	$.25	$.75	$1.50	$.30	$1.00
Year 4	$1.40	$.25	$.75	$1.40	$.30	$1.00
Year 5	$1.30	$.25	$.75	$1.40	$.30	$1.00
Year 6	$1.30	$.25	$.75	$1.40	$.25	$ .75
Year 7	$1.25	$.25	$.75	$1.30	$.25	$ .75
Year 8	$1.20	$.20	$.50	$1.30	$.25	$ .75
Year 9	$1.20	$.20	$.50	$1.30	$.25	$ .75
Year 10	$1.20	$.20	$.50	$1.25	$.25	$ .75
Year 11	$1.15	$.15	$.50	$1.25	$.25	$ .75
Year 12	$1.10	$.15	$.35	$1.25	$.25	$ .75
Year 13	$1.20	$.20	$.50	$1.20	$.25	$ .75
Year 14	$1.20	$.20	$.50	$1.20	$.25	$ .75
Year 15	$1.20	$.20	$.50	$1.20	$.25	$ .75

TABLE 8
Profit/Loss Statement for *The Daily News* (in Thousands)

| | Revenues | | | |
	Circulation	Advertising	Expenses	Profit/Loss
Last Year	9,554	29,659	41,504	(2,291)
Year 2	9,164	28,322	39,479	(1,993)
Year 3	8,735	27,891	36,675	(49)
Year 4	8,678	25,671	34,798	(449)
Year 5	8,082	23,827	32,729	(820)
Year 6	7,779	19,867	28,830	(1,184)
Year 7	7,194	16,710	25,735	(1,831)
Year 8	5,733	14,868	22,685	(2,084)
Year 9	5,293	13,360	20,154	(1,501)
Year 10	4,817	12,524	18,109	(768)
Year 11	4,116	11,096	16,019	(807)
Year 12	3,453	10,680	15,202	(1,069)
Year 13	3,510	9,706	13,320	(104)
Year 14	3,446	9,332	12,828	(50)
Year 15	3,400	7,784	11,304	(120)

TABLE 9
Profit/Loss Statement for the *Mount Pleasant Telegraph* (in Thousands)

| | Revenues | | | |
	Circulation	Advertising	Expenses	Profit/Loss
Last year	12,026	54,609	64,717	1,918
Year 2	12,121	56,610	64,693	4,038
Year 3	12,341	56,956	65,521	3,776
Year 4	11,931	56,111	63,345	4,697
Year 5	11,862	56,329	62,879	5,312
Year 6	11,122	57,736	61,122	7,736
Year 7	10,602	57,705	58,154	10,153
Year 8	10,703	56,029	57,234	9,498
Year 9	10,747	55,805	56,434	10,118
Year 10	10,442	55,310	53,989	11,763
Year 11	10,481	56,011	52,134	14,358
Year 12	10,561	55,929	51,234	15,256
Year 13	10,341	55,410	51,110	14,641
Year 14	10,214	56,148	50,845	15,517
Year 15	10,051	53,104	49,010	14,145

TABLE 10
Age of Population

Age Group in Years	City Zone	County Area Outsdie of City	State
Under 11	18.7	14.6	10.4
11 to 17	10.5	9.5	7.8
18 to 25	14.5	13.2	11.6
26 to 35	14.5	18.3	12.5
36 to 45	14.3	17.8	20.2
46 to 55	11.2	14.5	17.8
56 to 65	9.8	7.7	11.4
Over 65	6.5	4.4	8.3

TABLE 11
Income Per Household

Income in Dollars	City Zone Percentage	County Outside City Percentage	State Percentage
Under 10,000	4.9	2.8	7.2
10,001 to 15,000	6.7	5.2	10.1
15,001 to 20,000	11.6	10.8	14.6
20,001 to 25,000	15.3	12.8	15.7
25,001 to 30,000	21.9	22.1	23.2
30,001 to 35,000	15.8	18.8	10.3
35,001 to 40,000	9.9	10.7	8.9
40,001 to 45,000	5.8	7.1	4.3
45,001 to 50,000	4.9	5.2	4.0
More than 50,000	3.2	4.5	1.7

TABLE 12
Education of Population Over 18 Years of Age

Level of Education Completed	City Zone Percentage	County Outside of City Percentage	State Percentage
Grammar School	10.2	9.3	14.3
Junior High	14.6	15.5	18.3
High School	54.6	51.7	53.0
Bachelor's Degree	17.5	19.3	13.2
Postgraduate work	3.1	5.2	1.2

TABLE 13
Population

	City Zone	County Outside of City	State
Last year	350,400	348,160	3,103,345
Year 2	346,347	345,345	3,009,298
Year 3	344,555	338,234	2,978,234
Year 4	343,090	327,789	2,924,890
Year 5	341,998	311,822	2,879,345
Year 10	333,989	287,098	2,756,781
Year 15	321,340	273,099	2,567,213

TABLE 14
Number of Households

	City Zone	County Outside of City	State
Last year	125,591	140,021	1,120,222
Year 2	124,313	138,310	1,074,749
Year 3	124,027	136,606	1,063,655
Year 4	121,698	133,254	1,033,530
Year 5	121,785	130,291	1,010,297
Year 10	118,210	115,740	950,614
Year 15	114,050	98,333	885,247

THE CASE OF CHAOS IN CHATTANOOGA: THE WAR AT WOOF-TV

Robert Mitchell, station manager at WOOF-TV in Chattanooga, was concerned about the upcoming meeting he requested with Jeb White, group owner, regarding Mimi Howard, general sales manager. White, who owns White Broadcasting, a regional broadcasting group located in the South, bought WOOF 2 years ago. White is known for exploiting profits in the short term and then reselling a station after a few years. WOOF, a network affiliate consistently ranked second out of four stations in the market, previously was owned by Smith-Sharpston Broadcasting, a small group whose owner, Steve Sharpston, had died. Sharpston had been known for his keen business sense. He expected a great deal from his employees, but was understanding when problems arose. His heirs sold the small chain to White for a handsome profit. White now wanted to get his money back and Mitchell suspected that White was milking WOOF in order to support the group stations in Atlanta and Miami.

Mitchell called the meeting regarding Howard as a result of a number of problems that arose since she was hired 1 year ago. Howard had been hired to motivate the sales force, increase the station's advertising base, and develop new ways of selling WOOF to local advertisers and agencies. She was also the first woman in management at WOOF. Mitchell secretly feared that Howard soon would be promoted to assistant general manager and possibly replace him someday. He also felt she was being groomed for a future position in upper management in the group.

Mitchell felt that Howard had succeeded in motivating the sales force and increasing the advertiser base, but he did not approve of her methods and had personal reservations about the station's long-term interests if she remained. She had managed to meet quarterly sales goals, but by attracting different advertisers than Mitchell had envisioned. Mitchell told Howard to expand the local sales base by appealing to advertisers who presently bought time on competing stations, especially the local independent station. He told her to use Sales & Marketing Management's *Survey of Buying Power* to examine Chattanooga's index of buying power, demographics, and retail sales figures to develop leads and figure out how the station might attract established local advertisers. He told her to come up with ways to convince advertisers and agencies to include WOOF in their media mix for clients.

However, Howard did not follow his suggestions. She increased sales by attracting advertisers who had not advertised on television prior to deregulation. These new advertisers included Bubba's Guns, Bait & Tackle, the Today Sponge contraceptive, late night ads for The Roadhouse (a local bar and dance hall), 900 phone number ads for dating services, and ads promoting local radio stations. She also accepted 30- and 60-min "program-length commercials" or infomercials for hair restoration products for men, weight loss programs, investment opportunities, and time-sharing condos in Florida. Mitchell had noticed, by reviewing the acceptance dates on contracts and invoices, that these buys often were approved right before quarterly sales deadlines, making him suspect that Howard approved them to bolster her performance on paper.

This made her look good to the group owner and White periodically commented that Howard seemed to be accomplishing her assigned goals. But Mitchell was discovering that this course of action created other problems for the station. He had to keep on Howard to make sure the credit histories and backgrounds of these companies were checked out adequately. Early on in her tenure, a few had not paid within 60 days and their ad schedules had to be put on hold until payment was received. This still happened occasionally. The number of local complaints about advertising also had increased. And one program-length commercial about investment opportunities she accepted was later the subject of a large consumer-protection agreement in a neighboring state.

Mitchell was worried that WOOF's community image might suffer in the long run. He already had heard comments about these ads at the local Kiwanis luncheons he attended. And a local advertising professor told him that a recent study he had conducted suggested that viewer perceptions of television advertising had worsened over the past 5 years.

Mitchell was concerned that the FCC might take some sort of action against the stations that had accepted the investment program-length commercial. The FCC had begun to take action against radio stations with risque disk jockeys. As a result, he called White, explained the situation, and recommended that WOOF develop a set of station policies regarding advertising. White agreed, so Mitchell told Howard to expand WOOF'S acceptance standards and policies and to develop reasonably specific guidelines for major areas of concern, like political advertising, contraceptive advertising, and so forth. WOOF presently had written standards banning hard liquor advertising and a product protection standard guaranteeing at least 15 min of airtime between competing advertisements. WOOF also unofficially tried to keep total commercial time per hour below 16 min, the old NAB and FCC guideline. Mitchell also provided her with a national survey, conducted by an advertising professor at the local university, showing the types of standards most stations had. He also gave her data from the statewide study conducted by this same professor that suggested that public perceptions of television had worsened since deregulation. He told her to turn in a proposal in two weeks.

Howard's proposal demonstrated that she was not enthusiastic about developing advertising standards. She argued against developing written standards, suggesting that ads and advertisers should continue to be evaluated on a case-by-case basis. She also argued that it was not necessary to consult outside sources for making such decisions. She noted that if policies were formalized, it would take away the flexibility needed to deal with new sources of advertising income. She argued that it would be a waste of time to have to develop a new policy every time a new advertiser was recruited.

Mitchell was also concerned about how Howard managed the sales staff. She convinced White to reduce the base salary of the sales force and increased the salary percentage based on actual sales. Mitchell had opposed this move, telling White that they stood a good chance of losing their best salespeople to a competing station, which had higher base salaries. Howard also instituted higher quarterly sales goals for each employee and based her first year-end salary recommendations on each salesperson's ability to meet or exceed those goals. And some of the older salespeople were uncomfortable dealing with the new clients she had recruited. Part of the reason for the meeting with White was that two of the salesmen, who had been with the station for over 20 years, were threatening to quit or sue because they claimed they were not given advance notification of changes in sales policies. Both were well respected in the local community and active in civic affairs. Mitchell knew that how they were treated in this situation could affect WOOF's image in the local business community. Mitchell had developed a close friendship with both of these salesmen over the years and was concerned about how to present the situation fairly to White, given his personal feelings.

Mitchell also was concerned about how to broach another issue with White. He felt that there was some truth to Howard's claim that she had not attracted more established local advertisers because many were not comfortable dealing with a woman sales manager. Chattanooga still was rather conservative and Mitchell had had a tough time trying to break into the "old boy" network. Her assertive nature, although good in a salesperson generally, sometimes could be abrasive. This compounded her problems in dealing with advertisers and the sales staff. However, Mitchell suspected that she was using this to hide her failures with other, nonbiased, advertisers. Sure, there were a lot of "good old boys" in Chattanooga, but a number of the big advertisers who were not buying time on WOOF were companies owned and/or run by younger, more liberal, male and female managers. A few of these male and female managers told Mitchell in private conversations that Howard would not negotiate airtime rates fairly. Howard just could not expect to charge that high a price, given WOOF's ratings.

Mitchell and Howard had discussed these issues over drinks one evening after work. Howard said that she did not use the Sales & Marketing Management data because she felt she would show results more quickly by going after new business. She told Mitchell, "We both know how quickly White will dump you if you aren't meeting sales goals." She said that Mitchell had not told her specifically in writing what types of advertisers to attract, only to increase sales of airtime. She also acknowledged that some local advertisers were leery of her and that she had begun to realize that she could be abrasive. She said she had tried to tone down her approach and asked Mitchell for suggestions on how to accomplish this. She also pointed out that the two salesmen who had threatened to quit or sue had not met the sales quotas she set, whereas the other four met them easily. She argued that her quotas were not unreasonably high. It was just that these two had been resting on their laurels as they approached retirement and resented the fact that they had to hustle once again. She said she had told them verbally about the new sales quotas ahead of time. She noted that the problem was exacerbated by the fact that she had been selected for the sales manager job over both of them. She had tried to be friendly, but both seemed determined to undermine her. Mitchell conceded that the other four salespersons had met the new quotas easily.

One of these four salespersons, Adam Kagan, had told Mitchell privately that he was glad Howard was trying to get the two disgruntled salesmen moving again; both were indeed lazy, according to Kagan. Mitchell respected Kagan's opinion. He had been with the station for about 2 years and in that time became the station's sales leader, earning a well-deserved reputation for being hard-working, honest, and fair.

Mitchell was most disturbed by Howard's attitude regarding sales goals. Howard acknowledged that she had accepted certain ads only when it became apparent that sales goals for the quarter would not be met. She did not think this was wrong given White's attitude. She did not seem overly concerned with ad content, because the FCC had loosened requirements concerning deceptive advertisements. She reminded Mitchell that sanctions were not likely, which he had to concede was probably true. She felt that the number of complaints had not increased significantly and argued: "It's only the local prudes and fuddy-duddies who are complaining. I think you're overreacting."

Assignment

Read the following background sections and then answer each of the following questions.

1. How extensive should WOOF's advertising policies be? What recommendations should Mitchell make to White? What form should these recommendations take? Provide an advertising mission statement; explain which specific advertising policies should be included (if any); and tell what action should be taken when a special situation arises (e.g., when a "problem" or "controversial" ad is submitted for possible broadcast by an advertiser). Indicate who should be involved in this type of situation and why.

2. Should Mitchell submit his own proposal regarding advertising policies, Howard's, or both? Why?

3. How could White, Mitchell, and Howard have avoided some of the problems each are facing now? Explain your answer. Discuss what each manager should have done, if applicable.

4. What type of leadership style do White, Mitchell, and Howard each exhibit? Do you think White, Mitchell, and Howard are effective leaders? Why or why not?

5. How should the situation with the two disgruntled salesmen be handled? Who should handle this situation and why? What should be done? Should these actions be documented? If yes, how?

6. Were the techniques Howard used to motivate the sales force effective and appropriate? Why or why not? What other techniques or methods could Howard have used to motivate the sales force?

7. Should a formal system of communication be instituted at the White chain and/or WOOF-TV? Why or why not? If yes, what communication system do you recommend?

8. Should a formal performance evaluation system be instituted at the White chain and/or WOOF-TV? Why or why not? If yes, what type of performance evaluation system do you recommend?

9. Do any other organizational and/or personnel changes need to be made at the White chain and/or WOOF-TV? Why or why not? If yes, what changes do you recommend?

10. What are the major ethical issues White, Mitchell, and Howard each faced? Would you have behaved differently than any of these managers? Why? What would you have done?

Background on Deregulation

During the 1980s, the FCC deregulated commercial radio (Deregulation, 1981) and television (Revision, 1984). Policies and guidelines on ascertainment, program-length commercials, program logkeeping (program logs were the official daily record of all material aired on a station), and the amount of commercial time to air per hour were relaxed or eliminated. Shortly thereafter, other practices including guidelines regarding deceptive advertising (Elimination, 1985) and the Fairness Doctrine were deregulated (Inquiry, 1987; *Syracuse Peace Council v. Television Station WTVH*, 1987). Due to the relaxation of the deceptive advertising policy, local broadcasters no longer need to exercise particular care when deciding to accept advertising that is the subject of an unadjudicated Federal Trade Commission complaint, or to review the reliability of every prospective advertiser (Elimination, 1985). And the Fairness Doctrine required licensees to present alternate views on controversial issues in certain circumstances.

Local broadcasters now have more individual discretion in deciding how to serve the public interest. However, more discretion may be accompanied by greater uncertainty about whether a station is serving the public interest. Policies are now less specific about how public interest responsibilities are fulfilled. New broadcast managers have been advised to review the 1960 policy statement and ascertainment primers for guidance in determining how to meet public interest requirements.

The former National Association of Broadcasters (NAB) TV Code was the most important self-regulatory mechanism for local broadcasters, providing guidelines regarding commercialization, clutter, and clearance (e.g., reviewing ads prior to broadcast to determine if they are deceptive). The NAB Code Authority Board also cleared commercials for national and regional advertisers. Preclearance by the NAB was tantamount to network approval (although the networks still determined for themselves whether a commercial would be accepted) ("Agencies, Networks," 1983). After the

Code's demise, the networks assumed primary responsibility for clearance. However, concerns over clearance effectiveness were raised in 1987 when ABC, CBS, and NBC cut back their Standards and Practices divisions as a cost-cutting move (Davis, 1987).

As a result of the events of the past decade, individual station management has more commercial decision-making freedom than ever before. At the same time, station responsibility for ascertainment or determining how the local community views station policies was relaxed by the FCC. The FCC no longer concerns itself with ascertainment methodology, but only with how responsive stations are to community needs (Revision, 1984). So managers may decide what new policies to implement and how to determine what community views are of them.

Licensee discretion is essentially "penalty-free," as the FCC also eliminated license challenges based on commercial time considerations. Violations of the deceptive advertising policy are now considered only in "character" proceedings, which rarely occur (Policy Regarding Character, 1986). The FCC considers ascertainment satisfactory if "programming presented by the licensee satisfies its obligation" (Revision, 1984, p. 1101).

The FCC said that competitive market forces would regulate the industry adequately. For example, viewers would not watch and advertisers would not buy time on stations adding too many commercials. It noted a decline in public complaints about advertising as support (Commercialization, 1981; Revision, 1984).

Background on Deceptive Advertising Requirements

The FCC noted early on that it expected stations to investigate potential advertisers (KMPC, 1939). It originally attempted to regulate advertising content (Public Service, 1946), but later relinquished most of its responsibility in this area to the Federal Trade Commission (FTC, 1987; Liaison, 1987). However, the FCC noted that licensees did have obligations regarding deceptive advertising (Elimination, 1985): "Broadcasting licensees must assume responsibility for all material which is broadcast through their facilities. This includes all programs and advertising material which they present to the public. With respect to advertising material, the licensee has the additional responsibility to take all reasonable measures to eliminate any false, misleading, or deceptive matter . . . This duty is personal to the licensee and may not be delegated" (Report, 1960, p. 2303).

These clearance measures included taking reasonable steps to assure every prospective advertiser's reliability and reputation, and ability to fulfill promises made to the public (Licensee, 1961), especially those of "questionable character" (KMPC, 1939, p. 730). Broadcasters also had to exercise particular care when deciding to accept advertising that was the subject of an unadjudicated Federal Trade Commission complaint. The

FCC expected more diligence when a station employee prepared ad copy or directly examined ad claims, and acted when a station neglected to implement adequate clearance practices (NAB Legal Guide, 1984). However, most of these clearance requirements were eliminated in 1985. The FCC simply noted that stations are still responsible for all material that is broadcast on their facilities (Elimination, 1985). How stations choose to fulfill this responsibility is up to them.

Before deregulation, most stations had mechanisms for clearing deceptive advertising; many had standards dealing with traditional areas of concern like political and children's advertising (Linton, 1987; Wicks, 1991a). Larger stations probably have more policies for more specific areas of ad content or sales techniques, such as mail and direct-selling accounts (e.g., buying products by calling an "800" number). Perhaps this is because the FCC formerly expected stations of greater size and resources to make a correspondingly greater effort to screen deceptive advertisements (Center for Law & Social Policy, 1971).

Large-market stations, which are often quite profitable, sell more of their commercial time inventory to national or regional "spot" advertisers (Wirth, 1977). This also may explain why larger organizations have more advertising policies. They must deal with more types of advertisers.

Background on Broadcast Organizations

Commercial television stations depend on the sales of national, regional, and local advertising for profits, and also may receive funds from national commercial television networks. They may carry network programming, originate syndicated and paid programming, and compete with other stations for a share of the viewing audience. Historically, network affiliates have tended to sell more advertising and earn higher profits than independent stations. Other commercial stations include those that depend primarily on fund-raising efforts or direct sales for revenues, such as certain religious or Home Shopping Network stations.

Most stations have established mechanisms for reviewing ads. The Sales and Traffic departments typically monitor advertising content and preview ads before they air. The sales manager oversees traffic, but a station's general manager makes the final decision when an extraordinary question on whether to accept an advertisement for broadcast arises (Wicks, 1991a).

Most stations have policies for political advertising, product acceptance (e.g., whether ads for certain products will be accepted for broadcast), copy acceptance, advocacy or issue advertising, product protection (e.g., separating competing ads), and time standards. Larger stations may have policies for mail and direct-selling accounts, bait-and-switch advertising, contests and games, demonstrations, medical products, free offers, and guarantees (Center for Law & Social Policy, 1971; Linton, 1987; Rotfeld et al., 1990; Wicks, 1991a).

National advertisers generally review their own ads to avoid litigation. National advertisements initially are cleared within agency and advertiser organizations, including both the agency's and advertiser's legal departments, in storyboard form. Then, the media reviews an ad in storyboard form. The national television networks, and other print and broadcast media, have developed advertising codes. After an ad is cleared, it is produced, and final clearance begins. First, the agency grants final clearance, then the advertiser and its law firm, and finally the media. Regulation after broadcast or publishing is mainly the responsibility of the FTC, although there are a number of government agencies that regulate various aspects of advertising. The FTC also publishes guides that make recommendations regarding advertising for certain industries and products.

Stations might consult the NAB and the networks for advice. Larger stations may contact advertisers or visit a store. Stations might review ads by perusing scripts, storyboards, a product sample, or a label or package insert, before and/or after production. Claim substantiation, or authentication of demonstrations or testimonials, could be requested as well.

Station managers may find it necessary to resolve differences between competing advertisers. Commercials may be challenged by competing advertisers, who must present supporting data. Outside technical expertise may be called in, and ads withdrawn only if the complaint is found valid. Viewer complaints also may be investigated, and ads possibly discontinued until complaints are resolved (Miracle & Nevett, 1987; Zanot, 1985).

Stations vary in how their policies are communicated. Stations may codify policies in a manual, have mostly written policies, use mostly memoranda, use the last NAB Code, or convey policies verbally. Staff policies are communicated either through making their existence known, staff discussion, or encouraging or requiring the staff to read them. Generally speaking, policies are communicated verbally to employees on a day-to-day basis (Linton, 1987; Rotfeld et al., 1990; Wicks, 1991a).

Background on National Survey of Advertising Policies

A national survey of advertising policies was conducted by an advertising professor at a major university. A 62.6% response rate (482 of 769 commercial television stations polled nationwide) was achieved. Respondents represented a cross-section of stations, as responses approximated the natural proportion of VHF and UHF stations and network affiliates and independent stations.

At most stations, the sales manager is responsible for deciding whether or not to accept advertisements for broadcast on a day-to-day basis. Although the average time sales managers, as a group, spent reviewing ads was 5 hr per week, the most common response was 1 hr per week. About 84% of responding managers saw an ad they declined to accept for broadcast air on another market station. Most managers also convey advertising policy decisions verbally. The national breakdown of employees responsible for reviewing ads is found in Table 15.

The study indicated that the average station has 12 advertising policies. The percentage of stations having certain policies is shown in Table 16.

Most stations do not have formalized advertising policies. Regarding the form most policies were in, only 66 stations reported having policies codified in a manual, 56 had mostly written policies, 113 favored memos, and 139 conveyed policies verbally. Regarding the communication method used most often: 87 stations required their employees to read their policies; 34 encouraged them to; 139 communicated policies through staff discussions; and at 94 stations the supervisor told each employee individually about policies. Thus, the average station "stores" and "communicates" its policies verbally. Stations nationwide also tended to consult certain sources when making decisions about whether or not to accept a questionable advertisement. This study showed that the average station uses about five sources to make decisions regarding ads (see Table 17).

The average amount of commercial time aired per hour was 12:15, below the old FCC guideline. Only a minority exceed it (18 of 426 responding, or 4.2%). Stations also were asked if they accepted program-length commercials. Of the 470 stations responding, 77.9% (or 366) accepted them and 22.1% (or 104) did not. The average station airs five program-length commercials per month. The minimum was zero and the maximum was over 100.

TABLE 15
Employee Responsible for Clearance Review

Employee	Percent of Stations	Number of Stations
Sales manager	52.1	248
General manager	15.6	74
Program director	7.8	37
Operations manager	5.9	28
Station manager	5.7	27
Traffic manager	3.4	16
Broadcast standards	2.7	13
None	.5	3
Other	6.3	30

Note. N = 476.

TABLE 16
Station Advertising Policies

Policy Area	Percent Having Policy	Number Having Policy
Political advertising	96.6%	460
Product protection (separates competing ads by a certain amount of time)	85.1%	405
Contests & games (restrictions on how they are advertised)	84.7%	403
Movie trailers (bans or restricts the airing of violent or sexy movie ads)	82.8%	394
Mail order/direct selling (restricts the use of direct response ads)	80.0%	381
Product acceptance (bans certain types of products outright)	79.0%	376
Issue advertising (bans or restricts ads about controversial issues)	78.6%	374
Copy acceptance (bans or restricts certain copywriting techniques)	78.4%	373
Contraceptive advertising (bans or restricts contraceptive ads)	77.9%	371
Children's advertising	69.1%	329
Bait & switch (bans advertising one product at a very low price and trying to get the consumer to buy another, more expensive one, at the store)	67.4%	321
Time standard (limits the amount of commercial time to be aired per hour)	67.4%	321
Interruption standard (limits the number of commercial breaks per hour)	62.8%	299
Guarantees (restricts advertising warranties or guarantees)	49.6%	236
Free offers (restricts the use of free offers in ads)	48.9%	233
Medical products (bans or restricts how medical and/or health products are advertised)	46.4%	221
Demonstrations (guidelines on how to demonstrate products in ads)	25.8%	123

Note. N = 476.

Selected Questions from the Statewide Survey of Viewer Perceptions

The following four questions were taken from an advertising professor's exploratory survey of viewer perceptions of advertising on television. These questions were intended to examine whether viewers (in the state where WOOF-TV was located) perceived differences in television since deregulation, such as whether the number of commercials on TV increased, whether the number of program-length commercials increased, whether the number of deceptive ads increased, and whether the responsiveness of local stations decreased. The wording is as follows:

> The next few statements are about television today. For each statement, please indicate how much you agree or disagree.
> • There are more commercials on television now than there were five years ago.

TABLE 17
Station Policy Sources

Policy Source	Percent Usually Consulting	Number Usually Consulting
Station policies	75.6	360
FCC publications	66.0	314
Former NAB television code	61.6	293
National Association of Broadcasters	55.5	264
Group owner	42.0	200
FTC publications	39.5	188
Local or state consumer agency	34.0	162
Better Business Bureau	31.3	149
Network	26.5	126
Network code	19.3	92
Group code	17.9	85
BBB code of advertising	14.3	68
BBB ad review committee	6.9	33
NAD/NARB case reports	6.7	32

Note. $N = 476$.

- There are more programs on television selling products like real estate than there were five years ago.
- There are more dishonest advertisements on television now than there were five years ago.
- The television stations in my area are more concerned with viewer complaints about advertising than they were five years ago.

A 5-point Likert scale was used for each question, with values ranging from Strongly Agree (1) to Strongly Disagree (5). Responses are given in Table 18.

TABLE 18
Responses to Four Perception Questions

Value/Label	Percent	N
More Commercials Now?		
1 Strongly agree	42.4	329
2 Agree	41.5	322
3 Neither agree nor disagree	8.4	65
4 Disagree	6.1	47
5 Strongly disagree	0.9	7
Don't know	0.5	4
Refused	0.2	2

(continued)

TABLE 18 (Continued)

Value/Label	Percent	N
More Programs Selling Products Like Real Estate?		
1 Strongly agree	24.9	193
2 Agree	46.6	362
3 Neither agree nor disagree	10.7	83
4 Disagree	13.3	103
5 Strongly disagree	1.0	8
Don't know	3.4	26
Refused	0.1	1
More Dishonest Advertisements?		
1 Strongly agree	25.6	199
2 Agree	37.3	289
3 Neither agree nor disagree	11.3	88
4 Disagree	23.1	179
5 Strongly disagree	1.3	10
Don't know	1.2	9
Refused	0.2	2
Stations More Concerned With Viewer Complaints?		
1 Strongly agree	9.4	73
2 Agree	37.7	292
3 Neither agree nor disagree	11.7	91
4 Disagree	27.5	213
5 Strongly disagree	4.6	36
Don't know	9.0	70
Refused	.1	1

Note. N = 476.

THE CASE OF VIDEOTEXT AND *THE KOUGHTON POST*

Assignment

As an outside consultant, you are hired to investigate the videotext operation at the *The Koughton Post*. You have been asked to develop a 5-year strategic plan for Postext.

The company wants you to propose new initiatives that will help the service be "even leaner and meaner" internally as well as increase Postext's subscriber audience. The parent company wants to see this operation on firmer ground and is growing weary of the piecemeal, day-to-day, grind-it-out approach and vision of Post management regarding this service. They want an outside opinion (yours) as to whether their weariness is justified now—as well as in the long term. Here is what you find:

The Community. Koughton is the third largest city in the state with a population of 300,000. Often combined with Boiseville to form "the centerplex," Koughton lies about 35 miles west of its sister city in the center of the state.

Of the city's nearly 180,000 working adults, more than 100,000 work in technical, sales, administrative support, and blue-collar jobs.

A diverse economy helped the city withstand the problems that beset other area communities in the 1980s. In the last few years, the city attracted new industry and added more jobs.

The Newspaper. Koughton has only one daily newspaper, the *Post,* which publishes morning and evening editions, as well as Saturday and Sunday issues. The combined weekday circulation last year was 257,991, whereas the Saturday and Sunday circulations were 262,235 and 306,548, respectively.

Cosmo Corp. bought the *Post* and a local radio station from AC Publications, Inc., in the 1970s for more than $65 million in cash and notes. The newspaper is one of nine daily newspapers owned by Cosmo Corp., which also owns 20 weekly community newspapers and shopping guides as well as a cable TV network.

The slumping state economy forced newspapers to monitor more closely and thus curtail their operations. For example, the *Boiseville Trumpet,* although it increased its advertising market share, laid off employees last year. In September last year, just before TMC Corp. completed its sale to Ryan C. Hammeron, the rival *Boiseville Leader* also cut its work force.

The *Post,* which employs about 1,000 persons, planned to cut expenses by $2 million to $2.2 million last year via several austerity measures. The paper expected to lose about $1.5 million in revenue because of the closing of a major local grocery story chain.

Although the *Post* is the only newspaper in Koughton, it competes heavily with the Boiseville newspapers. Advertisers believe they can expose their product adequately to the centerplex by taking one Boiseville paper and adding the *Post* to the schedule. Neither Boiseville daily boast substantial circulation in Koughton and the Post has stronger coverage in the so-called mid-cities area between Boiseville and Koughton.

History and Innovation Process. Videotext technology has spurred much investment and speculation within the newspaper industry but also great disappointment.

But the finances of Postext, the consumer videotext of the *Post,* are relatively small—some $200,000 in capital investments through last April and operating losses of $120,000 before the break-even point. But from the beginning, the venture has been unique.

In the early 1980s, Koughton-based PerComp Corp. approached the *Post* with the idea of testing a videotext service. Under the arrangement, the newspaper provided the information and Percomp provided the service/technical management. Billed as an attempt to "bring news to the screen," Postext began offering subscribers unlimited access for $5 per month. After 5 months of operation, the service had only 25 customers. Postext ended its first year with 250 subscribers.

But the increasing audience proved too much for the PerComp software system. PerComp sold the service to the *Post*.

Since then, subscriber levels have reached about 2,800 out of a potential 60,000 households in West and Boiseville counties. Some 68% of the 2,552 year-end subscribers last year lived in West County whereas the remainder resided in Boiseville County.

Management has evaluated Postext from the standpoint of its profitability, its subscriber levels, and the acceptance of new services. The short-term goal is to get a good mix of services so as to appeal to each subscriber. Postext must walk an economic tightrope of offering a service that does not use much computer time while simultaneously having some value to subscribers because there is no charge for connect time. That situation prompted management to go slower with Postext than some hoped and, as a result, there is no formal timetable.

Start-up costs were estimated as $250,000 and initial annual cost projections were estimated near $60,000. As of last May, the service had 2,743 subscribers, paying an annual $119.40 basic rate on a quarterly, 6-months, 9-months or yearly basis. That equaled about $327,000 in revenue for the calendar year. However that figure fluctuates; the potential revenue could be significantly higher, because at least 2,665 users subscribed to at least one service beyond the basic Postext service.

Although the service has potential, manag· nent sees limits. For example, videotext requires some effort on the user's part. Only so many people–those willing to put the effort into it–will use the service. The general manager says that marketing and promoting Postext with hopes of increasing subscriptions to, say, 10,000, would necessitate changes in software architecture/capacity and organizational structure.

General Operational Background. Postext is driven by two large computers. In addition to updated news, Postext offers electronic mail, closing stock quotes, classified ads, an on-line encyclopedia, airline schedules, home banking, and subscriber columns.

For the Postext staffer/operator, the access procedure is more complex. For example, after a *Post* reporter completes a news item, the Postext copy editor retrieves the item and puts it in a Postext editing file. The copy editor then enters coded commands that allow the story to go to the Postext mainframe computer. The copy editor then writes a headline and assigns the story a space in one of the Postext news summary banks.

Throughout the day, there is the ever-present mandate to keep the news current for the user because Postext is an 18-hr-a-day service boasting current news. So constant and continuous scanning and recoding of the wires is needed.

Counting the two system programmers, a customer service rep and three full-time copy editors, Postext employs 6.5 nonmanagement employees. All others except the part-timer have worked for Postext for at least a year and for an average of 3.5 years.

Two of the full-time copy editors work the day shift, whereas the other full-timer and the part-timer work until 1 am. The news editor primarily handles customers' concerns, and copy edits when possible or if necessary. The job is supervisory in title only.

Employee Users and System Impact on Work

Direct Impact.   For Postext's full-time copy editors, working at Postext presents conflicts.

They are loyal, say they are happy in their jobs but indicate a certain frustration — such as inadequate time allowances, lack of specialization, job repetitiveness, and Postext's slow growth. But they see their jobs as meaningful, mainly because of their involvement with the news, the immediate feedback from customers, and videotext's potential. They also dislike being dependent on the technology. For example, when the system is not working, no one can see the copy editor's work, nor can the copy editor work.

Indirect Impact.   Copy editors believe many of their newspaper colleagues do not know them or view them inaccurately or unsympathetically.

Managers and System Impact on Work

Direct and Indirect Impact.   Only one manager consistently deals with Postext matters on a daily basis. That person, the general manager (GM), supervises all other Postext staff and reports to the *Post* vice president of operations. Unlike many newsroom middle managers, the GM supervises the marketing, budgeting, and programming aspects as well as the editorial functions.

Employee motivation is a vital part of the job. The relative lack of employee financial/career path incentives in the Postext operation necessitates that the GM spend considerable business and personal time communicating with the staff and planning social gatherings.

He considers these gatherings essential, particularly for editorial employees. (Their jobs are relatively unrecognized and anonymous—they receive no bylines—and they are somewhat impatient with Postext's slow growth.)

Motivation is particularly important at times. Prolonged problems quickly hurt morale. The GM often tries to help the staff "see the plateaus and stop and admire the view before we start climbing again."

The GM also helps market Postext. The tasks vary: stuffing envelopes, producing and distributing the monthly subscriber newspaper, attending various area computer user-group meetings, designing Postext ads, and giving presentations.

Of the five main functional areas of his job—overseeing the news, programming, financial, strategic planning, and public relations/marketing—he estimates he spent more time on the the latter (35% to 40%) than on any other area.

Within the news area, the GM treats the news product according to the same journalistic guidelines followed by the newspaper: truth, accuracy, and fairness, with an eye toward exploiting the videotext advantage of being able to quickly disseminate the news. In the traditional newspaper structure, copy editors serve as checks and balances throughout in regard to the quality and quantity of news. At Postext, to do so—in addition to the customer relations work—the news editor would have to monitor the VDT screen constantly. As a result, mistakes could become rather glaring.

To make amends, the GM attempts to stress accuracy in headline writing and in editing. But the time spent on such supervision is inadequate.

In regard to the strategic planning area, the GM sets aside time on an "as-needed" basis to discuss plans with his superior. Many planning ideas are developed away from the office and then placed in a weekly status report to the vice president. Decision making about plans often occurs spontaneously, though the general manager sees this as an asset.

Programming is another somewhat sensitive area, primarily because of the GM's lack of expertise in the area. But the GM sees technical knowledge as something that will become less important as videotext matures as an industry.

Environment and System Impact on Work

Postext staffers work throughout the main newspaper building in downtown Koughton, with offices on the first and third floors, at opposite ends of the building. What staff members lack in geographic proximity, they gain in a strong sense of cohesion. Staff meetings are jovial and cynical in atmosphere.

The staff considers the GM a good supervisor, primarily for his interest in them, flexibility, nondemanding demeanor, honesty, accessibility, and cheerleading attitude toward videotext. Still, they say the GM needs to improve in several areas: his tendency to "shoot from the hip" in making decisions about them, his delegation of additional work when workloads already are full, his lack of technical expertise, the amount of his time spent on marketing, and his infringement on employees' news autonomy.

Cosmo's Command to You. Specifically, Cosmo wants you to develop a strategic plan of action the result of which finally will see the *Post* managing the technology, rather than the technology managing the *Post*. Let these questions from Cosmo's Board of Directors be your guide:

1. What kind of managerial approach should we take to improve our situation and how would you recommend implementing that approach?
2. How do we get more people to subscribe? What can we do to make subscriptions double in 2 years and quadruple by the end of five years? What do consumers want that we are not giving them?
3. What changes, if any, should we make in content? Should these changes be gradual or sudden? What time schedule would you suggest?
4. What new steps have to be implemented to improve our efficiency of operations? What will it cost us in each of the 5 years? What staffing levels do you recommend for each year?
5. Can we introduce significantly more advertisers to our system? How?
6. Can Postext generate alternative revenues, that is, can we make money from more than just subscribers and advertisers? If so, how? Are there any new markets we can generate with the technology?
7. After 5 years, should we keep Postext or attempt to sell it? Should a newspaper be in the videotext business? Why? If not, to whom do we sell, or do we just declare a loss?

REFERENCES

Aaker, D., & Myers, J. (1987). *Advertising management* (3rd ed.). Englewood Cliffs, NJ: Prentice-Hall.

ABC's of the Fifth Estate (1990). *Broadcasting Yearbook.* Washington, DC: Broadcast Publications.

Adams, J. S. (1963). Toward an understanding of inequity. *Journal of Abnormal and Social Psychology, 67,* 422–436.

Adams, R. C., & Fish, M. J. (1987). TV news directors' perceptions of station management style. *Journalism Quarterly, 64,* 154–162, 276.

Adler, S. J. (1991, October 9). Lawyers advise concerns to provide precise written policy to employees. *The Wall Street Journal,* pp. B1, B5.

Agencies, networks battle over censor's role. (1983, November). *Adweek,* p. 52.

Alderfer, C. P. (1972). *Existence, relatedness, and growth.* New York: Free Press.

Altschull, J. H. (1984). *Agents of power.* New York: Longman.

AMA board approves new marketing definition. (1985, March 1). *Marketing News.*

Amendment of Part 3 of the Commission's Rules and Regulations with Respect to Advertising on Standard, FM, and Television Broadcast Stations, 36 FCC 45 (1964).

America, A. (1991, May). Anatomy of a libel suit. *presstime,* pp. 6–10.

American Association of Advertising Agencies (1956). *Agency service standards.*

American Association of Advertising Agencies (1962a). *Creative code.*

American Association of Advertising Agencies (1962b). *Standards of practice.*

Andrews, E. (1991, June 14). FCC is increasing local regulation of cable TV rates. *The New York Times,* pp. A1, C5.

Argyris, C. (1957). *Personality and organization.* New York: Harper & Row.

Argyris, C. (1962). *Interpersonal competence and organizational effectiveness.* Homewood, IL: Dorsey.

Argyris, C. (1974). *Behind the front page.* San Francisco: Jossey-Bass.

Ascertainment of Community Problems by Commercial Broadcast Applicants, 57 FCC 2d 418 (1976).

Associated Press v. United States, 32 6 U.S. 1 (1945).

Bagby, M. A. (1990, September). The heavier hand of government. *presstime*, pp. 22–27.

Bagby, M. A. (1991, March). White-collar crime jolts newspapers. *presstime*, pp. 6–8.

Bagdikian, B. H. (1990). *The media monopoly* (3rd ed.). Boston: Beacon Press.

Bantz, C., McCorkle, S. & Baade, R. (1980). The news factory. *Communication Research, 7*, 45–68.

Barnard, C. I. (1938). *The executive functions.* Cambridge, MA: Harvard University Press.

Barrett, G. (1984). Job satisfaction among newspaperwomen. *Journalism Quarterly, 61*, 593–599.

Bass, B. M. (1983). *Organizational decision making.* Homewood, IL: Irwin.

Bass, B. M. (1985). *Leadership and performance beyond expectations.* New York: Free Press.

Baumol, W. J. (1967). *Business behavior, value and growth* (2nd ed.). New York: Harcourt, Brace & World.

Baxter, R. (1983a, August 29). Avoiding liability in firing employees. *The National Law Journal*, pp. 20–21.

Baxter, R. (1983b, September 12). Managing the risks in firing employees. *The National Law Journal*, pp. 20–21.

Beam, R. (1990, July). *Impact of Group Ownership on Organizational Professionalism.* Paper presented at the meeting of the Association for Journalism and Mass Communications, Minneapolis, MN.

Bem, S. L. (1974). The measure of psychology and androgyny. *Journal of Consulting and Clinical Psychology, 42*, 155–162.

Bendix, R. (1956). *Work and authority in industry.* New York: John Wiley.

Bergen, L. A., & Weaver, D. (1988) Job satisfaction of daily newspaper journalists and organization size. *Newspaper Research Journal, 9*, 1–13.

Berger, W. (1990, September). Drug testing: Watchdog or witch-hunt? *Folio*, pp. 100, 102–106.

Berkowitz, E. N., Kerin, R. A., & Rudelius W. (1989). *Marketing* (2nd ed.). Homewood, IL: Irwin.

Berzins, J. I., Welling, M. A., & Wetter, R. E. (1978). A new measure of psychological androgyny based on the personality research form. *Journal of Consulting and Clinical Psychology, 46*, 126–138.

Beville, H. (1988). *Audience ratings: Radio, television, cable* (rev. ed.). Hillsdale, NJ: Lawrence Erlbaum Associates.

Bezanson, R., Cranberg, G., & Soloski, J. (1987). *Libel law and the Press.* New York: Macmillan.

Blackler, F., & Brown, C. (1985). Evaluation and the impact of information technologies on people in organizations. *Human Relations, 38*(3), 213–231.

Blankenburg, W. B. (1982). Newspaper ownership and control of circulation to increase profits. *Journalism Quarterly, 59*, 390–398.

Blonston, G. (1991, September 11). The white collar blues. *Boulder Daily Camera*, p. B1.

Bogart, L. (1989). *Press and public* (2nd ed.). Hillsdale, NJ: Lawrence Erlbaum Associates.

Breed, W. (1955). Social control in the news room: A functional analysis. *Social Forces, 33*, 326–335.

Broadcasters win retrans consent in S.12. (1991, May 20). *Broadcasting,* pp. 30–31.

Broadcasting/cablecasting yearbook. (1991). Washington, DC: Broadcast Publications.

Buchanan, D. A. (1985). Using the new technology. In T. Forester (Ed.). *The information technology revolution* (pp. 454–465). Cambridge, MA: MIT Press.

Burack, E., & Sorensen, P. F., Jr. (1976). Management preparation for computer automation: Emergent patterns and problems. *Academy of Management Journal, 19*(2), 318–323.

Burton, P. (1990). *Advertising copywriting* (6th ed.). Lincolnwood, IL: NTC Business Books.

Bushman, E. (1989, May-June). Wrongful discharge. *Case & Comment,* pp. 3–4, 6–9.

Busterna, J. (1988a). Antitrust in the 1980s: An analysis of 45 newspaper actions. *Newspaper Research Journal, 9*(2), 25–36.

Busterna, J. (1988b). Trends in daily newspaper ownership. *Journalism Quarterly, 65*, 831–838.

Buzzell, R. D., & Cook V. (1969). *Product life cycles.* Cambridge, MA: Marketing Science Institute.

Cass, R. T. (1978). Pattern for planning. In M. D. Richards (Ed.), *Readings in management* (5th ed., pp. 250–260). Cincinnati: South-Western.

Center for Law and Social Policy, 23 RR 2d 187 (1971).

Child, J. (1972). Organization structure, environment and perfromance: The role of strategic choice. *Sociology, 6*(1), 318–323.

Children's Advertising, *FTC final staff report and recommendation,* 43 Fed. Reg. 17967 (1981).

Children's Television Report and Policy Statement, 50 FCC 2d 1 (1974).

Commercialization on TV Stations, 49 RR 2d 391 (1981).

The Commission on Freedom of the Press. (1947). *A free and responsible press.* Chicago: University of Chicago Press.

Compaine, B. M. (1985). The expanding base of media competition. *Journal of Communication, 35*(3), 81–96.

Cooley, C. (1909). *Social organization.* New York: Scribner.

Copyright Office. (1980, September). *Copyright basics.* Washington, DC: US. Government Printing Office, Library of Congress.

Coulson, D. (1988). Antitrust law and newspapers. In R. Picard, J. Winter, M. McCombs & S. Lacy (Eds.), *Press concentration and monopoly* (pp. 179–195). Norwood, NJ: Ablex.

Court throws out FCC's 24-hour indecency ban. (1991, May 20). *Broadcasting,* p. 33.

Crable, R. & Vibbert, S. (1986). *Public relations as communication management.* Edina, MN: Bellwether.

Crispell, D. (1991, December 18). People patterns. *The Wall Street Journal,* p. B1.

Cyert, R. M., & March, J. G. (1963). *A behavioral theory of the firm.* Englewood Cliffs, NJ: Prentice-Hall.

Davis, L. (1987, July/August). Looser, yes, but still the deans of discipline. *Channels,* pp. 33–34.

Davis, R. (1957). *The fundamentals of top management.* New York: Harper and Row.

Del Vecchio, G. (1991, September 23). A question of loyalty. *Newsweek,* p. 8.

Deregulation of Radio, 84 FCC 2d 968 (1981).

Dietemann v. Time, Inc., 449 F.2D 245 (9th Cir., 1971).

Dominguez, C. M. (1990, December). A crack in the glass ceiling. *HR Magazine*, pp. 65–66.

Dracos, T. (1989, September). News directors are lousy managers. *Washington Journalism Review*, 39–41.

Drucker, P. F. (1983). The effective decision. In E. Collins (Ed.), *Executive success: Making it in management* (pp. 464–475). New York: Wiley.

DuBoff, L. (1987). *The law (in plain English) for writers*. Seattle: Madrona.

Dunn, S., Barban, A., Krugman, D., & Reid, L. (1990). *Advertising: Its role in modern marketing*. Chicago: Dryden.

Duscha, D. (1990, October). Plan newspaper estates early. *presstime*, pp. 58–59.

Elimination of Unnecessary Broadcast Regulation, 50 Fed. Reg. 5583 (1985).

En banc programming inquiry. (1960). 44 FCC 2303.

Etzioni, A. (1960). Two approaches to organizational analysis: A critique and a suggestion. *Administrative Science Quarterly, 5*, 257–78.

FCC endorses children's TV act. (1991, April 15). *Broadcasting*, pp. 90–91.

FCC puts two stations on indecency notice. (1991, April 29). *Broadcasting*, pp. 50–51.

FCC v. Pacifica Foundation, 438 U.S. 726 (1978).

FCC wants to raise radio ownership limits. (1991, May 13). *Broadcasting*, p. 29.

Fester, C. B., & Skinner, B. F. (1957). *Schedules of reinforcements*. New York: Appleton-Century-Crofts.

Fiedler, F. (1967). *A theory of leadership effectiveness*. New York: McGraw-Hill.

Fink, C. C. (1988). *Strategic newspaper management*. New York: Random House.

First National Bank of Boston v. Bellotti, 435 U.S. 765 (1978).

Fishman, D. B., & Chernis, C. (Eds.). (1990). *The human side of coporate competitive.* London: Sage.

Fleishman, E. A. (1956). A leader behavior description for industry. In R. M. Stogdik & A. E. Combs (Eds.), *Leader behavior: Its description and measurement* (pp. 104–119). Columbus: Ohio State University Bureau of Business Research.

Fletcher, J. (Ed.) (1981). *Handbook of radio and TV broadcasting*. New York: Van Nostrand Reinhold.

Fowler, G., & Shipman, J. (1982). Pennsylvania editors' perceptions of communication in the newsroom. *Journalism Quarterly, 61*, 822–826.

Francese, P. (1988). How to manage consumer information. In P. Wickham (Ed.), *The Insider's Guide to Demographic Know-How* (pp. 10–14). Ithaca, NY: American Demographics Press.

French, C. (Ed.). (1987). *The Associated Press stylebook and libel manual*. New York: Associated Press.

French, W. L. (1986). *Human resource management*. Boston: Houghton Mifflin.

Friedman, B. J. (1986, April). Videotext languor claims victims. *presstime*, p. 56.

Friedman, M. (1962). *Capitalism and freedom*. Chicago: University of Chicago Press.

FTC, FCC in liaison agreement on ads. (1987). *RR Current Service*, 2d, *11*, pp. 212–214. (Originally published April 27, 1972.) FTC v. Raladam Co. 283 U.S. 643 (1931).

Garneau, G. (1991a, April 20). Press freedom in deep trouble. *Editor & Publisher*, pp. 11, 44.

Garneau, G. (1991b, April 20). To err on the side of publishing. *Editor & Publisher*, pp. 9–10.

Gaziano, C., & Coulson, D. C. (1988). Effect of newsroom management styles on joutnalists: A case study. *Journalism Quarterly, 65,* 869–880.

Gellhorn, E. (1981). *Antitrust law and economics in a nutshell.* (2nd ed.). St. Paul, MN: West.

Gertz v. Robert Welch, Inc., 418 U.S. 323 (1974).

Giles, R. H. (1988). *Newsroom management.* Detroit: Media Management Books, Inc.

Gillmor, D., Barron, J., Simon, T., & Terry, H. (1990). *Mass communication law: Cases and comment* (5th ed.). St. Paul, MN: West.

Going to the mat over tough cable bill. (1991, May 13). *Broadcasting,* pp. 27–28.

Goltz, G. (1991, January). Disabled are knocking at door. *presstime,* p. 54.

Gragg, C. I. (1954). Because wisdom can't be told. In M. P. McNair (ed.) *The case method at the Harvard Business School* (pp. 6–14). New York: McGraw-Hill.

Graham, J. (1989, February 13). New VALS 2 takes psychological route. *Advertising Age, 60,* 24.

Granger, C. W. J. (1980). *Forecasting in business and economics.* New York: Academic.

Greer, D. F. (1980). *Industrial organization and public policy.* New York: Macmillan.

Griffin, R. W., & Moorhead, G. (1986). *Organizational behavior.* Boston: Houghton Mifflin.

Grunig, J., & Hunt, T. (1984). *Managing public relations.* New York: Holt, Rinehart & Winston.

Guide to understanding and using radio audience estimates (1987). *Arbitron radio market report reference guide.* New York: Arbitron Ratings Co.

Hacker, A. (1980). Loyalty and the whistle blower. In A. Westin & S. Salisbury (Eds.), *Individual rights in the corporation* (pp. 75–95). New York: Pantheon.

Hamner, W. C., & Organ, D. W. (1978). *Organizational behavior: An applied psychology approach.* Dallas: Business Publications.

Haney, W. V. (1973). *Communication and organizational behavior* (3rd ed.). Homewood, IL: Irwin.

Harrison, E. F. (1987). *The managerial decision-making process* (3rd ed.). Boston: Houghton Mifflin.

Head, S., & Stirling, C. (1990). *Broadcasting in America: A survey of electronic media.* Boston: Houghton Mifflin.

Heller, F. A., & Wilpert, B. (1981). *Competence and power in managerial decision-making.* Chichester, England: Wiley.

Hersey, P., & Blanchard, K. (1972). *Management of organizational behavior: Utilizing human resources* (2nd ed.) Englewood Cliffs, NJ: Prentice-Hall.

Herzberg, F. (1968). One more time: How do you motivate employees? *Harvard Business Review, 46,* 53–62.

Herzberg, F., Mausner, B., & Snyderman, B. (1959). *The motivation to work.* New York: Wiley.

Hofstede, G. (1980). *Culture's consequences: International differences in work-related values.* Beverly Hills, CA: Sage.

Hood, J., & Kalbfeld, B. (Eds.). (1982). *AP broadcast news handbook.* New York: Associated Press.

House, R. J. (1977). A 1976 theory of charismatic leadership. In J. G. Hunt & L. L. Larson (Eds.), *Leadership: The cutting edge* (pp. 189–273). Carbondale: Southern Illinois University.

House, R. J., & Dessler, G. (1974). The path-goal theory of leadership: Some post hoc and apriori tests. In J. G. Hunt & L. L. Larson (Eds.), *Contingency approcahes to leadership* (pp. 60-75). Carbondale: Southern Illinois University.

Howard, H. H. (1973). *Multiple ownership in television broadcasting: Historical development and selected case studies*. Unpublished doctoral dissertation, Ohio University, Athens.

Huber, G. P. (1980). *Managerial decision making*. Glenview, IL: Scott Foresman.

Inquiry into Section 73.1910 of the Commission's Rules and Regulations Concerning Alternatives to the General Fairness Doctrine Obligations of Broadcast Licensees: Notice of Inquiry, 2 FCCRcd 1532 (1987); Report of the Commission, 2 FCC Rcd 5272 (1987); Memorandum Opinion and Order. 3 FCC Rcd 2050 (1988).

Janis, I. L. (1982). *Groupthink* (2nd ed.). Boston: Houghton Mifflin.

Joffe, B. (1989, July). Law, ethics and public relations writers. *Public Relations Journal*, pp. 38-39.

Johnston, W. (1987). *Work force 2000*. Indianapolis: Hudson Institute.

Johnstone, J. W. C. (1976). Organizational constraints on newswork. *Journalism Quarterly, 53*, 5-13.

Joseph, T. (1983). Television reporters' and managers' preferences on decision-making. *Journalism Quarterly, 60*, 476-479.

Katz study says Birch, Arbitron paint different portraits of radio listening. (1988, July 11). *Broadcasting*, 71-72.

Keeton, W. (Gen. Ed.). (1984). Privacy. In *Prosser & Keeton on Torts* (5th ed, pp. 849-869). St. Paul, MN: West.

KMPC, The Station of the Stars, Inc., 6 FCC 729 (1939).

Kotler, P. (1980). *Marketing management: Analysis, planning and control* (4th ed.). Englewood Cliffs, NJ: Prentice-Hall.

Kreitner, R. (1986). *Management* (3rd ed.). Boston: Houghton Mifflin.

Lacy, S. (1988). Content of joint operating newspapers. In R. G. Picard, J. P. Winter, M. E. McCombs, & S. Lacy (Eds.),. *Press concentration and monopoly* (pp. 147-160). Norwood, NJ: Ablex.

Lacy, S. (1989). A model of demand for news: Impact of competition on newspaper content. *Journalism Quarterly, 66*, 40-48, 128.

Lacy, S. (1990). The impact of repealing the newspaper preservation act. *Newspaper Research Journal, 11*(1), 2-11.

Lacy, S., & Simon, T. F. (1992). *The economics and regulation of United States newspapers*. Norwood, NJ: Ablex.

Lancaster, K., & Katz, H. (1989). *Strategic media planning*. Lincolnwood, IL: NTC Business Books.

Latham, G. P., & Locke, E. A. (1979). Goal setting a motivational approach that works. *Organizational Dynamics, 77*, 68-80.

Lavine, J. M., & Wackman, D. B. (1988). *Managing media organizations*. New York: Longman.

Lawrence, P., & Lorsch,, J. (1967). Differentiation and integration in complex organizations. *Administrative Science Quarterly, 12*, 1-47.

Leavitt, H. (1965). Applied organizational change in industry. In J. March (Ed.), *Handbook of organizations* (pp. 1144-1170). Chicago: Rand McNally.

Leenders, M. R., & Erkskein, J. A. (1973). *Case research: The case writing process*. London, Canada: The University of Western Ontario.

Lewin, K. R., Lippitt, R., & White, R. K. (1939). Patterns of aggressive behavior in experimentally created social climates. *Journal of Social Psychology, 10*, 371–399.

Liaison between FCC and FTC relating to false and misleading radio and TV advertising, *RR Current Service* 2d. *11*, p. 201 (1987). (Originally published February 21, 1957).

Licensee Responsibility with Respect to the Broadcast of False, Misleading or Deceptive Advertising, 74 FCC 2d 623 (1961).

Likert, R. (1961). *New patterns of management*. New York: McGraw-Hill.

Linton, B. (1987). Self-regulation in broadcasting revisited. *Journalism Quarterly, 64*, 483–490.

Litman, B. (1988). Micoreconomic foundations. In R. G. Picard, J. P. Winter, M. E. McCombs & S. Lacy (Eds.), *Press concentration and monopoly* (pp. 3–34). Norwood, NJ: Ablex.

Locke, E. A. (1968). Toward a theory of task motivation and incentives. *Organizational behavior and human performance, 3*, 157–189.

Lofland, J. (1971). *Analyzing social settings*. Belmont, CA: Wadsworth Publishing.

Lublin, J. S. (1991, October 9). Thomas battle spotlights harassment. *The Wall Street Journal*, p. B1.

Maslow, A. H. (1954). *Motivation and personality*. New York: Harper & Row.

Mauro, J. (1980). Application of census data for circulation sales. In P. Hirt (Ed.), *Census applications in newspaper management and marketing* (pp. 11–17). Reston, VA: International Newspaper Promotion Association.

Mayo, E. (1945). *The social problems of an industrial civilization*. Boston: Graduate School of Business Administration, Harvard University.

McCavitt, W., & Pringle, P. (1986). *Electronic media management*. Boston: Focal Press.

McClelland, D. (1961). *The achieving society*. Princeton, NJ: Van Nostrand.

McCreary, E. A. (1978). How to grow a decision tree. In M. D. Richards (Ed.), *Readings in management* (5th ed., pp. 122–130). Cincinnati: South-Western.

McGregor, D. (1960). *The human side of enterprise*. New York: McGraw-Hill.

McKean, R. N. (1975). Cost-benefit analysis. In E. Mansfield (Ed.), *Managerial economics and operational research* (3rd ed., pp. 549–561). New York: Norton.

Meade, R. D. (1967). An experimental study of leadership in India. *Journal of Social Psychology, 72*, 35–43.

Mintzberg, H. (1979). *The structuring of organizations*. Englewood Cliffs, N.J.: Prentice-Hall.

Miracle, G., & Nevett, T. (1987). *Voluntary regulation of advertising*. Lexington, MA: Heath.

Misumi, J. (1985). The behavioral science of leadership. Ann Arbor: University of Michigan Press.

Morgan, G. (1986). *Images of organization*. London: Sage.

NAB legal guide to FCC broadcast regulations. (1984). (2nd ed.). Washington, DC: National Association of Broadcasters.

Moriarity, S. (1986). *Creative advertising: Theory and practice*. Englewood Cliffs, NJ: Prentice-Hall.

Nadler, D. A., & Lawler, E. E. III. (1977). Motivation: A diagnostic approach. In J. R. Hackman, E. E. Lawler III, & L. W. Porter (Eds.), *Perspectives on behavior in organizations* (pp. 26–38). New York: McGraw-Hill.

National Advertising Division. (1983, July 15). Self-regulation of national advertising. *NAD Case Report, 13*, 20–23.

New allegations complicate FM indecency case. (1991, May 13). *Broadcasting*, pp. 43–44.

New York Times v. Sullivan, 376 U.S. 254 (1964).

OSHA begins to promulgate repetitive motion guidelines. (1990, October). *presstime*, p. 38.

Ouchi, W. (1981). *Theory Z*. New York: Avon Books.

Pavlov, I. P. (1902). *The work of the digestive glands* (W. H. Thompson, Trans.). London: Charles Griffin.

Phillips, D. (1976). *A systematic study of the leadership process at the corporate level of two television group owners*. Unpublished doctoral dissertation, Ohio University, Athens.

Picard, R. G. (1988). Pricing behavior of newspapers. In R. G. Picard, J. P. Winter, M. E. McCombs, & S. Lacy (Eds.), *Press concentration and monopoly* (pp. 55–69). Norwood, NJ: Ablex.

Picard, R. G. (1989). *Media economics: Concepts and issues*. Newbury Park, NJ: Sage.

Pilenzo, R. C. (1990, February). Managing for survival in the 1990s. *Modern Office Technology*, pp. 25–37.

Polansky, S. H., & Hughes, D. W. (1986). Managerial innovation in newspaper organizations. *Newspaper Research Journal, 8*, 1–12.

Policies and rules concerning children's television programming, 6 FCC Rcd 2111. (1991)

Policy regarding character qualifications in broadcast licensing, 102 FCC 2d 1179 (1986).

Policy statement on deception (1983). Letter from then Federal Trade Commission Chariman James C. Miller III to Congressman John D. Dingell, 14 October 1983. Reprinted as an appendix to Cliffdale, 103 FTC 110 at 174 (1984).

Policy statement regarding advertising substantiation program, 49 Federal Register 30999 (1984).

Powell, G. N. (1988). *Women and men in management*. Newbury Park, CA: Sage.

Powers, A. (1990, November). *Theory applied to practice: A case study of the effect of management behavior on productivity and job satisfaction in local television news*. Paper presented at the meeting of the Speech Communication Association, Chicago, IL.

Powers, A. & Lacy, S. (1992). A model of job satisfaction in local television news. In S. Lacy, A. Sohn & R. Giles (Eds.), *Readings in Media Management* (pp. 5–20). Columbia, SC: Association for Education in Journalism and Mass Communication.

Preston, I. (1975). *The great American blow-up: Puffery in advertising and selling*. Madison: University of Wisconsin Press.

Preston, I. (1986). Data-free at the FTC? How the Federal Trade Commission decides whether extrinsic evidence of deceptiveness is required. *American Business Law Journal, 24*, 359.

Preston, I. (1987). Extrinsic evidence in Federal Trade Commission deceptiveness cases. *Columbia Business Law Review, 1987*, 633.

Preston, I. (1989). *Advertising claims: Using evidence to back them up*. Reference materials from seminar held November 16, 1989, Wisconsin Center in Madison.

Preston, I. (1990). The definition of deceptiveness in advertising and other commercial speech. *Catholic University Law Review, 39*, 1035.

Primer on Ascertainment of Community Problems by Broadcast Applicants, 27 FCC 2d 650 (1971).

Prosser, W. (1960). Privacy. *California Law Review, 48*, 383–423.

Public Relations Society of America. (1977). Code of professional standards for the practice of public relations. In R. Crable & S. Vibbert (Eds.), *Public relations as communication management* (pp. 114–115). Endina, MN: Bellwether.

Public Service Responsibility of Broadcast Licensees (1946, July 2). Public Notice 95462, pp. 45–47. (More commonly known as the "Blue Book").

Radding, A. (1991, February 11). Consumer worry halts data bases. *Advertising Age*, p. 28.

Radio broadcasters seek post-ban guidance. (1991, May 27). *Broadcasting*, pp. 41–42.

Radio-Television News Directors Association Code of Broadcast News Ethics. (1991). In P. Mayeux, *Broadcast news writing and reporting*, (p. 405). Dubuque, IA: Brown.

Rauch, H. (1991, January). Editors beware! Improperly handled complaints mean trouble. *Folio*, pp. 108, 110–112.

Ray, R. (1988, Spring). *The use of culture analysis to examine the management philosophies and leadership styles of radio station general managers.* Paper presented at the meeting of the Broadcast Education Association, Las Vegas, NV.

Redwood, A. (1990, January-February). Human resources management in the 1990s. *Business Horizons*, pp. 74–80.

Report and Statement of Policy re: Commission en banc Programming Inquiry, 44 FCC 2303 (1960).

Revision of Programming and Commercialization Policies, Ascertainment Requirements, and Program Log Requirements for Commercial Television Stations, 98 FCC 2d 1076 (1984).

Reynolds, P. D. (1971). *A primer in theory construction.* Indianapolis: Educational Publishing.

Rhea, J. (1970). *An investigation of relationships among specified variables in the management of television stations.* Unpublished doctoral dissertation, Ohio University, Athens.

Rich, O., & Martin, E. (1981). Qualitative data: The why of Broadcast Research. In J. Fletcher (Ed.). *Handbook of radio and TV broadcasting* (117–36). New York: Van Nostrand Reinhold.

Richards, J. (1990). *Deceptive advertising: Behavioral study of a legal concept.* Hillsdale, NJ: Lawrence Erlbaum Associates.

Ries, A., & Trout, J. (1986). *Positioning: The battle for your mind* (rev. ed.). New York: Warner.

Robinson, J. P. (1990) *American's use of time project.* Hilton Hotel Corporation Project.

Rogers, E. (1983). *Diffusion of innovation* (3rd ed.). New York: Free Press.

Rogers, E. (1986). *Communication technology: The new media in society.* New York: Free Press.

Ronstadt, R. (1980). *The art of case analysis.* Dober, MA: Lord.

Rosden, G., & Rosden, E. (1990). *The law of advertising.* New York: Bender.

Rosenberg, J. (1991, April 20). Out of the office, onto the shop floor. *Editor & Publisher*, pp. 30–32, 51.

Rosener, J. (1990). Ways women lead. *Harvard Business Review, 68*, 119–125.

Rotfeld, H., & Abernethy, A. (1992). Radio station standards for acceptable advertising. *Journal of Business Research, 24,* 361–375.

Rotfeld, H., Abernethy, A., & Parsons, P. (1990). Self-regulation and television advertising. *Journal of Advertising, 19*(4), 18–26.

Rotfeld, H., & Parsons, P. (1989). Self-regulation and magazine advertising. *Journal of Advertising, 18*(4), 33–40.

Rubin, M. (1991, March). Avoid truthful, but incomplete press releases. *Public Relations Journal,* pp. 26–27.

Sandage, C., Fryburger, V., & Rotzoll, K. (1989). *Advertising theory & practice.* New York: Longman.

Schein, E. H. (1985). *Organizational culture and leadership: A dynamic view.* San Francisco: Jossey-Bass.

Schoell, W. F., & Guiltinan, J. P. (1990). *Marketing* (4th ed.). Boston: Allyn & Bacon.

Schriesheim, J., & Schriesheim, C. (1980). Test of the path-goal theory of leadership and some suggested directions for further research. *Personnel Psychology, 33*(2), 349–71.

Schultz, D. (1990). *Strategic advertising campaigns* (3rd ed.). Lincolnwood, IL: NTC Business Books.

Severin, W. J., & Tankard, J. W., Jr. (1992). *Communication theories: Origins, methods, and uses in mass media* (3rd ed.). New York: Longman.

Shames, L. (1989). *The hunger for more.* New York: Times Books.

Sheppard, D. L. (1989). Organizations, power and sexuality: The image and self-image of women managers. In J. Hern, D. Shappard, P. Tancred-Sheriff, & G. Burell (Eds.), *The sexuality of organization,* pp. 139–157. London: Sage.

Sherer, F. M. (1970). *Industrial market structure and economic performance.* Chicago: Rand McNally.

Sherman, B. (1987). *Telecommunications management.* New York: McGraw-Hill.

Shoemaker, P. (1987). Building a theory of news content. *Journalism Monographs, 103.*

Simon, H. (1957). *Models of man.* New York: Wiley.

Simon, H. (1960). *New science of management decisions.* New York: Harper & Row.

Sissors, J., & Surmanek, J. (1982). *Advertising media planning* (2nd ed.). Chicago: Crain.

Skinner, B. F. (1953). *Science and human behavior.* New York: Macmillan.

Skinner, B. F. (1972). *Beyond freedom and dignity.* New York: Knopf.

Smith, G. D., Arnold, D. R., & Bizzell, B. G. (1985). *Strategy and business policy.* Boston, Houghton Mifflin.

Smith, P. B., & Peterson, M. F. (1988). *Leadership, organization, and culture.* London: Sage.

Society of Professional Journalists Code of Ethics (1991). (adopted 1926; revised in 1973, 1984, 1987). In P. Mayeux, *Broadcast news writing and reporting* (p. 404). Dubuque, IA: Brown.

Sohn, A., Ogan, C. & Polich, J. (1986). *Newspaper leadership.* Englewood Cliffs, NJ: Prentice-Hall.

Solomon, D. (1989, December). Media research tool box. *Marketing & Media Decisions, 24,* 122, 124–5.

Soloski, J. (1989). News reporting and professionalism: Some constraints on the reporting of the news. *Media Culture and Society, 11,* 207–228.

Soyster, M. (1991, May 4). Using a free-lancer: Who owns the copyright? *Editor & Publisher,* p. 30.

Spence, J. I., & Helmreich, R. L. (1978). *Masculinity and feminity: Their psychological dimensions, correlates and antecedents.* Austin: University of Texas Press.

Stewart, R. (1976). *Contrasts in management: A study of the different types of management jobs, their demands and choices.* London: McGraw-Hill.

Stewart, R. (1982). A model for understanding managerial jobs and behavior. *Academy of Management Review, 7,* 7–13.

Stigler, G. J. (1952). *The theory of price* (rev. ed.). New York: Macmillan.

Stoneman, P. (1983). *The economic analysis of technological change.* New York: Oxford University Press.

Strassmann, P. (1976). Stages of growth. *Danamation, 22*(10), 46–50.

Syracuse Peace Council v. Television Station WTVH, 2 FCC Rcd 5043 (1987); Order Requesting Comment, 2 FCC Rcd 794 (1987).

Tannenbaum, R., & Schmidt, W. H. (1973, May/June). How to choose a leadership pattern. *Harvard Business Review,* pp. 162–180.

Tausky, C. (1980). Theories of organization. In J. A. Litterer (Ed.), *Organizations: Structure and behavior* (3rd ed., pp. 11–33). New York: Wiley.

Taylor, F. (1947). *Scientific management.* New York: Harper.

Taylor, R.N. (1984). *Behavioral decision making.* Glenview, IL: Scott, Foresman.

Time, Inc. v. Firestone, 424 U.S. 448 (1976).

Tower, C. (1958). The structure of management. *Journal of Broadcasting, 2,* 179–81.

Tuchman, G. (1978). *Making news: A study in the construction of reality.* New York: Free Press.

United States v. National Association of Broadcasters, 536 F.Supp. 149 (D.D.C. 1982a).

United States v. National Association of Broadcasters, 553 F.Supp. 621 (1982b).

Van Fleet, D. D. (1991). *Contemporary management* (2nd ed.). Boston: Houghton Mifflin.

Veronis, C. (1990, March). Moving minorities up instead of out. *presstime,* pp. 23–25.

Vroom, V. H. (1964). *Work and motivation.* New York: Wiley.

Vroom, V. H., & Yetton, P. W. (1973). *Leadership and decision making.* Pittsburgh: University of Pittsburgh Press.

Walley, W. (1990, September 24). Nets force Nielsen showdown. *Advertising Age,* pp. 3, 60

Warner, C. (1989, November 27). Advertising case studies great station sales tools when written properly. *Television/Radio Age, 37,* 87.

Warner-Lambert Co. (1975). 86 FTC 1938. Affirmed in Warner-Lambert Co. v. FTC, 562 F.2d 749 (D.C. Cir. 1977). Cert. Den. 435 U.S. 950 (1978).

Weaver, D. H., & Wilhoit, G. C. (1986). *The American journalist.* Bloomington: Indiana University Press.

Weber, M. (1947). *The theory of economic and social orgnization.* (A. M. Henderson & T. Parsons, Trans.). New York: Free Press. (Original work published 1921.)

Webster's new world dictionary (2nd College ed.). New York: Simon and Schuster.

Wells, W., Burnett, J., & Moriarty, S. (1989). *Advertising principles and practice.* Englewood Cliffs, NJ: Prentice Hall.

Whiting, C. S. (1955, October). Operational techniques of creative thinking. *Advanced Management*, pp. 24–30.

Wickham, P. (Ed.). (1988). *The insider's guide to demographic know-how.* Ithaca, NY: American Demographics Press.

Wicks, J. L. (1991a). An exploratory study of television advertising practices: Do profitability and organization size affect clearance formality? *Journal of Advertising, 20*(3), 1–12.

Wicks, J. L. (1991b). Varying commercialization and clutter to enhance airtime attractiveness in early fringe: How TV sales managers may be responding to deregulatory freedoms. *Journal of Media Economics, 4,* 3–18.

Williamson, O. E. (1964). *The economics of discretionary behavior: Managerial objectives in a theory of the firm.* Englewood Cliffs, NJ: Prentice-Hall.

Willis, J. (1988). *Surviving in the newspaper business: Newspaper management in turbulent times.* New York: Praeger.

Wimmer, R., & Dominick, J. (1991). Mass media research (3rd ed.). Belmont, CA: Wadsworth.

Wirth, M. (1977). *The effects of crossmedia ownership on television and newspaper 'prices'.* Unpublished doctoral dissertation, Michigan State University, East Lansing, MI.

Witcover, J. (1971, September/October). Two weeks that shook the press. *Columbia Journalism Review*, pp. 7–15.

Zanot, E. (1985). Unseen but effective advertising regulation: The clearance process. *Journal of Advertising, 14,* 44–51, 59, 68.

Zuckman, H., Gaynes, M., Carter, T., & Dee, J. (1988). *Mass communications law in a nutshell.* St. Paul, MN: West.

Author Index

Simon, T., 34, 62, 133, 134, 145, 146, 147, 148, 149, 150, 151, 152, 153, 155, 156, 157, 158, 162, 165, 176, 182, 183, 185, 187, 376, 373
Sissors, J., 253, 381
Skinner, B. F., 112, 114, 375, 381
Smith, G. D., 217, 220, 381
Smith, P. B., 76, 381
Snyderman, B., 110, 376
Sohn, A., 132, 135, 142, 146, 147, 148, 236, 261, 262, 381
Solomon, D., 259, 264, 270, 381
Soloski, J., 47, 148, 373, 382
Sorensen, P. F., Jr., 309, 374
Soyster, M., 151, 382
Spence, J. I., 81, 382
Stewart, R., 72, 382
Stigler, G. J., 179, 382
Stirling, C., 273, 376
Stoneman, P., 314, 382
Strassmann, P., 314, 382
Surmanek, J., 253, 381

T

Tankard, J. W., Jr., 119, 120, 182, 381
Tannenbaum, R., 41, 70, 382
Tausky, C., 30, 31, 382
Taylor, F., 30, 37, 382
Taylor, R.N., 2, 4, 23, 382
Terry, H., 133, 145, 146, 147, 148, 149, 150, 151, 152, 153, 155, 156, 157, 158, 162, 165, 376
Tower, C., 43, 382
Trout, J., 256, 380
Tuchman, G., 46, 47, 382

V

Van Fleet, D. D., 102, 382
Veronis, C., 143, 382
Vibbert, S., 163, 374
Vroom, V. H., 14, 116, 382

W

Wackman, D. B., 43, 45, 237, 377
Walley, W., 267, 382
Warner, C., 269, 382
Weaver, D. H., 49, 105, 106, 107, 194, 373, 382
Weber, M., 30, 31 37, 71, 75, 382
Welling, M. A., 81, 373
Wells, W., 256, 383
Wetter, R. E., 81, 373
White, R. K., 67, 378
Whiting, C. S., 226, 383
Wickham, P., 258, 383
Wicks, J. L., 164, 361, 362, 383
Wilhoit, G. C., 49, 105, 106, 194, 382
Williamson, O. E., 178, 383
Willis, J., 252, 261, 383
Wilpert, B., 67, 376
Wimmer, R., 252, 266, 383
Wirth, M., 361, 383
Witcover, J., 13, 383

Y

Yetton, P. W., 14, 382

Z

Zanot, E., 362, 383
Zuckman, H., 146, 147, 148, 149, 150, 151, 152, 156, 165, 383

Subject Index